The Parent App

The Parent App

Understanding Families in the Digital Age

LYNN SCHOFIELD CLARK

OXFORD

UNIVERSITY PRESS

Oxford University Press is a department of the University of Oxford.
It furthers the University's objective of excellence in research,
scholarship, and education by publishing worldwide.

Oxford   New York

Auckland   Cape Town   Dar es Salaam   Hong Kong   Karachi
Kuala Lumpur   Madrid   Melbourne   Mexico City   Nairobi
New Delhi   Shanghai   Taipei   Toronto

With offices in

Argentina   Austria   Brazil   Chile   Czech Republic   France   Greece
Guatemala   Hungary   Italy   Japan   Poland   Portugal   Singapore
South Korea   Switzerland   Thailand   Turkey   Ukraine   Vietnam

Oxford is a registered trade mark of Oxford University Press
in the UK and certain other countries.

Published in the United States of America by
Oxford University Press
198 Madison Avenue, New York, NY 10016

© Oxford University Press 2013

Library of Congress Cataloging-in-Publication Data
Clark, Lynn Schofield.
The parent app: understanding families in the digital age /Lynn Schofield Clark.
p.   cm.
ISBN 978-0-19-989961-6 (hbk.: alk. paper)
1. Internet and families. 2. Internet—Social aspects. 3. Parent and child. I. Title.
HQ799.2.I5C59   2013
302.23'1—dc23   2012006687

1 3 5 7 9 8 6 4 2

Printed in the United States of America
on acid-free paper

CONTENTS

Preface: The Parent App and the Parent Trap   vii
Acknowledgments   xvii

PART I | Digital and Mobile Media: Cautionary Tales

CHAPTER 1   Risk, Media, and Parenting in a Digital Age   3

CHAPTER 2   Cyberbullying Girls, Helicopter Moms, and Internet Predators   28

CHAPTER 3   Strict Parents, Gamer High School Dropouts, and Shunned Overachievers   49

PART II | Digital Media and Youth

CHAPTER 4   Identity 2.0: Young People and Digital and Mobile Media   75

CHAPTER 5   Less Advantaged Teens, Ethnicity, and Digital and Mobile Media: Respect, Restriction, and Reversal   98

PART III | Digital and Mobile Media and Family Communication

CHAPTER 6   Communication in Families: Expressive Empowerment and Respectful Connectedness   125

CHAPTER 7   How Parents Are Mediating the Media in Middle-Class and Less Advantaged Homes   151

CHAPTER 8   Media Rich and Time Poor: The Emotion Work of Parenting in a Digital Age   174

CHAPTER 9 Parenting in a Digital Age: The Mediatization of Family
Life and the Need to Act   201

Appendix A: Methodology   227
*Appendix B: Parents, Children, and the Media Landscape:
Resources*   233
*Appendix C: Family Digital and Mobile Media
Agreement*   235

Notes   237
Bibliography   275
Index   293

PREFACE | *The Parent App and the Parent Trap*

I t's 2:45 p.m. and I'm late—again. My husband, Jon, already texted me to tell me that he was going to be at a meeting, a subtle reminder that it's my turn to pick up the kids today. I left my office on time, but I'd forgotten to allow for the construction project at the end of Evans Avenue, the main thoroughfare separating my office from the highway. So I've got my iPhone on the seat next to me, at the ready for when I hit the next red light, and I'm already scrolling through the list in my head. Should I call Delia? No, she's working on Thursdays; so is Suelita, and she always works until six. Keiko and Mike are at work, too, and Jodi's got to take her boys to baseball right after school. Laura, my friend who's a dedicated stay-at-home mom, just helped me out two days ago; I'm too embarrassed to have to ask her to bail me out again. Red light: what's the plan? I decide to call Margie, who works at the school's front desk, and ask her to catch my young family members as they exit the school and let them know I'm on my way. But I dread that, too: who knows what the school staff does with the dirt they have on chronically late parents like me? I suddenly find myself wishing, for the very first time, that my ten-year-old had a cell phone. Life would be so easy then, I muse. I could simply call Jonathan and tell him that I will be there ten minutes after school lets out, and ask him to alert his younger sister so that they can wait for me together. Such a call might have an added benefit, too: maybe I could forestall "the look" (any parent who's ever been late for pickup will know exactly which guilt-inducing look I'm talking about).

I quickly dismiss the idea of getting him a cell phone. I couldn't do that, because then eight-year-old Allison would be more convinced than ever that Jonathan was the favorite—unless I bought one for her, too. Which she'd no doubt lose within a week, since she'd really have no use for it. And anyway, their school doesn't allow them to bring mobiles into the classroom, so even if they both had one, there'd be no guarantee either one of them would remember to pick it up from the office and turn it on to check for a message from Mom. And then I had the strangest realization of all: the real reason that I didn't want to get them cell phones was that I felt unprepared for it. I didn't know enough about what getting them mobiles would *mean*: for them, for me, for our family. What would having a cell phone lead to? Is it sort of like the adult drug abuser's slide from beer to hard liquor to heroin, so that the next thing I know they're twelve-year-olds with a CrackBerry habit?

Especially strange was the thought that occurred to me in the next moment: how could I not know what having a mobile phone would mean? I've had a cell phone for more than a decade. What's more, I've been studying family uses of mobiles, the Internet, television, and a host of other media for the better part of fifteen years. I can rattle off statistics with the best of them: 95 percent of kids have access to the Internet by age eleven; 89 percent of families have multiple mobile phones, and 75 percent of twelve- to seventeen-year-olds have their own phone; the average age at which young people get a cell phone is around nine and a half, and children in single-parent families tend to get cell phones earlier than those who have two parents living in the same household; the average number of texts sent a month by a U.S. teen is well over three thousand.[1] I also know that it's parental concerns for safety, as much as kids' desires, that are fueling the growth of Xbox, PlayStation, Wii gaming, and portable game devices, since parents want kids to be supervised and kids who have fewer resources for or access to supervised outside activities are more likely to spend time inside with mediated entertainment. I know all about the defeat of the Stop Online Piracy Act and the Verizon-AT&T showdown over the iPhone. Like most moms, I'm sometimes unsure of myself, but shouldn't I, of all people, know what to expect?

I realized then that what all parents really need, or wish we had, is some way to discern the most caring, smart, sensitive, and effective responses to the dilemmas that digital and mobile media have introduced into the lives of our families. What we need is a Parent App. Is my thirteen-year-old responsible enough to handle a Facebook page? Check the Parent App. What will happen down the road if I allow my seven-year-old to download games onto my cell phone? Consult the Parent App. The house phone is ringing and ringing, but my twelve-year-old has decided that pounding out the Harry Potter theme on the piano is what he'd rather be doing right now. Parent App, can you help me out here? How about helping out with dinner, laundry, or after-school pickups while we're at it?

A number of companies have rushed in to address our felt need for apps that will help with parenting. Parents can diagnose children's aches and pains with the Portable Pediatrician mobile app, look to the Dinner Spinner for suppertime plans, or figure out what their teens are saying by checking the Teen Chat Decoder. There's even an app you can use if you put your child in time-out: it will remind you to take her out of it when her time is up. Additionally, parents can consult a number of social network sites for advice on parenting. Almost all of the most frequently trafficked have the word "mom" in the title. With sites such as CafeMom, Mamapedia, and MomsLikeMe, help is only a click away.[2] These apps hold the promise of making life more manageable and productive, especially for women who are expected to balance the demands of work and family and to move seamlessly between them. But does technology really make life easier for us? Is that how technology is changing family life today? Most parents instead are reporting that technology is making life with their children more challenging, not less.[3]

Parents have always had to face challenges. Yet digital and mobile media have put a fine point on the experience of living with preteen and teenage young people who believe they know better than their parents about how best to manage such things. I decided to name this book *The Parent App* when I said the title out loud and realized how much the voices of the young people in this book remind me of the perennially popular film with a similar name: *The Parent Trap*. Hayley Mills and, later, Lindsay Lohan brought to life a humorous fantasy with enduring appeal among generations of elementary, tween, and teenage young people, including me and later my own children. In those films, twins who were separated at birth discover a deep secret about their parents' past that is obvious to everyone who meets them. Then they connive to help their parents recognize and correct the mistake the adults made so long ago. Once the parents have realized that the kids were right, they all live happily ever after. The pink landline phones featured on the cover of the 1961 video version are replaced with mobiles in the 1998 version, but the theme is the same: young people are able to work around and ultimately correct their parents' wrongs because they are smart, they can pull together resources (including those of technology), and, of course, they knew all along what was best for everyone.

Young people thinking they know what's best for everyone: that may sound familiar to parents and to those of us who remember what it was like to feel that way. In the interviews with mothers and fathers that form the core of this book, this is the way that many parents of teens and preteens characterize the interactions they have with their children about mobile phones, social media sites, gaming platforms, and the Internet. Parents recognize that young people are growing up in a world saturated by digital and mobile media, and we often feel trapped because the context seems so different when compared with our own growing-up experiences. Yet, like the similarities between the 1961 and 1998 films, we also know that some aspects of the growing-up years remain the same. We just need help navigating the new situations.

But this book is not strictly an advice manual for parents. For one thing, digital and mobile media are changing so rapidly that any book could be outdated before it reached publication. Numerous websites and blogs exist that provide excellent advice on how parents can address particular situations they confront, and thus it's possible to find suggestions tailored to the unique challenges of individual families. Some of these resources are highlighted in Appendix B, and specific suggestions for parents are offered in the concluding chapter of this book. But in order to set those suggestions in context, this book explores the meaning behind the changes that we are all experiencing. It asks how families are experiencing and responding to the challenges, both new and old, of parenting young people through the late elementary, preteen, and teen years. Why are parents responding in the ways that they are? And perhaps most importantly, what will these responses mean for us as family members and as members of society?

In order to investigate these questions, in this book I bring together two different bodies of research. First, as a sociologist who studies media, I consider various theories that are helping to explain both the characteristics of today's new media and the ways in which these characteristics may be changing our individual and social experiences. Second, as a communication scholar interested in families, I look at how families have adopted various strategies for communication between family members, and how these strategies shape the ways in which digital and mobile media technologies fit into our lives as individuals and as families. I also bring to this book my perspective as a married working mother of a teen and preteen, with our family living in a middle-class neighborhood.

When I first realized my own hesitation about getting my son a mobile phone, I wondered where the nervousness was coming from. I wasn't overly worried about the risks that receive the most media attention: sexting, possible exposure to undesirable content, or contact with sexual predators. I just wanted to know whether a mobile would help me in my quest to be a good parent. Would getting him a phone help me achieve my goal of having positive connections with my son, or would it undermine that goal? I realized then that I didn't want to write this book solely about the risks of new media. I wanted to write about how digital and mobile media fit into this felt wish to be a "good-enough" parent.[4] Of course, my own context and family background shape what it means to me to be a "good-enough" parent. I *might* use a Parent App to help me locate a family-friendly restaurant, but what I could *really* use is a Parent App that would help me recognize risk as I define it, so that I can be the best parent possible in my own context, in relation to my own children, and in what often feel like unfamiliar situations.

In this book, I want to add to the numerous important studies exploring how parenting is changing in the United States, particularly with the rise of overparenting and the "helicopter parent," trends that are much in evidence in my own cultural milieu.[5] Some books, such as Margaret Nelson's *Parenting Out of Control* and Barbara Hofer and Abigail Sullivan Moore's *The iConnected Parent*, have argued that today's technologies make it altogether too easy for "helicopter parents" to spy on their children or remain too connected to let go as the children get older.[6] The temptation to be this kind of parent is surely there, but it's one that many parents in my study actively tried to resist.

I also wanted to consider insights from my field, media studies. It does have an important lens of theory to bring to these issues of how families are experiencing digital and mobile media in their everyday lives and how children and parents struggle together over the when and why of their practices involving media.[7] The field of media studies reminds us to think about communication technologies not as things we merely use but as innovations that evolve in specific contexts in relation to perceived needs and which continue to evolve in relation both to those needs and to practices that specific technologies discourage or make possible.[8] Technologies such as mobile and online communication do not only enable our connections with others and with information. They also add a new layer of meaning to those connections, and in doing this, they change our relationships with each other. New technologies make possible certain ways of being, and how we use technologies then further shapes our options for the future.[9] I wanted to look not only at how parents and their children were using technologies but also at how those uses made sense to us in relation to the rest of our lives.

The media-saturated context of our lives is undergoing change, and this provides an excellent opportunity for us to reexamine some of the taken-for-granted ways in which we have approached communication and communication technologies within our families. Some of our assumptions may be outdated given this new context; as this book will argue, they may even be having unintended consequences that we are not yet able to see. As Carolyn Marvin suggested in her book *When Old Technologies Were New*, "new practices do not so much flow directly from technologies that inspire them as they are improvised out of old practices that no longer work in new settings."[10] It's in the spirit of this observation that this book turns to how, exactly, families are improvising in the new settings inaugurated by digital and mobile media.

This book argues that two distinct patterns in how families communicate are shaping media use in the digital age, and each of these patterns is rooted in particular histories and is now evolving in relation to digital and mobile media affordances. Among upper-income families, I observe an *ethic of expressive empowerment*, in which parents want to encourage their children to use these media in relation to education and self-development and to avoid use that might distract them from goals of achievement. Among lower-income families, I observe what I term an *ethic of respectful connectedness*, in which family members want to encourage the use of digital and mobile media in ways that are respectful, compliant toward parents, and family-focused. Certainly upper-income families want their children to be respectful and connected, and lower-income families want their children to grow into expressive and empowered people, and there are many instances in which family members use these media in ways that end up being disrespectful or even disempowering. I use the term "ethic" to signal that there are guiding principles that help parents and young people determine a course of action in relation to communication practices. Even if our efforts fall short, we all act out of the limits of our practical situations and in relation to what we take for granted as the right or good way to do things. But I argue that families live in a cultural milieu that tends to value one approach or the other, and we find ourselves adopting or responding to the patterns that are taken for granted in our particular context. Because there remain what Sonia Livingstone and Elizabeth Helsper term "gradations of digital inclusion," and because U.S. families experience lives that increasingly isolated from the lives of those in different economic circumstances, the uses of these media are reinforcing rather than alleviating a troubling economic and social gap in U.S. society.[11]

What may be surprising is this: when you consider the stories people from differing economic backgrounds tell about how they incorporate technology into their family lives, those with the greatest access to skills and resources would find much to envy among the family communication ethics of those who have much less access to skills and resources. And yet the very embrace of a communication ethic of expressive empowerment may be undermining our ability to foster an ethic of respectful connectedness within our families and beyond them. Does this mean that middle- and upper-income families are actually losing something of value as we unconsciously embrace certain approaches to technology in our fast-paced and teleconnected lives? I believe that we are, and this is part of the larger story this book will tell about how technological advances and family communication patterns are working together to reshape the family and the communication environment in which we all live. What I will argue is that in the networked society, focusing on the empowerment of our individual children may be causing us to miss the bigger picture. We need to understand not only what's new about technology and how technology changes our children's environments but also how our traditional ways of communicating with one another in our families may be generating more work for us all, and may need to be rethought in the digital era.

Not all upper-income families engage in the same strategies for setting guidelines regarding digital and mobile media, and not all lower-income families are similar to one another, either, as this book will demonstrate. But I believe that the patterns of difference that are emerging now will continue to shape the landscape of the future. The ways in which families are now differently engaging in digital and mobile media use suggest that technology is playing a role not in leveling the playing field, as many of us had hoped it would, but rather in contributing to the income inequality that has been on the rise in most countries since the early 1980s.[12] Thus, this book will foreground three issues: (1) how new technologies are introducing new situations that parents and children confront in their daily lives, (2) how inherited patterns of communicating within families are shaping our uses of and approaches to digital and mobile media, and (3) how the ways we communicate with one another (and not only the ways we regulate or oversee the uses of technologies) may need to be reconsidered so that we can better understand and manage the changes we are currently experiencing. All three of these components are needed if we are to understand how young people and their families are experiencing the mediated environment today, what parents can and should be doing to help young people to prepare to face the challenges of the emergent digital environment, and what we might anticipate for our future together. I believe that for too long we have overlooked the connections between family, technology, and what researcher Roger Silverstone referred to as the "moral economy of the household"—the relationships between what we do in our individual households and what happens in the world at large.[13] We owe it to ourselves to understand both how digital and mobile media are reshaping family life and how family uses of these media are, in turn, reshaping our society. Ultimately, these interrelated issues inform what parents need to do with, for, and in relation to young people in the emergent digital environment.

In order to write this book, I relied upon both formal and informal interviews held over more than a decade with parents, young people, relatives, educators, and researchers. I also relied upon the excellent research being produced in the areas of parenting, digital and mobile media, and gender and technology, and am especially grateful for the many journalists who have worked hard to keep parents informed about the issues confronting parents and young people today. Although my research team and I analyzed interview and survey data that filled well over a bookshelf's worth of three-ring notebooks, this book is also informed by my own experiences. As my children have grown up, the issues of this book have taken on increasing urgency in my own family's life.

In this book, I write in a way that is consistent with what some scholars have called "women's ways of knowing," in which there is no harsh separation between research and life, and where what happens in one realm inevitably informs the other.[14] Researchers are charged with telling stories that help to convey new interpretations of data and to offer new insights into shared experiences. Similarly, when parents, and in particular mothers, are faced with parenting dilemmas that relate to digital and mobile media, we also share stories. Just as researchers contribute to an ongoing conversation in which they build upon or challenge existing understandings, parents listen to what others have done and we try to learn from the successes and foibles of other parents. Sometimes the stories that parents share with one another are laugh-out-loud funny; other times they're sad and deeply troubling. Sometimes they're not even our own stories, but stories that have attained a mythic level of resonance because they speak to deep fears or anxieties about what it means to be a human being who cares about others. We are symbolic animals, and by putting our experiences in story form for others we learn what to do and what our actions mean.

My own understandings of the role of digital and mobile media within family life have been impossible to separate from my personal experiences as a parent who now lives within the milieu of expressive and empowering parenting. They are also influenced by my own experiences of having been parented in a context that was a study in contrasts. I grew up in a household where one of my parents came from privilege and the other didn't; one liked television, the other liked reading. Members of my mother's Italian American family have lived their entire lives in an economically depressed rust belt city of the Northeast. Many members of my father's Anglo-American family moved from the New York City area to the upwardly mobile and progressive city of San Francisco. On my mother's side there are bankruptcies; on my father's, millionaires. I think my own complicated background is why the relationships between economics, technology, and family life have always fascinated me. I'm sure it's why I am uncomfortable with the term "working class" or even "lower middle class," as you will see in this book. Sociologists would refer to half of my extended family in that way, although my family would never use those terms themselves. Members of my extended family buy middle-class things; they do things middle-class people do. If things had worked out differently, they would have had middle-class incomes and security. Some of them do now; others might someday. That's the way they, and I, see it. Like most parents, and like my own relatives, I hope that my own children are able to craft a balanced life that is meaningful and not financially strapped, and I worry about today's economy and their future prospects. Today my children go to a school two blocks from a mobile home park and two blocks from mini-mansions, and I sometimes wonder if there will be anything in between when they are older. As much as anything else, my desire that there be something in between is behind this book.

Researchers often fail to acknowledge how our own stories connect with what we study and why.[15] I include these personal stories to provide a framework for evaluating what I say here. It may not make the stories in this book any more "informational" or "factual," but I hope the stories will be resonant and instructive.

I have structured this book as a series of stories because I believe that even as human beings are challenged to access, process, and manage information to a greater extent than ever before, we do not make decisions based on a formula that is rooted in algorithms. Having information is not the same as *knowing*. Knowing involves feelings and intuitions as well as logical analysis. Knowing is relational, and our past experiences shape what we think we know about our present. We do not need more information on how to parent, therefore: we need ways of knowing that can frame how we understand the changes we are experiencing, and how we might parent as a result.

This book is divided into three parts, and you are welcome to read them in the order that strikes you as most interesting or urgent.

The first section foregrounds the most well-publicized parental fears related to digital and mobile media. These chapters tell stories that highlight concerns about possible links between depression and overinvolvement in social network sites, cyberbullying and teen suicide, and gaming and dropping out of high school. They include a discussion of how young people experience some of the things parents fear most about digital and mobile media contexts: cyberbullying, sexting, and Internet predators. Most of these stories reveal that young people are capable of handling the new situations that emerge with digital and mobile media, yet they also reveal the benefits that can come from advocating for those who are most vulnerable.

In the second section, I turn to the stories of young people, particularly preteens and teens. These stories illuminate why digital and mobile media technologies have come to be so central in the lives of youth today, and what that looks like in the lives of differently situated young people. These chapters consider how these media relate to youthful needs for identity, peer relationships, privacy, and autonomy, as well as to young people's continuing needs to maintain relationships with family members, cultures, and traditions.

In the final section, I introduce the two ethics of communication that I observed among upper- and middle-class families, on one hand, and "would-be middle-class" and less advantaged families. I do this by discussing how communication technologies both contribute to risk and are used to resolve it, how parents' patterns of communication have evolved to be responsive to these risks, how parents mediate the media as a means of overseeing their children's media environment, and how parents strive to keep their own familial goals in mind as they parent in spite of the host of other pressures they feel. I explore the ways in which even technologies that seemingly save time can add to the workload of the primary caregiver, who is usually but not always the mother.

The final chapter reviews the main themes of the book and presents a map for building a Parent App that will suit the needs of different families as they address themselves to the challenges and opportunities that digital and mobile media present to us all.

I have no interest in contributing to the already healthy amount of anxiety that parents have about technologies. Instead, I'm interested in understanding what's new about new media technologies as well as how these technologies are being used according to patterns that came before, so that we better understand how both factors are contributing to the changes we are all experiencing.

ACKNOWLEDGMENTS

First and foremost, I could not have completed this book without the loving support of my life partner, Jon Clark, and the times of no interruption given to me by my children, Jonathan and Allison Clark. I dedicate this book to them. I also appreciate the encouragement I've received from my parents, stepmom, and in-laws, Gerald Schofield, Sandra Schofield, Crea Clark, Janet Clark, and Joy Pearson-Obitz, my brother Rob, and my sisters and brothers-in-law Katie Webster Lois and Larry Ramey, Jan and Wiley Bucey, and Carol and Stephen Pardridge. My nieces Amanda Ramey and Sally Bucey need to be thanked for reliably setting me straight on mobiles and social media, my nephew Jon for showing me that Halo might not be so bad, and my nephews Jimmy Bucey, Joshua Pardridge, and Nick and Alex Maccallini for introducing me and my kids to Ultimate Dog Teaser, I Love Cats, Rebecca Black, Harry Potter Puppet Pals, the Muffin Man, Charlie the Unicorn, and every other viral teen thing. Consider yourselves Rick-rolled.

I wish to thank the University of Denver for providing me with an outstanding intellectual home and a matchless group of colleagues in the Media, Film, and Journalism Studies Department and the Emerging Digital Practices Program. Friday happy hours were a lifesaver, as were trips to Boulder to scheme with Adrienne Russell and John Tomasic. Thanks also to the University of Colorado at Boulder, and particularly Stewart Hoover, for support in the initial years of this project's development and ever since. Thanks to the University of Copenhagen and the Danish Research Council for timely opportunities to serve as visiting professor and to test out ideas related to this book's development. I particularly want to thank Stig Hjarvard for offering such a hospitable intellectual environment, and

Christa Christensen, Line Peterson, Klaus Bruhn Jensen, Kevin Barnhurst, Knut Lundby, Mia Lovheim, Espen Ytreberg, and Norbert Wildemuth, who made my time there especially valuable.

Friends and colleagues associated with the International Communication Association have listened and responded to many versions of this work over the years as I have developed this project. Special thanks especially to Sonia Livingstone for her inspiration, friendship, and razor-sharp insights, and to Carolyn Marvin, whose intellectual lineage I'm very proud to claim. Thanks to Mara Einstein, Michele Rosenthal, and Diane Winston, true friends and comrades in this academic life. Thanks also to Nancy Ammerman, Elizabeth Bird, Levi and Sheindy Brackman, Annette Markham, Sharon Mazzarella, Horace Newcomb, Amy Nathanson, Gina Neff, Radhika Parameswaran, Janice Peck, Ellen Seiter, Terri Senft, Fred Stutzman, Zala Volcic, Rhys Williams, and David Yamane, as well as Jefferson Unitarian Church. Other noteworthy conferences and venues that gave me an opportunity to develop this book's theoretical arguments include the conference on Media Ecology and Mediatization organized by Fredrich Krotz and Andreas Hepp at the University of Bremen; the Nordic mediatization conference organized by Stig Hjarvard at the University of Copenhagen; the Digital Media and Learning conference organized by Mimi Ito, Heather Horst, and Henry Jenkins at the University of California, Irvine, and the University of Southern California; the conference on Media Ecology and Cultural Studies at Santa Clara University; and the conference on graduate student research organized by Yariz Tsfari at Haifa University. I also want to acknowledge the inspiration I've found in the work of danah boyd, Stephanie Coontz, Eszter Hargittai, Heather Horst, Arlie Hochschild, Becky Herr-Stephenson, Mimi Ito, Henry Jenkins, Annette Lareau, Joshua Meyrowitz, and Stephen Mintz, as well as Anne Collier and Lenore Skenazy.

For reading and offering prescient criticisms on various drafts of this book, I thank Diane Alters, David Brake, Heidi Campbell, Mara Einstein, Monica Emerich, Heather Horst, Amanda Lenhart, Sun Sun Lim, Rich Ling, Regina Marchi, Adrienne Russell, Rivka Ribak, Michele Rosenthal, Lisa Tripp, and Kelly Whitney as well as the anonymous reviewers who offered wonderful suggestions for improving this manuscript.

I also want to thank the collaborators who worked with me in the development of the book *Media, Home, and Family* (Routledge, 2004): Diane Alters, Joseph Champ, Lee Hood, and Stewart Hoover. This book develops many ideas that first emerged in relation to that one, and my partnership with you has had and continues to have a profound influence on my thinking and ways of doing research.

I'd like to thank the friends and troublemakers outside of university life who, over the years, provided inspiration, real-life stories, interest, and timely play dates and dinners when needed: Diane and Henry Tiberi, Carrie and Jim Borer, Shelly and Loren Pinkernell, Risa Kerns, Dot Brownson, Stephanie and Dave Gaw, Marla and Mike Tamburro, Denise Feasel, Colleen Reed, Darlene Mayhak, Kyra Schueppert, Theresa Worsham, Nellishia Cisneros, Rick and Sandra Fisher, Beth Bidwell, Liz Minyard, Peggy Mroz, Lisa and John Young, Jen & Michael Olin-Hitt, Katrina Sarson, Julie Janson, and Laurie Menzies.

I was fortunate to have many excellent research assistants over the course of this project. For working with me at the University of Denver, I thank Morehshin Allahyari, Art Bamford, Caroline Davidson, Jill Dierberg, Tess Doezema, Collette Holst, Emma Lynch, Alexis Lynn, Loosineh Markarian, Rachel Monserrate, and Nik Vukovich. For working with me at the University of Colorado, I thank Christof Demont-Heinrich, Monica Emerich, AnnaMaria Russo Lemor, Kati Lustyik, Andy Matranga, Dan Mercado, Michele Miles, Zala Volcic, Denice Walker, and Scott Webber.

Support for aspects of this project came from various sources. I am especially thankful for support from the Lilly Endowment, Inc., especially Chris Coble and Craig Dykstra, who served as outstanding and patient program officers. Material in this book is also based on work supported by Prime Grant No. 08-91257-00-HCD between The Regents of the University of California and The MacArthur Foundation. Thanks also to the University of Denver for a Partners in Scholarship grant, and to the University of Colorado for several Undergraduate Research Opportunities grants.

Parts of chapter 2 appeared in Lynn Schofield Clark, "Doing Reflexive Ethnographic Work Among Parents and Their Teenage Children," in Radhika Parameswaran, ed., *Blackwell's International Companion to Media Studies: Audience Studies* (Oxford: Blackwell, 2011).

A longer version of Steph Kline's story (chapter 3) first appeared in L.S. Clark, "The Constant Contact Generation: Exploring Teen Friendship Networks Online," in S. Mazzarella, ed., *Girl Wide Web* (New York: Peter Lang, 2005).

Discussions of Norma and Veronica Domentary (chapter 3) and the Blayne-Gallagher family (chapter 8) were previously published in L. S. Clark, "A Multi-Grounded Theory of Parental Mediation: Exploring the Complementarity of Qualitative and Quantitative Communication Research," in K. B. Jensen, *A Handbook on Media and Communication Research: Qualitative and Quantitative Methodologies*, 2nd ed. (London: Routledge, 2011).

A discussion of the relationships between parenting styles and parental mediation theory (chapters 3 and 7) were previously published in L. S. Clark, "Parental Mediation Theory for the Digital Age," *Communication Theory* 12 (2011): 323–43.

The stories of Tanya Cortez (chapter 3) and Montana Odell and Gabriela Richards (chapter 5) were first analyzed in L. S. Clark, "Digital Media and the Generation Gap," *Information, Communication, and Society* 12, 3 (2009): 388–407.

Lower-income families' approaches to digital and mobile media (chapters 3, 7, and 8) were first discussed in L. S. Clark, C. Demont-Heinrich, and S. Webber, "Parents, ICTs, and Children's Prospects for Success: Interviews along the Digital 'Access Rainbow;'" *Critical Studies in Media Communication* 22, 5 (2005): 409–26, and L. S. Clark, C. Demont-Heinrich, and S. Webber, "Ethnographic Interviews on the Digital Divide," *New Media and Society* 6, 4 (2004): 529–47.

The stories of immigrant and refugee teens (including Iskinder, Santosh, Tahani, and others), as well as other parts of chapter 5, were previously published in L. S. Clark and L. Swywj, "Mobile Intimacies in the U.S. Among Refugee and Immigrant Teens and Their Parents," *Journal of Feminist Media Studies*, 2012.

An earlier discussion of mediatization (chapter 9) first appeared in L. S. Clark, "Mediatization: Where Media Ecology Meets Cultural Studies," in Knut Lundby, ed., *Emerging Theories of Mediatization* (New York: Routledge, 2009).

Lastly, I want to thank James Cook, my generous editor at Oxford University Press, along with Rebecca Clark, Leslie Johnson, and Arun Sivaramakrishnan, who also worked to bring this book to its final form. I am forever appreciative of your help and support!

PART I | Digital and Mobile Media: Cautionary Tales

CHAPTER 1 | Risk, Media, and Parenting in a Digital Age

THIRTEEN-YEAR-OLD RENEE VENUZZO COULDN'T wait to tell me what had happened earlier that day. As she got in my car for the short trip to my house for her babysitting job, she told me: "Me and Tessie were at the mall and some guy took our picture. And he had a laptop and everything." The words came in a rush, including something about the police and harassment.

"Wait. What?" I asked, trying to make sense of what she was telling me.

Renee told me that she and her friend had been walking around the mall on Friday afternoon when "some guy" took a photo of them, then quickly left. Renee didn't know what to do, so she called her mom at work and Tessie called hers. After asking if the girls wanted to leave the mall (neither girl did), the mothers told the girls that they should find mall security and tell them that an unknown man had taken their picture. The girls did so and continued shopping, but then they saw the man sitting in the food court. Renee and her friend alerted mall security again. The security officers brought him in for questioning and then asked the girls to come in and give a statement so that the man could be arrested for harassment. It turned out they weren't the only girls he'd taken pictures of that day. "It was weird, because he looked like such a normal, fortysomething guy," Renee said. Normal, except that he was carrying around a camera and a laptop in a mall on a Friday afternoon, taking photos of thirteen-year-old girls.

What is happening to young people like Renee and Tessie as they live in the electronic world? How are today's digital and mobile media affecting their experiences in and views of the world? And what are parents doing to help their children prepare to live as happy, independent, productive, and caring human beings in the digital age? These are the questions that form the core of this book.

Renee and Tessie are members of what some have termed the "digital generation."[1] They can't remember a time when their homes didn't have laptops and mobile phones in addition to the more traditional electronic media of televisions, music players, and gaming consoles. They take for granted the freedom and independence that mobile connections have made possible for them, options that their parents and grandparents could not have even imagined.[2] These freedoms create more opportunities for young people to remain connected to their parents and other family members—and more opportunities for them to come into contact with potentially undesirable people from outside their immediate environment.

The events at the mall that day encapsulate several aspects of what it means to be a parent in the digital era, and they direct our attention to one of the primary concerns that all parents have when it comes to digital, mobile, and traditional media: they want their children to be safe, to be smart about any situation in which they find themselves. On one hand, there is the aspect of danger: who knew what the guy intended to do with the photos he'd taken of Renee and Tessie? Would he have tried to identify the girls? He might have planned to use facial recognition software to find other photos of them online so as to track who they were and where they lived or went to school. Or perhaps he wanted to post the photos online. Within minutes after taking them, he could have uploaded the photos, Photoshopped them, and even sold them as pornography. Digital media make horrifying things possible, often in ways we can't yet imagine—and wouldn't want to.

On the other hand, Renee and Tessie knew that in such an unknown and uncomfortable situation, they wanted to connect with their mothers—and because of mobile media, they were able to call them to ask for advice at a crucial moment. The girls' mothers could feel confident that they helped their daughters to address the situation in a way that would protect the girls' safety. And by reporting the man's actions, Renee and Tessie were able to avert potential danger for others as well.

Risks like these, involving digital and mobile media, are the focus of the first section of this book. This chapter begins by considering the current debates about how digital and mobile media heighten risks for young people, exploring research that has looked at the characteristics of these media and the social indicators that might point us toward particular areas of concern. The following two chapters then consider stories of young people who have experienced some of the dangers and difficulties that parents fear most in relation to these media.

In this book, I'm especially interested in how different families respond to what they perceive as the risks of digital and mobile media. Thus, although this chapter and those that follow look at the risks these new media present, I aim to place these concerns in sociological context. I suggest that in order to understand the risks of digital and mobile media, we have to consider the important role the news media have played in constructing both how we think about these risks and how we think about parental responsibilities in the face of these risks. We also need to consider the ways that economic resources structure risk and our responses to it. Our heightened sense of childhood risk is related to what sociologist Ulrich Beck has termed the rise of a "risk society" in which a 24/7 marketplace, facilitated by ever more efficient communication media, has introduced instability into various aspects of our lives. We now feel that we as individuals are responsible for mitigating risk, even as our interconnectedness and inescapable vulnerability have placed the prospect of eliminating risk permanently out of our reach. I'm interested in how this sense of risk plays out differently among contrasting families.

Too often, our research on digital and mobile media, just like our news coverage of its risks, has focused on the middle- or upper-middle-class experiences of these media. This book aims to see what happens when we think about digital and mobile media and their related risks in comparative perspective, which seems an especially relevant approach given the economic circumstances of the vast majority of people in the United States and the rest of the world. But this book also aims to help parents across the economic spectrum as family relationships transition in relation to the new digital reality. I am a social researcher of new media in family life, but I am also a parent. I cannot separate my interest in describing family life in the digital age from my felt need for what I've called a Parent App, or a way of finding help and direction as I navigate parenthood in a digital age myself. You may find that there is a sense of urgency as I review various theories of parenting and media here, then, because I'm writing this book as much for me as I am for you.

Digital and Mobile Media as a Risk Amplifier

When risk and safety in the online realm are mentioned, parents' thoughts usually turn to things such as cyberbullying and sexual predators. Parents might also think about how young people can become involved in activities that are potentially illegal, such as downloading music or sexting.[3] Some parents worry that spending too much time online or with entertainment media can contribute to a child's social isolation, declining social skills, and depression.[4] Others are concerned that constant immersion in digital media contributes to distraction, increases rates of ADD or ADHD, and leads to an inability to process information meaningfully.[5]

In many public venues, the Internet has come to be viewed as a "risk amplifier." People generally accept the idea that access to the Internet makes children more vulnerable to predators, that the Internet promotes and aggravates bullying, that it sexualizes, and that it corrupts through exposure to extremism. It's also believed that the Internet encourages anorexia and even suicide, and that it threatens academic and physical development.[6] Yet David Finkelhor, director of the Crimes Against Children Research Center, who put together this list of ways in which the Internet is thought to act as a risk amplifier, suggests that the idea that the Internet increases dangers for young people is largely unsupported by the evidence.[7] Finkelhor speaks about heightened "juvenoia" in relation to the Internet, noting that parents' fears tend to be articulated in relation to what the Internet makes possible rather than what has actually happened. Not only does the Internet afford predators easy access to vulnerable people, or so the thinking goes, but because it's easier than ever to be anonymous, people can act without regard to the moral norms that would otherwise govern behavior. And yet, as Finkelhor points out, in the years since the widespread introduction of the Internet, in the United States sex crimes against children have dropped dramatically, the percentage of teens who say that they have had sex has gone down, the number of teen suicides has declined dramatically (as has the number who have contemplated suicide), and we have even seen a decline in the number of young people who reported criminal victimization in school.[8] If the Internet were causing a major shift in the experiences of risk among young people, surely some of these indicators would show different results, Finkelhor argues. The main conclusion one can draw from this data, he says, is that bad things can happen to children online because they can happen *anywhere*.[9]

Parents are concerned that digital and mobile media heighten the possibility for risk, and yet all of the social indicators seem to suggest that these media do not create new risks or even increase the number of young people who experience negative consequences. Digital and mobile media may amplify the effects of problem behaviors, and they may also amplify the possibilities for addressing those behaviors insofar as they provide the means for young people and their families to find resources to protect themselves. What we need to attend to in order to evaluate risk, then, is how these media provide new means for amplifying, recording, and spreading information, as social media researcher danah boyd suggests, since these affordances of new media do change the landscape in which all human behaviors now take place.[10]

There are basically four characteristics of digital and mobile media that contribute to making problem behaviors more visible, as boyd has suggested, and what Renee and Tessie experienced illustrates these four key characteristics:

1. Digital media have introduced *persistence* to communication. Once uploaded onto the Internet, information (such as the photos of the girls taken in the mall) can be extremely difficult to remove. Contrary to the norms of interpersonal communication, on the Internet the norm is "persistent by default, ephemeral when necessary," as boyd has argued.[11]

2. Digital and mobile media are constantly changeable; they are *in perpetual beta*. It is now relatively easy to replicate, modify, and share materials online, making it difficult for us to distinguish originals from replicas, and creating new opportunities for those who wish to defame or defraud others.

3. There is a *scalability* to digital media. What might once have been an isolated prank can "go viral," whether the person who originally posted the content intended this or not. What's scaled is not necessarily "what individuals want to have scaled or what they think should be scaled, but what the collective chooses to amplify," writes boyd.[12]

4. Digital media are defined by *searchability*.[13] Anyone or anything can be Googled through a search engine, and with GPS and visual and voice recognition software, it is now possible for nearly anyone to be found and identified.

Parents need to understand how these characteristics of digital and mobile media have changed the environment in which teen actions occur, and they also need to figure out how to address their concerns about these changes. The chapters in this book's first section offer insights into how parents and their children are experiencing this changed environment. In the second and third sections of this book, we explore how parents respond to these changes, and how young people interpret those responses—sometimes in ways that differ from what their parents intended.

How the Media Participate in Constructing Risk

Parents across the economic spectrum wonder how they can keep informed about the risks that immersion in digital and mobile media may present to their children. Not surprisingly, perhaps, they turn to experts. Not only is there a burgeoning list of parenting blogs, websites, and self-help books offering help, but online and broadcast commentators are also quick to provide advice. This media attention to the subject isn't surprising either—after all, parents (particularly middle-and upper-middle-class mothers) make up a highly desirable demographic for publishers and producers to target.

Executives at legacy media such as television, radio, and print news know they can capitalize on parental fears by reporting on such potentially sordid phenomena as ChatRoulette.com, HotOrNot.com, and IsAnyoneUp.com, garnering desirable ratings in the process.[14] Sometimes news media attempt to advocate for young people, such as when the *Sioux City* (Iowa) *Journal* devoted the front page of its Sunday edition to an anti-bullying editorial in response to a gay teen's suicide, mentioning Facebook and cell phones as some of the locations where bullying can occur.[15] Unfortunately, the media do not always report accurately about children's and teens' use of social media, choosing instead either to make unfounded statements themselves or to find and quote experts or law enforcement officials who may make exaggerated statements for them. In this way, as Barry Glassner pointed out in his book *The Culture of Fear*, the news media along with advocacy groups and politicians have contributed to the perception that danger has increased in relation to these media, despite evidence to the contrary.[16]

Let me offer a brief review of one such example of questionable reporting from a Spokane, Washington, television news station, which broadcast a report titled "'Sexting' Takes on New, More Dangerous Form."[17] The segment begins with an older male news anchor noting that "Spokane County sex crime detectives say more and more people are using the Internet to prey on children." Then an attractive, young, and earnest female reporter offers this attention-grabbing introduction: "Every time you log onto a social media site, you open yourself up to a host of dangers, and it is even riskier for kids who don't have much online awareness." The report cites no evidence of an increase in predatory behavior, and no evidence that young people without "much online awareness" are at greater risk than their more technologically savvy peers. The Spokane County detective who speaks on camera for the story, in fact, does not discuss either of these issues. Nevertheless, the reporter then offers another unsupported statement: "Sexual interaction between children and adults is skyrocketing," she says, as the detective is shown researching possible Internet predators online. The report concludes with a familiar admonishment: "Unless more parents help to educate their children, this scary online world will stay a reality."

Imagine how this news story might have been presented differently if indeed sexual interaction between adults and children was "skyrocketing" in Spokane. Wouldn't a reporter be expected to back up this claim with evidence? Wouldn't viewers expect that such a story would feature information about the victims of these unwanted interactions and about specific law enforcement efforts to stop the perpetrators? Yet this story leads with the purported dangers of the Internet and concludes with the suggestion that responsible parents should attend an upcoming law enforcement workshop on social media. Given the lack of facts relayed in this two-minute segment, one might wonder why this story was thought worthy of attention. The reason may have been revealed in the reporter's seemingly incidental mention of the workshop on social media at the end of the segment: perhaps it was a news release from law enforcement rather than "skyrocketing" sexual interaction that prompted this story. In other words, the story may sound frightening, but it's a promotional announcement posing as news.

This story fits the general pattern of crime reporting identified by researchers, who have noted that magnifying problems of crime benefits both news organizations and law enforcement. Such reports strengthen the felt need to watch more news and suggests that law enforcement and news organizations share common purposes in keeping individuals safe and informed.[18] Modifying the age-old television news adage "If it bleeds, it leads," crime coverage researchers Brian Spitzberg and Michelle Cadiz summarize this titillating if misleading approach to news this way: "If it terrorizes, it mesmerizes."[19] Researchers have found that heavy news viewers are more likely than light news viewers to believe that we are living in a "mean and scary world," and therefore reports such as these contribute to our collective sense that new media should be a reason for concern.[20]

Because of the commercial structure of the U.S. media, there is a built-in incentive for news media outlets to churn out material warning about the dangers of sexting or highlighting arrests of Internet predators.[21] Books and editorials with titles such as *Endangered Minds: Why Children Don't Think and What We Can Do About It* or "Hooked on Gadgets, and Paying a Mental Price" provide the same promise of tantalizing information to an interested and concerned audience, thus ensuring that reports exploring the relationship between digital, visual, and mobile media and increases in attention deficit disorder, autism, and the inability to think critically will inevitably be a part of our public record for a long time to come.[22]

Whereas it's worth considering carefully how digital and mobile media have brought about changes in our lives, it's also important to recognize hyperbole. Even if the fears are not always warranted, the rise in the *perception* of fear is having real consequences in our lives. Fears about the

Internet, mobile phones, and social media are often related to a larger cultural anxiety concerning "stranger danger."[23] Journalist Lenore Skenazy has been tracking the rise of worries about "stranger danger." She argues that in the past several years we have seen an increase in the number of statutes, laws, and policies that purport to increase safety for young people but which actually may be making childhood more restrictive and parenting less effective.[24] We need to address this rising anxiety before it undermines our best parenting efforts.

Just as news organizations can benefit from fear-mongering, so too can others benefit as they lay claim to a moral high ground regarding parenting and digital and mobile media. Sometimes this claim of moral concern can be downright amusing if examined in context. For instance, consider the news report titled "Study: Parents Don't Care if Kids Play Violent Video Games."[25] After rhetorically chiding several parents who explain their reasons for allowing their children to play these games, the reporter goes on to cite a purported expert who exhorts, "Parents must take responsibility." Without irony, the article credits this precious insight to the head of a gaming trade organization—who benefits from taking the moral high ground while also selling games to those who allegedly shirk responsibility. What I'm especially interested in is the way in which moral discourses such as these—those that frame reports of "stranger danger" and mediated exposure to risk—feed into our collective sense of who should be taking responsibility for addressing these alleged problems.[26] Several voices in our cultural conversation emphasize that it's the job of the parent alone to address problems, regardless of a particular parent's access to support and resources to manage such problems on her own. The message in the media seems to be that because *some* children have encountered danger, we must *all* be vigilant, but only about our own children. And, by extension, the cultural message seems to be that if a child engages in problem behaviors, it's primarily the fault of the parent. It's easy to get involved in this discussion of morally correct parenting: just look at the comments section of the *New York Times* blog *Motherlode* for an example of how quickly people jump to judging the parenting philosophies and practices of others.

The problem with this judgmental approach, however, is that ultimately it does not help our own children, who live in a culture that includes children who struggle. Being the idealist I am, I wonder how different our collective lives could look if our first response was one of compassion rather than judgment toward other parents and the children who struggle (and I admit to participating in the judging). I also wonder how digital and

University students are wonderful sources of knowledge about morally correct parenting. Here's a sampling of what I've heard when I've discussed parenting and technology with them:

- "My parents didn't let me have a phone till I was fifteen, and that was a good decision, so I can't understand why any parent would consider getting their child a phone at a younger age."
- "No one younger than thirteen needs to be on social networking sites, so why would parents even consider allowing their kids to have access to Facebook?"
- "Why do parents let their preteens see movies like the *Hunger Games* series? Those films are so violent that it could damage vulnerable young people." (Sometimes this is followed with a caveat: "Well, I wasn't that vulnerable when I was that age, but I know that kids today are.")

Here's my response. We all tend to think that it's morally wrong to engage in certain kinds of parenting practices. But let's start with the big picture of what we agree on: physical, psychological, and emotional abuse of children is always wrong. Those are the most egregious risks that children face. Let's then also note that parents who engage in these activities are punished, both legally and socially. When we're talking about media practices, we're on a different level of moral decision making. Parents might make wrong choices about media practices (for me, the dad who fired his gun into his daughter's laptop in February 2012 comes to mind; see chapter 5), but these choices will hardly ever fall into the same realm of moral and legal infractions. Some choices might be indicators: a neglectful parent might allow a young child to watch television all day. But that doesn't mean that every mother who's allowed a youngster to watch *Teletubbies* in order to get a much-needed shower is neglectful or engaging in a morally question-able activity.

Let me simply suggest here that there are a lot of parental decisions that look clear-cut and morally wrong until you're a parent yourself. One of my best friends still loves to tease me about the pronouncement I made before I became a parent that my children were never going to watch Disney movies. I still remember her knowing smirk a few years later at my then-four-year-old daughter's Disney princess party. So I guess I've learned the hard way: parents usually are trying their best, and they have reasons for what they're doing when it comes to media. They may not always be what we think are good reasons, but I believe it's worth exploring why parents make the decisions they do. Just be slow to judge. Someday you too might find yourself hosting a Disney princess party.

mobile media might be utilized in partnerships as well as in individual families to help address problems of social inequity. In this book, after we have heard how families of differing backgrounds have addressed issues of digital and mobile media in their lives, we will return to these questions of compassion and social structure in the book's concluding chapter.

Somehow, despite all of the changes we are experiencing, most parents and their children are managing fairly well when it comes to the actual situations of risk they encounter, and our views of new technologies tend to become more tempered over time, as we will see in the chapters that follow. In fact, a recent study revealed that when considering how to limit their children's media use, parents reported that they were primarily concerned with the extent to which these media prevent their children from getting enough physical exercise or from spending time on other activities.[27]

But there is no question that news stories about Internet predators, cyberbullies, and Internet-related crimes that affect young people are articulating some very real parental concerns. Underlying our concerns about digital and mobile media is, perhaps, something deeper. Western society seems to have developed a discomfort both with the developmental processes of growing up and with the role of parents and digital and mobile media in these processes.[28] Perhaps parents are worried that they have not adequately prepared their preteens and teens for the adult world available to them through digital and mobile media. Maybe they do not quite trust their children to act responsibly and sensibly, or they worry that their off-spring will not know what to do under pressure, given all of the various mediated temptations they will encounter. Or perhaps parents across the economic spectrum are concerned that their children's peers, or even the commercial media industry itself, might have more influence over their children than they do. I believe that our contradictory feelings regarding digital and mobile media in our children's lives mask a more fundamental concern: we are worried about the process of growing up and becoming independent in a world dominated by risk and uncertainty, particularly in relation to a media environment that seems less familiar to parents than it does to their children.

Living in a Risk Society

The risks associated with growing up in today's world extend far beyond those of the online realm that young people encounter through their mobile phones or laptops. Discussions about risk relate to the media environment in two different yet intersecting ways. Communication technologies continue to shape the economic landscape of family life, as I explain below. They also provide the means through which parents can respond to the dilemmas that arise within that economic landscape as they seek to balance work and family needs.

First, media have significantly shaped the economic landscape in which parents work, and in which children themselves will someday work. Numerous sociologists have commented on the changes Western society has already undergone over the past hundred years as we have moved from being an agrarian and rural society to being an urban and industrialized one, and from a society organized by groups in physical co-presence to one in which social and media networks constitute the primary mode of organization.[29] Thanks to the interconnectedness of digital media, the work environment is increasingly shaped by a 24/7 networked global economy. And modernization, as the German sociologist Ulrich Beck noted, has introduced a series of new hazards and insecurities that arise from our heightened interdependence in this increasingly urban and networked society, as illustrated both by the prospect of coordinated transnational terrorist acts and the near collapse of the world's financial markets. Beck notes that we now live in what he terms a "risk society."[30] Sophisticated systems of communication technology have been employed to *control* risk, and yet these systems have also *contributed* to risk. For instance, the risk of human-generated disaster is heightened when people can decide in one part of the world to deploy chemical or biological weapons in another.[31] Accordingly, communication technologies have fundamental importance to the development of globalization, as labor, money, and correspondence travel easily from place to place, allowing relationships, both of enrichment and of exploitation, to develop in new ways.[32]

We have come to realize that there may be no permanent solutions to the problem of risk, and that in many ways, the more mundane uses of communication technologies—particularly those related to digital networks—are increasing exposure to risk on a global scale. The U.S. public has largely lost faith in the ability of societal institutions to manage risk, particularly in the aftermath of the 2008 financial crisis and the well-publicized 2011 failures of U.S. government bodies to reach bipartisan solutions to enduring problems. This heightens parental anxiety in general, as parents sense that they have less control than they might wish over the shape of their own lives and their children's lives. People now increasingly look for ways to put preventive measures in place to reduce their exposure to risk, at both the societal and individual levels.[33]

The second way in which risk in general is related to the media is more specific to media practices in the home. As adults in both single-parent and two-parent families feel obligated to work longer and longer hours in an increasingly unstable economic environment to reduce their family's exposure to risk, they rely on a variety of arrangements for supervising and engaging their children in activities while they address the demands of their work lives. The rise in media use among young people, therefore, is not unrelated to the demands of parents' work lives. At the same time, parents feel obligated to oversee and control their children's increased media use. As we will see in the stories presented in the third section of this book, many parents feel that leisure time spent with media is wasted time, and given the uncertain economy, they fear that there is no time to waste in preparing children for a competitive job market.[34] Even as U.S. middle-class income has declined in real terms since 2002, incomes have been surging in Brazil, Russia, India, and China.[35] As resources for schools and enrichment programs have become a battleground in the United States, young people have come to be viewed less as a resource in which society invests than as participants in a competition; it's "economic Darwinism," as Henry Giroux has argued.[36] And unfortunately, many of our young people are not faring very well in this competition. Risk, even risk related to digital and mobile media, looks quite different depending on one's economic circumstances.

Contrasting Stories of Risk and Resources

Just as the news media have played a role in constructing how we think about risk, these media have helped construct how we think about what it means to be middle-class. Commercial media stand to benefit by reaching those of us who prefer to think of ourselves as middle-class. We tend to put ourselves in this category if we have sufficient income to purchase at least some of the goods and services that advertisers—those who support the media—are trying to sell.[37] In reflecting our experience, advertising confirms for us our sense that we are a part of that group. Too, publishers know that those with higher incomes purchase more books, e-books, newspapers, and other reading materials than those with lower incomes, and this provides a built-in incentive to speak to middle-class audiences about middle-class experiences. The majority of people in the United States today, in fact, self-identify as middle-class.[38] However, most of us recognize that people have vastly different life experiences depending on their income, assets, education, aspirations, and occupation.

In contrast to this chapter's opening story of Renee and her friend's experiences with dangers that were vaguely related to the Internet, Gerardo Molinero, another young person interviewed for this book, was much more reserved when discussing his experiences with risk and the online environment.[39] His friends pressured him to join Facebook, he said, but he had refused. Adopting a stance of bravado among his mostly lower-income friends, he said he didn't care about sites like that. Later, however, Gerardo admitted that his mother, who had family members who had started the process of acquiring citizenship but were residing and working in the United States without documentation, had expressly asked him and his brother to refrain from establishing profiles on Facebook. Her fear was that such a public display might attract unwanted attention to their family. And so, because he wanted to protect the interests of his family, he did not establish a profile. He had also asked friends not to post pictures of him on their profiles, although that request often went unheeded. Gerardo wasn't especially worried about the fact that his pictures were on his friends' Facebook profiles—but he had chosen not to tell his mother about it, just in case.

Families from varied economic backgrounds experience and respond differently to the risks related to the introduction of digital and mobile media into their family's lives. Here's how the concerns of Gerardo and his mother relate to the four key characteristics of digital media. Gerardo's mother did not want photos or information about their family members online because she implicitly recognized the *persistence* of digital information: anything put online could be available online for a long time afterward. Moreover, both Gerardo and his mother recognized that the decision to avoid participating in social network sites was one that they would have to revisit over and over, as the nature of communication as something *in perpetual beta* meant that someone could put a photo of Gerardo online at any time, and Gerardo's mother wanted him to remain vigilant and request that they be taken down. *Scalability* was not a direct concern, but Gerardo's mother definitely worried about the *searchability* of digital information and the fact that a person who was so inclined could piece together stories of who they were and the circumstances under which they and their family members were living.

Gerardo, Renee, Tessie, and their mothers all recognized certain risks present in the digital environment, particularly in relation to personal safety. In each case, mothers felt justified in their fears that the Internet was a gateway to an outside world full of potential dangers: creepy people like the guy in the mall might find you, or law enforcement officials might use information about you to gain access to a family member who would prefer to remain hidden. However, in these examples we gain some insight into how people whose life experiences differ may consider digital, mobile, and even traditional media in some ways that are similar and in others that are quite different.

Families like Renee's and Tessie's live in a cultural milieu that responds to risk through what I will call an *ethic of expressive empowerment*. I use the term "ethic" to refer to the body of principles and values that are distinctive to a particular group. Among wealthy, upper-middle-class, and some middle-class U.S. families such as Renee's and Tessie's, "good parenting" is associated with raising children who are self-confident, caring, self-reliant, honest, and capable of expressing their views and emotions while exercising self-control. Intellectual curiosity and a desire to achieve are also prized.[40] Renee and Tessie were praised for using their cell phones in a way that demonstrated their self-confidence and their self-reliance. Ironically, they demonstrated this self-reliance by calling their mothers for advice.[41]

Other families appreciate many aspects of this approach to good parenting, but for them the emphasis is slightly different. Families like Gerardo's live in a cultural milieu that responds to risk through an *ethic of respectful connectedness*. Among these families are those that might be described as "would-be middle class" or "less advantaged" as well as some middle-class families, and for them, good parenting is associated with raising children who are loyal, respectful, patriotic, and caring toward both their families and their communities, because family bonds are seen as the greatest defense against risk. A good sense of humor, leadership, and resilience in the face of adversity are highly prized.[42]

Renee and Tessie were able to use their mobile phones to stay safe by remaining in contact with their mothers, just as Gerardo similarly maintained strong relationships with his family. Each of these young people lived in a family in which parents wanted to supervise their children and help them minimize their exposure to risk. Yet Gerardo was strongly encouraged to avoid social network technologies to safeguard not only himself but also extended family members living at the margins of society; he was expected to respect his family's needs and to want to help them to stay safe as well.

Reframing the Discussion of Media and Risk: The Digital Trail

Whenever a new communications technology is introduced, our lives as individuals and as a society are forever changed.[43] In many ways, then, this book seeks to follow the lead of communication scholar Joshua Meyrowitz, who several decades ago made a compelling argument about how television was reshaping family life. In his book *No Sense of Place*, Meyrowitz observed that television changed the "situational geography" of social life.[44] Before television, there were some situations that were simply inaccessible to certain people, whether for geographic reasons or because people behaved differently behind closed doors than they might in public. Electronic media tended to "expose many features of what was formerly the 'backstage' of social life," he argued.[45] Television made it possible for people to know more about situations that previously had been hidden from them. Because of television, it was harder for parents to keep certain aspects of adult life hidden from their children—a problem that policy makers, media literacy experts, and parents have been attempting to address ever since. What I liked about Meyrowitz's book was that it was attentive to the concerns that parents and others had about young people growing up in a mediated environment, and it also emphasized how important it is to consider the bigger picture of how social change happens when new technologies introduce challenges to existing patterns of social behavior. What I add to his approach, which he terms "medium theory," is a more comprehensive understanding of how parents and their children are actually incorporating new media into their lives, and how these patterns of use, as well as the characteristics of those technologies themselves, are shaping the emergent digital and mobile media environment and our lives within it.[46]

With the rise of television, Meyrowitz argued, children could see what adults might not have wanted them to see. With the emergence of the digital and mobile media environment, parents—along with everyone else—can also witness what children and those who wish them good or ill may not want anyone else to see. We have unprecedented access to children's experiences, a situation that produces both more knowledge about what is happening among a variety of children (information, for instance, about sexting, bullying, online predators, and human trafficking) and more anxiety about what could happen to our own children. This increased access to information gives parents greater opportunities to anticipate problems, but it also heightens anxieties about what could emerge that would make our own children vulnerable.

The information that parents can access about their own and other people's children pales in comparison to the vast array of information to which we *all* now have access. As economics and communication researchers Martin Hilbert and Priscila López have observed, our combined technological memory has increased exponentially over the past twenty-five years.[47] To illustrate, they note that if all of our technological memory were stored on double-sided paper, in 1986 all of the world's land masses would have been covered with a single layer of paper. Since then, our storage capacity for information has doubled roughly every three years. By 2007, the world's land masses would have been covered with one layer of books, and by 2011, with two layers of books.[48] Over the same period of time, our capacity for communicating with one another has also increased exponentially. In 1986, each person conveyed the equivalent of two newspaper pages of information per day to other people, and received the equivalent of 55 entire newspapers per day. By 2007, people were conveying to others the equivalent of 6 newspapers of information per day and receiving the equivalent of 175 newspapers of information.[49] We also have much greater capacity to process this information than ever before, and to do so more quickly. Hilbert and López observe that if 2,200 people carried out manual calculations from the big bang until 2011, they could execute as many instructions as computers could carry out in *one second* in 2011.[50]

Our ability to *access, process, and manage information* has become an important marker of mental development in the contemporary world, and it is related to how we must begin to rethink risk as well as parenting.[51] Parents, and in particular mothers, have much more to manage as a result of this change in technology. For women, technologies such as mobile phones can be useful, and they can seem liberating, as they allow women greater control over their means of communicating with others. But they may not necessarily lighten the workload for women, as historian Ruth Schwartz Cowan first observed in her study of household technologies "from the open hearth to the microwave."[52] Feminist researchers note that women use technologies in ways that sometimes challenge and sometimes reproduce power relations. These uses happen not as a result of conscious rational thought but as women seek to address particular situations in relation to their felt needs. In the realm of parenting, the rise of the information age has coincided with what Anthony Giddens terms the "reflexive self," and specifically with what my colleagues and I have called *reflexive parenting*.[53] Mothers are expected to make conscientious decisions not only about digital and mobile media but also about everything else that shapes the environment in a child's life. They do not make these decisions by rationally assessing risk; rather, they make them in relation to their interest in promoting their children's well-being, experiencing well-being themselves, and being a "good parent." Being a self-conscious parent is touted throughout the self-help literature for mothers: "think and then respond," or engage in "love and logic," as several popular parenting texts geared to middle-class parents exhort. This approach does not assume that people are rational; rather, it assumes that they are guided by emotions and must self-consciously adopt a rational position. Parenting advice books may be good indicators of the "emotion work" parents engage in as they manage life and information overload in the digital age.[54]

Of course, digital and mobile media have made communication multidirectional and about much more than just sharing information. Rather than simply being permitted to *observe* social behavior, as was the case with television, we are all *participating* in new forms of social behavior via communication technology platforms that bridge the private and the public. Every time we are online, we participate in creating our own digital trail: one that is visible to many, that is not created exclusively by us, and over which we cannot exert full control. This digital trail is part of who we are because it plays a role in how other people and organizations view us and interact with us, but it is also neither completely separate from nor completely aligned with our embodied selves. It is also not merely information but related to a kind of knowing.

In addition to children being inadvertently exposed to the vagaries of adult life, then, in today's digital and mobile media environment everyone is potentially capable of knowing a great deal about everyone else, and we all relate to one another through an ever-expanding repertoire of communication practices facilitated by digital and mobile media as a result. As sociologist Anthony Giddens has asserted, we are now all "communicatively interdependent."[55] This situation is reshaping our experiences of privacy, authority, identity, and tradition. It presents all of us with new challenges, and parents are on the front lines of enacting how these challenges are lived out in our most intimate relationships.

To figure out what children and parents are experiencing in the emergent digital environment, we have to pay attention to the fact that not everyone in society experiences the same thing when it comes to communication technologies, and that this in itself is part of a much longer-term change in our mediated environment. A mere half century ago, television was a homogenizing force in society. At least for a time, we all watched the same programs on the same few networks. Even if you were in a social community that didn't feel well represented (or represented at all) on television, or even if your family didn't have a television, you knew what the choices were: you could watch, or you could not watch and have a pretty good idea of what you were missing. In contrast, with today's plethora of communication technology options, the patterns of ownership and use of communication technologies seem almost limitless. In our own homes, four people can be seated in the same room engaging with four different forms of media.

The patterns of difference increase exponentially as we consider different patterns of communication and media use that are occurring in differing neighborhoods. Not all families have the same level of access and skill, and not all young people are "digital natives," as the popular phrase has it.[56] This book contends that we have to pay attention to these differences if we are to recognize how differing patterns of communication that existed prior to the emergence of the latest technologies are shaping their use today, and how, in turn, these new technologies are reshaping family life.[57]

Despite all the talk about how young people are more adept at technologies than their parents, what is much more obvious is an enduring *economic* gap in which both younger and older people who have greater access to resources are generally more adept and more engaged in the digital landscape than those who have less access to such resources. Simply put, some people are better situated than others to manage in the new communication environment. Whether it's because of the limits of time, limited space in the household, limited technological skills, or limits on how many cell phones or what kind of cell phone plan the family can afford, differences in usage patterns persist. This challenges the facile assumption that someday everyone will "catch up" and have the same experiences with digital and mobile media that the wealthiest in the United States, northern Europe, and East Asia now have. Evidence is mounting that technological advances are contributing to widening income inequality.[58] Therefore, as we think about the Parent App that is needed for our families and our society, we have to take into consideration the fact that families' experiences with technology vary greatly depending on how they are able to incorporate such technologies into their lives in the first place.

In the stories of Renee, Tessie, and Gerardo and their families, then, we can see that there are similarities and overlaps in how these families approach digital and mobile media in their lives. All of the parents aim to make themselves accessible to their children for support, and they expect that their children will contact them if a difficulty arises. There are also differences in how these families attach meaning to the cultural objects of digital, mobile, and traditional media. How they incorporate these things into their lives can't be directly tied to their economic situations. What the differences in these stories point to, and what we will see in the chapters that follow, is that there are certain patterns in how families are incorporating digital and mobile media into their lives. If we want to understand how these media are changing family life in the United States, we need to consider that perhaps families that are situated differently in relation to resources may be having incommensurable experiences with these media.

The resources to which parents and their children have access make a big difference, and they give a particular shape to the ethics of expressive empowerment and respectful connectedness that in turn shape parental approaches to digital and mobile media. Yet so far, most analyses of how digital, mobile, and traditional media are playing a role in family life have explored either middle- and upper-middle-class experiences or those of the digitally excluded; they have not compared the two.[59] Recent works by digital media researchers Sherry Turkle and danah boyd have included both middle-class and non-middle-class people in their studies, as have large-scale surveys, but these studies have not delved into the different patterns between these groups.[60] On the other hand, works that explore how digital, mobile, and traditional media are reinforcing economic barriers for the less advantaged have focused on individuals or on policy and large-scale statistics rather than on families.[61] I wanted to address this gap. In this book, I recognize one pattern among those who are wealthy, upper-middle-class, and middle-class, and a different pattern among those who are lower-middle-class, working-class, and working poor (whom I prefer to term the *would-be middle class* or the *less advantaged*).

Sociologists have long used the term "social class" as a way to understand groups of people in relation to a combination of factors—income, education, assets, and occupation—that influence their lived experiences.[62] In recent years, observers of social class in the United States have noted that even though upward mobility still exists, the opportunity for a significant change in class status has lessened significantly over the past thirty years.[63] As American cultural and literary historian Paul Fussell once noted of how this situation is experienced, "Because the [American] myth conveys the impression that you can readily earn your way upward, disillusion and bitterness are particularly strong when you find yourself trapped in a class system you've been half persuaded isn't important."[64] Even those most averse to looking at America's enduring patterns of inequality have been adjusting their perspectives. As Daniel Larison wrote for *The American Conservative*:

> Social and economic stratification is happening, reflected by growing income inequality, and it is being exacerbated by changes to the U.S. economy that are raising barriers to upward mobility and by the mass immigration of poorly educated, unskilled workers that are at risk of being trapped in a perpetual underclass.[65]

Today, people across the economic spectrum passionately disagree about what to do with regard to social stratification and limited opportunity, and they may also disagree about what the continued influx of immigrants means for society (for, contrary to Larison's statement, many are not poorly educated or unskilled), but few deny that such social and economic stratification exists.[66]

Middle- and upper-middle-class approaches to parenting have received quite a bit of attention lately, most recently with the 2011 publication of *The Battle Hymn of the Tiger Mother*, Amy Chua's celebration of the parenting-on-overdrive approach.[67] Chua discusses her own strict and uncompromising approach to parenting and relates it to her Chinese heritage, setting her approach in contrast to the indulgent and permissive "Western" style of parenting she believes is rampant in the United States today. Her memoir, which includes a fair amount of humor as well as some self-congratulation about the highly successful daughters she and her husband raised, generated a fair amount of controversy. But the debate that arose among the book's largely middle- and upper-middle-class readers wasn't about whether Eastern- or Western-style parenting is better; rather, it became a call to arms against overdoing what sociologist Annette Lareau termed "concerted cultivation."[68] Concerted cultivation refers to a parenting approach popular among middle-class parents in which parents encourage children, preteens, and teens to be involved in organized activities meant to provide them with opportunities to develop their talents and to enjoy the benefits of working as a team with their peers. My use of the term "empowerment" in the ethic I ascribe to middle- and upper-middle-class parents is meant to recognize the embrace of this approach.

Both the Western and Eastern styles of parenting that Chua describes emphasize the importance of empowering young people through such activities. U.S. middle- and upper-middle-class parents want their children to feel good about themselves, and they believe that children feel good if they're achieving; these parents also believe that childhood achievement leads to positive life outcomes (particularly economic ones). Middle- and upper-middle-class Western and Eastern parents both seem to worry a great deal about how children spend their time, and both encourage the productive use of time.[69] Critics consider Chua's approach, which involved renting music practice rooms while the family was on vacation and refusing bathroom breaks until a piece of music was perfected, as going a bit too far. But many also believe that most Western parents could stand to go further in our parenting efforts, as Hannah Rosin argues in the *Wall Street Journal* to her middle- and upper-middle-class readers: "We believe that our children are special and entitled, but we do not have the guts or the tools to make that reality true for them."[70] Certainly from Rosin's perspective, communication media are mostly a distraction and a problem, and Amy Chua would agree.

Among the would-be middle-class and less advantaged families interviewed for this book, there are some similarities to Chua's perspective, in particular the assumptions that children are strong, not fragile, and that children should respect their elders. Yet whereas Chua suggests that instead of softness, children need hard or heavy-handed concerted cultivation, the less privileged parents whose stories are told in this book see the goals of parenting differently. They voice the belief that the goal of parenting is to help their children become responsible for themselves, not to encourage them to push themselves in front of others in the race to high achievement. The less privileged parents I studied want to encourage young people to value their relationships with their family and community and to place goals of individual achievement, as well as their uses of media, within that wider framework. For families embracing an ethic of respectful connectedness, leisure isn't altogether bad. Indeed, one of the interesting reasons to foreground the ways in which digital, mobile, and entertainment media figure in U.S. family life is that it helps us explore the ways that U.S. society treats the relationship between work and leisure, and examine different attitudes about this relationship—attitudes that depend greatly on a person's place in the socioeconomic order.

There are, of course, a range of ways in which the would-be middle-class and the less advantaged could be defined. Yet the number of people in these categories and the choices and constraints under which they live does suggest the possibility of a *habitus*, to use sociologist Pierre Bourdieu's term, that differs from that of the upper-middle-class. A habitus is a set of norms imbued with a certain constellation of tastes and dispositions and associated with a complex array of resources, including access to certain social groups and to what might be called local knowledge or "street smarts."[71] It is important to pay attention to the variety of life experiences found among those whose income and other resources make middle-class life hard to maintain, and it is also important not to romanticize these differences. However, people in this group share life experiences and meanings that are not the same as those of the more financially stable and largely white upper-middle-class, and it is worth considering how they might be different.[72]

Sociologists of U.S. family life have been working for a long time to help construct better understandings of how families live within today's stratified systems and how such stratification reproduces itself through the practical actions of groups of people. Whereas there are some shared national traits of U.S. culture—a strong belief in innovation and in individual effort, for instance—there are also key examples of how members of a particular group within U.S. culture share certain taken-for-granted ways of seeing and experiencing the world that differ from the ways other groups see and experience it. We all exist within "webs of significance" that we ourselves spin, meaning that although we have the ability to create and modify our own lives, we are situated within cultures and communities that serve to define our worlds and give meaning to our actions.[73] Annette Lareau has argued that social class powerfully impacts childhood experiences, and she observes that at least two different cultural patterns exist in the United States that relate to the economic differences between families. Similarly, in a study of how parents buy consumer goods for their children, sociologist Allison Pugh has noted that parents with fewer means tend to invest in what she terms "symbolic indulgence," whereas those with greater financial resources engage in practices of "symbolic deprivation."[74] In observations closest to my own, sociologist Margaret Nelson has pointed out that whereas parents with fewer financial advantages tend to practice "parenting with limits," those in the upper-middle-class engage in what she terms "parenting out of control," particularly in their use of digital and mobile media as tools for surveillance of their children.[75] And sociologist Wendy Griswold has shown that although two groups of people in two different countries may read the same novel, they may interpret it quite differently based on their country's relative position in the world.[76] The same television program, fashion style, or (in this case) smart phone or laptop can be imbued with meanings that are quite different depending on one's particular community of identity.[77]

The Research for This Book

This book draws on research I have led for more than ten years, as my colleagues and I have been exploring how families experience and negotiate media use in their lives together and as individuals. The book reports the results of interview and observational research conducted with nineteen middle-class and twenty-seven less advantaged families with preteens and teens. More interviews and observations were conducted with an additional eighty-eight middle-class parents, twenty-six middle-class teens, and thirty-four less advantaged teens. Most of these interviews and observations took place in family homes and apartments located in urban, suburban, and rural areas of Ohio, Pennsylvania, New York, California, Colorado, Washington, D.C., and Illinois. Although I reflect on national survey data throughout thanks to the excellent work of the Pew Internet and American Life Project and other similar efforts, my research is qualitative. Stories produced and analyzed in qualitative research are, in researcher Brene Brown's characterization, "just data with a soul."[78]

Of the nineteen middle-class families, fifteen of the families had two resident parents, and single parents headed the other four. All of the parents in the two-parent households were married except for one same-sex couple; three of the couples were in their second marriage. Twelve of these families identified themselves as of European heritage, four were European and Hispanic/Latino, one was European and African American, one identified as Asian, and another was Asian and European.

The twenty-seven would-be middle-class and less advantaged families had annual household incomes of less than $50,000. Twelve of these families had incomes of less than $25,000 in the year in which they were interviewed. Thirteen families had two parents who were either married (first or second marriage) or cohabiting, and fourteen were single-parent families. Twelve of the families identified themselves as being of European ethnic heritage, one was Hispanic/Latino, three were European and Hispanic/Latino, and two were Hispanic/Latino, Native American, and European. One family was African American, three were European and African American, and one was African American and Native American. The final three families were Asian and European, recent immigrants from Eastern Europe, and recent immigrants from East Africa.

As a result of my interest in including families of all backgrounds in this study, my research team and I interviewed members of families that were affluent and members of families barely subsisting near the poverty line, although most fell somewhere in between and were either relatively more or relatively less advantaged. To complement our interview-based research, we attended seminars on parenting, went to book talks, guest-taught in schools in disadvantaged areas, and participated in media literacy events. We went to informal neighborhood gatherings and school events, were present at functions at churches and synagogues, and attended teacher-training sessions. We reviewed and consulted on nationally representative surveys designed to better understand parents, teens, and digital media uses and participated in international and cross-cultural comparisons. As my own children grew into their preteen years within an economically diverse school district, I became even more immersed in the questions of how media were

LOCATING MYSELF IN RELATION TO CLASS
AND BACKGROUND

Despite all my caveats about how the media construct the category, I consider myself middle-class, like most people. I'm one of the lucky ones: I have a full-time job, unlike many of my peers with Ph.D.'s and my peers struggling in the would-be middle class. My children go to public schools, and we have no aspirations for Ivy League schooling. My partner is a small business owner, and we live in a nice if rather unremarkable ranch house. I'm not as fashion-conscious or as confident as most of the upper-middle-class women you'd meet, and I talk about money all the time, which no self-respecting upper-middle-class or wealthy person would do.

My life experience is unusual only in one fairly significant respect: my mother was diagnosed with multiple sclerosis when I was about eleven years old. At the time it was a very unfamiliar and little-understood chronic illness, and my parents were understandably reluctant to tell many people about her diagnosis because people would inevitably protest that she looked so healthy. And so, throughout my own preteen and teen years, I was constantly on the lookout for what "normal" family life was like, so that I could participate in presenting my family and myself as such. Just as people around me were embracing their diversity and difference and I was participating in celebrating their uniqueness, I was busily concealing my own family's struggles. My family members and I did this for a variety of reasons, chief among them preserving my mother's dignity and living through the uncertainties of the illness ourselves. As a teen, I was independent and mature in some ways, developing a thoughtful, serious, and well-rehearsed response to the inevitable question "How's your mother?" But I was immature in other ways, acting out my rage at the injustices of chronic illness. I would like to say that I've learned to live in the moment as a result, but I think I also learned that time may not be on your side. Through the research I conducted for this book I learned that my personal struggle as a parent in a digital age is not really about figuring out the safest or most productive way to utilize technology for education or bonding. It's really about resisting the temptation to engage in technologically aided multitasking in order to make the most out of every moment simultaneously. A secondary struggle is about constantly worrying whether the parenting I'm doing is good enough. I've learned, however, that in their own ways each of these struggles can seriously undercut goals of connection. Whether it's trying to catch up on emails during family movie night or middle-of-the-night trolls through psychology websites to try to determine whether my children are healthy, digital and mobile media are implicated in my bad middle-class parenting moments as well as in my good ones. Like every story featured in this book, my own viewpoints are shaped as much by my social class as by my own experiences of parenting and being parented.

playing a role in the lives of middle-class and less advantaged families. Throughout this work, I have found that parents and their children have been engaging in a great deal of nuanced decision making, a fair amount of discussion, and a significant number of emotional exchanges when it comes to the role of digital and mobile media in their lives. How they manage these things has a great deal to do with the challenges they experience in relation to the economic landscape. Families look to digital, mobile, and traditional media to solve certain problems, even while these media seem to create other, new problems for them to solve. In the next two chapters, then, we consider how parents approach some of the problems that they perceive are most closely related to the risks of new media as their children grow up in a digital age.

CHAPTER 2 | Cyberbullying Girls, Helicopter
Moms, and Internet Predators

TUCKED AWAY IN A pleasant enough middle-class suburb on a street named
Waterford Crystal Drive, two mothers and their daughters in Dardenne
Prairie, Missouri, unwittingly became the focus of the world's first cyberbullying court case. *Wired* magazine named the case one of the greatest
threats to privacy and online freedoms because it attempted to utilize the
Computer Fraud and Abuse Act to convict forty-nine-year-old Lori Drew of
violating the terms of service of MySpace by registering to communicate
with others under a false identity.[1] Lawyers and cyberspace pundits were
especially interested in the ways in which this case has threatened to make
it a felony to create and experiment with online identities. But the case has
garnered far more attention—and vitriol—because of the toxic combination of teen nastiness, online social networking practices, and disturbingly
inappropriate parental actions that lay at its core. It's an unfortunate
example of what can go terribly wrong, and the reach of the story demonstrates that many people have found in it a compelling, perhaps epic story
both of the worst that can happen to teens online and of what it means to be
a "bad" parent in the digital age.[2] It also allows us to explore the various
ways in which the parents of teens respond to troubling online behaviors.

It all started in 2006, when Lori Drew's thirteen-year-old daughter
Sarah complained to her mother that Megan Meier, a former friend, was
bothering her. The two girls had had an on-again, off-again friendship;
both had engaged in name-calling and spiteful actions. Sarah Drew wanted
to learn what Megan was saying about her, so Sarah and Ashley Grills, an
older teen who worked for Sarah's mother, allegedly created a fake
MySpace account. Sarah's mother, Lori Drew, allegedly observed them.
The young women gave the fake account the name and identity of a fictional sixteen-year-old boy and named him "Josh Evans."

Once the girls had ensnared Sarah's ex-friend Megan in a romantic relationship with the fictional boy online, "Josh" began insulting Megan in true cyberbullying fashion, telling her that she was "mean" and "fat." Others joined in with the insults, ultimately sending a message to her that included the phrase "The world would be a better place without you."[3] Megan reportedly was devastated by this turn of events. After receiving that last message via AOL Messenger one day in mid-October 2006, she went to her room and hanged herself.

The facts of the case didn't come to light until later. Six weeks after Megan's death, Megan's mother learned that "Josh" had been a hoax, and that Sarah's mother, Lori, had known about it. Megan's mother and father initiated an investigation into the affair. Before the FBI had concluded its inquiry, bloggers and other observers close to the case began to implicate the Drews online, publishing their names, address, businesses, and phone numbers, beginning a witch hunt of sorts, full of demands for retribution.[4] People from all walks of life wanted Lori and Sarah Drew to be held responsible for their role in the cyberbullying that led to Megan's suicide. Onlookers vandalized the Drew home, left offensive messages on their voice mail, and in local newspapers called for their arrest and conviction. Then, in November 2007, the parents of Megan Meier went on the NBC *Today* show to tell their story. Megan's father told host Matt Lauer that the Drew family had "offered absolutely no apologies. They sent us a letter in the mail, basically saying that they might feel a little bit of responsibility, but they don't feel no guilt or remorse or anything for what they did."[5] Letters poured into that program and into the local papers, and the case continued to light up the blogosphere. The marriage of Megan's parents fell apart, but they continued to press for legal retribution in the case.

In late 2008, Lori Drew was indicted in a federal court on one count of conspiracy and three counts of accessing computers without authorization. Although numerous vitriolic blog posts and letters to the editor had excoriated Drew for her decision to allow her daughter to perpetuate the hoax and for attempting to cover it up afterward, the charges against Drew centered on whether her tacit approval of the creation of the "Josh" account violated the terms of agreement published by MySpace. If she had knowingly signed the consent to set up a fake account, or if people too young to sign the consent had done so as she observed them, she had committed fraud and could be held liable.[6] She was convicted of one misdemeanor count, but that conviction was set aside in May 2009 when a federal judge questioned the applicability of the computer hacking statute to the Drew case.

The Drew case prompted several jurisdictions as well as at least one U.S. state representative to propose legislation that would criminalize harassment over the Internet.[7] The hometown of the Drews and Meiers, Dardenne Prairie, Missouri, passed an ordinance making it a class B misdemeanor to harass someone over the Internet.[8] The state of Missouri later revised its statute regarding stalking to include harassment such as that of cyberbullying and to classify stalking as a class A misdemeanor.[9]

Through the publicity surrounding Megan's suicide and the court cases that followed it, curious and horrified onlookers got clear insights into an extreme example of what might be termed helicopter parenting in the digital age.[10] According to the police report, Lori Drew explained that she had "instigated and monitored" the MySpace interactions between the fictional "Josh" and Megan in order to find out "what Megan had been saying about my daughter." Drew stated that she believed Megan Meier had been saying untruthful and negative things about Sarah both online and in person. So in response, Drew claimed, she, her eighteen-year-old employee Ashley, and Sarah all took turns typing the messages to Megan, even after the messages became "sexual." Drew also stated in a later police report that she did "not feel as guilty" after learning at Megan's funeral that Megan had attempted suicide before that fateful day in 2006.[11] Apparently, Drew felt that the news relieved her and her daughter of some responsibility for the suicide, even while she seemed to be excusing herself and her daughter for participating in the cyberharassment of an emotionally unstable thirteen-year-old girl.[12]

Much media attention has focused on this and similar cases involving cyberbullying and sexting incidents that have resulted in suicide. Researchers estimate that between 20 and 85 percent of young people between the ages of ten and eighteen have been bullied.[13] However, Megan's case differed from what most people experience, as she had been under the care of a psychiatrist since third grade and was perhaps less emotionally resilient than the majority of young people who experience cyberbullying. Along with her onetime friend Sarah Drew, before her death Megan had been both a perpetrator and a victim of bullying both online and off.[14] Her story has been viewed as a cautionary tale of the excesses of Internet use and of parental overinvolvement in a child's life. Lori Drew participated or at least passively observed the harassment of a thirteen-year-old, prompting some to suggest that perhaps she should have been tried for psychological child abuse.[15] Sarah Drew participated in fraud by using MySpace's ability to act anonymously, creating a false person whom Megan came to trust and who later broke that trust.

Given the individualistic orientation in U.S. society, we're always tempted to assign blame to the individuals in scenarios like this, asking what went wrong, and what parents or young people could do differently to prevent something awful like this from happening in their own lives. As this book points out, the stories of individuals and of families do not play out in isolation, and when something goes horribly wrong at the intersection of young people, parents, and technologies, a constellation of factors is usually involved, just as the troubles of Megan Meier and the Drews surely preceded their fateful online collision.

Social media did not cause these problems, but they were not inconsequential in the story, either. However, before we consider the role of the media in this situation, we move next to the story of Kayla Torelli. The actions of Kayla, an upper-middle-class young woman raised in an environment of expressive empowerment, reveal that she too utilizes social media sites in ways that are harmful both to herself and to others.

Profile of a Troubled Cyberteen: Kayla Torelli

At eighteen, Kayla takes great pride in what she sees as her ability to take care of herself. When she describes her activities, her parents, Hanh and Chuck, are always relegated far into the background. What is in the foreground? Her friends and the interactions with them that take place on sites such as Facebook and Twitter. She is happy to serve as an expert in our study.

"If you had to dissolve your Facebook site, how would you feel?" the interviewer, Caroline, asks Kayla, who is a friend of hers.[16]

"Um, honestly I would feel really awkward. It would feel like I lost something very dear to me, like a baby or something."

Startled, Caroline laughs, and asks in semi-disbelief, "Like a child?"

"Yeah," Kayla replies. "I would feel so weird, and I really wouldn't know what to do. 'Cause I would lose contact with so many people."

How about if she lost her cell phone? Caroline asks.

It would feel as bad as "losing my car," Kayla says, implying that it would be figuratively immobilizing.

Caroline is surprised by Kayla's response. She knows that Kayla has had horrible experiences with social networking sites and has been a repeated victim of cyberbullying. Her Facebook page has gotten her into trouble at her former school, too. When the principal was told of her page, which features many photos of her either drunk or consuming alcohol, she was asked to take the page down. The page was even used as evidence against her when she was later asked to leave the school, because she hadn't taken down the page after the principal had expressly asked her to do so. So what was it about Facebook that could possibly make it seem so precious to Kayla? How has Facebook become woven into Kayla's daily life? How important is it to her identity?

In addition to Kayla's multiple personal pages, she has created a page specifically for her former school, and has created several humorous groups for others to join, such as one devoted to keeping a has-been teen celebrity from buying a home in Kayla's pricey neighborhood. Kayla's Facebook profile goes on for miles, including numerous quizzes, jokes, links to music sites, and more than a thousand wall posts. Kayla has been "tagged," or identified as a subject, in more than two hundred photos that either she or her friends have posted online in one year. During her final year in high school, she used the earnings from her after-school job to purchase an iPhone so that she could get online wherever she was. Now, working as a waitress, she pays for her younger sister's cell phone service as well as her own with her meager wages.

"I have a couple people on my limited profile," Kayla explains when asked whether she ever restricted people from viewing her online information and photos. "They can't see the pictures on my wall, or my mini-feed, but they can just see my profile and, like, if I'm in a relationship and like my birthday. That's it."

"I wonder if I'm on anyone's limited profile," Caroline muses with a laugh.

"You definitely know if you are on somebody's limited profile," Kayla responds in all seriousness. "It is not a good feeling. It hurts, believe me."

Another source of hurt has been the harassment she's received from ex-friends who have posted nasty things about her on social networking sites. Once, when she Googled her name, the first site that popped up was a profile of a former friend, and on that profile, under a list of past regrets, "it was like, 'I don't have any [regrets] except for when I met Kayla Torelli.' Her profile was basically a site devoted to bashing me." This same girl, Kayla says, also got onto Kayla's instant messaging account and deleted her buddy list. Another former friend also has a distaste for her, and at one point had written about it front and center on her own online profile: "Like when me and my friend Britta got in a fight last year, she [wrote], 'Fat people take up too much space, this means you, Kayla.'"

Kayla denies that she has written nasty things to other girls online, although this claim seems dubious when she adds that she didn't mean to say anything hurtful. "That's just me venting," she says, excusing herself.

Kayla still knows the passwords that allow her to access some of her ex-friends' and ex-boyfriends' Facebook pages, and she sometimes reads their comments to one another to see what they are doing and what they might have said about her. "Sometimes I'll look at [an ex-friend's] pictures to see who she's hanging out with now," she said. This was a sad voyeuristic experience, but Kayla says she can't help doing it; she wants to know what's being said about her and, apparently, what's being done without her.

Sometimes when young people go through negative experiences with one set of friends, they look to other friends, or especially to family members, to help them reestablish a positive sense of self.[17] This isn't the case for Kayla, unfortunately. Even though the hurt that she experiences through these online interactions is extremely painful to her, it is not something her parents know anything about, because Kayla does not discuss it with them.

It isn't that Kayla's mother, Hanh, doesn't worry about social networking sites. But in Kayla's view, she really doesn't understand them. "My parents didn't want me putting up any pictures" when she first signed up for an online profile, Kayla says. "But of course I did." That's an inevitable part of teen culture, Kayla explains:

> Believe me, if you go to any party, there's going to be at least twenty girls with cameras trying to take pictures. Because it's all about getting pictures on there now . . . to show like, "Oh, look what I did this weekend, look who I was hanging out with, look what I was wearing," that kind of thing.

Those pictures are not something she wanted her parents to see. And, in Kayla's view, "I don't think they want to see the pictures. Ever." Kayla believes that her parents really don't want to know about her life, and therefore she feels that by not telling them about her own experiences—even the painful ones—she is protecting them, in a way.

Kayla's parents are divorced. Her father, Chuck, a European American stockbroker whom Kayla idolizes (and idealizes), has seen her Facebook site and has expressed no concerns about it, nor much interest in it, either. Her mother, Hanh, a Vietnamese American single parent raising Kayla and another daughter on her own, is "overprotective," Kayla says. Like many parents interviewed for this book, Kayla's mother "overreacted a bit with it" when she first heard about social networking sites, according to Kayla, fearing that sexual predators could get hold of her contact information:

> She would just always be like [changes her voice to imitate her mother], "You're not using that book-face, are you?" And I would be like, "No." But

now she knows about it, and she thinks it's okay because that's how I communicate with a lot of people. So she thinks as long as I'm not putting personal pictures up there it's fine. But she doesn't know.

Actually, there's a lot Hanh doesn't know about her daughter's activities online and off. Kayla has never shown Hanh any of her online profiles, although she has shown Hanh other people's sites in an effort to defuse her mother's anxieties. Even this tactic, though, obfuscates more than clarifies things for Hanh, leading her to believe that social networking sites are an innocuous and occasional part of Kayla's daily life. In actuality, hardly a day goes by when Kayla isn't taking multiple photos and posting them in new online albums. She checks her phone "24/7," she says. "I get a message on my phone telling me when someone's written on my wall, and I'll just go on and see what they wrote. But if I have time I'll actually get on the computer and spend time browsing and snooping on people's things, seeing what they're doing." If someone writes on her wall, she is likely to see it and respond to it within fifteen minutes—which means she checks her site at least four times an hour, and often eighteen hours a day; she estimates that she checks for messages "about every three minutes." She did this when she was at school, and does it even now when she is working, and especially when she is hanging out or partying with her friends. Checking and updating her site is less obtrusive than talking on the phone, which is why she prefers social networking communication to phone calls during most of her daily activities. And although she successfully hides her excessive online attachments from her mother, she also assigns blame for her behavior to Hanh, saying that she "definitely lets me get on it too much. Like I'll get carried away when I'm trying to do my homework." But at the same time, her mother really couldn't limit her online time, since

> they've never put that many limitations on me, so doing something [like setting up rules] with the computer would be weird for me. But definitely, I wish they had because, I'm trying to do my homework or Google things online, I'll be on Facebook too, and then I'll get distracted and be on Facebook for an hour and then I'll be up all night doing my homework because I was on Facebook.

Like other middle- and upper-middle-class-parents, Kayla's mother was reluctant to set clear guidelines about media use, preferring not to infringe on her daughter's rights and viewing Kayla's ability to establish her own rules as an expression of her growing self-reliance.[18]

When Kayla got into trouble at her old school, she transferred and began spending more time at the home of her father and his second wife. But tensions between Kayla and her stepmother escalated, so when her father and his wife moved twenty miles away, they informed Kayla that she was no longer welcome to live with them. Kayla nostalgically recalls times in the past when Hanh, Chuck, and her younger sister took vacations together. "That was really the only time my dad had time off of work back in the day," she says. "I only got to have daddy-daughter time once in a great while." The problem wasn't that Chuck and his new wife are busy, however, according to Kayla. "They just don't care as much as most parents," she says, seemingly seeking the interviewer's sympathy for growing up with uncaring parents. But then Kayla continues, equating caring with taking the time to set boundaries: "My mom tries to [demonstrate care] but she is very naive when it comes to setting boundaries, and my dad is too scared to set boundaries for me." At one point Kayla's mother did know that she was "smoking pot, drinking, and having sex," Kayla says, "but she definitely has no idea what I do now. Honestly, she's the easiest person to hide things from." Kayla sees Hanh as permissive and ineffectual, whereas she excuses Chuck for being uninvolved. In a sense, Kayla's views of her parents allow her to dismiss them as possible sources of perspective that could counter what she views in her ex-friends' online writings about her.

Kayla's mother is clearly overwhelmed with her tasks as a single mother, a situation exacerbated by the fact that Kayla's father remains largely uninvolved in the lives of Kayla and her sister. Her mother certainly wasn't choosing to be uninvolved, as evidenced in the conversations she'd tried to have with Kayla about the all-important roles that her friends and their contacts through digital media were playing in Kayla's life. But Kayla interprets Hanh's lack of confidence in setting and maintaining boundaries as a lack of caring, and as a result surmises that, to some extent, she is on her own.[19]

Kayla's desires for attention and ultimately for meaningful relationships are at the root of her desire to remain connected to peers at all times, even if such connections are painful. Young people like Kayla rely upon the media tropes of celebrity and the commercial realm and learn to act like a "star" in the dramas that are their own lives—often in ways that can undermine their other, more relational goals. Kayla's story of "live fast, die young, leave a trail of glory online in your wake" is part of an old story of the celebration of youth in Western culture, and it is also part of a more contemporary cultural message: it reveals what it means to grow up in the context of a digital age in which technologies both enable meaningful relationships even as they can also exacerbate and undermine our ability to maintain those meaningful relationships.

Kayla sees herself as having a right to participate in harmful actions and in self-harm as well. Hanh, like Lori Drew, seems to have difficulty distinguishing appropriate boundaries between and for herself and her daughter. Hanh may feel confused or ambivalent when Kayla makes requests or even demands of her, because she doesn't trust her own emotional responses. She may be choosing a more permissive route that contrasts with the strict and punitive upbringing that she herself experienced. She would probably prefer to have a warmer relationship with her children than she had with her own parents, but it may be that she is uncertain about when to assert parental authority, or how to do so without anger and control. Hanh is in need of support in her parenting efforts. As a single mother, she probably feels as if she is on her own, a message reinforced in a culture that tends to think of families as separate and independent units. Even when extended families help, resources can be limited as single mothers try to meet the need for child care, health care, or even a living wage. Hahn did not have extended family in the area to help her meet household and family needs and, perhaps more important in this case, needs for emotional support for both her and Kayla. Digital and mobile media did not cause the family's problems, but Kayla's self-destructive media practices exacerbated and amplified her negative experiences.

Kayla's story demonstrates the need for parents to understand the mediated environment, as parents who don't are likely to be parents who are uninvolved, even if they don't recognize themselves as such. Facebook and other online networking sites have become an important avenue for living out teen lives and identities, and sometimes limiting online time is a way that parents can provide loving support for their teens in distress. Stepping in and helping teens recognize the need for time offline is now an important part of digital parenting. The challenge for parents, of course, lies in gauging a young person's maturity: *Can my child recognize and avoid negative or potentially dangerous online situations, and if not, how can I help her or him to do so?* Rather than take for granted that their children can recognize troubling situations, parents need to have conversations with their children about these things. Too often parents overestimate their children's abilities in relation to new media, as Hanh seems to do. But sometimes they underestimate them, as we will see in the next story.

Privacy, Credibility, and Safety: The Internet Predator

Parents and adults are often concerned that young people might place too much trust in the words of those they encounter online, and this, it's believed, not only empowers cyberbullies but also leaves young people vulnerable to predators. Not all young people are quite so vulnerable, however, as the stories below will suggest. Rather, researchers have found that young people involved in risky behaviors online are not naive, but are young people who appear to be looking for trouble to begin with.[20] Kayla seems to be one example of this kind of young person.

Still, parents wonder why there is no regulation that would limit adult access to young people's sites and information online. And when parents realize that such regulation would run into the issue of Internet censorship, they then wonder why young people seem willing to ignore the privacy settings that many social networking sites now make available to them, choosing instead to open themselves to contact from individuals they may not know at all. Yet young people have generally felt that parental concerns about privacy, credibility, and their own personal safety are overblown, as Kayla mentioned above.[21] Overwhelmingly, young people over the age of twelve have reported that they know how to protect themselves from predators when they're online.[22] Young people have also become quite savvy about increasing the privacy levels on their Facebook and other online profiles.[23] Dealing with strangers online seems to be a fairly common and rather mundane occurrence for young people between the ages of thirteen and seventeen across all economic categories.

In one group discussion among sixteen- and seventeen-year-old friends from a middle-class suburban area, a seventeen-year-old named Brian notes that it's common to receive friend requests from people whose names you don't recognize but who might attend your school or know you because you have friends in common:

> And you're just like, okay. Then maybe you start talking to them, but probably not. Then every now and then you'll get like one really creepy one that you know is crazy.

Flipping into a mode in which he starts entertaining his friends by describing the stereotypes out there about such "creepy" would-be friends, Brian continues, "Like you get this old guy's picture, he's bald, his name's like Jed or something. So then you're like, 'No thanks.'" After the laughter subsides, Brian's sixteen-year-old friend Kelly notes that she, too, has received messages like that:

> I've never had someone be like, "We should meet up." But I got this really weird message from some guy. It was a picture of his abs, and the message was, "Hi, I was looking at your pics and you're a really gorgeous girl. Do you have any naughtier pictures that we can trade?" And right away I went and blocked him and made sure he couldn't contact me.

This reminds Brian and Kelly's seventeen-year-old friend Ashley that she received a very similar request:

> Some guy who was in his mid- to late twenties sent me a message and said that I was the most gorgeous girl he'd ever seen, and he wanted to talk to me. I was kind of creeped out. So I got rid of him.

And sixteen-year-old Rhianna, another friend in this group, then speaks more generally about what she has done when she receives invitations from people whose names she doesn't recognize:

> I know for me, my [social networking] profile is on private, so I get a lot of random people requesting me to friend them. They can't look at my profile, so I ask them who they are and why they want to friend me, and I give them a week or so, and if they don't say anything, I go back and delete them.

Then Brian elaborates on his earlier comments:

> I've had like the Jed guy. It was just a picture of his face, and he was bald and had these glasses and this smile. And then I've had girls my age or younger try to contact me. Like this one girl, who didn't even give me her real name, she like gave me her number and said, "I'm gonna be in your town next weekend. Wanna hang out?" I just never messaged her back.

This same kind of discussion about strangers asking to be Facebook friends occurred in a different group discussion among middle-class young people. Sixteen-year-old Adele notes that she has received the same kind of solicitation:

> I had this really weird guy ask me to friend him. He had all these weird pictures of him in a Speedo. All his friends were little boys and he was in his mid-twenties. I denied him.

Sixteen-year-old Suzanne agrees with her friend Adele, noting, "I don't usually friend people I don't know, especially if they're from a different state or if they're older. You never know."

Their sixteen-year-old friend Erika nods. "People these days are really weird, so I'm really careful."

Many older teens feel that parents worry too much about this issue of strangers seeking out ways to develop relationships with them. "I only talk to people I know or go to school with," sixteen-year-old Adele says.

"I think there are a lot of unknowns for the parents," observes Andrea, the college sophomore who is helping to interview the teens.[24]

"Yeah," Adele's friend Suzanne agrees, "but they should know that we're not *that* dumb."

Meeting strangers online just isn't what most young people look for in their online relationships. They know that it can be good to have online friends who might eventually become more than strangers or acquaintances. But if those friends give any indication that they are phony, insecure, or just strange, most young people will distance themselves, as the teens in the above discussions did. Even younger teens are mostly interested in using the technology to communicate with their friends, not with strangers, and overwhelmingly they report that they know from their parents what to look for and what to avoid.[25]

Thanks to an increasing number of programs in schools and communities as well as increasingly informed parents, young people know about the dangers of posting information that could be read by unintended audiences, and are also aware of parental concerns regarding mistakes that might be made out of innocence (or ignorance). In addition to talking about the strangers who tried to friend them, young people also talked about the problems that might emerge when other adults, such as coaches, college recruiters, or employers, find out about them from their online profiles. The problems, young people felt, arose when young people wanted to put up "way too much information" about themselves and their lives—or when those adults in their lives seemed to seek out too much information. As will be discussed in chapter 4, young people sometimes interpret sharing or desiring "too much information" as a sign of insecurity. But it also could have repercussions in areas of life beyond what peers think of them, as seventeen-year-old Sarah notes:

> You have to be responsible. Like, don't put anything online that you don't want other people to see, because anyone can look at it. I think that

companies are starting to look at potential job applicants, so you just have to think about who's going to be looking at it and what you want to put out there.

Sarah's seventeen-year-old friend Peter agrees, noting that young people need to remember that both future employers and college recruiters might be looking at their pages:

I've heard a lot of kids getting in trouble with scholarships for having pictures of alcohol on their pages. They'll get blacklisted with all the colleges for that. You've got to be really careful about what you post.

One of the key challenges of parenting in a digital age is that both children and technology are constantly undergoing change. As children age, they become both more familiar with technology and more mature when confronted with new technologically enabled problems. Whereas young people now seem to be able to recognize the oddness of a stranger who wants to trade pictures, knowing how to interact with the other adults in their lives is fraught with greater ambivalence. Do you friend an employer if he or she makes a request? And what are the consequences if you ignore the invitation? Some young people give such adults only limited access to their profiles. And some adults who regularly interact with young people develop one site that can be accessed by friends in their private lives and another that can be accessed by those younger people with whom they work.[26] Others, such as some public school teachers, are forbidden from using social networking sites to keep in contact with students or even former students—a policy that shuts them out of what potentially could be positive mentoring relationships.[27] Clearly, we are still working out the social norms for social networking sites. There are no easy answers about how to protect our young people from harm while allowing them to maintain relationships with adults who matter to them. What is clear, however, is that parents need to be aware of these issues so that they can discuss appropriate and inappropriate online interactions with their children. As these discussions about Internet predators demonstrate, it seems fairly common for parents to underestimate their teenagers' online sense. Teens are figuring it out, just as their parents are, and sometimes parents will be pleasantly surprised when they discover their teens' knowledge and common sense.

The Temptation to Overparent

Concerns about cyberbullies, suicides, Internet predators, and sexting dominate the discussions about what parents should worry about when it comes to the digital environment, as discussed in chapter 1. Whereas young people and many parenting experts increasingly suggest that parents should not panic about these topics, public discussions advocating more parental oversight can become the source of another kind of cautionary tale: that of the overbearing parent and the young person who must respond.

Technology makes it easier than ever for parents to find out where their children are and what they are doing, and certain surveillance technologies are quickly gaining increased acceptance among middle- and upper-middle-class families.[28] Thanks to GPS tracking, parents can now utilize apps such as WhereAreYou, which sends a text to the parent's phone with the location of a child's phone displayed on Google Maps. Parents can also install SafetyWeb, which provides parents with reports on their children's social media posts, cell phone calls, and text messages. Sociologist Margaret Nelson relates the growth of these technologies to the desire on the part of middle- and upper-middle-class parents to monitor their children. The impulse to monitor is not always rooted in a desire to be intrusive or prying, however. Some parents want to maintain control, but parents also may wish to make use of these technologies to identify and address potential problems their young people may be facing.[29] One mother told me that from their online monitoring program she learned that her ten-year-old daughter was looking at weight loss sites, prompting her to initiate a conversation with her daughter about healthy eating habits. Another learned of her daughter's pot smoking and casual sex exploits by surreptitiously reading her daughter's text messages, claiming that this activity enabled her, similarly, to initiate conversations and to restrict her daughter's freedom until she felt the problems had been addressed. A third said that she has no hesitations about using a GPS tracking system, based on her own memories of the lies she told her mother about her locations as a teen. Each mother saw her use of these technologies as a tool that could enable her to be more caring and responsive to her daughter's needs. They wanted to empower their daughters to be self-reliant, but like Renee and Tessie's mothers, introduced in the first chapter, they also wanted their daughters to see them as resources and guides during the years that these mothers viewed as prime for questionable decision making within a "mean girl" culture.

Many have observed that teen girls in particular describe feeling uncomfortable about how their mothers want to supervise their social networking sites, text messages, or phone calls.[30] What parents imagine as an effort to protect young people from harm, some young people perceive as an invasion of privacy.[31] Overbearing oversight sometimes results in outcomes that are exactly the opposite of the ones parents hope for. Sixteen-year-old Kelly, for instance, tells a story about one day a year earlier when her middle-class mother said to her a propos of nothing, "Oh, I saw your online profile." Then, Kelly reports, her mother continued, "Be careful on there. Do you talk to people you don't know?" Kelly immediately felt uncomfortable in this conversation. Her mother, perhaps misinterpreting her daughter's discomfort, continued quizzing Kelly, who felt increasingly accused, although she wasn't sure of what. At this point Kelly's mind was reeling, she reports. First, when she realized that her mother had accessed her online profile without telling her, she felt "weird": "She'd seen all my friends' comments and all my pictures and stuff," she says, noting that it was weird because, "you know, you're so much different than your parents know." Then, she began to feel angry, surmising that her parents didn't trust her. After a few weeks, things got even worse. Her parents decided to block the website so that she couldn't go to it anymore. Kelly was angry about their decision to block her access to the site, but she didn't argue with them about it. She abided by their rules and never accessed the site from her home and in their view again. Instead, she says, she began spending more time at a friend's house so that she could participate online from there. Kelly's parents' decision to block her access to social networking sites didn't lead her to never use those sites again; it just prevented her from visiting them on her home computer. Her parents' attempt to protect her actually drove her activities to a more secretive location and did not stop her use of social networking sites. Kelly learned that her parents didn't trust her, and that therefore she needed to reveal even less to them than she had before.

When Kelly and her friends were asked about what they thought might be the best way for parents to approach their uses of social networking sites and other digital media, seventeen-year-old Brian was the first one to respond:

> I like that they trust me. My parents really don't bother me because they know they can trust me with it. Every now and then my mom will walk in and see what's on my page, but they don't really bother me much with it.

Female teens had more mixed reactions to their parents' attempts to oversee their social networking and digital media use, however. "I think checking a person's profile page isn't going to do anything. I think you should talk to the actual kid," sixteen-year-old Suzanne notes.

"My mom checks mine all the time," a chagrined seventeen-year-old Chelsea says, sounding unhappy; "I think they should ask permission first," she adds.

Sixteen-year-old Cate, who has grown up with two mothers, similarly bemoans that one of her moms "keeps trying to add me [as a friend] on Facebook" and once looked through her photos when she'd inadvertently left her Facebook page pulled up after she'd left the computer. "That was a little sketchy," Cate says.

In recent years, more and more adults have been creating online profiles on social networking sites such as Facebook. But teens differentiate between parents who create these profiles to keep in touch with their own friends and parents who seem a little too interested in developing an online profile as a way of knowing what is going on in young people's lives. As sixteen-year-old Adele notes with clear disapproval: "Melody's mom has an online profile, and she comments on [Melody's] page more than Melody's friends." She then continues to describe this mother's online posts on her daughter's page: "She's like, 'Oh my God, you're so cool, girls!' I've read some of her comments, and I'm thinking this mom is trying to be a kid."

"My mom probably wouldn't be able to get on if she wanted to," sixteen-year-old Erika notes in response with a laugh.

"And you wouldn't show her?" the interviewer asks.

"Oh, I showed her," Erika replies nonchalantly. "She asked to see it. Then she was like, 'Are those your friends?' And so I showed her my friends' pages. That's about it, though."

The teens we interviewed were largely in agreement that they preferred to be asked to show their online profiles to their mothers or fathers. Like sixteen-year-old Erika, teens seemed to find that when they did show their pages to their mothers, the mothers' worries quickly dissipated, and both mother and daughter found that social networking sites were "no big deal," as Erika observes. But when a mother or father "snooped" on the pages, anger and misunderstanding would often result, and the young people then focused on the feelings that their privacy had been invaded; they had a hard time being sympathetic to the parents' desires to protect them from potentially troublesome situations. Sixteen-year-old Chelsea relates a story that was quite insightful on this point:

One time, we were texting each other and Patrick's mom was asleep and he wanted to go to the store to get some ice cream. This was at midnight or twelve-thirty. So Suzanne texted Liz and then we all went out and got Patrick and got the ice cream. And then we got home and Suzanne wrote on Liz's wall, "Last night was fun." Then Liz's mom read it, and Liz's mom wouldn't let me hang out with her for three months.

"How did Liz respond then?" the interviewer asks.

"Liz's mom is psycho," Chelsea replies. "Liz has to be careful no matter what she does. Now she doesn't even have a social networking profile. Her parents made her delete it."

Now, let's pause here for a moment. We're talking about four teens who reportedly made a last-minute, late-night plan to leave their houses and drive to get ice cream. This was probably not the best instance of good judgment on the teens' part. What upset the teens afterward was not that they received punishment for their actions but that Liz's mother had found out about their activities by snooping on her social networking profile. Surely the teens could have expected to suffer some kind of negative consequence as a result of their ill-considered action if their parents had found out about it. It is the fact that the mother found out about the outing from reading an entry on a social networking site that complicates things, which is my point here. Rather than learning from consequences, the teens focused on what they believed were the inappropriately intrusive actions of the mother in this situation. What they learned instead was that Liz's mom was a "bad parent," a "psycho," and that Liz needed to be careful or her actions would be heavily controlled. This reminded me of another teen who was asked whether parents should have the right to read their teenagers' texts. After suggesting that reading text messages is like reading a diary and is therefore experienced by teens as a serious invasion of privacy, she added this:

Final piece of advice: if you choose to pick a fight over these things [e.g., things you learn from snooping in their text messages], I wouldn't tell your teen that you got the info from their cell phone. Find some other creative way of knowing. Because I'll bristle over the privacy invasion and will have switched off before we get to the real discussion.

These kinds of situations certainly present parents who would prefer not to "overparent" with a dilemma of sorts: should parents scout out information on their young people to ensure that they are abiding by parental expectations? That kind of awareness does tend to be prized by other adults. Yet at what point does it become counterproductive to the overall goal of helping young people learn from their mistakes, because it allows them to focus on the putative mistakes of their parents rather than their own? This concern relates to a much larger shift, and struggle, in how we collectively think about authority today, and how parents approach issues of strict parenting and develop trusting relationships, as we will discuss in chapter 3.

Conclusion

Digital and mobile media continue to be a double-edged sword in the lives of families. The same software that makes it possible for parents to decode teen slang can be used by predators to pose more effectively as younger peers. On the other hand, while texting might make it easier for peers to know when and where a fight breaks out, it can also enable parents and teachers to learn of problems and to respond to them more quickly and effectively. Colleges are now encouraging those who work in freshman dorms to monitor Facebook sites and are teaching them to recognize when signs of sadness in status updates might be signs of depression.[32] Over time, communication technologies have come to be viewed less as a site for danger and risk and more as an integral if risky part of growing up. Helping young people to learn to navigate these possibilities is not unlike helping them learn to drive a car. Parents need to remember that young people are not reckless because they underestimate risks but because they overestimate rewards. Young people are utilizing digital and mobile media to accomplish developmental goals of establishing independence, and they need guidance in recognizing the relationship between risks and rewards.

As we saw in the story of Lori Drew that opened this chapter, new media technologies make it easier than ever for parents to engage in surveillance and overinvolvement in their children's lives. At the same time, parents also feel unprepared for the challenges digital and mobile media present to their teens and their relationships with them, as illustrated in the story of Kayla and her mother. How do parents find a middle ground? What's the Parent App we need to address these situations? Based on my research and my experiences, I believe that parents do well when they are willing to exhibit trust and when they do not stop there. Parents can ask their children to teach them about the media environment in which they're immersed. We saw this in the story of Erika, the young woman who was able to defuse her mother's concerns when she showed her mother her online identity at her mother's request. But we also need to know when to step back and let them make decisions—even bad decisions—without our overinvolvement. If we let them share their media expertise with us, we can then share our own insights about its uses and possible consequences with them. This interaction will help prepare them for making good decisions on their own, which is what the majority of parents want most for their children,

The desire to protect our children from harm is an understandable one, but it has actually become a problem of epic proportions in the United States, as the Harvard psychologist Richard Weissbord has pointed out.[33] He argues that we fail our children when we privilege protecting their individual happiness and well-being over their ability to develop a sense of what is good and right in relation to others. We might shield them from the consequences of their own behavior because we don't know how to (or we don't know that we need to) confront them, as in Kayla Torelli's case, or because we want to spare them pain, as in the case of Sarah and Lori Drew. Either way, we do them a disservice.

There is a role for parenting in the situation of the teen who's being cyberbullied, but it's not a matter of either ignoring the problem or jumping in and taking over in an attempt to shield a young person from pain. Most teenagers are actually much less vulnerable and more resilient than we give them credit for. We can only wonder what might have happened if Kayla Torelli's mother had been more insistent about understanding her daughter's situation, or if Lori Drew had allowed her daughter to talk about and then simply feel miserable about the failed relationship with Megan rather than encouraging and co-plotting retribution. What if these parents had encouraged their daughters to use their own feelings of pain and suffering to think about how wrong it was to say hurtful things to others, so that they might empathize with those on the receiving end of nastiness? What if these parents had modeled positive relations by expressing concern yet staying out of their girls' altercations? Unfortunately, Kayla's mother was so preoccupied and undersupported, and Lori Drew was so intent on defending her daughter against the pain of mean-girl interactions, that neither could acknowledge her own daughter's participation in teen nastiness, nor muster any understanding or compassion for the other girl and her family. Moreover, both seemed incapable of teaching their daughters to take responsibility for their actions, online or anywhere else.

Whereas the Drew case has concluded, stories of cyberbullying continue.[34] Currently, legislation penalizing cyberbullying or digital harassment has been introduced in thirteen states.[35] In 2008, the California state legislature became the first to give school administrators the authority to discipline students for bullying online or offline.[36] And in at least one case, young people engaging in bullying online and off were charged with a violation of civil rights resulting in bodily injury, and now face years in the courts and juvenile justice systems.[37] In 2012, the United States witnessed another troubling cyberbullying case when Dharun Ravi was found guilty of privacy invasion, tampering with evidence, and bias intimidation related to the suicide of his Rutgers University roommate, Tyler Clementi.[38] Advocates for young people argue that such legal decisions are important, but it is increased respect for self and others, rather than increased fear of penalties alone, that may ultimately change cyberbullying behavior among young people.[39] Young people may learn respect for themselves and for others in several locations, but it is important to observe and experience such respect in the home. Kayla Torelli, who engaged in cyberbullying as well as in several other risky behaviors both online and off, seemed to be acting out in response to a difficult home environment. Research has found that participation in online harassment and risky behavior is more common among those who grow up in households with conflict and poor child-parent relationships.[40] Unfortunately, Kayla's mother, Hanh, seemed to lack the self-care or the will that would be needed for her to intervene in Kayla's life; she did not know how to intervene to help Kayla through her difficult teen years. And, schooled in the belief that parents are solely responsible for their children's problems, she blamed herself rather than seeking out available resources that could provide her with the support she needed. Other parents, such as Kelly's mother as well as Sarah Drew's mother, seemed to be consumed with fear for their daughters. Kelly interpreted this impulse toward protection as her mother's lack of respect for her. Perhaps Sarah Drew has similarly wished that her mother had trusted her ability to handle her own problems. Like Hanh Torelli, each of these mothers could have benefited from living in a society in which they sensed support rather than potential blame in their role as mothers.

Stories like that of Megan Meier's suicide can encourage parents, and in particular middle-class mothers, to be like helicopters: hovering nearby, ready to swoop in and save children from dangers that they presume their children are incapable of understanding or addressing. Stories of cyberbullies, Internet predators, sexting, and other experiences of young people's heightened vulnerability can unwittingly provide support for parents to preach and react rather than to listen and respond, and thus can undergird the culture of fear that pervades and informs the ethic of expressive empowerment that we find in the U.S. upper-middle-class, as noted in chapter 1. But what young people need from their parents is not fear or heroes who can save the day when things go wrong. Such efforts only prepare young people for their place in a society of surveillance and containment.[41] What they need instead are parents who are part of a community of people that looks out for them, listens to them, asks permission to gain insights into their lives, and models supportive relationships both within and outside their immediate families. These are the building blocks for a society in which cautionary tales remain outliers and real resources are devoted instead to problems that truly matter.

CHAPTER 3 | Strict Parents, Gamer High School Dropouts, and Shunned Overachievers

U.S. SOCIETY HAS TENDED to view young people either as vulnerable and in need of protection or as a potential menace to be controlled and contained.[1] When we think of children as vulnerable and in need of protection, we want to offer them warmth and support. In contrast, when we think of children in relation to problem behaviors, we consider the benefits of regulation and control. These two components—warmth/support and regulation/control—guide parenting behaviors, and research suggests that the best parenting practices involve finding a balance between responsiveness (warm and supportive parenting) and demandingness (regulating behaviors).[2] This balanced style is termed *authoritative parenting*, and it contrasts with the less desirable styles of *authoritarian* (demanding but not warm), *permissive* (warm but not demanding), and *neglectful* (neither demanding nor warm) parenting.

In the previous chapter, we considered the stories of parents who perhaps viewed themselves as authoritative but were inclined to be either overinvolved (helicopter parents), trying to control their children's digital and media environment, or underinvolved, underestimating the role of digital and mobile media in their children's lives. So far, research says little about parental under- or overinvolvement in digital and mobile media, but existing studies do suggest that authoritative parents, or those who are deemed successful in balancing responsiveness and demandingness, tend to talk about digital and mobile media use with their children more than do parents who are less warm or more restrictive, and also tend to place more restrictions on their use.[3] Most parents report that they spend at least some time restricting and overseeing media use, talking with their children about the Internet and remaining in the same room when their children are online.[4]

Note that research indicates that most parents *report* that they engage in restricting and overseeing media use. Parents readily acknowledge that they should place some restrictions on how their children use the Internet, whether they access the online environment with mobile devices or with computers located in their homes. Yet in-depth and observational research into family life suggests that parents may engage in less restriction of media use than they care to admit.[5] This, in fact, is consistent with a larger U.S. trend away from a regulatory approach to parenting among upper-income parents. Upper-middle-class and wealthy parents tend to equate restriction with a lack of warmth, as sociologist Margaret Nelson found in her research.[6] Several mothers in her study contrasted their own warm and supportive parenting style with what they viewed as the overly restrictive and rigid styles of their own parents.

Nelson also found that less well-off parents, those I term would-be middle-class and less advantaged, were more likely than their wealthier counterparts to embrace a strong view of parental authority that emphasizes regulation and control.[7] These less privileged parents might also embrace warmth, but they discuss parenting in relation to boundary setting and restriction, which they see as important given the challenges they face.[8] As noted earlier, these families tend to embrace an ethic of respectful connectedness, emphasizing the need to respect authority and placing a high priority on family loyalty.

Sometimes young people view strong parental authority as an important part of a loving parent-child relationship in that it expresses the parents' concerns for children who face tremendous odds. But in other families, this strict oversight shades into intrusiveness, and not surprisingly, young people in these families find overly restrictive rules frustrating, particularly when they don't sense that a degree of warmth and support accompanies those restrictions. Digital and mobile media then often become sources of tension and misunderstanding between parents and their children.

Most of the parents I have spoken with want to see themselves as warm and supportive of their children, regardless of how many restrictions they put on their children's media use. What might make teens understand restriction and discussion of media as indicating a lack of warmth? And, given the new challenges presented by digital and mobile media, are there occasions when warmth appropriately balanced with regulation (authoritative parenting) may not be quite enough? To get at these issues, this chapter continues chapter 2's discussion of problem behaviors related to digital and mobile media. I pay particular attention to young people who may seem to their parents to be rebellious or inordinately interested in digital and mobile media. How are parental choices related to these behaviors? To frame this issue, we begin with stories of how young people experience strictness or regulatory parenting today.

Strict Parenting and Digital and Mobile Media

Carmen Rodriguez, a sixteen-year-old Latina who lives with her sister, brother, grandmother, and both of her parents in a lower-income neighborhood, sounds fairly comfortable with her father's authoritarian approach to her digital and mobile media use—at least initially. She explains her use of digital media in this way:

> I'm on the phone all the time at home, because at school I don't really have time to be with my friends, 'cause I have school, two sports, and when I get home, it's usually around six, and so I want to talk to my friends or my boyfriend. But I have a limitation [on my phone use], because I haven't been with my family and they want me to be with them, not on the phone all the time. They say I have to choose one or the other. So during dinner, I have to turn it off. And I have a curfew, and I can't be on past that time.[9]

Many families interviewed for this book had rules about turning off the phone during dinner and about not talking on the phone past a certain time, with some parents keeping the cell phone charger in their bedroom or in the kitchen so as to subtly remind young people when it's time to turn it off. These were some ways in which parents established rules that demonstrated respect for everyone in the household. What was interesting in Carmen's case surfaced when she said more about how her parents, and in particular her father, enforced the family's rules, and then again when her friends and peers reacted to her father's approach.

First, she tells a group of her classmates about how her parents enforce rules about her mobile phone use. "They just look at me and say [mimicking a stern, low voice], 'Turn off your phone. *Now*.' They scare me, so I turn off the phone," she says somewhat sheepishly. Later in the conversation, Carmen notes that her father reviews her text messages: "He wanted to see them, and I just leave my phone laying around. It's not like I say anything bad, so it's okay."

As some of Carmen's friends and peers seem to bristle in their seats at this comment, I ask her, "So it was okay with you?"

"No," she says, it wasn't okay that he read her text messages, "But he just grabbed it. He tends to snatch things, and he looked at it." At this point, others in the group exchange glances and a few give incredulous looks. Noticing this, Carmen adds uncomfortably: "It's no big deal."

"That would suck!" another seventeen-year-old, Cassandra, bursts out.

"Has anyone else had their parents do that?" I ask, to see if I can help Carmen find support for her father's position. No, apparently not.

"They *trust* me," another sixteen-year-old named Victoria explains, clearly equating Carmen's father's actions with a lack of trust in Carmen. When Carmen later notes that she didn't like to use either her cell or the house phone when she was in her house "because my dad listens in," seventeen-year-old Alejandro turns to me and says emphatically,

> See, that just doesn't happen in my house. It's about *trusting* you. Like there's things in text messages, they're personal. If I feel comfortable, then I'll show them. Otherwise, no. Just grabbing it, that would bother me.

Carmen is blushing and looking uncomfortable, and her classmates are reacting to her father's actions in consensual disapproval. "My dad just worries," Carmen says with a shrug, adding somewhat unconvincingly and almost as a question, "But he trusts us."

Some of the acquaintances and friends in Carmen's discussion group similarly talked about how they had a trusting relationship with their parents. But others were frustrated with what they believed were their parents' attempts to control their uses of mobile phones or laptops with Internet access. Seventeen-year-old Winona, a Latina who lived in Carmen's lower-income neighborhood, adopts an aloof smirk as Carmen talks about her family's experiences with media. She was not interested in complying with the group interview, frequently providing only one-word responses to questions and offering a judgment of raised eyebrows when others contributed more. Winona seems to have a relationship with her own parents that differs from Carmen's:

INTERVIEWER: Do your parents pretty much know what's going on online?
WINONA: Nah, 'cause I'm never on the computer.
INTERVIEWER: So you use the phone more?
WINONA: Yeah.
INTERVIEWER: And how do they feel about that?
WINONA: They just get mad 'cause I'm on the phone all the time.

INTERVIEWER: So, are there restrictions, then? Like, maybe they say you have to get off the phone during dinnertime?

WINONA: No.

INTERVIEWER: No? So you can just text and talk all the time?

WINONA: Yeah. 'Cause it's my phone and they can't take it away.

Whether or not Winona's parents try to exert parental authority over her, and whether or not they do so in a way that they think expresses warmth, Winona clearly seeks to assert her own authority over her mobile phone. Similarly, when seventeen-year-old Eduardo is asked if his mother, a single parent, takes his mobile phone away when he is grounded, he says, "No, 'cause I pay for my cell phone. [I would tell her,] 'No, you're not paying for it, I am, so it's mine.'"

"Yeah," his eighteen-year-old friend Jose agrees. "I mean, they can't take it away from me. If you pay for it, it's yours." Paying for the technology becomes a way for young people to assume authority, at least in the minds of those we interviewed. But regardless of who pays, technologies such as mobile phones are often a battleground for teens and parents who disagree on who has the final say over how and with whom young people will interact.

Carmen, Winona, Eduardo and others in their group all live in a busy city neighborhood where unemployment has been higher than the national average and houses that have been abandoned serve as magnets for substance abuse.[10] Parents living in such locations often feel the need to exercise greater protection over their children because of their concerns about the immediate environment in which they live.[11] Carmen's father's impulse to read all of her text messages was probably rooted as much in affording a protected space for childhood as it was in exercising a certain kind of discipline. One of the problems, though, is that the young people in Carmen's circle of acquaintances do not see his actions in this way. And young people's friends and acquaintances are apt to work fairly hard at helping young women like Carmen see the errors of their parents' ways. Even if young people like Carmen see their family as warm and are not inclined to resist their parents' authoritarian approaches, they can find plenty of justification among their friends for thinking about situations in which they feel less trusted and more controlled, and can wonder about when parental actions cross over from setting limits to intrusive behaviors. Carmen works hard to defend her father's actions, perhaps because she does not necessarily see his approach as lacking warmth, even if it is very restrictive about her cell phone use.

Caleb: Finding a Workaround

Caleb Baylor doesn't need his friends to tell him that his parents place an awful lot of restrictions on him. The very environment of his home, with its two small bedrooms for four large teenage boys and a single piece of technology that functions as both television and computer screen, is a constant reminder. Caleb lives with his mother, stepfather, and three half brothers in a neighborhood of small houses where the rate of unemployment is well above the city's average.[12] The boys share one car and one cell phone, and they rarely go anywhere without Caleb's mother, Donna, or with another sibling.

Donna believes that films have a negative influence on young people, and so she prefers that the boys—ages fifteen, sixteen, and seventeen—only watch movies she has seen before so that she can be reassured that there aren't "bad parts," as she says. Caleb's family is very involved in a conservative Christian church. Although his mother and stepfather express warmth, Caleb finds his parents' restrictions frustrating. "It's hard not to be able to talk about R-rated movies that everyone has seen," he says. "But when people are talking about PG-13 movies, it's even harder because I'm sixteen and I still can't see those kind of movies." Caleb's mother is equally restrictive of games, insisting on reading reviews of games before allowing her sons to purchase and play them. Her strictness sometimes becomes a source of good-natured humor in the family. Once, after Caleb tried unsuccessfully to convince his mother that he should be allowed to purchase an online game called Bloody War, he started referring to it as "Not So Bloody War." Despite the joking, however, the game didn't get purchased, and Caleb quietly resolved to play it only when he was at a friend's house.

The summer before he participated in an interview with one of my research team members, Caleb went on a trip to a camp in the Midwest. It was the first time he'd been out of his home state of Colorado, and it opened up new relationships for him. One person he met there was a girl his own age from Ohio. Like Caleb, she came from an extremely restrictive family, and like Caleb, she wasn't so sure about all of her family's rules. As Caleb says of how the relationship started, "We were both having a very hard time with different spiritual issues, so we just kind of talked it all out, vented toward each other, and that's one of the main reasons we became friends."

In previous generations, such relationships might have been maintained, at least for a while, through letter writing and the occasional phone call. In the age of the Internet, however, friends can remain on each other's buddy lists and keep up with each other's goings-on through their Facebook pages, thus remaining in closer and more immediate contact than was possible before. This has a real advantage for young people, who tend to live in the present and desire immediate connection with and feedback from their peers.

Caleb and his online friend have remained in frequent contact in part because of their shared reservations about their families' restrictions, but also because each has come to serve as a sounding board for the other in a way that entails less social risk than geographically bound friendships might. As Caleb notes,

> I'd rather talk to her and ask her some questions than someone I know who might judge me. . . . She's halfway across the country, so if she decides never to talk to me again because she decides she hates me, oh well. I like her, but the chances of us ever meeting face-to-face again are not very good.

In Caleb's life, social networking sites have afforded him with the opportunity to extend his interpersonal network beyond what his parents would have approved of. He has been able to build an intimate, trusting relationship that would have been difficult to cultivate in his immediate environment and under his family's near-constant supervision. Social networking sites, carefully and quietly used, have enabled Caleb to have a work-around that counters his parents' extreme restrictions. He can use the limited online time he has to cultivate a relationship with a friend who is different from anyone in his social circle, and most likely different from anyone his parents would approve. He can appear to be fully participating in his family's crowded life while carving out a psychic space apart from that family. Caleb has found a way to rebel even while remaining safely within his family's protected realm. In effect, he is protecting his parents from the knowledge that he is rebelling against them. In the process, he greatly reduces the influence and quality of the relationship his parents can have with him. Even though Caleb seems less interested in challenging parental authority than Carmen's classmates Winona, Eduardo, or Jose, his story is another example of the unintended consequence of parental strictness and how it can be undermined as the wider digital and mobile environment provides new avenues through which teens can test their limits. In these cases, it's not clear that young people in even the most restrictive families see restrictions on media use as a sign of a lack of warmth. This is an important point, and we will return to it later in this chapter. First, however, we turn to a family in which restriction outruns warmth, and the consequences play out beyond digital and mobile media use.

Norma and Veronica: Rigidity and Distance

Like Caleb's parents and Carmen's father, Norma Domentary similarly describes herself as a strict single parent. Norma, a European American woman, is a part-time checkout clerk at a major grocery chain. She lives in a small inner suburb of Seattle with her only child, eighteen-year-old Veronica.[13] She notes that because of depressed housing values she cannot move from the modest 1950s ranch that she owns. She wishes she could, though, as she describes her neighborhood as "poor," plagued with gang activity, and too close to the busy nearby streets that are lined with Chinese, Korean, and Cambodian restaurants and food markets. Norma and her ex-husband, who is Filipino, both grew up in this neighborhood, and Norma's sister and brother-in-law live nearby.

Norma has encountered many problems in her daily life, and she wants her daughter to respect her. She wishes that Veronica appreciated the many efforts she's made to support her welfare. Like many parents, Norma wants her daughter to both know and agree with her way of seeing the world.

In large part, like the Baylor family, Norma expresses concern about how television's portrayals are at odds with her lived experiences of economic instability and disadvantage. Norma believes that, as a parent, it is her responsibility to counter what Veronica sees in the media and to inculcate in Veronica the views that she herself embraces: that no one is entitled to anything, and that you need to work hard for what you want out of life. Yet she also believes that, at eighteen, Veronica is old enough to be trusted to make her own decisions regarding media use. Rather than actually imposing restrictions on digital and mobile media use or reading the text messages on her daughter's phone, as some other parents in this study have done, Norma prefers to offer criticism regarding media behaviors of which she does not approve. She uses the instance of the interviews about family media use as an occasion to convey her views to her daughter, providing opportunities to analyze the interactions between mother and daughter regarding media use.

Veronica, who identifies herself as biracial and Asian American, is a well-liked student whose friends are similarly high achievers at her diverse urban high school. Although Veronica, like many young people, uses her cell phone constantly, she also speaks of television as a primary source of leisure time activity.

Veronica agrees with many of her mother's views, noting that she thinks there is "too much" sexuality on MTV and VH1 and that she, like her mother, believes that such representations can influence the ways that teens feel about and engage in sexual activity. But she also implicitly disagrees with her mother's views that such negative assessments should result in restrictions on television viewing. "We don't have cable and we don't get good reception," Norma explains proudly when asked about how much television they watch together as a family. As a result, says Veronica, "there's nothing *to* watch, so I don't spend my time with television." At least, Veronica means, she does not spend her time with television at her own home. "I probably would be home more if there were things to watch. But instead I try to go out," she clarifies, noting that she watches television at her friends' houses instead. Like Caleb Baylor, Veronica has found a way to work around the limitations on media that she experiences in her home life. She then adds thoughtfully, "It's kind of weird, 'cause like every day after school I go to my friend's house. We go over there and hang out and watch BET [Black Entertainment Television], MTV, you know." When the interviewer, seeing the surprised look on Norma's face, asks Norma about this, Norma replies, "I didn't know that until just now!" and laughs uncomfortably.

"You know that I go to friends' houses," Veronica counters.

"Well, I know you go to friends' houses, but I didn't think you'd be sitting there in front of the TV!" Norma replies.

"What do you think we do there?" Veronica asks incredulously.

Her mother replies defensively, "Well, you say sometimes you go to play tennis. You say you go sometimes to get something to eat. You just say you hang out."

"Watching TV *is* hanging out," Veronica says.

"Not talking?" asks her mother imperiously.

"I don't know! I guess," Veronica says with increasing frustration. "We eat, we talk, and we watch TV!"

At this point the interviewer, sensing the rising tension, asks Veronica's mother to share her concerns about television viewing. Norma seems to relish the opportunity to discuss this topic:

Oh, my goodness, I can tell you why [she doesn't like Veronica to view too much television]. Because every time you turn it on you see something that grieves your spirit. I mean, half the shows— Everything that is not normal is made to look normal. I mean, it is so distorted on TV that it is not real life. There are a few good shows on. I like news shows—*60 Minutes*, *20/20*, you know, informative shows. Animal Planet. There is some good-quality TV. But these sitcoms when everyone is putting each other down and it's funny and the alternative lifestyles that are made normal and cool and funny, that's not how the real world is. No one has any money problems. I mean *The Real World*. I watched an episode of *The Real World* one time and the whole episode was about this one girl borrowing this other girl's shirt but not asking, or she stole it and— That is *not* the real world, when your biggest problem in life is someone wearing your shirt without asking. I mean, they are living in this Las Vegas casino with these clothes. That's not the real world. That is distortion.

After this diatribe against television, Veronica, ignoring her mother's comments about young people's sense of entitlement and the concern that on television "no one has any money problems," responds animatedly that she did not believe that television programs depicting homosexuality were offensive: "Because, I mean, we do have to be accepting to everybody else's lifestyles and not be stuck up to the fact that other people live differently. You know? So, it's just like you are seeing a different view. There are a lot of different things going on." Television content, just like whether or not Veronica chooses to watch it, becomes one more stage on which Veronica and Norma duel over whose views of people and their actions are "right."

Veronica is also conscious of her mother's disapproval of her participation in the online spaces of social networking sites. Veronica likes to post information about herself on her profile, and when online, she has sought out forums that enable her to make connections with the Asian part of her identity. But she expects her mother to disagree with her online communication, as is evident in the aside to her mom as she tells this story:

> We were online and said, "What are you doing tonight?" And we were both doing the same thing [going to the same club] and it was, "Cool. I'll see you there." And then there is this other—[To her mom:] You are not freaking out, are you?—[Returns to the interviewer's question about whether or not she interacts online with people she did not know beforehand] But there is this other thing, my friend, his sister is doing this modeling thing. He wants to do a photo shoot of me. So I have connections through that with other people, too.

Veronica is enthusiastic about the possibilities that can grow out of making acquaintances online. Veronica's mother, in contrast, expresses little interest in either the online realm or the mobile phone. She believes that if she improved her computer skills, it might be beneficial for her professionally. Yet, she says, she would rather read books or speak to someone in person than be online or on a mobile. She does wish that Veronica would be more forthcoming about what she does online, however, and complains that whenever she walks into Veronica's room, Veronica quickly exits the screen on which any conversation is taking place.

What starts as discussion of differing views about social networking sites then seems to escalate into yet another disagreement in their joint interview:

> NORMA: I would rather see people, see their facial expressions, do an activity together, not sitting there talking online or on the phone.
>
> VERONICA: I would too, but it's just like when they are online you can talk to twenty people at one time. I don't like to talk on the phone either but it is just more convenient. You can talk to all these people at one time. So that is kind of beneficial.
>
> NORMA: But sometimes you are talking to people, if you are in a group of twenty people, it would be so much more interesting to see their faces, to feel their spirits, to see if they were real because sometimes people are just fake on these things.
>
> VERONICA: At ten o'clock at night?
>
> NORMA: I don't know! Does time make a difference?
>
> VERONICA: Yes! I'm at home at eight p.m. talking to people, that is my hobby. I'd rather go out and talk to them, but if it it's ten p.m. and I'm getting ready to go to bed, then it is just convenient to talk to them there, you know?
>
> NORMA: I personally feel like I am tired of talking to people and by ten at night I'd rather be in my room or—
>
> VERONICA: It is just like "Hey, what did you do today?" or "What's new," you know?

In this exchange, Norma makes several statements expressing her belief that face-to-face communication is preferable to conversations that take place online or by text, perhaps in an attempt to help Veronica to know and appreciate her views. Veronica, who does not challenge her mother's 8:00 p.m. curfew (with, perhaps, time in her room after 10:00 p.m.), argues for the benefits of being able to continue communication when within the confines of her house. Veronica sees her use of digital and mobile media as a way to maintain her ties with her peers while she is under her mother's supervision. Norma might prefer not to communicate with people later in the evening, but it is clear that Veronica feels differently. Unfortunately, Norma seems to be so interested in expressing her preferred way of doing things that she is unable to hear, or even express interest in, Veronica's friendships, her day-to-day practices, or her desire to follow her mother's household rules, much to the detriment of their relationship.

The interviewer returns to Veronica and Norma's modest home for a follow-up interview about three months later. At that point Veronica, who had recently graduated from high school, had moved out of her mother's house and into an apartment with a relatively new boyfriend. Veronica and Norma are not speaking to each other as a result of the move. Veronica explains the move in relation to the fact that her mother does not trust her. Her mother, on the other hand, attributes her move to outside influences such as the media, which, Norma feels, have given Veronica a set of unrealistic aspirations and a sense of entitlement.

Norma is especially indignant about the fact that when Veronica moved out of the house, she took their computer with her. Veronica's secretive removal of the computer from Norma's house was, to Norma, one more sign of Veronica's sense of entitlement. This makes Norma angry, and perhaps this is why she insists again in the individual follow-up interview on the benefits of face-to-face communication over computer- or phone-mediated conversation. In keeping with her approach to socialization, which emphasizes recognizing right and wrong through criticism, Norma wants Veronica to get the message that she disapproves of her daughter's choice to move in with her boyfriend. She is therefore withholding contact as a way of voicing her objection. It is another way in which she is attempting to express strict expectations of appropriate behavior.

The research literature on parental mediation, or parents' rules about media use, has little to say about a case like Norma and Veronica's, in which rigidity seems to outweigh warmth. That literature offers suggestions as to why a self-described strict parent like Norma might engage in restricting media—but she herself does not. And although the literature suggests that the most effective means of mediating media involves engaging in discussions with children about their media practices, Norma's efforts at talking with Veronica about her media choices demonstrate that such parental talk is not always well received by children, nor is it effective in achieving parents' intentions regarding the mediation of media use. Young people like Veronica can experience such talk as less about connection and responsiveness and more about regulation and demandingness.

The story of Norma and Veronica suggests that the theory behind parental mediation—the belief that it is the parent's responsibility to provide judgment about media, which are presumed to be largely negative influences in the lives of young people—can provide justification for ineffective parental mediation strategies, such as those embraced by Norma in her relationship with Veronica. Unfortunately, Norma did not listen to Veronica's experiences in order to understand them on Veronica's terms. She felt justified in her inflexible responses to Veronica because she viewed media as a source of disruption to be mediated through argumentation. She thought she was helping Veronica to attain a more realistic sense of what to expect from life, whereas Veronica thought her mother was not able to appreciate her own relationships and aspirations. Whether or not the media were to blame for what Norma interpreted as Veronica's sense of entitlement, the alienation between Norma and Veronica had lasting consequences for Veronica, who was not able to afford to pursue classes at the local community college without her mother's help. Her story is somewhat different from those of other young people, but the closing down of future options is one sad consequence that it shares with many others.

Strict parenting is not necessarily parenting without warmth. In fact, young people can view strictness as a sign of parental concern, even as some pushback to strict parenting is to be expected as teens test their limits. However, Veronica and Norma's story reminds us of how young people and their parents can interpret parental intentions quite differently. When parents impose rules or voice criticisms about media use without inviting their children to share their experiences, young people may experience their parents' words and actions as devoid of warmth. This can eradicate the parental goal of fostering respect and connection between parent and child.

Dell Sealy

Unlike Norma, Caleb's parents, or Carmen's father, Meghan Sealy does not describe herself as a "strict" parent, preferring to say that she maintains high expectations. She and her son, Dell, have always had a close relationship, and she has felt the need to look out for him because he has a learning disability and has always struggled with traditional schooling.[14]

Meghan, a single parent for nearly all of her son's life, earned a four-year college degree while Dell was growing up and she was working full-time. She and Dell's father split up when he decided to leave the state to avoid a warrant for his arrest; Dell was less than two years old at the time. Meghan and her sister have now both earned college degrees, although neither of her parents had any experience with higher education. Her brother, who trained and worked as a police officer, now works for UPS because the benefits and hours are better, and all of the extended family members live fairly near Meghan and Dell in the same small city. Meghan and her son live in the lower- to middle-income inner suburbs, in a small apartment with well-worn furniture.

Dell dropped out of high school a year earlier, at the age of sixteen. Meghan is frustrated about this but believes that, as an adult, Dell must make his own decisions, and she trusts that he will learn from them. She sees her role primarily as providing support for him. Dell, who has taken a variety of jobs in automotive repair and in seasonal landscaping, expresses lukewarm interest in going back to school, and he hasn't followed up on his stated plan to pursue a GED. "Yeah," he says with a sigh. "I might do it. I don't know. I'm just working right now." He shrugs, suggesting that he is less interested in pursuing a long-term plan than in hanging out.

Hanging out, after all, is a reasonably entertaining way to spend free time. Dell watches movies and music videos when his mother is at work. He used money from one of his jobs to purchase a new computer, which he uses to download music, play games, and communicate with friends. In the evenings, Dell goes out with friends when he has money to spend and a car that is working. For Dell and other young men like him, digital media become part of a home environment that's comfortable and difficult to leave, and they also fill the time that's left available due to a lack of work or school commitments.

Dell says that he does want to support himself and he doesn't like relying on his mom, but he isn't excited about her suggestion that he consider the military, except for the sign-in bonus: "Then I could get a really nice car," he says. Dell spends a lot of time indulging his interest in cars at websites such as StreetRacing.org, a social networking site in which people share car images and stories of races they've been in or witnessed. Through his constant involvement in this site, Dell engages in what researchers have called "interest-driven participation," or a deep level of engagement that has led him to become involved in a passionate subculture supported by an online community.[15] Dell particularly likes meeting young women there who share his interests. A sensitive and soft-spoken young man, he believes that the young women in his own neighborhood are "really stuck up" and he finds it difficult to talk with them. He prefers thinking about and working with cars. But overall, he says, he is "bored" with surfing the Internet. "Well," his mother interjects, "that's because you've really limited yourself in terms of what you're looking at." When the interviewer asks what she means by that, Meghan replies:

> That he's so into the line of looking into street racing that he's not thinking that maybe he could learn about the country of Brazil on the Internet or just

look at different things. You know, I think he gets bored and so all he's thinking of is, "Well, let's go back to the street racing and see what's new." As opposed to really looking up other things online.

Protesting his mother's statement that he isn't looking at a variety of things online, Dell replies,

Well, I do really like car information. Like I just downloaded this engine program where you can just look at your engine specs. It helps you calculate torque from horsepower, from horsepower to torque. Just like your gear ratios.

This leads Meghan to encourage Dell to follow up and look into how his interests might be parlayed into the development of a career:

I don't think it's that difficult to get certified, Dell. See, these are things that you could look into. You could probably find this information on the Internet. If you took the time!

Dell mumbles something unintelligible, to which his mother replies with a laugh, "See. I cut your boredom in half already and you don't even know it!"

Meghan is very interested in encouraging Dell to consider his options, and uses these interviews as yet another opportunity to get Dell to think about what he might do with his time and how he might use access to the Internet, among other things, to pursue better options for himself. Meghan is a believer in higher education, as the completion of her degree meant that she'd been able to move from a low-level clerical position to a supervisory job in a nursery in which she oversees the planting and growth of trees and shrubs for sale. So she knows the value of self-motivation and of following one's interests into a rewarding career path.

With her limited income, Meghan finds that family time usually means watching television together. This is often a positive opportunity for her to interact with Dell, as she notes: "I think television gives us opportunities to be together. Sometimes there'll be music videos that he's watching, and he'll go, 'Mom, you gotta see this!' So I'll sit through it, and we'll talk about it or stuff like that. You know, that does open doors for conversation." She says she tries to use discussions about television to discuss "moral character and behavior" because "as a parent, you always look for opportunities to discuss good moral values."

But television was also a way for them to spend time apart in the limited space of their apartment, with him watching television in his bedroom and her watching it in the living room. "You watch entirely too much TV," Dell says to his mother.

"Yeah," she agrees. "Both of us watch too much TV. But I want to get a bike so I can get out of the house more."

"And I want to get out more, too," Dell adds, "but both of my cars are broken down now"—another good reason Dell gave himself for allowing his life to be in limbo and free of decision making.

When talking with the interviewer on her own, Meghan discusses some of the challenges she has encountered as a single parent. She says that Dell's decision to drop out of high school was painful for her, not only because she knew it would hurt him later in life but also because she felt that it showed he "lacked self-esteem," and she therefore took some responsibility for his choice. When she'd first heard that he was skipping school, she changed her work hours so that she could drop him off at school every day before heading to her own place of employment. Later, she learned that he was walking home after she'd dropped him off. She regrets that she wasn't able to monitor his attendance more closely, but she notes that "if I don't work I don't get paid." Thus she couldn't "take a week off from work and say, 'I'm going to go to school with you every day and we're going to make sure you follow through with this.'" She did, however, take one day off and showed up in each of his classes to make sure that he attended them. "That embarrassed him," she says. But once she had to go back to work, he went back to "ditching" and eventually stopped attending altogether. She likes the idea of having him join the military, she says, because then he "would get the discipline a father would give him, and maybe that would calm him down and help him feel more secure," she reasons.

Because Dell spends a great deal of time online, the interviewer asks Meghan whether they have filtering software. Meghan replies candidly:

> Sometimes I wish I had one of those spy programs that followed him so that I knew where he was looking. You know, when I walk into a room and he changes the screen. I'm like, "Where were you?" I'd just like to know. Not that I'm going to berate him or anything. It would just help sometimes. So would mind reading [laughing]. But I don't think that's going to happen.

Like many other parents, Meghan wants to trust Dell, and she is very intent on treating Dell with respect. She describes her views on "how people should treat each other" as a guiding principle for how she makes decisions and how she hopes to raise Dell as well. She is also intent on not overparenting: she prefers allowing him to make choices and to experience the consequences of those choices. He doesn't like that she encourages his independence, however:

> The one thing he hates the most is when I make sure he knows that these are his choices and that what's happening is the result of the decisions he's made. It's not happening because I was too mean or I wasn't mean enough or I wasn't caring enough to do anything. I've always been really straight with him—even when he was little. Because I figured that was the best way to have a relationship.

Dell trusts and respects his mother, and she is a truly remarkable and reasonable woman. He asks her for advice, speaks openly with her about his concerns involving friends and young women, and clearly recognizes both her warmth and the strong set of expectations she has for his behavior. "I just think that the honesty that I've always tried to have be a part of our relationship has helped him feel comfortable coming to me for advice," she says, adding, "And then that helps me kind of gauge where he's at and what I can help him do to get him closer to accomplishing his goals." Sometimes, she says, "it just chokes me up because, I'm like, 'Oh my God, I don't think he can do this!' But I don't tell him that because this is his goal. And I don't want to hamper his decisions and how he's going to do that."

Meghan is quite aware of Dell's lack of options, and although she isn't entirely in favor of his extensive media use, she is concerned that if he wasn't inside, he might be finding even more negative, and possibly even self-destructive, ways to spend his free time while she is at work. She sees a relationship between her economic situation and the difficulties both she and Dell are facing in the job market. "I think our society is becoming more of the haves and the have-nots. Either you're poor or you're rich," she says. She is well aware of the lack of support she and Dell have as well as the sense in the United States that if you aren't economically successful, there is something wrong with you, not with the system itself.

Meghan is trying her best to be a respectful, authoritative, and egalitarian parent who is not overly strict, overly involved, or neglectful. She is also trying her best to be a part of his network and to see his experiences from his point of view. However, Dell is being disrespectful of his mother without even realizing it, because he is putting his needs before hers. This isn't entirely his fault, as the economic disadvantages of his home life and his lack of ability in traditional schooling have led him to have fewer opportunities to pursue for self-support. Nevertheless, his reliance upon her is exhausting, and the lack of support they each had from the school and from other social support systems only makes it worse. In many ways, it seems as if Dell is taking advantage of his mother's good intentions. Because she is intent upon being a "good" parent, Meghan feels that she has no option but to allow him to do this. After all, how can she be vigilant in overseeing her son's life—including his media life—when she's got to continue to be the main earner for the household? And what if his use of media in the home is an alternative to other, less safe, more self-destructive paths? Dell Sealy finds escape and sustenance in his uses of digital and mobile media. His lack of motivation combined with his truncated education means that he most likely will be a victim of downward mobility and will encounter new struggles in his years ahead. But foregrounding his mother's approach to parenting or even his own shortcomings does not provide an adequate explanation for this outcome. In other words, something is missing in our assumptions about how parenting styles, approaches to technologies, and outcomes relate to one another.

Tanya Cortez

Tanya Cortez is the antithesis of Dell Sealy. Like Dell, Tanya is fortunate to have a mother who wants to be supportive and who has made great sacrifices in order for her to pursue opportunities. But unlike him, Tanya is a strong student whose academic excellence has been recognized in her lower-income school. At twelve, she tested into a gifted and talented program, but the closest school with such a program was several miles from their home. Her mother, Louisa, made the difficult decision to switch Tanya as well as her two younger siblings to the school that had the gifted and talented program, which means that Louisa and her husband, John, have needed to patch together a complicated system of driving their unreliable car when it was workable, using public transport otherwise, and relying on Louisa's brother to get them to and from school as an emergency measure.

Everyone in Tanya's immediate family is happy with the new school and particularly with the support Tanya has received from her new teacher, and Tanya's parents take great pride in their children's success in the program. But a problem quickly emerged: in order to do her sixth-grade homework during her second year at the school, Tanya needed to have high-speed Internet access, and Tanya's family's computer equipment was outdated and their cell phone did not have data access. Louisa's brother offered to let Tanya come to his house to use their family's computer, so Tanya began alternating between going to her uncle's house after school and heading for the public library to use the computer there.

Tanya's uncle has remarried, and there are two sixteen-year-olds, his daughter and his wife's daughter, living at their home and attending the school system that Tanya and her siblings left. Both of these young women badger Tanya about her explicit desire to succeed in school. They see Tanya's interest in participating in interviews about digital media as yet another example of something she is trying to do in order to better herself, particularly when Tanya agrees to organize a discussion group with these two cousins. During the discussion group with the three of them (to which the two cousins showed up more than an hour late), one of Tanya's older cousins demands that Tanya rather than the cousin answer the interviewer's questions. Speaking to Tanya, she says: "Go ahead, Miss Professional." At this, the other cousin turns to me and explains:

COUSIN 1: We make fun of her 'cause of the way she's been talking to people [such as the interviewer].

TANYA: Because I present myself in a professional manner.

COUSIN 2 (MIMICKING TANYA): "I present myself in a professional manner." [Both cousins then look at each other and laugh]

It is not difficult to imagine the kind of resistance Tanya might encounter as she attempts to use the computer at her cousins' house for homework. It is clear that her interest in using the computer for online access, along with the decision to attend a school outside the neighborhood, marks Tanya as different from her cousins. For Tanya, using her uncle's or the library's computer for online access is already difficult given her family's transportation difficulties and ongoing financial challenges. She holds on tenuously to the hopes her family and her teachers have invested in her, which put her at odds with her cousins and the peers in her neighborhood who attend her old school. She has asked her parents to consider getting online access at their home, but because she realizes that they cannot afford it and because she has no other alternative, she makes do with what she has.

Tanya's desire to use the library's and her uncle's computer arose pragmatically as a result of her school's homework expectations, but quickly her cousins vested her practices with a symbolic weight. They see her as aspiring, which in turn they view as a negative judgment about their neighborhood. This slight needs to be addressed through intimidation and bluster so that the cousins can save face at Tanya's expense. Tanya's wish to use digital media for her homework and possibly for the betterment that her parents and teachers desire of her is admirable. It is also not without poignant emotional costs. Tanya finds herself weighing future promise against present discomfort, which is a difficult calculus for young people, whose limited life experiences lead them to privilege immediate gratification over longer-term benefits. What Tanya wants in relation to digital, mobile, and traditional media is rife with conflicts whose outcomes potentially have great consequence for the eventual life chances she will encounter.

Tanya's experiences were not unlike those of Carmen, the young woman whose father was considered by her peers to be overly strict. Carmen weathered the slings of criticism from her peers, just as Tanya did. Both Carmen and Tanya seemed appreciative of their parents' high expectations or "demandingness," as did Dell, the young gamer who couldn't quite get his independence under way. And note the difference in the conversations about television and gaming that occurred among some of these parents and teens. Caleb, the young man from a highly restrictive family, had discussions about television and gaming that were not unlike those between Dell and his mother but were quite different from the troubled conversations between Veronica and her mother. The young people whose stories were told in this chapter seemed quite capable of recognizing the difference between warmth and lack of warmth. They did not automatically equate restriction and strong parental authority with a lack of warmth, as some of us inclined toward warmth over restriction (including me) might have feared that young people do.

The discussion among Carmen and her peers illustrates something important about strict parenting, as the young people in that conversation assume that any kind of parental restriction is going to be overly intrusive and authoritarian. Whereas earlier I equated this with upper-income families, it's important to note that this tendency to balk when faced with overly restrictive parenting has a long history. Beginning in the middle of the twentieth century, when Benjamin Spock popularized the idea of the nurturing parent, the focus on parenting has shifted from questions of how to maintain authority in a hierarchical arrangement to how to develop relationships of trust and mutual respect. This may explain why Carmen's peers used the word "trust" to contrast Carmen's relationship with her father to their relationships with their own parents. Today's emphasis within authoritative parenting seems to lie in agreeing upon clear rules and expectations, so that a young person will come to see consequences as a result of his or her actions rather than resulting from parents' arbitrary use of power.

It's important to note that Tanya's experiences also share some similarities with those of Carmen's peers, who expressed rebellion against parental authority and who badgered Carmen about her father's restrictive and intrusive style when it came to the cell phone. We can't know the extent of warmth present or absent in the families of those young people, or why those teens equated purchasing their own phones with claiming the right to challenge parental authority (although that's an interesting question for future research). However, even a parenting style involving a great deal of both warmth and restriction may not be enough to counteract other negative factors in one's environment, as we saw in Dell's and Tanya's stories. Rebellious acts can be understood as logical responses to curtailed opportunities and freedoms. "Deviance," as sociologists have long argued, is an outgrowth of social conditions: when young people feel limited, they act out, expressing their frustration in ways that challenge authority, in order to claim some power and agency for themselves.[16] Given that cell phones and social networking sites afford young people access to locations and people that are not always accessible to parents, they can serve as an important avenue for escape and for the creation and maintenance of life apart from supervision, as we saw in Caleb's story.[17] In other words, it's important to recognize that even though parents have a significant influence on the lives and behaviors of young people, there are also factors in young people's environments that are beyond parental control. Studying the outcomes of digital and mobile media in the lives of young people is always going to involve looking at these practices in larger contexts. We need to explore what young people themselves experience and how embeddedness in culture plays a significant role in the risks that digital and mobile media might enable or amplify—and this is the subject of the next two chapters.

Conclusion

The young people and parents in this chapter have differing views regarding the role of parental authority and of how media might fit into their lives collectively and individually, even as each of these families could be said to exist within a cultural milieu of respectful connectedness. Carmen

Rodriguez is compliant in her father's efforts to curtail her freedoms and exercise his right to view her text messages and listen in on her phone conversations, viewing this in relation to the expectation that her father's parental authority is to be respected. Her friends and school acquaintances, however, are less sanguine about his approach, reacting to her disclosures with seeming indignation. It's possible that their reactions are related to the fact that they may find themselves in similar situations. Some of them may feel that they are forced to assert themselves and rebel against their parents, as Carmen's peers Winona, Eduardo, and Jose have done. Or, as Caleb Baylor does, they may develop work-arounds that enable them to attain a sense of agency in the midst of strict parental oversight. Feeling trapped in a life he experiences as too restrictive, Caleb feels compelled to utilize digital media to work out the differences between his views and his family's commitments. Caleb acts in self-preservation but, perhaps, at the expense of the relationships with his family members. Tanya Cortez, too, finds herself in the untenable position of being asked to choose between her relationships with her family and a chance at greater life opportunities. And Dell, whose future is perhaps the most precarious, is choosing inaction in the face of scarce opportunities, utilizing digital media as an escape from facing the problems that confront him.

Veronica Domentary, like Caleb, is frustrated with her mother's attempts to express parental authority through criticism of Veronica's digital and mobile media practices. Their exchanges demonstrate the limits in their ability to listen to and communicate effectively with one another. Like Kayla Torelli from chapter 2, Veronica engages in some risky behavior both online and off. Veronica was once a popular high school student whose circle of friends included college-bound high achievers. Yet when she moved out of her mother's house, her mother severed ties with her, effectively limiting Veronica's ability to pursue higher education in the crucial years following high school. Veronica is expected to be on her own now, and any decisions she makes about higher education will be her own responsibility.

In the last two stories, of Dell and Tanya, a different aspect to the cautionary tale emerges. In those cases as well as in the stories of many other young people from would-be middle-class and less advantaged backgrounds, parents provide as much emotional support as they can and strive to engender healthy relationships with their children—and yet this still does not seem to be enough, on its own, to overcome the difficulties their children face. Even with a focus on a particular interest and passion, as Dell expresses in his love of streetcar racing, and even with a school that promises to provide academic support, Dell and Tanya find many additional challenges in their immediate environments. Access to technology is one problem in Tanya's case, although this is complicated by close relations who seem intent on undermining or ostracizing her, illustrating the cultural costs of stepping outside expectations. For Dell, there are too few social connections between his interest-driven online participation and prospects for future (or even more immediate) employment.

Engaging in overly intrusive behavior isn't a unique practice of middle-class, would-be middle-class, or lower-income parents. Lower-income parents may engage in overly intrusive behavior that takes the form of rigidly preaching to their children about the perils of the media, as Veronica Domentary's mother did, or assuming the right to access all of a child's text messages, as Carmen Rodriguez's father did. But it's important to recognize that healthy and supportive parenting is not the sole answer to the problems facing the growing number of young people who must deal with challenges in their personal lives—challenges that often involve issues of how digital and mobile media fit into their leisure, schooling, and eventual work lives. Foregrounding the role of new media in relation to long-standing problems of societal inequity can focus us on real issues of disengagement, as represented in the stories of Tanya and Dell, as well as possibilities for intervention rather than blame, such as in Kayla Torelli's story from chapter 2. These cautionary tales reveal that young people need many and varied sources of support as they grow up, and not just from parents. In other words, a Parent App might need to go beyond questions of what a parent does in her own household, as our actions within families are inevitably linked to a larger public. New media technologies such as mobile phones and laptops with Internet access may be changing the ways that teens encounter challenges and opportunities in their lives, but they do not ruin young people's lives. These technologies, just like individual parents, also cannot be expected to solve long-standing social problems on their own.

PART II | Digital Media and Youth

CHAPTER 4 | Identity 2.0
Young People and Digital and Mobile Media

IN THE PREVIOUS SECTION of this book we considered several cautionary tales related to digital and mobile media in contemporary family life. We reviewed stories of young people who engaged in cyberbullying, limitless gaming, and excessive Facebook use, and we considered teen experiences with Internet predators and sexting—all practices that have received a great deal of attention in the news media because they represent lamentable ways that digital and mobile media have amplified some of the troubling aspects of teen life. We also discussed under- and overinvolved parents, many of whom acted out of anxieties about digital and mobile media, and who displayed varying degrees of warmth in their approaches to restricting their older children's experiences with media. But one thing we have not yet addressed is the question of why these media have become so central to the experiences of growing up in contemporary Western societies. Understanding the perspective of young people is an important part of parents' relationships with their children. In this chapter and the one that follows it, therefore, we turn to the stories that young people themselves tell of how these media have become embedded in their lives and experiences. We see how various communication media play a role in providing mythic, pragmatic, and symbolic cultural resources for young people as they strive for recognition, connection, and meaning. But first we begin with a story that reminds us that young people and their parents often view these media quite differently.

In sixteen-year-old Steph Kline's home, the family's laptop sits at the back of the formal living room, near the kitchen and family room.[1] It now resides there rather than in Steph's room, Steph's father, Fred, explains, because he and his wife, Isabella, want to monitor her Internet use. "She was spending a lot of time on the computer and away from us," her mother noted, "and we did not know what was going on and I heard a lot of things about teens getting into things on the computer." Referencing the horrific Columbine tragedy that occurred not far from their neighborhood years ago, Isabella says that the case of the two teen killers frightens her because "those parents thought they knew their kids, too." So, because of Steph's parents' fears about the dangers of the online environment, they mandated a new and more public place for the computer.

As noted in the previous chapters, upper-middle-class and middle-class families like Steph's are investing a great deal of energy in parental oversight of leisure out of their desire to create what they believe is a caring and empowering atmosphere for their children. But Steph does not see her parents' decision to move the laptop in this way; rather, she views the move as a sign of her parents' lack of trust in her. A chatty, articulate, and attractive young woman, Steph juggles a demanding school curriculum, extracurricular activities, and a part-time job. She remains in constant contact with her friends through the use of her cell phone and the family's Internet connection at home.[2] Her mother, Isabella, is a Latin American woman born in Guatemala who works as an outreach worker for the county health department, and her father, Fred, who is of European American heritage, works in sales and distribution. Because her parents don't use the laptop much for their own work, and because her seven-year-old brother, Sam, finds little use for computers, Steph tends to think of the computer as hers. After all, she notes, it was purchased years earlier so that she would be able to complete her school assignments.

When the computer was in her room, she'd had more freedom to spend as much time as she wanted conducting conversations either on the phone or through instant messaging and social networking sites. Now, she says, her parents "always want to read all my conversations." She protests, "I'm not doing anything wrong, but it is just that I want to talk to my friends!"

Steph and her parents are not alone in their disagreement about the role that digital and mobile media should play in the lives of family members. In a cross-generational study of how parents and teens differ in their views about digital and mobile media, researchers from Harvard University found that parents and teens viewed media differently in relation to five concerns: identity, privacy, credibility, authorship and ownership, and participation. Teens in that study tended to approach ethical issues related to these areas in terms of individual concerns; they think about how a decision would affect them personally, not about how a decision might affect someone else. As a result, when using digital and mobile media, young people tend to emphasize the freedoms to which they feel they have a right, rather than considering the responsibility they might have to protect the rights of others.[3]

In U.S. society, young people have been encouraged to think of themselves as capable of making their own decisions. Moreover, they have learned that the way to connect to and garner respect from others is through self-expression and achievement, and they have been encouraged all of their lives to consider themselves special and capable. Once children reach the age at which peers become more important in their lives, parents are concerned that this desire for connection will undermine their relationships with their children and erode parental influence. Some parents are nervous about the role that digital and mobile media come to play in young people's lives, associating these technologies both with a loss of parental influence and with the potential dangers parents see in peer influence. Parents wonder if they should curtail or institute more supervision over their children's media practices, as Steph's parents did. From the perspective of teens, however, these media are a taken-for-granted and natural part of their environment. They are not distinct from the other places in their lives where they meet, posture, fight, and create intimacies with their peers.

Each of the stories in this chapter reveals some things about what young people want from digital, mobile, and traditional media, things that relate to much longer-standing practices of identity formation and peer belonging that have defined the elementary, preteen, and teen years. As in years past, young people today want recognition and acceptance for who they really are and who they believe themselves to be, they want to be found attractive by prospective intimate partners, and they want to experience themselves as belonging. But new challenges to all these desires have arisen because of digital and mobile media, and this chapter will focus on the following three:

1. The need to judge how much about yourself to reveal online: enough to seem accessible but not so much that you come across as needy and insecure

2. The need to reveal something of yourself so that those you care about will recognize and acknowledge you, yet to make those revelations without relying so heavily on commercial products that your friends and acquaintances might see you as overly narcissistic or cocky

3. The need to engage in digitally enhanced interest-driven pursuits such as gaming or academics without alienating yourself from peer cultures that might not offer support for such practices

This chapter considers how teens encounter the digital and mobile media environment and do there the "work" of being a teen.

The Digital and Mobile Media Environment for Young People

The everyday experience of most U.S. young people today is deeply ensconced within the media environment. An often-cited study conducted by the Kaiser Family Foundation in 2010 found that young people under the age of seventeen were spending an average of seven and a half hours a day utilizing various media devices—an increase of nearly an hour and a half over the time they spent with media devices just five years earlier.[4] When "media multitasking" is taken into account, most adolescents are actually consuming closer to eleven hours of media content a day.[5]

More than 93 percent of all U.S. teens between the ages of twelve and seventeen use the Internet, and almost three-quarters of all teens who are online have created a profile on a social networking site such as Facebook.[6] More than a third of all online teens have uploaded photos where others can see them, and more than 80 percent have commented on photos uploaded by others.[7]

Lower-income families, as well as black and Hispanic families, spend more time with all kinds of media than white and higher-income families do.[8] Boys also spend more time in front of the screen than girls do, with most of their time devoted to video games.[9] Texting remains popular across the economic spectrum, as half of all U.S. teens sent an average of fifty text messages a day, and one in three sent more than one hundred a day.[10]

Media exposure has increased in similar ways around the globe. By 2010, mobile phone use around the world had doubled compared with a decade earlier, and developing countries experienced the greatest growth over this period.[11] There were more than five billion mobile phone users around the world by 2010,[12] and India alone was adding six million mobile phone subscribers each month as early as 2007.[13] What all of this means for most families is that the volume of personal contacts and information they are able to access from home and elsewhere is growing exponentially, as is the variety of information sources and the speed at which they are able to access those sources.[14]

Most of the media content received in people's homes via the Internet or television originates or has some connection to the "big six" global media conglomerates: General Electric, Disney, Viacom, Time Warner, News Corporation, and CBS. Other big players in the realm of digital and mobile media include the Internet and cable service providers AT&T, Verizon, Comcast, and Cox, as well as electronics and related media conglomerates Sony, Apple, Microsoft, and Nintendo. Each of these corporations aims to develop a market for children and young people through its various offerings. Each spends a great deal of money discerning what young people want and attempting to create products that will both satisfy those wants and create more desires.

I don't mean to suggest that the advertising and media industries are wholly responsible for manufacturing desires. After all, as Colin Campbell has suggested in his study of the Romantic era, the roots of today's consumerism are to be found not so much in the processes of production as in the human desire to experience ourselves as self-creating beings.[15] This desire is what the media industries capitalize on: a wish to *feel*, to experience life, to express ourselves, and specifically a wish to feel loved, accepted, and capable of maintaining both a sense of ourselves and a sense of our relationships with others. A Romantic sense of self is not reserved for adults, either. Children, too, want to feel and experience themselves as self-creating and in relationships with others; this is a key part of how young people come to understand themselves and what they want from digital and mobile media.

Digital, mobile, and traditional media play three interrelated roles in the lives of young people and in their identity construction processes. First, television programming, books of fiction, video games, mobile phones, and other media products become cultural resources that do the work of allowing young people to express to others and to themselves who they are. In this sense, media, and entertainment media in particular, have long functioned *mythically*, as they provide stories that resonate with us, giving us all an opportunity to feel and offering us meaningful, anchoring stories, music, and cultural touchpoints that we can then share with others in our everyday interactions.[16] Second, digital and mobile media also function *pragmatically*, as they provide a conduit for young people to remain in constant contact with others through cell phones, text communication, and digital communication.[17] But mobile phones are "doubly articulated," as communication researcher Rich Ling notes, and thus they also function *symbolically*, as young people own commercially produced products such as mobile phones, televisions, and MP3 players or iPods that say something to others about who we are.[18]

The very youngest children do not have the direct purchasing power necessary to buy media for pragmatic or symbolic purposes, but with access to television, films, and music, they are able to participate in its mythic dimensions and to convince their parents of the pragmatic and symbolic value media might hold in their lives. They and their parents are heavily targeted by the television, book, film, and music industries as a result. Sociologist Allison Pugh has argued that parents, recognizing that children of all ages have a need to belong within their peer groups, acquiesce in buying things (including media products such as Nintendo DSi and Sony PlayStation) not because they want to indulge their children but because they want their children to be able to participate fully in their peer culture.[19] Pugh therefore helps us understand an important connection between childhood, parenting, and the context of the commercial environment. She recognizes that whereas the advertising industries have indeed worked to make certain products seem necessary for childhood, it is the culture of children themselves—and the desire of parents to see their children fitting into this culture—that drives how buying things becomes a means of conveying caring. She also points out that this is how media-related products themselves come to be related to the symbolic needs and peer cultures of children, pre-teens, and teens.[20]

Each of the stories in this chapter explores how young people utilize digital and mobile media in relation to identity goals of finding recognition and acceptance among their peers, establishing and maintaining connections, and ultimately finding meaning in their lives and in their relationships with others. For example, we'll see here why sixteen-year-old Taylor changed his social network profile—and in doing so, we'll gain insight into how young people perform an identity for the particular (and often changing) audiences of their peers on social networking sites such as Facebook. Too, in a discussion among fifteen-year-old Korinna and her friends, we learn how oversharing is frowned upon among teens even as texting is a constant pressure. And, among fourteen-year-old Joe and his friends, we hear about why and how voyeurism is widely practiced.

We begin our teen stories with Jennifer, who is currently a college student. Jennifer recalls what it was like growing up with the gaming site Neopets and how she believed that her involvement with that site influenced who she became as a young adult. Each of these stories reveals differing aspects of how young people experience themselves as individuals and as members of peer groups whose identities are co-constructed with and through the pragmatic, symbolic, and mythic dimensions of communication technologies.

Growing Up with Neopets

Like many of the commercial products that become part of life for young people, Jennifer Yu, a bright and enthusiastic Asian American student at a prestigious university, first learned of Neopets from her peers. She explains that when she was ten years old and growing up in the U.S. Midwest, "Neopets.com was a huge fad at my school." Her interest in the game began when a teacher provided the opportunity to play Neopets as an incentive for completing coursework:

> All the children in fourth grade had to take a computer class to master basic skills such as word processing. Although we were not supposed to be in the computer lab unless we had class there, we found out one day that a custodian always unlocked the lab a few minutes before class, toward the end of lunch break. Fairly soon, all of us were wolfing down our lunches early in order to spend time on Neopets.com before the teacher arrived. When the teacher found out what was happening, she struck a deal with her students: if we paid attention during class and finished our lessons, she would let us spend the rest of class time on Neopets.com. We became very conscientious from then on, and the final fifteen minutes or so of each class were always spent in happy playing.[21]

Wanting to be a part of the "fad" in her classroom, Jennifer developed a junior account on Neopets and created a pet named Yinna that took the form of a cat-like creature called a yellow wocky. She began playing minigames to earn Neopoints, the form of currency within Neopets. With the Neopoints she'd earned, she began furnishing her pet's Neohome.

In her fourth-grade classroom, classmates would call out to each other and would cheer each other on as they competed in the site's Tug-of-War game, each of the classmates sitting at a different terminal so that they could log in individually and participate with their own pet. Jennifer, who grew up in an upper-middle-class family that embraced an ethic of empowerment, found that she could play Neopets at home within limits. Her parents set up a rewards system similar to that of her teacher: Jennifer could spend thirty minutes on the Neopets site after her homework was completed.

As Jennifer got a bit older, Neopets enabled her to experiment with structures of the adult world, introducing her to the economic system of capitalism. As communication scholars Mimi Ito and Heather Horst have observed of Neopets, "Just as in our capitalist real world, wealth is generated through labor, investment, and commerce. In turn, capitalist exchange drives endless diversity in consumption, identity production, and social distinction."[22]

With her accumulated Neopoints, Jennifer opened a Junior Saver bank account, and once she'd saved even more points, she was able to qualify for a higher return on her investment. She saw a direct connection between her game play and her education about finances. As she noted, thanks to her involvement in the "complex society" of Neopets, "when I earned my first paycheck from a work-study job in the real world, I understood that my income, though small, was part of a much larger system." Financial education was a by-product rather than a goal of the fantasy play that is at the heart of Neopets, however. As she became engaged in the site's opportunities for caring for her pet, she also became deeply immersed in the mythical dimension of the game, inserting herself into the preexisting storyline and feeling that she was creating something new within its borders.

Once she reached thirteen, Jennifer and her peers also began to discover the site's Neoboards, a feature that is limited to participants who are over thirteen because it opens communication between participants in the game.[23] Contacts she made through these boards enabled Jennifer to begin to see the site's potential beyond the play she'd initially enjoyed. She also learned from these boards that her chosen pet "wasn't cool enough," as she says, so she began to "morph my pet into an elite species-color combination, get her stats up, equip her with powerful weapons, acquire more pets, expand her item gallery, and build an impressive Neohome."[24]

Jennifer, who was a high achiever in school, was drawn to the opportunity to create a distinctive and impressive Neopet in a virtual world. She developed skill in the site's games but then also went on to learn how she might gain more Neopoints through investing and reselling goods on the site. By the time she was fourteen, Jennifer had acquired an elite avatar that garnered her the attention and respect of others on the site. Jennifer found a great deal of symbolic value in Neopets as her own needs for belonging and support changed and developed through her early and middle teen years. As she noted, "Returning home after school to a handful of friendly Neomails was always a wonderful experience for me."

Although her parents continue to see the value in her participation in Neopets, her decision to remain a part of the Neopets world didn't come without social costs. Because most of her college-age peers regard the game as a children's diversion, when Jennifer is among her university acquaintances she rarely admits to playing the game. To do so would be to place herself in a precarious position with her peers, who might consider her interest in Neopets a sign that she is immature or more interested in childhood interests than in those deemed more appropriate by her older peer group. Through her online activities, though, Jennifer is able to expand her social network and make new friends who share her interests in writing and who do not share her peers' negative view of Neopets.

Her use of the digital realm at this stage in her life is consistent with what Mimi Ito and her colleagues identify as "interest-driven" media use, allowing Jennifer to carve out a space for herself that is apart from the context of school and peers, and in which she can develop and experience a sense of self-identity for which she finds affirmation and support.[25] Jennifer participated in a storytelling competition, and at sixteen she began contributing regularly to the *Neopian Times*. When she joined the *Neopian Times* Appreciation Guild, she met others who enjoyed writing as much as she did. From her experiences writing for the site, she notes, "I learned to receive and respond to criticism from my readers," and she believes that her ability to take criticism "has also served me well in my later ventures into academic writing." Over time, she developed acquaintances online as she and others shared stories, and she has come to see herself as a role model for younger members of the site.[26]

Through her engagement with Neopets, Jennifer has developed a confidence in her ability to present herself differently among varied groups of people. She has gained a sense of her right to interact with others on her own terms, and to develop her own identity and interests apart from the expectations of a peer culture's dominant norms that might disparage her interests. In this sense, the gaming site Neopets has provided Jennifer with the pragmatic benefits of connecting with others who share her love for writing, as well as the symbolic benefits, at least among other Neopians, of serving as a leader within the Neopet community. It has also provided her with the mythic benefits of offering stories that enable her to reflect on her own developing narrative as a young person figuring out who she is and who she wants to be. As Jennifer participated in the virtual world of Neopets, she enacted changes in her sense of self, and thereby found a platform for this performance that differed from that of her everyday life.

Being Part of the Group, Yet Distinct

Conversations with eighteen-year-old Taylor Billings similarly illustrate some of the work teenagers do as they try to figure out who they are, who they want to be, and whom they want to relate to in the context of a commercialized youth culture.[27] Although he does some gaming, his primary interest is in interacting with peers his age through texting and social networking sites. An amiable young man of European American heritage with stylishly messy hair and an easygoing smile, Taylor indicates that he approaches social networking sites (SNSs) both pragmatically and symbolically: they are an important way in which he can be in touch with his friends, and they give him a means to be recognized by his peers for who he is.

Taylor recognizes that the profiles he creates on SNSs give him visibility among a wider network of peers, for if he had no profile, he would appear uninterested in and uninteresting to his peers. So when Taylor first put up a profile on a social networking site at age fifteen, he wanted to convey the image that he was a "punk skater who was against everything mainstream." His profile "had a lot of skate company layouts and I would always put on punk metal songs," he said. "I would always post pictures of skating and snowboarding." He wanted to be seen by his peers as someone who was fun, athletic, active, and "not mainstream," so he used his online profile to portray a certain "look."

How did Taylor know that "look"? He had grown up surrounded by images of fun, athletic, non-mainstream celebrities such as snowboarders Tony Hawk, Shaun White, and Ryan Sheckler, and was aware of the more crude and daring versions of non-mainstream celebrities such as Johnny Knoxville and the stars of Cartoon Network's *Dude, What Would Happen?* as well as mainstream celebrities such as Ashton Kutcher. He'd seen the "look" imitated and repackaged over and over in reality television programs such as *Survivor* and MTV's *The Real World*, on sports programs such as ESPN's *X Games*, in numerous music and sports videos, in men's magazines, and in ads for video games, candy, soft drinks, and clothes. Taylor borrowed from those images and sounds to say something about who he was and how he wanted to be understood. Without a trace of irony, he spoke of how he drew upon these elements of mainstream commercial and celebrity culture to portray himself as "non-mainstream."

Taylor sought to use the profile on his social networking site pragmatically as a means of connecting with his peers and as a means of existing in peer culture. He also drew on traditional media's mythic dimensions, borrowing popular cultural references from skateboarding magazines, programs, advertisements, and celebrities to say something about himself.[28]

That was early in his high school years. Later on, Taylor said, he found that his online profile was turning people off. "A lot of people" told him that they thought he was cocky and vain based on his online profile. So, he says,

I took off all the shirtless pictures of me. Now I have more pictures of me in choir, more pictures of me showing that I'm the loving boyfriend, that I'm the loving brother, all that. I used to not have anything to show that I was caring or loving.

Conscious of the fact that his peers spend time looking at the profiles of others online, Taylor changed his profile to better reflect who he thinks he "really" is and how he wants others to understand him. Although his "good friends" already know him, he recognizes that social networking sites permit acquaintances to look at his profile and consider whether or not they want to get to know him better, so he alters his online profile to better suit the needs and expectations of this larger circle of acquaintances. As he has grown older, he has come to share his acquaintances' negative views about borrowing too heavily from the commercial realm when putting together an online profile, and he looks with some disdain at other young people who do what he once did:

There are so many girls that post pictures that are all skanky, that have them posing in bathing suits, and then they have depressing suicidal poems. I'm sitting here thinking, "You're a happy person, you're not a slut, what the hell are you doing?"

Be authentic to who you are, Taylor seems to be saying; you don't have to be a mook or a midriff, to borrow language that's been used to describe the archetypal teen images of the goofy and fun-loving guy and the sexy but troubled girl.[29] Presenting yourself digitally as you are "in real life" is something that takes some time and thought, as evidenced in Taylor's own transformation from someone who borrowed from the mook image to say something about himself to someone who criticizes those who do such borrowing. Young people like Taylor do a fair amount of experimenting online in their early teen years, and much of it is directed toward adjusting the presentation of self to achieve the desired results from their peers—in other words, to receive positive reinforcement from their peers about who they "really" are. Today's parents used to do this same kind of identity work by adopting Madonna-inspired wavy bleached hair and multiple bracelets or a Run DMC–inspired jumpsuit and Adidas sneakers. Young people like Taylor are simply adding online expression to the long-standing teen portfolio of efforts designed to better perform the self they would like to be and to seek recognition and acceptance among peers.[30] Social networking sites in particular are helping young people to accomplish this task as they pursue what they believe is their right to construct, display, and perform their own identity.

As he grows older, Taylor has also started to think differently about the way he approaches social networking sites. Now he sees social networking sites such as Facebook not so much as places to display some image of himself but more pragmatically, as a place where he can communicate with his friends. Although he says that this is the main point of his time spent on social networking sites, he is still aware of how his status updates and other online postings "play" for an imagined audience that is not limited to his close friends. For instance, when asked if he ever changes his status specifically because he wants one or more of his friends to comment on it, he replies adamantly, "*No.* I'll tell people how I'm feeling. I don't care if you comment on it or not. I'm not putting it out there for a specific person to see. I'm putting it out there for *everyone* to see." Even when discussing the benefits of relating to close friends through social networking sites, therefore, we see the influence of symbolic participation, voyeurism, and celebrity culture in Taylor's comment that "everyone" is the intended audience for what he posts online. Taylor wants to be accepted and recognized by his close friends, but the public nature of social networking sites means that he is also somewhat cognizant of the fact that a large audience can form an impression of him based primarily on what he posts. Sites such as Twitter, Facebook, and YouTube help people create and enhance their status as a "micro-celebrity," and like many young people, Taylor prefers to cultivate this possibility rather than consciously limiting access to his online persona to only his close friends.[31]

Another study of teens and their views on doing identity work online found similar results.[32] In relation to researchers' questions about how the online realm represents potential problems in relation to identity, for instance, one teen notes:

> People are different online because they want to be. Why continue to be yourself when you can turn yourself into somebody you would rather be? It's like how everybody always chooses the prettiest or best picture of themselves to put as their profile pic. We don't have to be ourselves online; we have the freedom to be who we want others to believe we are.

Young people in that study speak of why they might be motivated to present themselves differently, just as we see in Taylor's story. In contrast, adults interviewed in the same study are more likely to think about the implications of such false or misleading self-presentations. As one adult notes, "I think it's important that people be themselves all the time, everywhere. It doesn't benefit anyone to try to be something or someone you're not." In contrast, few young people in that study express concern about how others might feel deceived or harmed when someone creates an inauthentic profile.

In Taylor's comments, we can see examples of the public, commercial, and celebrity-driven aspects of the contexts—often social networking sites such as Facebook and Twitter—in which young people today figure out who they are, how they want to be recognized, and whom they want to relate to. Taylor's story illustrates how challenging it can be to escape the commercial realm that permeates and feeds on contemporary youth culture. Corporations such as Viacom and News Corporation have long worked to associate certain products with desirable youthful lifestyles, and thus young people frequently and unconsciously draw on the commercial realm to convey something about themselves, whether it's in digital form or in older ways such as wearing branded T-shirts or buying certain products. Even those who seek to depart from commercial influence can run into difficulties and have to work at being "logo-free"—something that usually happens only when young people conscientiously join the anti-globalization, anti-corporate movement.[33] It is easier for young people to simply ignore the associations between corporate brands and lifestyles than to consciously reject them.

Taylor's story certainly points to the influence of the celebrity-driven culture in which young people are growing up. Teens and preteens may or may not want to be famous, but they do want to be thought of with respect and admiration, and they understand how social networking sites can serve as an invitation for further interaction. Although young people increasingly set limits on who can access all of their information, they still are aware that people they may not know might Google or Facebook them to look at their photos or writing at any time. They can set limits to some things, but they also are growing up in a context where they know that they have to deal with the potential for their online lives to be viewed by anyone. And with the prospect of future friends or girlfriends/boyfriends on the line, they often have more incentive to be open to "everyone" than to limit access. Because they have long had to navigate this line between private life and life that is available for public consumption, celebrities serve as models for how young people go about drawing these lines for themselves. Young people today experience themselves in ways that are like celebrities' experiences, managing their private lives and what they are willing to make available for public or semi-public consumption. This creates new dilemmas as they seek to manage their identities and their relationships with others, particularly in the area of how to share enough but not too much information about themselves online.

Navigating Mediated Friendships: Being Needed but Not Needy

It's not difficult for a fourteen-year-old to accumulate five hundred "friends" on Facebook. What's harder is figuring out what to share with whom, how often, through which medium—and what it all means. Can you break up with a romantic partner by changing your Facebook relationship status? It saves you grief, but it's frowned upon. What do you do when your friends start fighting on your profile page? What if your friends get mad or feel hurt about a comment you say was a joke?

Facebook and other social networking sites provide some unique challenges in this regard because young people can't observe the social cues that help them make sense of face-to-face interactions. Among other things, participants have to figure out ways to present themselves as open without revealing too much. And there are social costs to getting it wrong. Being too revealing can be interpreted as a sign of neediness or insecurity, as sixteen-year-old Korinna's comments suggest:

> My friend—well, she's *not* my friend. Marta, she, like, writes, "Today was horrible. In math class I couldn't figure out this problem." She, like, went through her whole day, like people care. Like honestly, I don't. People may. Their comments are, like, for her good friends. It's like, no one cares to read this except your close friends.

Korinna made this comment as part of a group interview with fifteen- and sixteen-year-old friends who were talking about social networking sites.[34] Korinna's not-friend Marta was using social networking sites in a way that Korinna deems inappropriate, revealing too much of her personal life in what Korinna considers to be a public forum. Marta, of course, was not present to hear this feedback. Yet after Korinna makes the disparaging remarks about her not-friend, an interesting discussion emerges.

"Caitlyn posts stories and poems online," Adriana points out, referring to another girl in the group being interviewed.

Another friend, Bella, agrees that it's not good to share too much online and then challenges Caitlyn directly: "Yeah, why *do* you want the whole world to read your diary?"

Korinna piles on: "Yeah, diaries are where you keep your secrets. I don't share those with a lot of people."

Bella, anxious to switch the subject, says, "Anyway, I get bored reading people's blogs."

Adriana quickly agrees, "So do I," seemingly in an attempt to end the disagreement.

But then Caitlyn defends her own practices of online writing. Distancing herself from the overly self-revelatory writing style of the non-friend Marta, she discusses her own writings in more of a mean-girl tone that, similar to Korinna's comment, made fun of not-friends who make too much information available online:

> I've blogged about, like, breakups. About Hannah's breakup, and how she blogged about it for like a year after they're still broken up. And every day there's something new about it. That's pretty much it. I usually don't read them. It gets kinds of dramatic, and it gets kind of boring after a while.

Others then chime in that they, too, read other people's profiles and blogs only when they're "really bored." Anyway, as Korinna later points out, she doesn't use social networking sites as much as she used to. "I don't really have the time," she says, and her friends all agree.

"Everybody got into it, but it just kind of died down," her friend Adriana observes.

They talk about their use of these sites in a way that is in keeping with the norm of an appropriately busy teen life. "I'm way too busy, I don't have the time, like with homework and church and stuff," Selena, a young Latina from an urban high school, explains when asked why she didn't use social networking sites regularly.

"It's a cool way to keep in touch with people who are far away," Nora, a young European American woman from a middle-income background, notes with a shrug. In contrast, caring too much about one's online or offline identity certainly isn't cool.

Somehow, young people need to determine for themselves the "right" amount of time they are spending on social networking sites, texting, tweeting, or IMing. In a different group interview, teens Joe and Rashad roll their eyes at the "drama," and Joe comments, "It's always the people who are attention-deprived who post all this relationship stuff. 'Oh my God, I hope my baby's not bad at me,'" he says, mimicking what he suggests is a typical post. But then Joe says that texting and social networking sites create new dilemmas about sharing, because how quickly you decide to respond is a measure of how much you care. He says, "If you have somebody who doesn't text you back, you can go and stalk their profile and if they've posted something recently but they're ignoring you, then you know something's up." Joe inadvertently demonstrates the tyranny of having to show that he is paying attention to his friends: he texts throughout the interview and estimates that he writes eight thousand texts a month, which is well above the norm of three thousand a month.[35] He does not want to appear needy, but he does want to be needed. I was reminded of the joys of being needed when my seventeen-year-old nephew crowed with pleasure at the number of texts he received from friends just after midnight when we were together on New Year's Eve. "I'm so popular," he said, half joking, half pleased, thumbs flying as he dutifully replied to each text.

Like Taylor, many young people say that they use social networking sites mainly as a way to stay in touch with friends, and some also mention their interest in following musicians, athletes, and celebrities they like.[36] In each of these situations, digital and mobile media provide both a pragmatic place for communicating with peers and a symbolic space for sharing one's representation of self, and these new spaces engender new questions about how to negotiate relationships of identity in relation to others.

Identity in a Digital Age

What does it mean to say that young people want to establish an identity and they use digital and mobile media in relation to this desire? The social psychologist Erik Erickson first popularized concern with the individual identity of young people in his 1968 book *Identity: Youth and Crisis*.[37] Building on the earlier work of anthropologist G. Stanley Hall, who first coined the phrase "storm and stress" as a characteristic of adolescence, Erickson argued that adolescents had to go through an "identity crisis" that enabled them to think about who they were as distinct individuals.[38] Once the identity crisis was resolved, adolescents would have a clearer sense of their role in society, and, he believed, they would have a more stable adult identity as a result. Erickson thus viewed adolescence as a key time in which young people may be influenced by a variety of sources, an idea that has been the foundation for research into how young people might be negatively influenced by media.[39] Erickson's ideas are also central to considering how young people might use digital media spaces for self-reflection and experimentation, and how these online sites become locations for much of the "storm and stress" and "crises" of adolescence.[40]

However, Erickson was subsequently criticized for not paying attention to the different ways in which social class, gender, and ethnicity are important contexts that shape young people's roles within society and their perceptions about those roles.[41] Obviously, there are things about these identifications that we do not choose. In addition, young people's choices are often limited by occurrences over which they have no control, such as a parent's divorce, a parent's job change or loss, changes in a family's financial picture, or even changes in a family's geographic location. Thus, identity has come to be understood as something enacted by people of all ages in relation to the situations we encounter, both those over which we have some control and those over which we do not.[42]

Our relationships and our identifications not only affect how others see us but also help shape our unconscious, taken-for-granted understandings of how we think things should be done.[43] Identity, therefore, has come to be seen less as something that we *are* or *achieve* and more as something we *do* or *perform* in our relationships with others based on what we believe about ourselves and who we wish others would believe us to be.[44] In this sense, it is related to the expressive self that we have inherited from Romantic-era, Walt Whitman–like ideals of what it means to be human. Taylor's efforts to redesign his social networking profile and Jennifer's decision to conceal her active late teen involvement with Neopets both illustrate this performative and expressive nature of identity. These are taken for granted as natural and important processes in the cultural milieu that supports an ethic of expressive empowerment.

The understanding of identity as a process of understanding oneself in relation to others is key to what sociologist William Corsaro has termed *interpretive reproduction*: the process through which children create and participate in their own cultures by appropriating things from adult culture to address their own concerns in relation to their peer culture.[45] Families of origin play an important role in interpretive reproduction, as they provide the first context in which young children come to learn about the cultures in which they live. But peers are also important, and children begin to participate in peer culture at an early age. Children and adolescents are members of social groups that have their own systems of hierarchies and patterns of inclusion and exclusion.[46] As they learn to navigate those systems, they are doing identity work, figuring out who they are in relation to others.[47]

Some researchers, such as danah boyd, have argued that social networking sites are key locations where young people produce their identities, since they are places where young people write themselves and their communities into being.[48] Young people work on social networking site profiles, boyd has noted, in order to participate in what sociologist Erving Goffman has called "impression management," figuring out how to develop a digital presence that echoes, or maybe reshapes, the impressions that are given to others through their flesh-and-blood bodies.[49] They consciously choose how to represent themselves, but they also choose whom to add as "friends," as this, too, is an exhibition of who they are: it shows whom they know and how they relate to other social groups. Representation, then, takes on a whole new level of importance when people can intentionally construct and perform who they think they are online, and when others can support or contest a person's online identity.[50]

As young people develop and maintain digital self-representations, they do so in the context of a peer culture that has long been shaped by voyeurism and celebrity culture.[51] The names of celebrities such as Katy Perry, Nicki Minaj, Brad Pitt, and Justin Bieber were among the most frequent Google searches in 2010 and 2011, demonstrating the staying power of music, film, and television-driven celebrity culture in the new digital environment.[52] The contemporary media industries both subtly and not-so-subtly encourage young people to utilize resources from commercial culture in the construction of their own identities.[53] As digital, mobile, and more traditional media have become a transparent and taken-for-granted part of the lives of young people, practices of identity creation occur in relation to the public, celebrity-driven, and commercialized aspects of the larger context of youth culture, and give shape to what young people want and how they interpret themselves and what they want in relation to others.

Negotiating Parents, Media, and Identity

Like their parents, young people are immersed in a particular milieu that supports sometimes conflicting values of self-worth and self-promotion, leisure and productivity, compassion and social hierarchy. They may choose to rely on their parents for both modeling and for advice, and they may also choose to resist that modeling and advice. The point is that these choices are theirs, and in the teen years parents often find themselves in a position of reacting to those choices rather than feeling as if they are steering their children as they intend. Young people have largely internalized their parents' and their environments' values of expressiveness and empowerment, and when they make choices parents find troubling, such as putting their own rights in front of the rights of others or assigning values to a social hierarchy, they are making visible some of the problems inherent in this approach.

Young people have been negotiating identity in relation to a commercialized and mediated youth culture for a long time, but it may be that today their immersion happens earlier and is more individualized than it has been in the past. In 2005, the average age at which children began using electronic devices was 8.1 years. Only two years later, the average age had dipped to 6.7 years.[54] With the rise of virtual-world sites such as Webkinz, Disney's Club Penguin, and Neopets, children ages eight and younger have spaces online that are welcoming specifically to their age group.[55] Apps and mobile games for children are also on the rise. My own iPhone features Pet Shop, Tiny Zoo, and Fruit Ninja Lite, all downloaded by my then ten-year-old. Today, the majority of families that share a smart phone have fewer than twenty child-related apps downloaded, but 7 percent of them had more than sixty apps for a child, demonstrating the potential for growth in demand for these products.[56] Such venues help online and mobile media to become integrated into the everyday lives of young people. Whereas adults have tended to focus on the teen years as a time for identity construction, new research is pointing to the importance of considering the ways that technologies and identities of young children are co-constructed in this emerging environment.[57]

Each of the young people discussed in this chapter engages in identity work as he or she seeks to negotiate self-concepts, digital and real-life self-representations, and understandings of peer expectations. This identity work is rooted in two desires that coexist: the sense that they want to belong, and the wish to view themselves and to be viewed by others as distinct and distinctly attractive individuals. Digital, mobile, and traditional media provide young people with the pragmatic, symbolic, and mythical tools for expressing themselves and significantly shape the context in which such interactions and negotiations between peers take place.

Jennifer found in Neopets both a place in which she could participate in the peer culture of her school when she was in her upper elementary years and then a place where she could experiment by learning skills—first with game play and now with creative writing—in order to fulfill her desire for achievement. As a ten-year-old, she needed to demonstrate to her parents that she could maintain a good homework routine in order to earn the right to devote thirty minutes a day to game play. As a teen, she needs to engage in emotional work with her peers, keeping her interest in Neopets largely hidden and enjoying her Neopian experience as something that is apart from the pressures of peer culture and rewarding for its contributions to her self-concept as an emerging writer. Rather than change her self-concept as a member of the Neopian universe, she changes her self-presentation, guarding her interests so as to maintain a positive impression among her school peers. In doing this, she adopts a new narrative that takes pride in her accomplishments as a writer and helper of other, younger participants in that virtual world.

Taylor, too, engages in identity work in the negotiations between self-concept, digital and real self-representations, and peer expectations. In his early teen years, he wanted to represent himself in a way that was considered acceptable to his peers, adopting a certain "look" from commercial culture in the construction of his Facebook page. Yet when he received negative comments from peers, he adjusted his self-presentation. He, too, adopts a new narrative in his later teen years, making negative judgments about those who are too involved in worrying about their presentation (as he once was) in order to draw a contrast between them and himself. At the same time, however, he also developed a more self-conscious approach to how he wants to be perceived by others, engaging in a studied casualness when he distanced himself from those who were too concerned about appearances.

Marta's not-friends Korinna, Caitlyn, Ariana, and Bella were engaging in identity work as they discussed Marta's use of her online profile. Korinna criticized Marta passionately as a way to distance herself from what she perceived as a violation of peer norms of not offering too much information. Bella's challenge to Caitlyn about her own online diary made it necessary for Caitlyn to engage in emotion work, trying to save face by distancing herself from Marta's practice and finding her own way to criticize those who overshared.[58] The friends eventually found a less emotionally fraught topic to agree on, and all asserted that more often than not they were "bored" with social networking sites and only visited them when there was nothing else to do. But Joe reminds us that even if young people do not want to appear needy, they do want to be needed, and they feel compelled to show affirmation and acceptance to their friends by replying to texts and online postings promptly. Like Taylor, among many teens there is a studied casualness in how they describe the role of social networking sites and texting in their lives, belied by their clear attention to who was doing what in various online spaces.

Conclusion

This chapter argues that young people utilize digital, mobile, and traditional media as sources and sites for identity construction, and approach such identity work as practices that are performative, expressive, and an outgrowth of self-empowerment. Although aware of the risks that their parents associate with these media, they are invested in navigating a different set of risks related to peer group culture, and therefore they feel that it is necessary to assert their right to participate in digital, mobile, and traditional media culture in spite of their parents' reservations. Like Jennifer Yu's parents, many parents recognize the need for their elementary-age children, preteens, and teens to participate in commercial culture as a means of participating in peer culture. However, many, such as Steph Kline's mother, Isabella, view such participation with a great deal of ambivalence and trepidation. Their fears are often related to stories of what can go wrong in these locations, as were discussed in the preceding chapters.

This chapter also presents young people who view their engagement in identity construction and use of media as their right. Steph Kline expresses her desire for freedom from her parents' surveillance and expresses dissatisfaction with what she felt was an invasion of her privacy as she seeks to maintain contact with her friends outside of parental supervision. Taylor Billings experiences his construction of a digital self-representation and his borrowings from celebrity culture both as a right and as a necessity for participation in his middle-class peer culture. Jennifer believes that she has a right to explore online virtual worlds, to develop her own skills and identity within the game, and to control how those in different peer contexts

---

A DIFFERENT PERSPECTIVE ON RISK

Children and young people do not view risk in the same way that adults do. Research shows that young people tend to overestimate benefits and underestimate risks. But they also may have a different idea about what constitutes risk. I once asked a group of middle school students what they didn't like about digital and mobile media, hoping to elicit some examples of how they had experienced risks such as cyberbullying or surveillance. Instead, one boy thought for a moment and said, "I really don't like it when my dad texts on the phone all the time during my soccer games. I wish he would just watch me instead." This boy demonstrated that just as parents think about how technologies can be a source of connection to a world beyond our families, our children similarly feel that technologies can pull us, and our attentions, away from *them*.

will or will not have access to her gaming experience. Finally, Korinna believes that she has a right to have access to information about peers in her school, including "not-friends" such as Marta, and that these peers' personal expressions can be used to construct boundaries around appropriate and inappropriate teen behavior.

In addition to figuring out how to negotiate with their parents over their right to have an online presence, and figuring out how to represent themselves digitally, young people also have to figure out how to exercise their right to express themselves in relation to the risks of being judged inauthentic, weird, needy, or in other negative terms within their peer circles. As social media heighten the pressure to construct the self and to digitally reconstruct relations with others on an ongoing basis, these media also increase the risk for individuals, thereby underscoring a growing need that young people feel to focus on the self and on the peer group as a source of identification. In this sense, it may be that the new digital environment is encouraging a heightened form of narcissism.

In her book *Alone Together*, Sherry Turkle expresses concern about the ways in which social media seem to foster an approach to relationships that differs from that of the past. "Intimacy without privacy reinvents what intimacy means," she writes.[59] In part, the problem is that young people today may be engaging in the right to express themselves and the right to define themselves according to the prerogatives of digital, mobile, and traditional media—but at a cost. As Turkle notes:

> Online, we easily find "company" but are exhausted by the pressures of performance. We enjoy continual connection but rarely have each other's full attention. We can have instant audiences but flatten out what we say to each other in new reductive genres of abbreviation. . . . We have many new encounters but may come to experience them as tentative, to be put "on hold" if better ones come along.[60]

The ways that young people experience their relationships with one another may be changing, in part because of the voyeuristic tendencies of youth culture inherited from previous eras, and in part because the technologies of the mobile phone and laptops or tablet computers with Internet connection make it easier than ever for us to manage our relationships with others instantaneously. Often these media seem to answer a need for entertainment or interaction. But young people like Taylor, Jennifer, Korinna, Joe, and Steph implicitly acknowledge that their engagement with media contributes to an already-full to-do list and does not always provide satisfaction. These media can encourage the development of an other-directed self: a self that is more concerned with how others perceive things than with a sense of inner purpose and worth. They may have to step outside the norms of their peer culture, as Jennifer did, to develop a sense of inner purpose, and this may mean also stepping away from social networking sites, the dominant locations for identity construction and relationship maintenance among peers.

As young people increasingly rely on others to validate who they are, they may be more prone to cultivating fragile and narcissistic personalities.[61] On the other hand, in this new environment, they need to learn how to navigate the possibility for more negative input than is healthy. With digital and mobile media, they can seek support from those who offer it freely and can limit their contact with those who undermine it. They can create expertise within constructed realms in which others appreciate and respect that expertise. They can text rather than talk on the phone so as to avoid the possibility of feeling rejected if their friend elects not to answer. To exist in digital space is to exist in peer culture, especially for teens, and the role of parents is both to understand and to act as sympathetic guides as their children navigate this environment as it expands into digital spaces.

CHAPTER 5 | Less Advantaged Teens, Ethnicity, and Digital and Mobile Media

Respect, Restriction, and Reversal

WHEN MIKE FIRST ENTERED the computer lab at Denver High School, he wasn't sure what to expect. He was taking my undergraduate class Critical Approaches to Digital Media, and he had been asked to serve as a volunteer tutor who would work with students who did not have access to the Internet in their homes. An experienced Web and game designer, Mike had thought that he would walk around the room to help various students with their projects. To begin, he sat down next to fifteen-year-old Asad and suggested that he start by titling his project "My Digital Profile." As Mike relates, "He typed 'My dihgitel profil' onto the screen. I never ended up getting out of my chair to help the other students."[1]

Mike learned that Asad had grown up in Somalia and had been relocated to Denver several years ago when he and his brother sought to escape the violence in his homeland. The two young Somalis had arrived in Denver with little money and limited language skills. After participating in an English Language Acquisition program at a local high school, Asad had been integrated into the school's curriculum and is currently completing his degree, with hopes of continuing his education in college. Asad and his brother share a mobile phone, and Asad likes to use his school's computers to locate and read online news from his hometown. And although Mike was impressed with how quickly Asad learned basic digital skills, we both wondered about the daunting gap that separated Asad's opportunities for developing those skills from Mike's own opportunities.

This chapter focuses on the experiences of young people like Asad who encounter limitations in relation to the digital and mobile media environment. Like the young people in chapter 4, they discuss the ways that they use digital and mobile media to remain in contact with their friends and family members, and the media do provide mythic, symbolic, and pragmatic cultural resources for these young people. But the teens highlighted in this chapter talk about digital and mobile media in relation to educational opportunities and parental desires as well as social needs.[2] They are concerned about how to maintain the trust of their family members, and how to use these media in ways that maintain rather than disrupt their family's traditions and values. These are stories that take place among young people who are part of what I've termed the "would-be middle class": those households that think of themselves as middle-class although their household income, disability, or other issues create challenges. In many of these families, young people have far more familiarity with media and often greater digital proficiency than their parents, unlike young people in middle- and upper-middle-class families. Thus, the Parent App needed in these situations calls for recognition of young people's needs and experiences as well as an understanding of how digital and mobile media fit into and shape certain constraints of everyday life. This chapter provides background on ownership of and access to digital and mobile media among less advantaged families, and introduces young people who are recent immigrants as well as those born in this country to explore how what I term an ethic of respectful connectedness—a way of communicating that emphasizes the importance of respect for authority and loyalty among family members—is made manifest in these families.

In lower-income families, access to digital and mobile media can be restricted because of financial constraints. Among these families, some parents also maintain much more restrictive rules about the use of these media when compared with middle-class, upper-middle-class, and wealthy families, as we saw in chapter 3. Many of these parents have concerns about the risks that their children will encounter, but the patterns of restriction and risk differ among these families. In order to understand this, we must consider racial and ethnic differences among less advantaged families.

A significant number of Hispanic/Latino, African American, and multiracial households are part of the middle or upper-middle-class.[3] But wealth and privilege remain concentrated among European American families in the United States. A 2009 study from the Pew Research Center found that the wealth gap between white households and their black and Hispanic counterparts was wider in 2009 than it was in 1984, when the government first began collecting such information.[4] This study found that the median wealth of white households was almost twenty times that of black households and eighteen times more than Hispanic households.[5] The recession worsened the wealth gap; in particular, the decline in housing values hurt black and Hispanic families the most. From 2005 to 2009, wealth fell 66 percent among Hispanic households and 53 percent among black households, whereas whites saw a decline of 16 percent.[6]

Some of the middle- and upper-middle-class families in this book are nonwhite, but most of the families in this chapter on less advantaged families are both not wealthy and nonwhite. In the United States, higher incomes remain concentrated among European American families; though the level of diversity among wealthy families is increasing and a large proportion of less advantaged families are European American, there is still greater ethnic diversity among less advantaged families.

The Role of Respect Among Differing Ethnic Groups

According to 2010 Census categories, the largest ethnic groups in the United States are white, not Hispanic or Latino (64 percent); Hispanic or Latino (16 percent); black or African American (12 percent); and Asian (5 percent). New immigrant communities are expected to provide most of the U.S. population gains in the near future, and in 2009 13 percent of the U.S. population was foreign-born.[7] Each of these demographic groups has been shaped by unique cultural attributes and specific histories within the context of Western societies, and whereas each warrants its own much lengthier treatment, I sketch out some basic differences that research within these communities supports.

For African American families in the United States, the family is a central organizing feature, and mothers play a dominant role. Although wealthier African American families share some common experiences with wealthier European American families, among the most impoverished African American communities a long history of oppression, discrimination, and lack of economic opportunity contributes to higher incidences of violence, criminal activity, and incarceration, particularly of African American males.[8] Parents and especially mothers work hard to protect their children from the risks of this environment. By the same token, older children in these environments, especially boys, place greater trust in their families than in their friends.[9] More-egalitarian parent-teen relationships have evolved, as young people must assume adult responsibilities at a younger age.[10] Respect for parents is important in these families, but financial instabilities mean that male father figures are often absent from extended families and communities, either temporarily or permanently. Mothers remain primarily responsible for the oversight of education, discipline, and leisure time as well as for household-related purchases. This has implications for what respect and connectedness looks like in relation to digital and mobile media use in these families, as we will see in the story of Deshonelle later in this chapter.

Families are also very important in Latino communities, but gender roles within the family are quite distinct. These gender differences are purported to have roots in the historical conquests of indigenous Americans by Spanish and Portuguese, as Iberian men mated with Indian women and as men, under the control of colonizers, worked long hours in the field while women tended to the home and children.[11] Families, pride, and *respeto* (respect) are key values, and tend to be filtered through the *machismo* that is central to this culture and the accompanying ideal of the self-sacrificing mother.[12] This means that as fathers set and enforce the rules for digital and mobile media use and expect that these rules will be followed as a show of respect for parents, it's the mothers who oversee the day-to-day realities of the household, including those related to media, as seen in the story of Carmen Rodriguez (chapter 3).

Among the many recent immigrant communities that constitute the fastest-growing proportion of the U.S. population, the father is often the unquestioned authority. He presumes to have authority over whom children can befriend and what they are permitted to do with those friends.[13] Recent immigrant communities include those who have come from Mexico and a number of Asian countries, including the Philippines, China, India, and Vietnam.[14] Other large migrant communities include families from Latin American and African countries. In families from these cultures, as Brown and his colleagues note, "children are expected to be respectful, compliant, and family-focused."[15] A great deal of research has explored the tensions that emerge as second-generation immigrant children contest the authority of their parents.[16] Immigrant parents share many frustrations in relation to what they often view as the overly sexualized, commercial, and disrespectful youth culture of their new home society. At the same time, young people in these families struggle to uphold their family's values while also adapting to some of the values of the peer culture that is a part of their everyday environment.[17] They serve as translators and interpreters for their parents, a role that places them in a position of some authority relative to their families and their new cultural context. In some of the extreme situations of refugee and immigrant families, young people live with extended family members rather than parents, and while they are expected to be respectful of these family members, they are of necessity also assuming adult roles and responsibilities. This, too, shapes their experiences of digital and mobile media, and their approaches to respect and connectedness.

The Digital and Mobile Media Environment for Less Advantaged Families

According to policy makers, the digital divide was officially "closed" in 2002, when President George W. Bush accepted an optimistic report from the U.S. Department of Commerce titled *A Nation Online*.[18] Following in the wake of two earlier national reports, *Falling Through the Net: Defining the Digital Divide* and *Falling Through the Net: Toward Digital Inclusion*, the 2002 report documented the rapid growth of Internet use among the U.S. population, highlighting the fact that from August 2000 to September 2001, Internet use grew substantially faster among African Americans and Latinos than among whites or Asians.[19] Concluding that federal support for the narrowing of the technology gap was no longer necessary, the Bush administration used the release of this report to announce its plans to zero out funding for two community-based programs that linked technological education and opportunities with education among disadvantaged communities.[20]

In the years immediately following that report, evidence existed that divides were still present. Digital proficiency correlated with ethnic background, educational level of parents, and income.[21] Blacks and Latinos were much less likely to have access to computers, and much less likely to have Internet access at home, than were white non-Latinos, and income disparities between black and Latino households and white non-Latino households accounted for some but not all of this difference in usage.[22] These different patterns in access and usage have continued but have taken different forms as families have adopted new technologies.

Research into the digital divide shifted course in the first decade of the 2000s to focus on how people came to use the Internet in meaningful ways in relation to their access to social, economic, and digital resources.[23] This new research uncovered associations between lower wages and online avoidance, suggesting that patterns of digital and mobile media use could contribute to social inequality.[24] Associations also existed between education levels and digital media use. One 2010 study on laptop distribution found that whereas four out of five eighteen-year-olds whose parents were highly educated had laptops, only half of eighteen-year-olds whose parents had a high school education or less had laptops.[25] Another study found that lower-income parents were less likely to utilize the Web to find information about children and families, and when they did go online, they demonstrated less sophisticated search skills.[26] In addition to what researchers term "gradations in digital inclusion," what's also come to be of interest is the "participation gap," as some young people have less access not only to technologies but also to the opportunities for participation that they enable.[27]

In 2011, more than a fifth of the U.S. population remained offline.[28] Almost 20 percent of U.S. teens living in lower-income households did not have high-speed Internet access at home or through mobile phones.[29] One-quarter of young people were sharing a mobile phone with someone else, often a parent or sibling.[30] With the rise of mobile phones and then smart phones, members of some communities first began receiving Internet access via mobile rather than through a laptop or tablet.[31] This has been especially true among young African Americans and Latinos, groups that are highly represented in lower income segments. But analysts are divided on whether this is a positive or negative direction for young people, as Internet access and production of original content is easier to manage with a laptop or tablet than on a phone.[32] Lower-income young people are more likely than their middle-class counterparts to have a prepaid cell phone plan and to pay for it themselves, further accentuating gaps between parents and teens in lower-income families, and between first-generation, Spanish-dominant adult Latinos and their Latino children in particular.[33]

Today, young people from less advantaged backgrounds are still more likely to lack access to broadband at home, to attend schools that have outdated equipment, to share a computer or cell phone, and to have fewer people in their social circles—and in particular, fewer parents and adults—who are active in the digital realm.[34] Additionally, some online sites, such as Facebook and Twitter, have been adopted more slowly by nonwhites than by whites.[35]

Digital and mobile media are less readily available to young people from less advantaged backgrounds than to those in middle-class, upper-middle-class, and wealthy families. Mobile phones, laptops, readers, and tablets, as well as older media such as televisions and game systems, are more frequently shared with other family members or used in smaller home spaces where privacy is harder to come by. Sometimes the young people whose stories are highlighted in this chapter check in online at the homes of their friends, as Raju does, or they use school, library, or community center computers, as Iskinder does, although they often face limits on when and how they can use these. Like Laticia, a sixteen-year-old from

Mexico, many young people have to turn over the mobile phone as soon as their mothers return from work, or like Iskinder, they have to use it when parents or guardians are at home and not using it.

We turn now to some of the stories of young people and their families as they negotiate digital and mobile media in their lives. As noted in the previous chapter, young people from less advantaged backgrounds are interested in developing strong relationships with their peers and in formulating a sense of self that is distinct. But they do so within specific material contexts and in relation to parents and cultures that embrace connectedness with family and respect for parental authority. Because the experiences of immigrant children are perhaps least familiar in existing research on digital and mobile media, we begin with these stories, highlighting the ways that Iskinder, Bina, and other recent immigrant children experience respect, restriction, and reversal in relation to digital and mobile media.

Young Immigrants and Digital and Mobile Media: Respect, Restriction, and Reversal

Iskinder Hagos is a sixteen-year-old who moved with his father from Ethiopia to the city of Denver eighteen months ago. Bina Dahal is a fifteen-year-old who moved with her parents and younger brother from Nepal to the United States three years earlier. Bina lives in Pittsburgh, to which her family moved from Denver after a friend helped her father find a job there.

Iskinder and his father live in a one-bedroom apartment in a modest apartment complex in a Denver neighborhood where the household income hovers around the state's average.[36] The area has the city's highest concentration of immigrants from North Africa, the Horn of Africa, and Eastern Europe, as well as a relatively high concentration of recent immigrants from Mexico. Iskinder and his father, who does not speak English, had been separated from his mother six years earlier during a local outbreak of ethnic violence; they have never been able to learn whether or not she is still alive.[37]

Iskinder explains that as he comes from a "more traditional" society, he feels that it is important to show respect to those who are older and in positions of authority, and he has been surprised by the lack of respect that he's witnessed in certain places in the United States. Once, when he was playing baseball on a local team, one of the opposite team's players became very upset when an umpire called a strike and it seemed very obvious that it was a ball. The player "said a lot of bad words to the umpire,"

Iskinder recounts. "That was really crazy." He describes his home country as both more traditional and more religious than the culture he's observed in the United States. His father wants to reinforce Iskinder's relationship with the traditions and religion of his home country. Often he and his father visit with friends from their region, preparing food together and listening to traditional music on holidays. His father worries that Iskinder will lose connection with his traditional culture; as he said through Iskinder's translation:

> He says like if people come here before they're fifteen years old or if they are born here, [U.S. culture] absolutely changes them. They follow all American culture and they even forget the language. But if you come older, like above eighteen, it doesn't much change them.

Iskinder's father's observation about changes in the children of first-generation immigrants is well supported.[38] But his father also strongly encourages him to develop his English-language speaking skills. "He wants me to get a good education, and so he encourages me a lot," Iskinder says.

Iskinder and his father share a mobile phone, and that sometimes makes it difficult for them to be in touch with each other. Iskinder recalls a time when he wanted to stay after school but hadn't told his father in advance:

> I was late, and he was crazy. He called the school and he called a lot of my relatives. Then when I came home he was really mad at me. Because I didn't tell him. The reason was I had something after school to do at school, and I didn't tell him and he called the office and they told him I left, so he was worried that something happened on the way. He is very nervous about car accidents.

After that incident, Iskinder says, he no longer even considers joining his friends in spontaneous after-school gatherings and now goes straight home instead.

Because Iskinder and his father do not have a laptop or smart phone, they rely on friends from their home country to keep them updated on relevant news from their area. Iskinder goes to a friend's house when he wants to go online, or he uses the computers in his school or in the public library. Iskinder set up a Facebook page, and he has tried to locate friends from his native country. But after close to a year of occasionally searching the site, he has only located a few of his friends from communities near where he used to live outside Addis Ababa. He has also found that among his new friends who have also relocated to Denver in recent years, few are using Facebook. Iskinder says that he likes that Facebook allows him to chat with his friends, but he also says he isn't using it very often, as so few of his friends are there. Another sixteen-year-old, Kamlai Niratpatanasai, who moved to the United States from Thailand just over two years ago, similarly says that she does not use Facebook much herself, although she enjoys seeing photos that are posted by other Thai young women she met in a Thai refugee camp. With her new friends in Denver, she uses texting more often, as many of those she knows do not have Internet access at home.[39]

Iskinder prefers to call his friends rather than texting them, since he doesn't want his father to end up receiving his text messages, as his father usually takes the phone with him to his work. His father has told him that he doesn't like some of his friends, and so Iskinder is not to call or text those friends when using their phone. Iskinder's father is like fathers from other recent immigrant communities, as noted earlier, in that he assumes the right to decide who Iskinder's friends will be and how his son will interact with them. Once, when Iskinder had called one of the forbidden friends, Iskinder says, "my dad heard me and he yelled, '*Why* did you call that boy?' He was really mad at me." His father did not allow him to use the phone for the rest of that day. Iskinder feels that it was an appropriate punishment, he says, "because he is just trying to protect my life and he is only thinking to do good things for me." Still, Iskinder isn't always pleased with his father's interventions. "My feeling is that [parents] shouldn't try to control you and all the things you do," he says.

Young people in immigrant families are acutely aware of the different expectations that shape parenting in new and in their former cultural contexts. Iskinder notes that in his home country, "we don't talk that much with our parents." Bina Silwal similarly observes that she has a closer relationship with her parents in their new environment than in the old. She observes, "People are more open here [in the United States]. In Nepal, teens have a hard time talking with their parents. They see their parents as much different from them," she says.[40] Parents have strict rules and expectations for daughters in particular, according to Bina.

Because both of her parents work "a lot," she says, Bina helps her mother with housework and meal preparation, and helps her brother and father with their English language skills. Like Iskinder, Bina has observed that U.S. teens are less respectful of adults than young people were expected to be in her home context. Also like Iskinder, in the new context Bina chooses to embrace traditions rather than to test out new possibilities for authority within interfamilial relationships. In fact, both felt that they were experiencing freedom in other ways. Bina expresses overwhelming enthusiasm for what she describes as the "freedoms" of her new home and the use of technology within it, clearly highlighting differences between her old and new contexts regarding gendered expectations and restrictions. Contrasting the strictness of her former context with the freedom she experiences in the United States, Bina comments that in Nepal, young women "can't go out and they are forced to spend time only with their families. And they get into trouble." In the United States, she continues, she *chooses* to spend free time with her family, which she believes is much better than feeling "forced." Bina, who was one of the few immigrant fifteen-year-olds we interviewed who has her own mobile phone, notes that the one thing that would cause her parents to take away her phone was a show of a lack of respect for her parents or older relatives.

Although some young women from restrictive societies who move to more gender-egalitarian settings do find ways to exercise freedoms apart from their parents and their families, Bina is not interested in this. She agrees with her parents about the cultural context of the United States, noting a difference in what is available in entertainment media. She observes, "In Nepal they censor all of the bad stuff. In America, the bad stuff is on TV and you can watch it, but we choose not to." For the most part, she says, in their new context her parents are worried about "drugs. And they don't want us ditching school. They always say just avoid bad company." Like Iskinder, Bina and her brother have "promised" her parents that they will not lose their home culture, and Bina explains that her desire to maintain traditional authority relations with her parents has to do with her family's felt need to rely upon one another more in their new context than they had in their old.

Respect for the wishes of one's family plays a strong role in how the young people we interviewed presented themselves both online and offline. Another young woman, seventeen-year-old Tahani Sabri, says that she chooses to wear the veil both in her new school and in her Facebook profile photo, even though her Muslim Iraqi family did not demand that she do so. "It's just like I don't want to be the only girl in the family not wearing it when every girl wears it," she says. Maintaining traditional language and dress is important to all of her family members, Tahani says, yet like Bina, she also believes that since moving to the United States her family has embraced the idea that young people can be "independent and open-minded"—and that, she says, has changed their family life a great deal.

Immigrant young women like Bina and Tahani embrace self-censorship when it comes to digital and mobile media practices, adopting restrictive approaches that they believe are in keeping with their desire to demonstrate respect for their parents and for the religious and cultural traditions of their home cultures. Sixteen-year-old Raju similarly places restrictions on his mobile phone use in the context of his family's Nepalese background. "We have real hard rules. We're from different customs," he explains. Raju was only allowed to receive phone calls; he was not permitted to make outgoing calls. His fourteen-year-old sister was not allowed to have a Facebook page, a restriction with which Raju agreed. His parents, he says, "don't want us to be crazy about the Internet." Yet Raju also notes that he is not always compliant, particularly when his parents insist that he finish a conversation or online activity in order to participate in a family activity. They have to enforce the rules every day, he says, and they do so by "staring" at him until he accedes and ends the conversation or goes offline. Raju is quick to approve of their oversight, however, pointing to their move to the United States as evidence that his parents have his future in mind.

Seventeen-year-old Josna Khan, who is also from Nepal, notes that she, too, has strict rules to follow regarding her phone use, as her mother only allows her to speak with her sister, although her mother and father allow her to text friends occasionally.[41] "We, like, have to erase the history," Josna explains, suggesting that she and her sister sometimes text more than is allowed and then remove the traces of these infractions before their parents can see them. Josna also is only permitted to have a Facebook profile that she shares with her sister, which limits her ability to communicate with friends apart from her family members. Similarly, Sunita, a fourteen-year-old who spent the early years of her life in Nepal and has been in Denver for four years, is not allowed to have a Facebook site and never speaks on the cell phone without her mother's supervision. Like Raju, Josna and Sunita defend these restrictive practices. Josna equates these restrictions with her parents' concern for her; as she says, "If the parents did not care about us, then we would chat with everyone that we don't know, and we would just make friends" and not get schoolwork and cooking tasks completed. Josna's parents want her to focus on her studies instead.

Some immigrant young people avoid Facebook and other social networking sites because they have experienced racial slurs or other forms of inappropriate communication from school acquaintances. Seventeen-year-old Josna, who wears a hijab and maintains a modest style of attire, recounts a time when someone Photoshopped pictures of her face and her sister's face onto "naked bodies." After that, she decided to raise the privacy level of her Facebook profile and has only added as friends those she knows very well. Some young people decide to limit access to their mobile phone's number for similar reasons. A fourteen-year-old high school boy originally from Kenya recounted harassment he'd experienced, saying of one text he received, "They used the *n*-word but I don't understand because that is not my nationality, but it really hurt me."[42] He then blocked the perpetrator's contact information so that he would receive no further calls from him.

Santosh Sadasankar's story embodies several similar tensions and negotiations. "I don't want to broadcast me," seventeen-year-old Santosh notes when asked why he doesn't update his Facebook page very frequently. He reports that he uses social networking sites to communicate with friends rather than set up a profile that could be viewed by those he does not know well.[43] Santosh is only online about once a week, as he has fairly limited access to both a cell phone and a computer. The family's one cell phone usually stays at home with Santosh's mother, and the computer is kept in his brother's room for his use with college assignments.

Like many other recent immigrants to the United States, Santosh has experienced various levels of harassment both online and off.[44] When one of his online friends referred to him on his Facebook wall using a racially loaded term, Santosh decided to ignore it, even though he found it "painful" and "horrible." He is hoping this friend will stop using that word, he says, because otherwise "there would be some problems."

Santosh takes it upon himself to warn his parents about the dangers of Facebook, telling his parents that his younger sister should not be permitted to have a profile on a social networking site until she is sixteen. He thinks his parents are right about both mobile phones and the Internet. "Cell phones, the Internet, is one of the ways of getting the drugs through," he says, recognizing that drug users frequently contact their suppliers via phone or social networking sites. Santosh opted not to tell his parents about the incident on Facebook. He also has not told them that he has three hundred friends on the site.

Santosh, like Iskinder, Raju, and Bina, speaks about the value of using digital and mobile media for keeping in touch with family and with home cultures. Santosh says that he communicates with his cousins in Nepal and shares what they say with his parents. His parents often look at his site with him, but as they are not literate in English, they can only understand the comments he writes in Nepali and in Hindi. Santosh has also helped his parents figure out how to watch Nepali television over the Internet on their computer. Young people in these families often serve as conduits and interpreters of the new home culture, and they are often the experts in the house when it comes to digital and mobile media. Because Iskinder's father does not speak English, he is unfamiliar with computer keyboards and is unable to read the screen in locations that make online access publicly available.[45] Like Santosh, Iskinder plays a key role in helping his father maintain connections with people in their home country. When his father wants to send a letter to a friend from their home country, he accompanies Iskinder to the library and sits with him while Iskinder types and then sends the email using Iskinder's own account. Iskinder has also helped his father to use the Internet to search for movies from their native country. Similarly, Mateo Lopez, a sixteen-year-old who lives with his mother, father, and brother, acts as a conduit to the online realm and expert for his family. Mateo, who has almost unfettered access to his family's computer with Internet access, considers his Facebook page an important way for his entire family to stay connected to the extended family they have in Mexico.[46] The family has one mobile phone that they share, and that is usually with Mateo's mother. His mother often sits beside him when he is on Facebook so that together they can chat with her sister and with Mateo's cousins back in Mexico. Like Santosh's and Iskinder's families, Mateo's family also uses the computer to watch news about their home country together online.

Like many young people, Santosh has made calculated decisions regarding what he shares with his parents about his activities online and what he shares with his peers via social networking sites. Santosh is also not alone in his desire to limit the amount of information about himself that he shares online with those he does not know well. In contrast to middle- and upper-middle-class young people who might find in Facebook a place where one can explore the possibilities of developing an acquaintance into a friendship or a romantic relationship, young people from marginalized backgrounds—including those marginalized because of economics as well as race and ethnicity—have reason to be more cautious.

In each of these stories, we hear some familiar concerns about digital and mobile media as potentially distracting to schoolwork, echoing parental concerns from across the economic spectrum. We also hear evidence of heightened restriction, which exists in relation to access, cultural prerogatives, and self-restriction as a response to harassment. Parents are concerned about the prospect of cultural loss and about opportunities for their children's futures. Sensing that their parents have their best interests in mind, young people are compliant with restrictions on digital and mobile media use, and they are also compliant regarding rules about friends. They see themselves as voluntarily participating in the maintenance of traditions through their choices of dress, food, and gender roles, and they use digital and mobile media in ways that maintain ties to their families and traditions. They select modest dress for online profiles, use online resources in their schools to read and then relay news about their home countries, and help their parents to maintain contact with their families back home. They teach their parents and younger siblings about the online environment. They talk of the respect they have for their parents and their own cultural backgrounds, their willing compliance with parental restriction on digital and mobile media, and their own engagement in self-restriction for privacy reasons; they also experience some reversal in adult/dependent roles, assuming adult responsibilities as they help their parents manage their new situation.

Respect, Restriction, and Reversal Among Less Advantaged U.S.-Born Young People

There are many differences between the experiences of these young recent immigrants and those young people who were born in the United States. Some of the young people, particularly young women in recent immigrant families, face more severe restrictions on from their parents than U.S.-born young people do.[47] Some born in the United States live in families that have undergone a decline in their economic fortunes in recent years, or have extended family members whose economic fortunes differ markedly from their own, or live in families that have experienced several generations of poverty. But there are also some similarities among these groups that are worth highlighting here, notably the central role placed on extended family and tradition among lower-income families from a variety of ethnic groups, as contrasted with the middle- and upper-middle-class (and largely European American) emphasis on individuals, immediate families, and progress. In part, these values are a functional response to the often difficult financial situations of these families, as family members can be called upon to assist with child care, lend money, provide transportation, and serve as sources of information about job opportunities.[48] Extended families are therefore key to both financial and emotional stability.

"You have to stay in contact with your friends and family!" Deshonelle Williams laughs as she explains why she sends "a *lot*" of text messages every day.[49] Like most fourteen-year-olds, Deshonelle also spends some time on Facebook, checking for messages, reading other people's status updates, and writing replies. But like the immigrant young people introduced earlier, her time online and on the phone is limited. Deshonelle is an African American young woman who lives with her mother, Laretta, and her younger sister. She shares a smart phone with her mother, and her mother has the phone with her most times. Because they don't have a computer with Internet access in their home, on most afternoons Deshonelle accesses Facebook from her friend's house.

Deshonelle lives in a two-bedroom townhouse in a community where the median income falls just below the average for the city and the rate of single-parent households is about double the city's average. Most people in her neighborhood are white, and a sizeable number are Latino. Few households are below the poverty line, and most parents in the area hold jobs, largely in the areas of sales, transportation, maintenance, construction, or, like her mother Laretta, office work. Most adults in the area, like her mother, have a high school degree or its equivalent; a number have completed some college. Because the high school that serves her neighborhood has been recognized as a low-performing school with a high incidence of violence, every day Deshonelle's mother drives her a half hour to an urban school in Denver that participated in an EXCELerator School Improvement Model project funded by the Bill and Melinda Gates Foundation.[50] The high school she attends also has a diverse student population, one-quarter of which is African American, and Deshonelle and her mother appreciate the school's self-identification as a culturally diverse community.[51]

What is especially striking about Deshonelle is that whenever she is asked about her media use, she mentions not only her friends and peer group, as the middle-class young people in the last chapter did, but also her family. When asked about how she uses Facebook, she replies that she chats with her friends, meets new people, "and then my family, I have a lot of family." She thinks other people, too, probably use Facebook mostly "to connect with friends and family." Deshonelle says that she watches the news "with my family," which includes her grandmother and grandfather. She describes her mother as her "best friend." When asked what she'd do if someone she knows was cyberbullied, Deshonelle replies, "I'll have to stick up for my friend or my family." She says she'd tell the perpetrator, "Like, that's not cool, dude. Just stop, you're making a fool of yourself, and it's really rude and disrespectful. I know your mom knows you better than that." Deshonelle's experience demonstrates the importance of family and in particular the importance of her mother in her life. Unlike many of the immigrant young people, Deshonelle has very few restrictions on her media use. Yet because many of her friends similarly have to share mobile phones with mothers or siblings and they, like her, do not have Internet access at home, her ability to communicate with her friends via digital and mobile media is somewhat limited.[52]

Fifteen-year-old Monique Coleman similarly found that texting is a more effective way to reach her close circle of friends than social networking sites because her friends go onto those sites infrequently.[53] She says, "If I really can't see the person I'm talking to, I text. Other than that, I go for a visit or something." Unlike the children of first-generation immigrants, Monique has rarely traveled outside Denver with her African American single mother and brother. Because Monique has had few opportunities to meet people beyond her immediate circle of neighbors and friends, she does not have many of the more distant friendships that Facebook enables for immigrant young people.

Like some of the immigrant young people who spoke of harassment, some lower-income young people and their parents similarly talk about a desire for privacy and a desire to maintain control over their own information and self-expression, and they, too, relate these desires to concerns about economic and racial/ethnic discrimination. Sometimes parents encourage a high level of self-censorship, as noted in the story of Gerardo Molinero (chapter 1), whose mother discouraged him from creating a Facebook profile to protect their family. Monique Coleman shares her mother's suspicions regarding social networking sites as well as everything else related to the online realm. She is concerned about not putting too much information on her Facebook profile, and, following her mother's suggestion, she has never downloaded anything onto the family's computer or onto her mobile phone. She also chooses not to post status updates very often on her Facebook page. "I don't put stuff like 'School was boring today,'" she says. "That's the kind of stuff you keep to yourself."

Like the immigrant young people, native-born young people of non-white backgrounds experience ethnic, economic, and religious slurs both online and off.[54] In comments submitted anonymously as part of an urban classroom discussion, one high school girl notes, "My friend experienced cyberbullying when [we] were at a basketball game and someone we all knew started arguing with her and then called her a racial slur over text."[55] Another high school girl worries about a friend who she says had been cyberbullied. "What I did was I tried to convince her that the skin color doesn't matter as long as your heart is pure, that every skin color has its own beauty . . . But she was deeply hurt and couldn't get over it."[56] Some young people also report slurs related to lower income as signified by clothing or personal hygiene.[57] These experiences lead young people and their families to approach digital media in particular with a great deal of suspicion, carried over from their experiences of discrimination in the offline world. "I just talk with my friends [and not strangers] on Facebook," seventeen-year-old Isabella Garcia replies when asked whether she has tried to make new friends on the social networking site.[58]

Lower-income young people aren't the only ones concerned with privacy. In 2009, after Facebook had started to receive attention for its controversial decisions to lower privacy default settings that resulted in more sharing of participant profile information, 71 percent of young adults ages eighteen to twenty-nine on the social networking site reported that they had changed their privacy settings.[59] Young people are more likely to have their profiles set to "private" if their friends also have private profiles.[60] However, social media researchers Eszter Hargittai and danah boyd have found that the least skilled population of Internet users, which includes many young people from lower income backgrounds, may be least likely to understand privacy settings.[61] This may explain, in part, why some young people choose to engage in self-censorship as a means of moderating what is made available to others online. Some young people may also be dissatisfied with privacy setting options, or may not wish to trust their personal information to sites such as Facebook.

Parents in lower-income families often have less experience with digital and mobile media than their children do, as noted in chapters 1 and 2. These parents rely on older and more technologically savvy siblings or cousins to look out for younger and less experienced members of the family. And when a technological question arises, they look to their own children to address it—something that young people sometimes disdain.[62] Sixteen-year-old Montana Odell, a biracial Native American and European American young woman, oversees the online experiences of her younger brother, Thad, and cautions him against making purchases over the Internet.[63] As she notes: "There is definitely stuff that I will be surfing through and I will notice something and think immediately, 'What if my brother saw this?' and how awful that would be." Montana believes that Thad will one day be thankful that she "shelters" him from things that he doesn't need to see:

I worry that he has access to this. Some of the stuff, I feel like I am old enough to know because I made my own decisions about morals and stuff like that. But for someone his age, he is growing up and he is more influenced than I would be. So it bothers me that he has access to a lot of stuff that, I don't know, it should be on late at night or something. If parents don't have a proper block then kids can just have access to it.

She worries that her mother does not have much knowledge of the online environment, and thus Montana sees herself as needing to take particular leadership with Thad in that area. As she notes, "I was telling him before he downloads music that he needs to ask me because a lot of weird stuff comes up sometimes. It's not totally bad but it will be girls in bikinis or something. He doesn't need to see that." Her family has a distaste for uncouth language and inappropriate situations, and she feels a need to model appropriate media behaviors for him, she says.

Montana's family does not discuss restrictions on digital and mobile media use in the same way as do many recent immigrant families, instead speaking of the need for "trust" between mother, daughter, and son. Later, when speaking with the interviewer on her own, Montana equates her mother's willingness to trust her with her mother's lack of experience online. "One of my best friends is the same as me. Her parents aren't really—I don't know, they don't use the computer much, I don't think." She adds, "My mom teaches us what is right and wrong but she doesn't set limits 'cause she trusts us." Montana's mother has a close extended family, and they all live in the city of Cleveland, arguably the heart of the rust belt area of the United States. Whereas some members of the extended family own their own small homes, a number have experienced serious financial difficulties, chronic health issues, or imprisonment, and they are each other's support system in relation to parental concerns. Yet none of the family members has much experience with digital media. As Montana's thirteen-year-old cousin Gabriela explains about the grandparents she resides with because her birth mother is in prison:

> They are older and they don't know a lot about technology. I think they are worried that if you use it a lot what you are actually doing. They don't know *what* you are actually doing. I don't think they are as dependent on it as we are now, so they think you don't really need to use it so much.[64]

Like Montana, Gabriela does not see her grandparents as permissive. But both girls are aware that their lack of oversight is directly related to their mother's or grandparents' lack of experience with the digital realm.

As suggested earlier, the reliance on extended family in Montana and Gabriela's families may be related to ethnic norms, but it is important to note that this strategy of relying upon family for help in the areas of communication technology does not seem nearly as prevalent with the higher-income families we interviewed, regardless of their ethnicity. That is consistent with previous research confirming that families from lower income levels and from recent immigrant communities look to children for leadership and adult-level responsibility.[65]

Montana Odell, her cousin Gabriela Richards, and other young people whose experiences with digital and mobile media outstrip that of their parents often seek to address their parents' concerns by sharing their online or text-related practices with them, taking on the role of educating both parents and younger siblings about digital media. Sixteen-year-old Cristina Mendoza, a lower-income biracial young person, relates a story that echoes those of Montana and Gabriela. She notes that when her parents saw a television news feature on privacy levels and social networking sites,

> they freaked out about it. They were like, "Is [your page] on private? Can they see everything?" I was like, "No, everything's like on confidential." And sometimes I'm on it and my dad goes into his home office 'cause that's where the computer is, and I'd be, like, talking to somebody, and he's like, "Oh, who's that you're talking to?" And I'm like, "Oh, that's my friend so-and-so, and look, he put up a new picture." And, like, my parents know my friends on there.

Cristina has calmed her parents' fears about social networking sites by engaging them in conversation and showing them what she does on her profile page. Seventeen-year-old Jessica Moran, a European American teen from a lower-income background, similarly tells her mother about the people she talks with online, emphasizing to her that she only talks to relatives and to friends she's known in person.

Extended families are often a source of additional supervision and advice, especially when a young person's parents are less savvy about social networking sites and mobile phone use than their teen children are. "My aunt has a Facebook page," Sofia Hernandez, a Latina young woman from a disadvantaged neighborhood, says. "She tells the grandparents what's going on [with me]. . . . It's not that I don't want them to see; it's just weird to think, 'Oh man, my aunt's watching,'" she says.

Perhaps because parents in less financially advantaged families often lack knowledge of the online and mobile phone practices of youth peer culture, as was the case in Montana's family and also in the family of Santosh from Nepal, older siblings sometimes take responsibility for younger siblings in relation to digital media. As seventeen-year-old Rosalia Jiminez notes, when she first learned that her fourteen-year-old sister had an online profile,

> I got mad. I was frustrated because, like, I don't know, I didn't want her talking to some people that she didn't know, and, like, I looked at her page and I seen her friends and there was guys from [Rosalia's high school] that requested [to be added to her list of friends]. And she would have them as a friend and she's only, like, an eighth grader. So that made me mad, and I was just going crazy on her. So I told her that if she was going to have a profile, she could only have people that she knew, she couldn't have people that she didn't know . . . And, like, I made her page private and everything.

Rosalia's younger sister was "mad" that Rosalia had intervened, and she had protested that "it's her page, she could do whatever she wanted." Her younger sister was even angrier when Rosalia reported the whole thing to their mother. "I told my mom to look at the page and look at the guys, how old they were," she says. Then, according to Rosalia, her mother told Rosalia's sister "that if she didn't delete the guys she had to delete her profile, so she deleted everybody that she didn't know." Rosalia continued to check on her sister's page after that incident. About six months later, when she found that her sister had again friended someone Rosalia didn't know, Rosalia got angry with her sister again. "She goes, 'Well, all right,'" Rosalia reports, and her sister again deleted the stranger from her friends list.[66]

Sometimes parents directly encourage—or, rather, enforce—this kind of ethic of siblings who look out for one another. Seventeen-year-old Violeta Moran, a Latina from a low-income neighborhood, relates this story:

> Well, there was this case when my sister, she had this boyfriend, and she would be always texting him like at four in the morning, she would stay up with him till six. So one day my dad caught her and he got really mad. So me and my sister got our phones taken away, we had to put them in their room, or sometimes in the kitchen overnight. Because if one of us gets in trouble and the other one knows about it and doesn't tell our parents, the other one gets the phone taken away, too. So they punish us both.

Violeta, then, has an incentive to keep her sister from "disrespecting the rules" of the family, as she says. After she tells this story, several of her friends chime in to note that their parents similarly enforce a rule of siblings looking out for one another, and two of them related this to having to go everywhere with their siblings.

Some parents, such as Gabriela's grandparents and Iskinder Hagos' father, make significant efforts to expand their children's opportunities to counteract the deepening separation between the families in their own neighborhood and those in higher-income communities, seeing in educational achievement a possibility for greater economic stability in the future. Like other parents in would-be middle-class and less advantaged families, these parents seek to maintain a strong relationship of respect and connection with their older children, believing that such strong familial bonds are an important means of protecting them for the present and for their future.

The Ethic of Respectful Connectedness and the Problem of Disrespect

It's important to remember that when I am describing communication ethics, I am referring to the guiding principles that parents and children bring to their digital and mobile practices. These are therefore not styles of parenting, but are the ideal of what parents and young people consider to be "good" parenting. Of course, practices often don't live up to the ideals. The young people we interviewed were not always respectful toward their parents, nor were parents consistently respectful toward their children, as we have seen in earlier chapters and we will see again in later ones. But in the middle-class, would-be middle-class, and less advantaged families, the most frequent conversations that seem to go on between parents and their teens are about how to use digital and mobile media in ways that are "appropriate." Use of such media is a privilege and a responsibility, parents reminded their teens. The media are important lifelines to peers, teens reminded their parents. Perhaps the most striking and illustrative recent example of how this ethic of respectful connectedness may be the mainstream approach to digital and mobile media, I think, is the story of the viral video "Facebook Parenting."

The video was created by a middle-class father who, frustrated with his fifteen-year-old daughter's public rant about her parents on her Facebook page, decided to create a video message for her. As the video begins, the North Carolina father reads a printout of his daughter's profanity-laced post. Her post complains about how hard her life is because her parents make her do household cleaning chores and expect her to make coffee for them. As the father reads her note, he makes editorial comments that express his frustration and anger, berating her for being lazy and disrespectful. After about seven minutes, he turns the camera toward the ground and explains, "That right there is your laptop. You see it right there on the ground. This right here . . . is my forty-five," referring to a .45-caliber gun. He then proceeds to fire several rounds into her laptop to demonstrate how he has decided to solve this problem of disrespect.

This video was posted in February 2012 and after three months online had received more than thirty-three million views. The video also received extensive coverage in mainstream media and in specialized outlets for parents. What was especially interesting was that the video immediately generated visceral feedback from parents and others across the country in a variety of fora. The conservative *American Digest* praised the father's wisdom and noted that the video had received more than a hundred thousand comments within four days after it had been posted. The *New York Times* blog *Motherlode*, a clearing house of sorts for progressive mothers (and to a lesser extent fathers) seeking parenting advice, similarly hosted a heated discussion about the father's actions, querying whether or not the father's gun use and public criticism of his daughter was appropriate.

All of this attention to a father's frustrated response to his daughter's online display of disrespect seems to speak to the importance many parents place on creating an ethic of respectful connectedness in regard to digital and mobile media use. This case tells us that parents desire the respect of their children, and that children desire the respect of their parents. We definitely do not agree on how to garner respect from each other, and digital and mobile media may exacerbate our experiences of these tensions. We tend to see mobile and digital media as important platforms in which struggles for respect play out. For this reason, future research needs to consider not only how different parents within U.S. society attempt to garner respect from their children in the online realm, but also what a difference it makes for all of us when platforms such as YouTube can make such personal discussions about respect more scalable, searchable, and persistent than ever before.

Conclusion

"Let Them Use AOL," read a blog post that reported on a study of how upper-income families had migrated to the search engine Google by 2008, whereas lower-income families, in contrast, preferred AOL Search.[67] The title of the blog entry implies that upper-income families recognize that there are different technologies available for differing groups within society and accept this as natural or inevitable. The consumer marketplace supports this view, too, as iPhones, MacBook Pros, BlackBerrys, and Android phones are promoted as items of choice and status, whereas Dell computers as well as the Net10 and other prepaid cell phones are viewed as inexpensive and simple alternatives. This emphasis on consumer choice has made it difficult for families of differing economic means to engage in discussions about access to digital and mobile media as a need versus a luxury item. It's especially challenging for families to describe what they mean by computer and online proficiency, particularly when lower-income families have much more limited experiences with various educational and business software packages and online applications than higher income families do.

Several themes emerge in the stories of Iskinder Hagos, Deshonelle Williams, Montana Odell, Gabriela Richards, and other young people growing up in lower-income households. Respect for one's parents and one's cultural traditions is heard throughout these stories. Each young person experiences limits and restrictions on media use, whether that entails having to share a mobile phone, having to go to a friend's house for Internet access, needing to negotiate television viewing in cramped household spaces, or something else. Not every young person experiences the same set of limitations, but as many within their friendship circles experience similar limits, these young people do not always find texting and social media sites to be reliable ways to get in touch with their friends. Moreover, many of these young people experience the online environment as a continuation of their offline experiences with discrimination. This, along with fears of heightened surveillance, contributes to concerns for privacy expressed by both young people and their parents, and in turn supports continued self-restriction when it comes to the online environment.

In many of these stories, we also see stories of reversal, or of young people who recognize that they are more adept in the uses of communication technologies than their parents are. Parents rely on young people to help them navigate online resources, and rely on older siblings and extended family members for advice about and even enforcement of appropriate limits to online sites. In several cases, young people are frustrated that parental lack of expertise contributes to their parents' reluctance about technologies as well as their inability to understand certain key parts of their growing-up experiences. Montana Odell and Gabriela Richards discuss the fact that their parents and guardians trust them, but they are also aware of how a parent's lack of experience can contribute to mis-understandings and anxieties that, in turn, can lead to greater restrictions. For each of these teens, their parents' lack of experience contributes to what the young people perceive as a rift in understanding between parents and young people over the role of technology in their lives.[68] None of the young people in recent immigrant families discussed concerns about their parents' inability to understand their experiences, although several, such as Bina, Raju, and Santosh, commented on how different their own experiences were from their parents'. In those families, technologies such as mobile phones and the Internet provided opportunities to help parents connect with families and traditions, thus providing a reinforcement of family norms.

Montana Odell, Gabriela Richards, and Iskinder and Bina come from very different life situations and circumstances. What these young people have in common, however, is this: their experiences are quite different from the experiences of some middle- and upper-middle-class young people. These differences obviously relate to limits of ownership and access to digital and mobile media. But they also relate to the importance of respecting their families and their traditions within a context that they feel marginalizes their experiences on the basis of economics, race or ethnicity, and religious background. This makes a difference in how these and other teens respond to the strategies their parents adopt with regard to digital media use, and how parents might think about the Parent App appropriate for their own situations. Other studies of young people from disadvantaged backgrounds have similarly found that when parents maintain a positive attitude toward sharing and supporting their children's Internet use, they are able to enhance their children's opportunities in a variety of venues even in spite of their own lower level of expertise.[69] Of course, as would-be middle-class and less advantaged families overwhelmingly use these technologies to connect with one another, they may be reinforcing bonds with their primary communities, sometimes at the expense of developing relationships that could expand their networks, thereby limiting the opportunities that they and their families might encounter. This difference between upper- and lower-income families, and the differences in how parents and children communicate with one another within those families and therefore in how they approach and utilize digital and mobile media, will be the subject of the book's next section.

PART III | Digital and Mobile Media and Family Communication

CHAPTER 6 | Communication in Families
Expressive Empowerment and Respectful Connectedness

WHEN SEVEN-YEAR-OLD GEMMA WELTON found that the backpack she'd inherited from her nineteen-year-old half sister contained a long-forgotten cell phone, she was thrilled. Gemma's mother and father had told her that she wasn't going to be allowed to have her own phone until an unspecified later time. And yet, once her half sister helped her locate the charger, here was an unclaimed and highly prized accessory that could be her very own, already loaded with several game applications and a working camera. Gemma's mother, Tammy, was not nearly as enthused about this unexpected turn of events as Gemma. Attempting to argue her way out of allowing Gemma to keep the phone, Tammy exclaimed, "Gemma, you're seven years old! You don't need a cell phone!"

"Well, Mommy," Gemma replied, "then when are you going to get me a cell phone?"

On impulse, Tammy declared: "You can have a cell phone when you can name for me five kids your age who have working cell phones." Right away, Gemma named four. And shortly thereafter, she got to keep the phone.[1]

Tammy and her husband, Larry, upper-middle-class parents in a biracial family living in a suburban community in the greater Denver area, related this story with both laughter and some discomfort. They recognized immediately that they might have chosen to keep the cell phone from their younger daughter for a few more years. Turning more serious, Larry reflected on why he felt that this might have been a good idea. He noted that his main concern about cell phone use, when compared with other media, was that he found texting to be "so exclusionary." You can see what a child's watching on a computer or television screen, but texting is easier to use in secret; it can be used to "completely circumvent others. And that's a potentially ominous and negative thing," he said. Tammy agreed. But after contemplating this for a moment, she observed that texting is not that different from the other forms of conversation between childhood peers to which they, as parents, don't have access. The same could be said about Facebook and other social networking sites, she pointed out, "'cause they're all about socializing without us." Both parents then began recalling how much they had felt the need for greater independence when they were preadolescents and adolescents. Keeping secrets from adults was a big part of their own growing-up experiences, and they didn't want to deny their children this same freedom. Yet something told them they should be concerned about this new turn of events.

Middle- and upper-middle-class parents like the Weltons have long been concerned about the role of media in family life.[2] As noted earlier, in order to understand the changes in our lives together as families and the changes in our children's lives that are related to the new media environment, we need to consider the characteristics of digital and mobile media and the new situations they introduce, as we have explored in the previous sections of this book. We have pondered the risks that parents fear are related to characteristics of digital and mobile media, as well as what young people themselves say about these media. We now need to consider the patterns of communication that existed within families *before* these technologies appeared and that continue to shape the uses of these technologies.

This chapter focuses on the factors that shape parents' perspectives on the risks and opportunities afforded by digital and mobile media. Here I delve more deeply into two different approaches: what I have termed the ethic of expressive empowerment and the ethic of respectful connection. In the next chapter I explore how these differing ethics relate to the ways that parents attempt to mediate the media in their family's lives, or how they attempt to mitigate the risks and maximize the opportunities that digital and mobile media afford. In the third chapter of this section, I highlight the fact that families, and in particular mothers, might be best understood as making decisions about media use not in relation to a logical assessment of risks but in relation to what they take to be "good parenting," which is an assessment that takes place in reference to values, emotions, and practicalities rather than solely in reference to rational decision making. We begin to get hints of how the ethics of expressive empowerment and respectful connectedness relate to assumptions of "good parenting" in this chapter, and the Weltons are an interesting example of how some wealthy, upper-middle-class, and middle-class families embrace and articulate an ethic of expressive empowerment.

The Ethic of Expressive Empowerment

For the most part, digital and mobile media play a secondary role in the lives of the upper-middle-class Welton family. Tammy and Larry view their three daughters' use of cell phones, it turns out, much the way they and other upper-middle-class parents view television and films, video gaming, commercially available music, and YouTube and Web-based surfing: these less desirable activities fall to the background as young people participate in what parents think of as preferred, and usually highly organized, activities. In the Welton family, these preferred activities include gymnastics, math tutoring, swim lessons, piano lessons, and soccer. Tammy and Larry Welton engage in a style of parenting that sociologist Annette Lareau has called "concerted cultivation." This refers to a pattern of encouraging their children to be involved in organized activities meant to provide them with opportunities to develop their talents and enjoy the benefits of working as a team with their peers.[3] Between school, participation in these activities, and the unstructured moments of interaction with peers that occur while their teenage daughter waits for transportation or their younger daughters are in after-school care, as well as in the more formally arranged play dates with other children, the Welton family has relatively little time for media-related pursuits.

The Weltons and other upper-middle-class parents like them are especially concerned to create empowering and expressive relationships with their daughters. In addition to facilitating highly programmed lives full of empowering activities, the Welton parents encourage their daughters to talk about their feelings and to share their ideas, both within their family and beyond it.[4] This emphasis on encouraging children to voice their views is what, in part, led Tammy to change her mind and let her daughter Gemma keep a cell phone at age seven. After all, she and Larry reasoned, as children each of them had had opportunities to explore independence, and thus surely they owed Gemma the same.

The main challenge for parents like the Weltons in the digital age might be thought of as a question of balance. How are parents to balance the child's right to explore her world and express herself with the parents' responsibility to prepare and empower the child for the future? These are the questions that tend to guide parent decision making about digital and mobile media; they shape what parents like the Weltons might seek in a Parent App.[5]

Developers have been on the lookout for ways in which parents' concerns might be translated into technological applications that can assist parents in their desire to engage in the concerted cultivation style of parenting. While the Weltons installed the software program Net Nanny to filter and block inappropriate websites, other middle-class parents have turned to cell phones with GPS systems and free iPad apps such as iStudiez, which enables parents to help their children keep track of school assignments and due dates. In my own family, my thirteen-year-old son uses Smart Music software as a means of improving his viola skills while practicing. That program signals when he is playing out of tune or off tempo, obviating the need for a parent to provide direct supervision during sometimes squeaky sessions.

There are more than half a million apps for the Apple iPhone and close to that number for Android phones, and apps meant to appeal to toddlers and preschoolers are both the most popular and the category that has experienced the fastest growth, according to a 2012 study.[6] These technologies help provide parents with a sense that their children's media use is being supervised, limited, or appropriately harnessed for educational purposes. Such media should be used primarily for educational or at least for age-appropriate purposes, according to the Weltons, and only when other, more worthwhile activities aren't available. Middle- and upper-middle-class parents also utilize references to media as the basis for discussions that help older children understand their parents' views about the world, or to learn about their preteen and teen children's interests.[7] These parents often see mobile, digital, and entertainment media as useful in contributing to the expressive relationships between parents and children that middle- and upper-middle-class parents tend to value, and as something they can use or curtail in the interest of their children's empowerment. In these families, digital and mobile media can be viewed as helpful in facilitating a middle-class family life in which communication is both empowering and expressive. But these media also facilitate *efficient* communication in the increasingly busy lives of these families, as well as communication that can be *narcissistic*, because these media can encourage a preexisting emphasis on self-expression and individual rights, as we will see.

Families like the Weltons live in a cultural milieu that embraces an ethic of expressive empowerment. Among families like these, good parenting is associated with raising children who are self-confident, caring, self-reliant, honest, and capable of expressing their views and emotions while exercising self-control, as first described in chapter 1.[8] Families like the Grantmans, to be introduced shortly, live in a cultural milieu that embraces an ethic of respectful connectedness. For them, good parenting is associated with raising children who are loyal, respectful, patriotic, and caring toward both their families and their communities. A good sense of humor, leadership, and resilience in the face of adversity are highly prized in these families as well.[9]

Communication researchers Stephen Chaffee, Jack McLeod, and Dennis Wackman outlined parallel differences in family communication patterns in 1973, when they argued that some families tend to be *concept-oriented*, encouraging children to express ideas, whereas others tend to be *socio-oriented*, emphasizing the importance of getting along with others.[10] Roger Silverstone and Eric Hirsch made similar observations about differing patterns of family communication, explicitly relating patterns to economic differences and suggesting that perhaps better-off families embraced concept-oriented approaches, whereas those less well-off embraced socio-oriented approaches.[11] The patterns of family communication related to digital and mobile media that I observed in my study echo and expand upon these earlier findings, as they also draw upon recent research in cultural sociology on family life and economic difference.[12] All of this is to say that differences are not emerging because of digital and mobile media; rather, there are patterns that existed before these latest media appeared on the scene, and these patterns give shape to the approaches parents consider appropriate as they address themselves to the new situations digital and mobile media introduce.

Communication researcher James Lull laid the groundwork for relating family communication patterns to uses of communication technology in his study of the social uses of television. He noted that socio-oriented families used television for "social" purposes such as initiating conversations between parents and children, reinforcing values, and providing family togetherness time. In contrast, concept-oriented families found almost no redeeming values in television viewing, and instead of seeing television time as togetherness time, they viewed television as a problem that needed to be regulated through the parental expression of authority.[13] Some of these same patterns emerge when we look at how families deal with the new situations brought about through digital and mobile media. To illustrate some of the differences in how families approach digital and mobile media use in relation to what they deem to be good parenting, we turn to a story that offers some contrasts with the Welton family's ethic of expressive empowerment.

The Ethic of Respectful Connectedness

Several hundred miles away from the Welton family, in a cramped apartment in urban San Francisco, Avis Grantman sits watching her favorite television program with her fifteen-year-old daughter, Nina Lane. There is one mobile phone in the room and Avis and Nina share it, although, as usual, it is next to Avis. Many afternoons and weekends pass this way at the Grantman home. As Dr. Bobby Jones of the *Bobby Jones Gospel* program begins introducing his program and guests, Avis, a woman of African American and Native American descent, turns to Nina and excitedly tells her to call her twenty-one-year-old sister Jasmine, who lives across town. "It's a gospel celebration!" Avis exclaims as she turns up the volume. Recounting the occasion later, Avis explained, "I get really pumped up and excited and it lifts me up," adding that she wanted to share the experience with Jasmine, who also enjoys the program's music. Avis notes that she and Jasmine frequently watch and talk on the phone until the singing begins, at which point they say a quick goodbye and hang up until the next commercial break.

Nina adds, "Then they get on during commercials and say, 'Did you see what he did?'"

"Mm-hmm!" Avis agrees enthusiastically. "The girl the other day was no more than six or seven and she was belting out that song, so I called my daughter and said, "'Did you hear that?'"

Avis and Nina also frequently interact while watching television programs and movies. "We like to make fun of the ads," Nina says, and Avis nods, fondly recalling an insurance advertisement they'd found especially funny.[14]

Like most of the parents interviewed for this book, Avis has concerns about how the Internet and the cell phone might be a source of risk for her fifteen-year-old daughter. But those concerns are fairly far down on the list of things she worries about. Avis would not be comfortable referring to her family as "poor" or even "working-class," as she has a stable (if low) income, she completed college, and she does not work in a blue-collar job. Avis and other families like hers might prefer to think of themselves as "would-be middle-class," as they set their sights on achieving a financial stability that at times seems quite distant and at other times seems just beyond their grasp.[15] But financial stability isn't the only thing that concerns Avis.

Nina, a high achiever at her school, lost seven friends and neighbors in drug-related violence the previous year. Avis is determined to have Nina see that she is not destined to suffer the same fate as those around her. Following the same ethic of concerted cultivation that drives middle-class mothers such as Tammy Welton to enroll their children in activities that may help them in their path to achievement, Avis takes Nina to several activities during the week and tries to serve as her advocate at school. When Avis asked about computers at Nina's school, she learned that there was a special program for those with digital aptitude. So Avis petitioned the school to allow Nina to enroll in an advanced computer programming course, even though the Grantmans do not have a computer in their home and Nina had little experience with them. Realizing that she couldn't give Nina much direction in the area of computers, Avis relies mostly on her older daughters, Jasmine and Shironna, to help Nina learn to navigate the Internet and use the computer. Nina's mother also seeks out opportunities for Nina to pursue a connection with her Native American heritage. She arranged for Nina to get a scholarship to attend a camp where Nina learned some traditions and met others of her heritage, developing friendships that Nina continues in a Native American youth program through the city of San Francisco and through social networking sites.

Nina experiences Avis' advocacy as an expression of her mother's respect and high hopes for her, and she is clearly devoted to her mother. Still, with their tight finances, Nina is somewhat limited as to the organized activities in which she can engage outside of school. Her mother works long hours as an HIV prevention educator in a community-based outreach center that is within walking distance of their apartment. At the end of the school day, as Nina waits for her mother to return home from work, she often spends time on the phone with friends, and sometimes even shares a television program with a friend much as her mother and older sister frequently do.

Less advantaged and would-be middle-class parents view television, music, movies, gaming, and other mediated entertainment as sources of bad influence, just as middle-class parents do. These media are not seen as a desirable or "natural" part of growing up.[16] Parents like Avis Grantman consider technologies such as laptops and tablets potentially useful for their educational benefits, but feel that they too could encourage time wasting or be a source of bad influence. Still, in contrast to middle-class families who feel that they could or should be doing something "better" with their time than watching television or talking on the phone, families like the Grantmans often associate television and cell phones with "family time," as was the case with Avis, Nina, and her older daughter's telephone-mediated viewing of Avis' favorite gospel program. Even when television isn't a part of family togetherness but rather something to do while waiting for others to come home, it is an activity that's safe compared to many other alternatives.[17] It's a regular source of entertainment, an excuse to stay away from less desirable activities, and a respite from the pressures of life. When Avis said that she often encouraged Nina to use their shared cell phone to seek out her friends in the evening hours, she admitted half jokingly that part of the reason was that "then the TV is all mine!"

Whereas families like the Weltons emphasize idea sharing, in families like the Grantmans, conversations tend to focus on establishing and reinforcing connectedness, as illustrated in the conversation Avis and her older daughter shared about their common appreciation of gospel music.[18] They enjoy conversations about dramatic events, and media often provide the fodder for these discussions. They share interpretations of how others respond to dramatic events in relation to their own ideas of what is good or bad, smart or silly. Children like Nina are expected to participate in or at least be present for these discussions, and to spend time and often share media with their siblings and parents. Although her sisters and mother are all hopeful that Nina will use education to help her find a path to greater financial security and fewer stresses than Avis and her older daughters have encountered, they also all share a level of suspicion toward the schools and after-school programs in their area, as such programs could easily be closed down or fail them in other ways. As a result, they feel a sense of deep connection and loyalty to their family members and close friends, and a sense of isolation and distance from those beyond their immediate circles.[19] In spite of their potential problems, communication media such as cell phones as well as television, music, and sometimes even gaming often play a key role in maintaining these strong bonds between family and close friends, keeping their circles tight-knit—and largely isolated.

Middle- and upper-middle-class readers of the preceding paragraph are likely to have some reservations about the story of the Grantmans. Most parenting experts, including the American Academy of Pediatrics, recommend limiting media use or "screen time" to no more than two hours a day.[20] Study after study demonstrates that there is a relationship between high media use and negative outcomes for children.[21] It will sound to some, then, as if by sharing the Grantmans' story I am providing a justification for seeing value in how some families engage in more media consumption than others. Yet this book has not suggested that increased immersion in entertainment media experiences is a positive development for young people individually, or for childhood in general. By presenting the stories of how less advantaged families approach digital, mobile, and entertainment media in ways that differ from the approaches of middle- and upper-middle-class families, however, the book aims to widen the discussion about how we might understand the role of media in the changing lives of U.S. families. In this sense, I am intentionally following sociologist Annette Lareau's approach in her book *Unequal Childhoods*, which successfully enables readers to consider why less advantaged families embrace what middle-class readers might otherwise consider to be an "inferior" approach to parenting.[22] This is also why, in this section of the book, I have replaced the language of parenting styles (over- and underparenting, or authoritarian, permissive, authoritative, and neglectful) with the language of an ethic of family communication. I use the term "ethic" as a way of recognizing that there are always reasons and guiding principles that provide orientation for the choices parents and their children make. Talk of parenting "styles" tends to imply that some styles are better than others (it's better to be authoritative than permissive, for instance, or better to be balanced than either under- or overinvolved). In contrast, a focus on an ethic encourages us to consider the positives and negatives of differing approaches. It also encourages us to think about how our choices relate to what might be called the cultural toolkit that we bring to our parenting tasks.

Like the middle-class Weltons, Avis Grantman and other would-be middle-class and less advantaged parents want to help their children achieve. They too believe in the importance of empowerment. But because they often couldn't count on concerted cultivation opportunities, they felt that the best way to encourage their children's development was through creating a relationship with their children that was respectful and connected. Avis, a recovering drug addict whose early life had been defined by abuse and life in a series of foster households, talks fervently about wanting to be a role model for her daughters. She wants to teach her daughters self-respect by being present in their lives, which she sees as a means of protecting them from the bad decisions around them, as daughter Nina notes:

> See, some people's parents are either on dope or they work so much that they can't be in their kids' lives. That's when they go out to the streets looking for friends and trying to be popular and stuff. When I was being brought up my mom say, "Don't listen to nobody that's going to tell you to do something that is going to hurt you."

Parents like Avis Grantman want the respect of their children, and in turn they want to be able to trust their children to do the right thing and make good decisions. *Trust*, rather than *rights*, often came up as a theme in discussions between parents and children from would-be middle-class and less advantaged families, particularly when it came to digital and mobile media. Trust came up in middle-class families as well, but in would-be middle-class and less advantaged families, parents believe that they have a great deal more at stake and their children have a great deal more to lose when this trust is broken, which may be why it was such a common theme in discussions about the risks and opportunities of digital and mobile media. Additionally, siblings and extended family members often act as trusted resources for parents in less advantaged families. Parents like Avis Grantman frequently work in jobs that don't require them to use BlackBerrys or iPhones to check their email and voice mail. They tend to have much less knowledge about digital media and the Internet than their children do, so they rely on close friends or family members as advisors and assistants in their parenting efforts.[23] These connections are key to how parents like Avis Grantman manage the unknowns in their children's experiences with digital and mobile media.

The challenge of the digital age for parents like Avis Grantman, therefore, is also one of balance, as it is for middle-class parents, but of a different order. Parents in less advantaged and would-be middle-class households need to find a balance between their lack of knowledge and experience in a digitally saturated world and their desire to help their children. They wonder how they can help foster a relationship of trust with their children when their children are living large swaths of their days within an environment the parents do not find trustworthy. Like middle-class parents, these parents also see that digital and mobile media represent access to opportunities and risks. Yet as they think about the present safety of their children and their future prospects, they believe relationships of *respect* and *connectedness* will help their young people weather the inevitable storms they will encounter in their lives. These relationships of respect and connectedness are largely limited to their own immediate circles. As a result, among the would-be middle class and the less advantaged, digital and mobile media are helping to facilitate an experience of family life in which communication is respectful and connected but can also be isolated and isolating.

Relating the Ethic of Expressive Empowerment to the Risk Society

"I don't think either of us is very concerned about media," Larry Welton responds when asked about how he and his wife, Tammy, supervise the use of digital, mobile, and traditional media by their daughters. His words echo the dismissive way in which the well-heeled "concept-oriented" parents of

Lull's study discussed television. The Welton parents are less concerned about media per se than about leisure time in general. "It's not like we're overly cautious," he continues. "It's just that TV or computer, they're the less ideal way to spend our time. I'd rather they get involved with things themselves rather than expecting to be entertained by the media."

Like many other middle-class parents interviewed, Larry Welton associates media with passive consumption and with what he considers to be idle socializing. He prefers that his children find something productive they love to do with their free time. He relates this to his hopes that they will one day find work that is both meaningful and enjoyable. Tammy adds: "You have to be able to enjoy what you're doing, 'cause once you enjoy it, you will succeed, and as you succeed, it just continues to progress." For the Weltons, who do not watch much television, even the few television programs they do enjoy reflect this desire for personal empowerment and fulfillment through work. "They love *Project Runway*," a program that purports to anoint future career success for the most talented among would-be fashion designers, Tammy says of her nineteen-year-old daughter and her two seven-year-old daughters. "They *love* the whole challenge of the project of each episode!"

This prompts Larry to tell a cautionary tale about a friend of his who has been miserable in his job as a lawyer due to what Larry sees as a lack of passion. This friend's parents had, according to Larry, limited his options, expecting the friend to be either a lawyer or engineer. Larry, who owns a successful marketing consulting company, then begins to reflect on the children from his first marriage. He wants to ensure that his children with Tammy are better prepared for a fulfilling career than the children from his first marriage were, he says, expressing sadness that his son and daughter from his first marriage never pursued college. They were passive in their approach to their work lives, Larry felt, due to a lack of interest in schooling. At this point, Larry's story takes an interesting turn. Rather than talking about whether the children from his first marriage found something they enjoyed and were passionate about, he says that he regrets that he didn't do more to inculcate a love of reading in his children. In this part of his story, then, the key to success no longer is tied to having a passion for doing something you enjoy; rather, Larry has linked success differently, so that it now lies in doing well within the framework of schooling. Dropping his earlier reference to passion and enjoyment, Larry seems to be suggesting that education is an important route to a desirable career path. "I feel like education is the great divider," he says, "and I worry about the future for that reason." In lamenting that the children from his first marriage didn't like school, Larry essentially questions whether their schooling had somehow failed them.

He also expresses pride in the fact that Tammy closely monitors her daughters' educational efforts. He and Tammy have enrolled their younger girls in structured opportunities such as music lessons and sports that they hope will both develop desirable skills and give the girls opportunities to experience enjoyment and passion through their participation in these activities. Larry clearly sees a link between participation in these concerted cultivation activities and his children's prospects for success. "We want to get them to pay attention to what they enjoy, but not be heavy-handed and say, 'I think you should do such-and-such,'" Larry says.

"Aside from going to college," Tammy quickly adds.

For the Weltons, a rewarding job is also the kind of presumably well-paying job one gets only if one has a college education. As another middle-class father said, in what was perhaps the most obvious statement of class distinction, "I hope they end up in some profession that is somewhat prestigious, in that they can feel proud of themselves and enjoy work and not be checking in at the factory every day." Enjoyable middle-class work, then, allows for autonomy in the workplace, which is a hallmark of professional-managerial positions that are better-paying than many other potentially "enjoyable" professions.[24]

Like the Weltons, Kevin and Freda Nelson encourage their children to pursue a host of enriching activities.[25] Eleven-year-old Casey Nelson plays four instruments and writes creative stories after school; fifteen-year-old Eddie also plays an instrument, is on a soccer team, and excels at math. Both children have mobile phones, which their parents consider a necessity given the various arrangements involved in transporting Eddie and Casey to and from activities. Like the Weltons, these children have few restrictions about their mobile phone usage, in part, their parents explain, because they want Casey and Eddie to learn to make "good decisions" regarding their use of time. Like Tammy and Larry Welton, Freda frames their family's approach to television as one of good choices:

> We'd rather do other things. We just haven't made it [television] a central part of our lives. . . . Casey will spend hours writing stories, for example. That's fun for her—more so than watching television. She can use Power-Point and make presentations out of them.

But computer time for PowerPoint presentations is somewhat infrequent, as neither watching television nor playing around on the laptop fits easily into the lives of these busy young people. Children in the Nelson family, like the Welton children, are encouraged to engage in empowering activities apart from the family, and to turn off their mobiles and talk with their parents over dinner on the infrequent evenings when they are all in their home together. The Nelson family rarely spends time together watching television or movies. According to Casey and Eddie, this is in part because of their different media preferences, but also because their parents "work too hard," as both of their jobs require long hours and, in Freda's case, trips that often take her away from home for a week or longer.

For the Nelsons, television is both a source of problems as well as the solution to the risk the family experiences in relation to their own family economy. In a strange irony, Kevin Nelson, who professes to hate television, works as a software engineer in a plant that manufactures high-end television sets. He and Freda, who works as a scientist in a government research center, decided against cable television for their own family. They employ a system of parental controls that enable them to limit viewing time and to block programs that they believe are inappropriate for Casey and Eddie. Kevin doesn't find his work personally rewarding because he believes that television fosters commercialism and greed. But in his critique of television, he feels out of step with his co-workers, many of whom he describes as "hard-core TV junkies." According to Kevin, the ideal job for him would instead be one that fosters intellectual curiosity and benefits from his strong sense of duty by allowing him to contribute to others in society. Television, in contrast, is "not constructive to society." And yet at the same time, Kevin Nelson got his job and has kept it because he feels that it is important to support his family. By shoring up his family's financial security, he seeks to buffer his family from risk; financial security trumps all other concerns about rewarding, enjoyable, or constructive work. The Nelsons do not seem to be alone in their decision to pursue financial security, as they live in an upscale neighborhood where most of the homes have more than 3,000 square feet of living space. Eddie Nelson attends a large high school renowned for its excellent scores in the state's accountability tests; close to 95 percent of the graduating class attends college. Their neighborhood is 95 percent white and is one of the highest-income neighborhoods in the area. As Kevin says about his hopes for his children, "I hope they find something they love to do because work takes up so much of our lives." Echoing his father's wishes, fifteen-year-old Eddie Nelson aims, not surprisingly, to find a job that will be "rewarding" and "make money too."

As the economy has shifted and as enjoyable professions that offer a living wage have become more rare in the United States, a job that is both fulfilling and lucrative has become less of a reality for most people—even those who, like the Welton and Nelson parents, seem to be on the right path toward getting one. Leisure, including not only mediated leisure but also a range of non-career-enhancing activities, can be seen as something that potentially can undermine one's prospects for enjoyable, personally rewarding, and lucrative work. Middle-class families therefore associate leisure with the risks of what Barbara Ehrenreich describes as falling out of the middle class.[26] Engaging in too much media use can therefore be a problem in a middle-class culture in which people vie for employment opportunities in the ever-diminishing pool of remunerative, if not always rewarding, work.

The Polanskis and the Risks of Childhood

In contrast to the rather unselfconscious ways in which the Nelsons and Weltons place a great deal of hope in the idea that their children's education and participation in extracurricular activities may eventually lead them to work that is rewarding and fulfilling, Jim Polanski is very conscious of the risks and uncertainties related to his daughter and son's education. Despite good grades and hard work in school, his son, Blake, graduated from their area's regional high school with no significant scholarship offers, and the Polanski family has few resources to help him pursue college. Jim and his wife, Sarah, both of European American heritage, grew up in a struggling rural area and have worked hard at their jobs in shipping and livestock in that same area. But they lost money when a family-owned farm business went under a few years back, and they are still working to recover their losses.[27] They are members of the would-be middle class, for they believe that as soon as they get back on their feet financially, they will have a secure financial life like the one they knew before. Unfortunately for Blake and Katie, that move to the comfortable middle class probably will not happen while they are still living as dependents in their parents' home.

Blake, who at eighteen is demoralized by the fact that his choices include going into debt or relying on his already overburdened parents to help finance his education, has decided to take a year off from school before going on to college. Blake's mother attributes his decision to "burnout." She worries about how Blake's decision will affect his younger sister, Katie, who is also a high-achieving student and is facing graduation in two years.

Like many families whose incomes make it difficult to sustain what they think of as a middle-class lifestyle, the Polanskis want to maintain oversight with regard to their children's uses of digital, mobile, and traditional media, although sometimes this is difficult given their somewhat inflexible work schedules. Like the Weltons and Nelsons, the Polanskis say they do not have many rules governing their children's media use, a point to which we will return in a moment. Rather than viewing media use as a "waste of time," as the Nelson and Welton families do, the Polanskis think of entertainment media as a form of what Jim Polanski terms "cultural pollution." The Polanski parents describe themselves as part of a "tight-knit" family living in a once-rural area that has been turning into developed neighborhoods thanks to new construction. The Polanskis are very interested in creating a family culture that will envelop their children in a loving environment in which they, as parents, serve as the protectors of their children against the wider backdrop of a corrupt culture.

Parental protection and a warm family environment are only part of the environment in which Blake and Katie Polanski are growing up. Even though Blake attended a high school that was, by state standards, just barely acceptable, he felt tremendous pressure to succeed in school. "You've got to go to the best college, you've got to get the best grades," he says. Academic excellence needs to be accompanied by excellence in other areas as well, whether that includes sports, music, the arts, or something else. Blake doesn't feel like he fit in amidst this school culture oriented to individual empowerment, though; in fact, he and his family tend to see the school as a victim of the same cultural corruption that they want to combat within their family life. Drawing a connection between this pressure to succeed and an ethic of individualism that he resists and equates with self-centeredness, Blake says, "Everyone's just so worried about their own business and what their future is going to be that it's just like I can't worry about the next person. I'm worrying about myself . . . It's like tooth and nail. They're just going for like the best."

Blake associates this desire to be the best with the sense of entitlement he sees among his peers. The culture of high achievement in Blake's high school encourages placing one's own rights above the rights or rules of others. Echoing his father's conservative political viewpoints, Blake also uses this language of rights to resist what he feels is the incursion of "political correctness" in his school: "It seems like kids have so many rights nowadays. Everyone has so many rights, and everyone has to be so free that no one's really free because you can't really say anything now. You don't want to step on anyone's toes, so it's like 'let kids be who they are,' and they just run amok."

It isn't clear that the kids about whom you couldn't "say anything" are the same ones who were "running amok" and who showed little care and respect for others. The point, from Blake's perspective, was that the pressure to succeed and the orientation toward individual empowerment are not serving all students and may not have been the best approach for him; after all, even success by the school's own standards was not enough to guarantee Blake access to the "best" universities. Part of the problem, according to the Polanski family, was that the school didn't support a range of career goals or a wider set of cultural values beyond individualism and achievement. Between the unrelenting pressure, the limited career options supported, the rights that were claimed by those both more and less advantaged than he was, and the failed promises, "they took the fun out of education," Blake's father, Jim, says, sighing.

Neither Jim nor Sarah views their work as a rewarding job or a "career." As Sarah puts it bluntly, "I just work for the benefits and the money. I don't get any rewards from my job."

"It's not like a rewarding job," Jim similarly says of his work, "I just focus on this group at home as far as influencing or anything like that." Indeed, Jim and Sarah both agree that their priorities lie in spending time together as a family and supporting their children. Their daughter, Katie, feels and appreciates this support: "They work real hard to help me or Blake. We have whatever we need, I guess. Like they'll do anything. I mean, if one of us needs twenty dollars, then they'll give it to us. I guess they provide a lot for us, and they work real hard."

Sarah and Jim Polanski say they don't mind working "real hard"; as Jim notes, he wants his children to know "what a good day's work is," a phrase that he uses in conjunction with his days growing up on a farm. "If they want to go to college and get into something they really like, I'm all for that," Sarah says; "I just want them to enjoy it and not end up like us." Like the Nelsons and the Weltons, the Polanskis hope that their children will find enjoyable work, and like Kevin Nelson, they too hope that it will be more enjoyable than their own work situations. However, the Polanskis do not put their faith in either the school system or the extracurricular activities their children pursue, in large part because such structures do not seem to be supporting them in the ways that they would like. Instead, they embrace a fairly traditional set of beliefs about religion as well as about age and gender roles within the family.

The family's approach to digital, mobile, and traditional media, then, plays out in relation to the assumption that children need to respect the authority of their parents. It also grows out of a perceived need to protect family members' personal safety, but they clearly see this task as within the traditional role of parental authority. Jim Polanski, for instance, explains that he and Sarah waited until just the year before to purchase two "starter" cell phone plans for Blake, who is eighteen, and sixteen-year-old Katie. "We consider them a safety kind of thing," explains Jim. "That's why they have them. If she's ever in a position that she's not comfortable with, I want her to be able to let me know and I'll come get her. He was that way too," Jim adds, suggesting that Blake's cell phone has helped his parents to feel that Blake can call anytime he needs to be removed from a situation of discomfort. Dangers are part of the environment beyond the family, the Polanskis believe—as do many parents. The mobile phone, though, rather than being viewed as a portal to those dangers, is instead seen as a means by which parents can retain their influence and connection with their children as the children gain more independence. This expression of a need to protect their children's safety and the desire to continue to influence their children were striking given Katie's age, and, even more so, given Blake's age. Most middle- and upper-middle-class parents with teenagers seem to believe that their children have already gained good decision-making skills, and they are thus less concerned with continuing to influence their children than with figuring out how to manage consequences when children stray from what they and their parents would agree is good common sense.

True to the family's dependence on the father's authority, in the Polanski family the parents, and specifically the father, decided upon and purchased the cell phone plan for the two teens, even though in some middle-class and less advantaged families, older teens purchase their own cell phone plans with money they have saved up.[28] In this family, Jim and Sarah Polanski's decision to continue paying for Blake's mobile phone is seen as natural and done with the best interests of Blake and Katie in mind: it is done to extend the family's circle of protection as Blake and Katie more frequently come to interact with the outside world. Thus the decision reflects the fact that these parents see themselves as mitigating what they interpret as risks.

Jim notes that they do not have any restrictions regarding either time or content that might come up online. They use Internet filtering software and periodically check their children's phones, "but after that we go on the basis that we trust what we taught them. They'll know if they are in the wrong location. Now, do I sometimes check where the websites are? Yeah. But otherwise . . . there are no rules." After Katie interjects that she has "nothing to hide," her father continues, noting that "the only other restraint is that at ten p.m. she shuts down whatever. I don't care what. She's still going to school, and at ten, everything's lights out. But otherwise, no, if she wants to be on the computer for two hours and we don't need it or I don't need it," she can continue to use it. Thus, one other practice that might also be considered a rule is this: if one of the parents needs to use the family computer when Katie is on it, the policy is "Katie, get off," as her parents laughingly acknowledge. As her mother explains, "I mean if she's doing a project at school, then we won't." But if she's on Facebook, "that's just messing around." The implicit understanding in the family is that parents have the ultimate authority over how the computer is to be used and that Blake and Katie are to conduct themselves in a manner that maintains their parents' trust. Katie and Blake do not raise any objections to this understanding.

When asked about the risks they see related to the online realm, the Polanski parents discuss the need for cultivating in Blake and Katie a sense of discernment that will enable them to navigate a "culturally polluted" environment. To help in this task, Blake is a part of an "accountability group" through his church that gathers young people together once a week, and on another evening he attends the church's larger youth meeting. He rarely communicates with the people in either of these groups via cell phone, text, or IM, he says, preferring instead to communicate face-to-face. He isn't always confident about his relationships with his peers, however, because he feels that his commitment to his conservative Christian faith is stronger than that of his friends. "Some of them you can totally tell that they're kind of on the same page as where I'd be; some are kind of wishy-washy," he explains. This sense of questioning his friends in light of their different perspectives also informs the way in which Blake uses digital technologies. Whereas other young people talk about seeking the advice of their friends online, Blake and Katie approach the Internet as a place where they can encounter different authoritative sources. Neither of them maintains a profile on a social networking site such as Facebook or Twitter; they use the Internet as a resource to reinforce the values of the religion in which they have grown up. This is especially evident in a story Blake relates about his process of locating a college to attend.

Blake spent several days searching the Internet for information on colleges that would help him in his goal of becoming a missionary. The website of the first school he viewed, which was in the local area, indicated that the school was "too expensive." Then, he cast the net wider, searching in "one of those college finder search things" on "Christian colleges" and "missionary colleges," and found a place that we'll call Missionary College. In the college website's emphasis on "godly character" and in online testimonials from directors of several conservative Christian organizations, Blake recognized the rhetoric of his own family's viewpoints.[29] "I just kind of saw this and was like, whoa. I just had a good feeling about it right away," he says.

Blake notes that his parents have been supportive of his decision, although he also adds: "People have been like, 'Well, make sure you're checking all your options, type of thing, and, you know, don't close your doors.' I'm kind of a stubborn person, so I'm kind of narrow-sighted. So, I'm like, 'No, this is it,' so I kind of run full-headed at it"—a statement perhaps indicating that some people in his life have questioned his decision to attend a narrowly focused, unaccredited program that trains fewer than ninety students on its "campus" of a few buildings in the suburbs of a small midwestern city. Consistent with Blake and Katie's parents' view that young people must learn to protect themselves from the negative influences of the outside world, Blake chose a college based on rhetoric that encapsulates a worldview he recognizes as consistent with his own.

As we can see in the case of the Polanskis, family members utilize some communication media to meet their personal and familial goals and to mitigate risk, and how they manage this has a great deal to do with how they conceptualize authority relationships within their family and beyond it.[30]

The ways in which risk is mitigated thus differs quite a bit between the Polanski parents and the Nelsons and Weltons. Whereas the Nelsons and the Weltons are concerned about education and the proper use of leisure time—as such pursuits are instrumental to attaining an enjoyable job—the Polanskis, who see these pursuits as ineffective in furthering their aspirations, emphasize the importance of raising their children with the values that they themselves embrace. These values include respect for authority and family connections, and thus share some similarities with the less advantaged and would-be middle-class families. However, the Polanskis' values are also shaped by and articulated in relation to their involvement in a conservative Protestant church.

Why Blake and Katie's father wishes to present the family as one of "no rules," then, is an interesting question, given that some would consider the use of Internet filtering software, occasional checking of phones and website histories, and a 10:00 p.m. "unplugged" policy to be rules. Children in this family are expected to respect the authority of their parents and risk punishment if they fail to do so, and neither Katie nor Blake questions their father's right to supervise their media use, just as they did not question the fact that he bought their mobile phones and supervised their use. Perhaps because strictness has fallen out of favor even among religious families with a fairly traditional approach to gender and parental authority, it seems important to the Polanskis to stress that "policies," rather than rules, govern their family's media use, and that maintaining trust, rather than avoiding punishment, is the goal of parent-child relationships.[31]

The Polanskis thus come across as both more traditional and in some ways more connected than members of the middle-class Nelson and Welton families. In many ways, the inflexibility of the Polanskis' work situations necessitates these mobile phone connections. Like the Nelsons and Weltons, the Polanskis believe that they are in professions they have chosen at least in part out of necessity. They want their children to have better opportunities and better choices in the work world than they themselves have had, but they have experienced both the failed promise of higher education and an inherent conflict between the drive for individual achievement and their own family's emphasis on respect for relationships. Rather than worrying about the effects of digital, mobile, and traditional media in displacing more preferable activities, therefore, the Polanskis worry about the heightened risk that they associate with the dangers lurking outside their tight-knit family and their religious community, coupled with concerns about the stalled opportunities of the anxious would-be middle class. From their perspective, leisure isn't the problem; the problem lies in the "polluted" cultural environment and in the structured inequities that have made college unattainable and any hopes for earning a living wage without college seem unrealistic. For the Polanskis, these anxieties are articulated in relation to the failings of Blake and Katie's school, the disdain for what they see as others' determination to secure their own economic foothold at the expense of all else, and their sense that traditional religious values can provide a better societal environment than what they see as the dominant culture's emphasis on individual empowerment.

Whereas Blake and Katie might be able to pursue higher education in the future, other families see such opportunities as almost completely beyond their grasp. Digital, mobile, and traditional media play a role in how these families navigate what they see as their children's experiences with risk, as is the case in the story of the Cruz family.

More Media, More Risks: Judy and Dave Cruz

Judy Cruz, a Latina single parent who lives with her youngest child in subsidized housing, describes her fifteen-year-old son, Dave, as "very intelligent" and with a taste for the finer things in life.[32] As such, she has high hopes that he might make a decent living one day. He has been thinking about joining the Marines or the Air Force so that he can earn a college degree and pursue his dream of becoming a computer game developer.

Dave's father died when he was much younger, and as a single-parent family living on Judy's meager disability payments, the Cruzes doesn't have much money for leisure activities or special programs that can help Dave pursue his dreams. But Judy doesn't necessarily see this as a problem: "If you just hang out with your son or daughter, or you watch TV with them, just do normal things with them, talk with them, go for walks . . . that's what's remembered the most," she says. Like the Polanskis and the Grantmans, Judy Cruz wants to ensure that Dave grows up in a home in which he feels loved and cared for. Like Avis Grantman, Judy doesn't express a great deal of anxiety about Dave's extensive media use; instead, she is glad that Dave chooses to do things in the house that involve media, since that means that he isn't choosing to do something else, like the irresponsible and excessive drinking she says some of his friends are known to do. "In a way I kind of programmed him to sit here instead of being over there all negative," she says, adding that she also avoids alcohol so as to provide him with a positive role model.

Dave Cruz is an avid game player and aspires to be a game designer someday. Judy encourages this interest. As they say in an interview:

> JUDY: He knows a lot about them. I was explaining to him that that would be a good field for him to get into.
> DAVE: I love computers.
> INTERVIEWER: Where did you learn so much about them?
> DAVE: Just people. My friends, mostly. I would usually go down to their house and they would have games like Doom and all them other games that I like.

Dave likes to download and play games "all day." He first started learning how to create computer games from a friend when he was nine years old, although it sounds like he and this friend have done more playing than creating. They continue to hang out and play games together quite a bit, as Dave shares enthusiastically: "[My friend] sits there 24/7 and just stays there [in front of the screen]. All summer that's all he did. He can just type eighty words a minute. He's real quick. He's fast on the computer. He wants to develop his own games."

But had his friend actually created his own games or taught Dave how to do it? Well, his friend is working on it, Dave says. And so is Dave; or at least, he says, he *could* be working on it, as there are computer classes offered in his high school, which has a high proportion of low-income students. But those classes are "boring," in his view, mostly focused on developing keyboarding skills and typing up essays. Dave got in trouble when the classroom monitors found that he was trying to download information about games or downloading the games themselves. "I'd be bored half the time and then I would just go and play putt-putt golf online. All they teach is how to type," he complains. "I want to learn how to do other stuff."

Finding out how to do "other stuff" isn't always easy because their lower-income neighborhood is "behind the times," as Judy says, although Dave is not very interested in after-school activities, anyway. "I would get too bored in after-school activities," he says.

But isn't he bored sitting at home? the interviewer asks him. He isn't, he replies, because he can always watch television. When the interviewer asks if he's ever looked into some of the courses that might teach him game design, he replies, "I haven't had the time." Self-motivation doesn't seem to be Dave's strong suit, although it's also easy to see a disconnect between his stated interest in computer game development and the lack of people in his social network who might support the cultivation of his interest beyond game playing.[33]

Whereas parents like the Weltons might consider it helpful to have filtering software to monitor online activities, Judy Cruz has a different take. "We're monitored on everything we do, we're watched," she says. "Now they're going to come out with these little gadgets where people can use their phones to see where you are. . . . There's no more privacy anymore, and that's very frustrating." Apparently Judy feels Dave deserves to have some privacy. But Judy Cruz also feels that the amount of fantasy in the games her son likes to play could be a problem. "They're presenting fantasy," she says. "That doesn't help them with their vocabulary or their expectations. They use slang words all the time and I think that has a lot to do with computers," she adds.

Dave Cruz knows that he wants to do something with his life that will please both him and his mother. But even at fifteen, there are signs that he will have a difficult time overcoming his lack of interest in school and his inability to find people in his social network who can help him.[34] Like many less advantaged single parents, Judy Cruz is frequently exhausted. Her debilitating illness keeps her in the house most days; she "likes to keep to herself" anyway, as she explains.

The Nelson and Welton families would probably view digital media as one more obstacle that was getting in the way of a better path for Dave Cruz's life, as media such as video games help reinforce a passive approach and distract from the pursuit of more productive goals. As is clear in the stories of Dave Cruz, the Polanski family, and the families introduced in chapter 3, parents worry that the options outside their homes are not likely to be clearly under their—or anyone's—supervision. Thus, the digital and mobile media that are a part of these young people's lives could be viewed as giving them something to do in a world in which there are limited constructive options and many opportunities to involve themselves in self-destructive activities. Perhaps, then, media use is a good way to prevent worse habits. In the case of Dave Cruz, heightened risk led his mother to see the benefit of *more*, not *less*, media use.

Digital media also seem to serve another purpose in the financially stretched Cruz family: game playing could lead to game design, thus enabling Dave to overcome the risks of alcoholism, gang participation, depression, and underemployment that surround him. Perhaps he is simply justifying his immersion in game playing, but Dave and his mother hold out hope that he can learn something online that can lead to what the Nelson and Welton families might call enjoyable or rewarding career choices later. It is clear, however, that what is lacking to some extent is a network that could help Dave establish linkages between his passions and the skills and credentials that would be necessary for him to pursue them.

Dave Cruz's interest in computers and in gaming could be cultivated in important and affirming ways if he was given the opportunity to participate in a school that fostered his creativity.[35] Unfortunately for Dave, most schools in the United States have been forced to emphasize standardization, thus leaving thoughtful experiments in game design as pedagogy to select charter schools.[36] At this point, individualized learning is largely the province of school systems that can afford better student-to-teacher ratios and creative enrichment opportunities, and the school system that the Cruzes live in is not able to afford these options.[37]

The stories of the Cruz and Polanski families serve as reminders that many of the well-publicized risks related to the online realm seem less relevant to the majority of U.S. young people than the risks associated with failing schools and a shifting economic structure. What parents need more than education about the risks of the online world is a reduction in the risks related to society's structural failings. When the structures to support parents in their efforts aren't there, their jobs as parents are made significantly more difficult due to the risky environments in which their children are growing up and over which they have little control.

Conclusion

The Polanski and Cruz families have experiences that are vastly different in many ways. Yet both of these families are confronting the challenge of raising children in a risk society in ways that differ from those of the middle- and upper-middle-class Nelson and Welton families, and both are embracing an ethic of respectful connectedness. The middle- and upper-middle-class families worry that too much time spent in unproductive leisure and socializing might undermine their children's prospects for a fulfilling life, as defined in relation to enjoyable and well-compensated work. Kevin Nelson, for instance, does not question the fact that some enjoyable jobs are less lucrative than others. He also does not question the idea that work is the thing around which people should organize the enjoyment they get out of life. He doesn't consider the idea that some might seek and find fulfillment outside work rather than in work; an adult who values helping people, enjoys engaging in outdoor activities, or prefers spending as much time as possible with family might choose a job that allows him or her to pursue those interests. Digital, mobile, and traditional media, though, certainly offer the wrong kind of enjoyment or passion, in middle- and upper-middle-class parents' minds; consumption of media is believed to encourage passivity, and incessant use of mobile devices leads to too much unproductive socializing. These uses of communication technologies detract from time that could be spent in what middle- and upper-middle-class parents consider more productive pursuits. Parents like the Weltons and Nelsons are seeking a Parent App that will help them limit the time their children spend in what they consider unproductive or less valuable activities related to digital and mobile media, or that will enable them to harness these technologies to help their children achieve excellence in education.

Families like the Polanskis view middle-class families like the Weltons and Nelsons as too concerned with careers, sometimes at the expense of their relationships with family members, and too willing to let their children's right to expression mean that they can "run amok." In the would-be middle-class Polanski family, "hard work" is understood in the context of sacrifices parents make for their children, suggesting an orientation toward a family's overall best interests that is consistent with an ethic of respectful connectedness. The Polanskis view the desire to find work that is enjoyable as a luxury related to seeking pleasure, and they seem to relate this to the culturally polluted environment that they view as fostering worldviews different from their own. The Polanskis are seeking a Parent App that will inculcate a shared worldview among family members and thus reinforce family connectedness. Like the middle-class families, they too want to avoid some things related to mobile phones and the Internet, but they also seek and find in these technologies reinforcement for their ways of seeing the world and a means by which to strengthen their family connections.

The Cruz family worries less about cultural pollution or time wasting than about the risks associated with poverty and disadvantage. Thus, the Parent App they seek is perhaps less related to the technology and more related to the structured inequities they face in everyday life. In addition to concerns about relatively high dropout rates among high school students and higher-than-average rates of incarceration, Judy Cruz worries that digital and mobile media could serve as one more avenue for surveillance and control. Like the Polanskis, the Cruz family has encountered difficulties in locating schools and enrichment programs that would help them address their needs, reinforcing a sense that support comes best and most reliably from family members and close friends. To the extent that digital, mobile, and traditional media enable Judy and Dave to remain in close contact with each other and away from what they perceive as the risks of their immediate environment, these media are not sources of risk so much as they are potential mitigators of what the Cruzes perceive to be far more critical and immediate risk. Whereas the Nelsons and Weltons mitigate risk by seeing that their children are enrolled in top schools and in empowering extracurricular activities, the Polanskis and the Cruzes seek to embrace an ethic of respectful connectedness, relying upon those in their immediate circle for support and help in the face of risk.

It's important to point out that both middle-class families and less advantaged ones have found in digital, mobile, and traditional media some sources of support for their familial goals.[38] Accordingly, experts are beginning to recognize that the Internet and mobile phones may actually be *protective* of youth rather than contributing to an increase in risk.[39] After all, they can be a source of hope and enjoyment that can foster bonds of friendship, as seen with David Cruz; they can become a source of conversation that helps parents speak with their children about what they value, as observed in the Polanski family; and perhaps most important, they can provide means by which parents and young people can remain in touch through challenging times. Yet parents recognize that even with these benefits, it is their job as parents to mediate the media, which is the subject of the chapter that follows.

CHAPTER 7 | How Parents Are Mediating the Media in Middle-Class and Less Advantaged Homes

AT ELEVEN YEARS OLD, Danielle Oliver was a campaigner. Danielle often disagreed with her single mother, attempting to convince her mother to see things as she did. One of the things they disagreed about was that Danielle believed that she needed a mobile phone; her mother, Nancy, was firmly opposed to this idea. But Danielle insisted anyway, using the occasion of an interview about their household's media use to argue that she needed a mobile in order to keep in touch with her mother at all times—for instance, when her mother was at the grocery store. Nancy countered that, given her demanding schedule of work, household maintenance, and transporting two children to and from school, she actually enjoyed the fact that she could be unreachable for a while, leaving Danielle at home with her younger sibling, Adam, for an hour while she completed the grocery shopping. "If you can't get a hold of me, you can't get a hold of me," Nancy said with a shrug. Not to be deterred, Danielle whipped up what she hoped would be a frightening scenario in order to change her mother's mind:

> DANIELLE: But what if I saw a car in front of our house and the door was wide open and these guys were carrying stuff out of our house and I needed to contact you, and I didn't have time to run over to Kelsey's?
>
> NANCY: Well, Danielle, a cell phone's not going to fix that, I don't think—
>
> DANIELLE (INTERRUPTING): It is, though, Mom! It is![1]

Unfortunately for Danielle, her mother remained firm in her resolve, and Danielle did not get her own mobile phone for several more years, when she was able to buy one for herself.

Marcia Richter had been similarly hesitant about buying her two sons their own mobile phones. But as her oldest approached the age of eleven, that purchase struck her as largely inevitable. In her family's upper-middle-class neighborhood, almost every young person older than eleven had a mobile phone, and most of those were smart phones. For Marcia, a software engineer who regularly left for work before her sons left for school and who often worked long hours including weekends and evenings, mobile phones had rather quickly seemed a necessity, as they allowed her to remain in contact with her sons and husband when she wasn't at home.

Every parent or set of parents has to decide either when to purchase a mobile phone for their children or when they will allow their children to purchase the phone for themselves. Most young people now receive their first mobile by the age of twelve, but parents initially pay the bills, making it a decision that has not only social but also financial and moral dimensions.[2]

Nancy Oliver wants to delay the initial purchase for her daughter, Danielle, in part to preserve her own freedom and in part because she wants to avoid having the extra expense. Marcia Richter sees no upside to delaying the purchase of mobile phones for her sons, as she views mobile communication as another way for her to extend her mothering duties and overcome what Arlie Hochschild has termed the "time bind" of working parents: the need to manage work from home and home from work.[3] Nancy Oliver, like many other lower-income families and single parents, is faced with the same need to manage the demands of work and family, but she is finding ways of managing without paying for individual phones for herself and for Danielle. Both the Oliver and Richter families find the mobile phone useful in their lives together, but, like the families introduced in chapter 6, they had different reasons for resisting the technology initially, and they also have different reasons for why and how they manage mobiles as well as more traditional media such as television, music, games, and films in their lives together. In part, as this chapter will argue, these differences in media management relate to the distinct challenges these families and families like them face based on their work/family demands and on their economic circumstances. These differences also are evident in how parents view family relationships and the wider environment in which they find themselves.

This chapter considers how parents like Nancy Oliver and Marcia Richter seek to make decisions about digital and mobile media in their home lives. It introduces the topic of what media researchers term *parental mediation*, or how parents mediate the media in their children's lives. It considers why some parents are more vigilant in this process of parental mediation and why others seem to devote less energy and anxiety to their children's media use. The chapter reviews how different parents restrict, discuss, and use media with their older preteen and teen children. These practices are considered in relation to the different parental approaches to communication introduced in chapter 6: the ethic of respectful connectedness and the ethic of expressive empowerment. The ethic of expressive empowerment is connected with an inadvertent emphasis on children's rights and on the importance of helping young people to make their own decisions. Yet this interest in rights, as we will see, sometimes comes into conflict with the preference for restrictive approaches to media. Sometimes these conflicts are resolved as young people are encouraged to pursue their own rather than joint family media activities, as this chapter will highlight.

The would-be middle-class Conner family, who will be introduced later in this chapter, experiences some limitations that are similar to those of the Oliver family and the Grantman family from the previous chapter. They live in much closer quarters and have fewer financial resources to support extracurricular activities. These families tend to have fewer media restrictions, as well as fewer conversations about media, even though they engage in more joint family media activities. We begin with the story of the Olivers.

The Olivers and the Richters: Same Media, Different Stories

Nancy Oliver made her decision regarding her children's ownership and use of mobile phones based on what she perceived to be the family's needs, including her own need for some degree of privacy as well as the need for the family to stay within a fairly strict budget. The Olivers are a family of European American heritage who live in a three-bedroom townhouse in a suburb whose median income matches that of the larger region and whose racial/ethnic background is about 85 percent white and 15 percent Hispanic. Prior to Nancy's divorce five years earlier, the family lived in a middle-class neighborhood of single-family homes. After the divorce and the sale of their house, Nancy completed her college degree in night school and eventually obtained a job in data management for a large travel company. As she was awarded sole custody of the children, she raises Danielle and Adam on her own, and after her divorce she wanted to pay off her student loans before attempting to buy a single-family home again. They are a would-be middle-class family, as their household income was higher before the divorce, and the family's situation could improve (for example, if Nancy continues to advance in her career or if she comes to share the household expenses with another adult, and if everyone in the family remains healthy).

Marcia Richter and her husband, John, have quite different economic circumstances. They live in a homogenous neighborhood in a largely white suburb with a median income well above their region's average. Marcia and John, both of European American heritage, work as software engineers in what they describe as stressful jobs in the defense industry.[4] At seventeen and fifteen, John and Marcia's sons, Trent and Dale, are several years older than Nancy Oliver's children. Yet like the Olivers, the Richter family also find themselves negotiating new ways of relating to one another because of the introduction of the mobile phone into their lives.

Like other middle- and upper-middle-class families that embrace a communication ethic of expressive empowerment, the Richter parents articulate a great deal of concern about their children's media use and present themselves as somewhat strict parents who are conscientiously engaged in overseeing it. They want their children to know that parents have a right to go through their sons' rooms and view their online profiles. They also have a rule that forbids texting during dinner—although as John notes, "I don't know—it's such a part of their life that they feel guilty if they don't reply within seconds if someone sends them a message." John further says that although they "tried to maintain the no-texting rule at restaurants" during their frequent dinners out, interruptions still happen.

Marcia Richter, like other middle- and upper-middle-class parents interviewed for this book, finds that she often ends up in difficult situations as a result of the mobile phone. Once she called her son Trent when he was at school, thinking that she would be able to leave a message on his voice mail about transportation home after his sports activities. Instead, her son answered the phone during class. When he saw that the call was from his mother, he stood up and quickly explained to his teacher that the call was from his mother and that it was an "emergency," and the teacher allowed him to leave the classroom in order to take the call even though answering phones during class was against school policy. When he found out that his mother had called merely with transportation details, expecting to reach his voice mail, he returned to the class, thanked the teacher for allowing him to answer the phone, and told her that he was going to handle the "emergency" later. He did this, he explained to his mother afterward, so that the teacher wouldn't confiscate his phone. Once a phone is confiscated for a violation of phone rules (and having a phone turned on during class is one of those rules), one of the student's parents has to go to the school to sign a form indicating that they are retrieving it on the student's behalf. Because he didn't want his parents to have to interrupt their workday, he said, he had taken the "easier" route of, essentially, opting to lie about why he had answered his phone and received his mother's phone call.

Trent's mother, Marcia, reports this story with a great deal of ambivalence, as she clearly feels complicit in her son's lie. Yet she also indicates that being constantly available for contact by her sons is something she lives with despite its inconvenience to her during her own workday. She strives to make their calls to her "the most important thing" in her day:

> If they call me, I can walk out of my meeting or whatever to answer it, and if I can't talk to them I'll answer and say, "I'm in a meeting, I can't leave, I'll call you in five minutes" or whatever.

Marcia Richter may have felt complicit in her son's lie because she believed she had always emphasized to her sons that it is important for family members to be available to one another. However, by letting the lie stand, she is also allowing her son to consider his own rights above the rights of others and even above the rules. Just as Dale and Trent have the right to interrupt her at work for any reason, so too does Trent effectively assume that he has the right to break school rules in order to answer a phone call, and the right to decide on behalf of his parents the best way to handle this infraction (e.g., by "saving" them from the hassle of having to retrieve his phone, and perhaps from the embarrassment of not knowing the school rules about not taking phone calls at school).

I do not describe the Richters' lenience about texting or Marcia's ambivalence about her son's use of the mobile phone in school to highlight the fact that upper-middle-class parents may wish to present themselves as being stricter than they really are. Indeed, as this chapter and the ones that follow will suggest, many middle-class parents strive to be quite restrictive and definitive in the guidelines they set forth regarding the media rules in their children's lives. However, I begin with these examples to illustrate the argument laid out in the chapter 6: middle-class families like the Richters tend to approach digital, mobile, and traditional media in their children's lives through an ethic of empowerment and expressiveness. They want to support their children by helping them develop their own unique talents and perspectives, and they want to encourage their children to express themselves as a means of engendering positive relations both within the family and beyond it. And mothers like Marcia Richter sometimes are so intent on making themselves available to their children that they do not know how to respond when their children seem to believe they are entitled to special treatment from others. Marcia Richter shares some common ground with the helicopter parents Margaret Nelson discusses in her book *Parenting Out of Control: Anxious Parents in Uncertain Times.*[5] Whether intentional or not, an emphasis on the child's empowerment and on his or her self-expressiveness tends to result in a foregrounding of children's rights, sometimes resulting in a sense of entitlement emerging among middle-class children.[6] This respect for children's rights occasionally comes into conflict with parents' best intentions, as we will see in the stories presented here.

In contrast, less advantaged families like the Olivers approach digital and mobile media differently, emphasizing the rights of the family as a whole and respect for family rules. Even if Danielle Oliver had a mobile phone, she has been schooled in the importance of respecting her mother's authority (even as she also vocally tries to challenge it) and probably never would have considered breaking school rules and answering the phone during class. And if she had answered the phone, her mother would have been angered that her daughter had broken school rules and would have been surprised that her daughter had chosen to break the rules rather than allowing the message to go to voice mail, as had been her mother's intent.

In many ways, of course, the Olivers' limits to mobile phone use are guided as much by financial limits and the pressures of single-parent life as by some idealized version of what it might mean to respect family rules. But the fact remains that in a certain sense, the differing situations in which the Richters and the Olivers find themselves create differing patterns of response to the digital, mobile, and traditional media in family life. Trent Richter can leave his phone on at school and violate school rules, and that might lead to a discussion with his parents, but it doesn't result in greater restrictions, in part because he has succeeded in demonstrating that he is a capable decision maker who takes care of problems decisively and independently, and those are things that expressive and empowering parents value. Yet when he does take care of this problem, his mother feels unsure of herself, because what she values in her son's decision conflicts with her own desire to see herself and her husband as having strong parental oversight when it comes to their children's media use. Their desire to be parents who emphasize empowerment and expressiveness and who parent using discussions about good decisions has won out over their desire to be parents who restrict media use.

In contrast, Danielle Oliver can't have a phone because it doesn't fit in with her mother's view of their family's needs, effectively curtailing Danielle's rights by placing the needs of the family above those of the individual. Danielle and her mother do not discuss her desire for a mobile phone; rather, Danielle makes an argument and her mother closes down the discussion by asserting her authority in the decision not to get a phone. Nancy Oliver does not feel ambivalent about her decision to wait on the mobile phone purchase. She is the sole person responsible for managing the family's meager finances, and she also wants to protect her own right to privacy during the small amount of time she's carved out for herself while she is completing what is surely the less than personally satisfying task of grocery shopping. She restricts phone use by not allowing Danielle to have a phone, but at the same time she imposes fewer restrictions on other media than the Richters do, as her children's television viewing and game playing give her time to carry out the many responsibilities of a single working mother.

Should the Richters have insisted that Trent take responsibility for leaving his phone on during the school day? Should Nancy Oliver have made other sacrifices in order to ensure that her daughter had a way to remain in contact with her at all times? Every parent has experienced the challenge of trying to make the right decisions for the family as a whole and for the individuals within that family, and the process of making those decisions will be reviewed more fully in the next chapter. The point is that there are patterns in how parents respond to these challenges, and those patterns have to do with the parents' economic situations as well as what they take for granted as the commonsense way of responding to them.

Parental Mediation

Since the earliest days of communication research, scholars have been interested in parental efforts to mitigate negative media effects on children.[7] Experts have recommended limiting television viewing time, cautioning that parental role modeling is an important aspect of a child's socialization into media use and that media use informs children's desires for commercial products.[8] *Parental mediation* is a term that came into use in media studies as a means of recognizing that parents take an active role in managing and regulating their children's experiences with television, although today the term is used in relation to how parents regulate their children's use of the Internet and mobile phones, too.[9] Parents engage in at least four different strategies of parental mediation: *active* mediation, or talking with young people about the content they saw on television or online; *restrictive* mediation, or setting rules and regulations about children's television viewing and Internet use; *coviewing*, which generally refers to simply watching television with children; and *participatory learning*, in which children and parents learn together (or parents might learn from children), such as when playing video games or working on homework assignments online together.[10]

Researchers have found many benefits associated with parental mediation. When parents talk with their children about how violence and aggression are represented in television, film, and music, they can help to encourage their children to engage in critical thinking and can help to promote a moral compass for thinking about aggression.[11] Additionally, when teenagers hear from parents about their own interpretations of television programs, this increases the teens' ability to be skeptical about television content and to be more interested in what adults consider "good" media, such as educational television and online news.[12] In general, researchers find that there is less familial conflict and a more positive environment for children in families where conversations between parents and their children are highly valued.[13] Middle-class families like the Richters, the Weltons (from chapter 6), and the Dykstras (who will be introduced in a moment) give priority to creating warm and expressive relationships through ongoing conversations about what both parents and children think and what they value.

Researchers have also found benefits associated with restrictive mediation, which amounts to setting limits on engagement with media. Parents are encouraged to set firm rules for children regarding what media they are allowed to consume, when, and for what length of time, as this kind of boundary setting allows children to feel secure.[14] But if parents provide too much restriction, especially as children enter their adolescent years, their efforts can backfire.[15] Too much restriction can lead teens to feel hostile toward their parents, and overly restrictive expectations also seem to encourage teens to engage in more secretive behavior, making teens more likely to engage in forbidden actions, such as texting late at night or viewing forbidden content with their friends, when they are out of their parents' purview.[16] As is the case with other rules within family life, children need to accept and internalize rules about media in order to abide by them willingly.[17]

Restriction was a key strategy in many of the middle-class homes in this study. Often the mantra of media use in these homes was, as one middle-class mother exclaimed, "Schoolwork first!"[18] Middle- and upper-middle-class children, preteens, and teens lead lives of concerted cultivation that are highly structured around school and organized activities, and this also provides a form of restriction upon leisure time that might otherwise be devoted to playing video games, watching television, texting friends, or listening to music. As noted in chapter 6, upper-income parents also were likely to use a timer or programs such as Microsoft's Family Safety to limit screen and gaming time.

Mothers, more-educated parents, higher-income parents, and parents of younger children engage in more parental mediation strategies than fathers, less-educated parents, lower-income parents, and parents of older children.[19] Most parents in the United States say that their preferred parental mediation strategy involves *talk*: they believe that talking with their children about their media use is more effective than either simply consuming media along with them or restricting media use through a firm set of rules. (As a comparison, in the Netherlands, more parents seem to prefer simply consuming media together.)[20]

Despite parents' stated preference for talking with their children about media, however, experts remain surprised how little of such talk actually seems to go on in U.S. families.[21] Previous research offers several clues as to why there might be less talk about media among parents and children than experts might expect or recommend. For one thing, parents often underestimate the influence of media on their children when compared with how they estimate the influence of the media on other people's children. This is called the "third-person effect" and might be stated as, "I'm too smart to let the media affect me, and my child is too smart to be affected, but that third person—who is someone else's child—is definitely more vulnerable to the media's effects than we are."[22] A parent may view her own child as more mature than most and may be overconfident in that child's ability to make her own rules regarding how much media to interact with and for how long, or the parent may overestimate the child's ability to discern for herself the messages from either television or the Internet.[23] Some families don't engage in such talk about media for other reasons. Some, such as the Weltons (chapter 6), consider media use to be fairly inconsequential. Texting, mobile phone use, television viewing, music listening, or video game playing does not warrant discussion unless some problem arises. Other families simply do not have much time for such talk. This is especially true among would-be middle-class and less advantaged families in which parents work in jobs that offer less autonomy than, say, Marcia Richter's job, which allowed her to take personal mobile calls that interrupted her work. Parents with heavier or less flexible work schedules may be less available for discussions and less capable of enforcing restrictions than middle-class parents, and research suggests that the amount of time young people spend alone with media increases as parents' availability decreases.[24]

In the next section, we consider two families that discuss why talk—what researchers term *active mediation of the media*—is so important to them, relating these values to the ethic of expressive empowerment that seems to characterize the ethos of life in the middle, upper-middle, and wealthy classes.

Talking About and Restricting Media in the Dykstra Family

"We're big on communication," Janice Dykstra replies when asked how she and her husband would describe themselves as parents. Janice notes that she and her husband, Mark, who are both of European American heritage, don't try to "hide" the world from their two teenage daughters, Kirsty and Laurel, ages sixteen and eighteen.

"My parents weren't like that," Mark adds, noting that whereas his parents tried to protect him from the world, he strives to give his daughters "lots of freedom." In order to present himself as responsible and not permissive, he quickly adds, "But you can't let them make fatal errors."[25] As is the case with many middle-class young people, the "freedoms" that the Dykstra girls experience are actually fairly constrained by their full schedules of sports, homework, music, and church-related activities.

The Dykstra family lives in a large suburban area consisting of single-family homes. Half of the households in their neighborhood have children under the age of eighteen. It is an extremely homogenous area—almost 95 percent of the area's residents are of European American heritage—located ten miles from a diverse urban center. The median family income in the area places this community squarely in the upper-middle-class. A small number of homes in the area are located within an exclusive gated community, less than 2 percent of households are living in poverty, and most families have household incomes in the six figures.

Laurel and Kirsty Dykstra agree with their parents that theirs is a family that loves to talk about their feelings and experiences. Even though both parents work and both girls have sports activities after school, the family has dinner together almost every night. Usually "none of us want to make dinner, so we go out to eat a lot," Laurel explains. Over dinner, they like to talk about school and politics, and they also talk about their aspirations for the future. Laurel, who is headed to college next fall, notes that she loves sports and wants to combine that with her interest in financial analysis. Her father says that many of the conversations he has had with his two daughters have related to their shared love of alternative rock music. Mark, who was a teen himself in the late 1980s, continues to enjoy the music of the Replacements and the Violent Femmes and seeks out music by those groups' early influences, such as the Velvet Underground. Admitting that he doesn't always appreciate his daughters' love of Pink and Lady Gaga, he shrugs and says, "But that's okay," as he believes that his daughters have a right to their own opinions and is glad that they readily share them with him. He is not interested in trying to tell his daughters what "good" music is, and doesn't see that as part of his parental role or responsibility.

The family does not have many rules regarding media use, although, like the Richters, the daughters are not allowed to text during dinner. "They sometimes still use them," Janice admits, "and they say, 'Suzie just texted about this, can I text her back?'" However, Janice adds quickly, as if to assure the interviewer that they are conscientious overseers of their children's media use, "They don't have computers in their rooms. Or TVs."

Kirsty and Laurel text their mother several times each day, including when they are finished with school and are on the way to their extracurricular activities and when they are heading home. Like Marcia Richter's sons, both of the Dykstra daughters text to ask questions or to share information about schedules, plans, transportation, and purchases, and Laurel often texts her mother for both sisters when they are together. When asked if they'd ever had any trouble with the girls' use of their phones, Mark replies:

> They got in trouble for instant messaging once. Some stuff they shouldn't have been doing. They have the Facebook pages, too. We tell them to be smart about it. That employers and others can see these things. When they put stuff on the Web it is available to the world.

Rather than employing rules about how and when they can use their phones, Mark and Janice prefer to emphasize that their daughters are trusted to make good decisions about their mobile phone use, just as they have been encouraged to make good decisions in other areas of their lives. Mark is especially concerned that the girls understand that their privacy is at stake, and he says that he encourages them to be vigilant about whom they allow to access their social network profiles and other online materials. As was discussed in the previous chapter, Mark's concern about exposure to risks online—particularly as such risks might relate to one's future—is common among middle- and upper-middle-class families.

But even though Mark sounds knowledgeable about the online environment, Laurel and Kirsty point out that they had to teach their parents how to text and how to lock their laptops. In a separate interview, Laurel also admits that she has "manipulated" her parents by texting them after she knew they would be asleep so that later she could say, "Well, I texted you, but you never replied." Like Trent Richter, Laurel has learned how to abide by the rules, but she has also learned how to claim the right to do what she wants: she just needs to establish a pretense that she did act responsibly, and then she can suggest that perhaps her parents had been less attentive than they could have been. Sometimes that confuses the issue enough that her parents won't challenge her decision to bend their rules. Kirsty and Laurel's mother, like Marcia Richter, seems to be responsive to the idea that mothers should be responsible for and attentive to their children's needs at all times, and that technology should be used to facilitate this.[26]

Laurel has discouraged her mother from getting a Facebook account and has told her mother that she would not accept a friend request from her if she did join Facebook. Like many other middle- and upper-middle-class young people (and especially young women), Laurel Dykstra thinks of Facebook as a place that is rightfully populated by young people, not by parents, and she believes that she has a right to this online space apart from adult supervision.[27]

When asked what kinds of media were a part of their own lives growing up, both Mark and Janice Dykstra note that they grew up in homes where they read the newspaper and discussed it with their parents. "We were very aware of what was going on the world," Janice says, a tradition that she strives to continue as she often engages her daughters in discussions of local and national politics. The older daughter, Laurel, continues that tradition, claiming to read the daily newspaper online every morning. Her decision to read the news is not motivated by a desire to be "aware" so much as it is consistent with the need that she feels to be a good student. She is expected to read it, she says, because her economics teacher often has current-events quizzes and discusses news events at the beginning of class each day. Thus, her media practices relate to her aspirations for the future and to her vision of herself (and her parents' vision of her) as someone working toward self-empowerment.

The Dykstra parents do not talk much about restrictions on media use, but they do restrict media indirectly by not allowing their daughters to have phones or laptops in their bedrooms and keeping their schedules filled with activities. But even as Mark and Janice emphasize how important it is to talk about media and other choices, the daughters in the family find many ways to use media to distinguish themselves from their parents and create a space apart for themselves, as illustrated in Laurel's use of texting to imply that perhaps her mother was not as available as she could be or in her restriction of her mother's ability to contact her through Facebook.

Talking About and Restricting Media (or Not) in Would-Be Middle-Class and Less Advantaged Households

Unlike the mini-mansions and expansive Tribeca apartments of middle- and upper-middle-class families, the majority of U.S. families, who are in less privileged economic situations, live in smaller homes, often with more people sharing the space and with fewer spaces for privacy. Children in lower-income households are also more likely to share technologies such as mobile phones and laptops.[28] Therefore, when discussing how parents restrict or talk with their children about media use, explanations are often framed in relation to the whole family, as noted in the stories of Avis Grantman and Nina Lane (chapter 6) and Nancy and Danielle Oliver. When asked about restrictions on television viewing, for instance, Jill Allen, a single mother of two children, remarks that if she doesn't like something, "I just say we can't watch that and we watch something else," a recognition of the fact that if the children want to watch television, they will be doing it in the apartment's living room. That is where the family's one working television is located, and if one of her children is in that room, Jill is likely to be in the room as well or in the small kitchen from which the living room's television can be easily observed.[29]

Thirteen-year-old Jeremy Conner does have a game system, television, and DVD player in his room, a setup similar to the media-rich homes of upper-middle-class families. And like Marcia Richter, his mother, Roxanne, seems so interested in respecting his rights that she lets him have a great deal of leeway with his media choices. Despite these similarities, the Conners' experiences with digital and mobile media are quite different from those of the middle-class Dykstra and Richter families.

Jeremy and Roxanne Conner live in a home situation that is in some ways similar to that of the Oliver family's. Roxanne owns a small two-bedroom house in a quiet suburban neighborhood where Jeremy, a some-what reticent teen, often practices his skateboarding techniques. They have no extended family in the area and therefore have few resources to rely upon for help with child supervision. Their financial situation is also similar to that of Nancy Oliver and Avis Grantman, as Roxanne, a college graduate, has a low-paying on-and-off-again job as a graphic designer; her ex-husband pays child support, and her occasional live-in boyfriend, who works full-time in sales, helps her out with food expenses.[30]

Like Nancy Oliver, Roxanne Connor put off the purchase of a mobile phone for her son, Jeremy. Yet once Roxanne finally got Jeremy a mobile phone earlier in the year, she was surprised by how much relief it gave her. As she recounts: "The cell phone has been a tremendous help because then he's not just out and I'm wondering where he is," she says. It has proven especially important in the after-school hours, when she is at work and he no longer needs to attend an after-care program because he is old enough to be on his own.

Roxanne and Jeremy own a computer that is five years old, but when-ever possible, they use her boyfriend's newer laptop for their computer needs. Roxanne has regular use of a computer with Internet access in her workplace, and her boyfriend usually doesn't need his laptop in the even-ings and on weekends, so during those times Jeremy frequently uses the laptop to play games and download music. In addition to the older com-puter and the newer laptop, Jeremy has a cell phone with a basic service plan, a PlayStation 2, and a TV with a DVD player in his bedroom, along with a large collection of skateboarding DVDs that he watches regularly. When asked about their media policies, Roxanne says,

> Well, initially, and ideally, you know, there's no TV until homework is fin-ished. That's the policy. But Jeremy bucks the policy all the time, and—oh, the arguing about it! Finally I say, "Okay! Just turn it down low, get your homework done!"

Jeremy's mother laughs, explaining how he wears her down until they reach the "compromise" he had favored to begin with. Roxanne expresses concern about the media environment but also is not terribly uptight about it. Part of the reason for this is pragmatic: like Nancy Oliver, Avis Grantman, and other less advantaged parents, she has limited means to offer alternatives. Part of it also may be because she puts less trust than the middle-class Dykstras and

Richters do in the idea that traditional education and extracurricular activities can increase Jeremy's life chances. School is important, but it is not viewed as a route to a more financially secure future. After all, there is little evidence in their immediate social circle that enthusiastic participation in school, sports, and community activities leads to outcomes that are different or better than the home-based leisure alternatives he prefers.

Like Marcia and John Richter, Roxanne Conner tries to be diligent in her oversight of the games Jeremy plays and the programs he watches. But like Nancy Oliver, Roxanne relates Jeremy's movie, television viewing, game playing, and cell phone use to the issue of child care and supervision:

> I'm surprised at, I guess, how lenient I am about the whole media thing knowing that when he was little, I thought, "Oh, I'm *certainly* not going to park him in front of the TV, I'm *never* going to be one of those parents." And it's just—[*She shrugs.*] There aren't many other options.

When Jeremy spends his leisure time with media, she believes that he isn't doing something negative or self-destructive. Plus his engagement with media enables her to fill a need she has for time for herself. Her reasoning that her lenience is related to her basic belief that she does not want to "shelter" Jeremy from the world sounds in some ways similar to Mark Dykstra's desire to raise his daughters in a manner less protective than his parents used with him. Roxanne has found that her views are similar to those held by the parents of Jeremy's friends: "We sort of, just let the world expose itself, media-wise, to our kids. But we talk to them about it a lot and we do pay attention to what they're doing." From Jeremy's perspective, such conversations aren't very common or particularly consequential. At any rate, Roxanne says, the "expert advice" on media that suggests that parents should know all about their children's media use is unrealistic and overly onerous:

> There is so much in the news about parents not knowing what their kids are playing or doing and all that. You can't possibly sit down and play these games with the kids and you know, know how they work or how much blood and gore because it's just— First of all, it's not interesting to me at all. And they're so friggin' good at it! It's not fun!

She laughs, and then, more seriously, she adds, "But you know, still you look and you know what they're doing and what they're renting." Roxanne may be justifying her lax media restrictions in relation to her own dislike for the games and her lack of time, but she also has few options given the demands on her time as a single working parent. She is implicitly critical of overparenting or helicopter parenting, and she sees "expert advice" as perhaps lending support to overparenting.

In a separate interview when Jeremy isn't present, Roxanne confesses that she isn't especially concerned about the sex or even the violence that Jeremy might encounter in the media. What concerns her is representations that are disrespectful—"if it's demeaning to women, or men even," she says. In terms of the violence, she argues, "I think it's more important to talk about what he's seeing rather than trying to keep it turned off all the time." She doesn't think that watching violent media will cause him to be violent, because she's observed that many of the games he likes to play look very violent to her and yet "I think he's a normal boy, he and his friends, they're like banging on each other. But he loves babies and kittens, you know," she says, smiling, recognizing that Jeremy probably would rather have died than have that statement repeated to his friends. What is most important, according to Roxanne, is that children are surrounded by "friendship, love, caring, and compassion." She prefers to emphasize connectedness in the present day, and, like Avis Grantman, she views television, music, movies, and games as providing opportunities for her to talk with Jeremy about what she values and what she hopes that he will value, too.

Roxanne, continuing on the topic of media policies, notes that in the past she has cut back on his computer time as a form of punishment for infractions. They have also talked about her wish that he not view pornography online, she says, and Jeremy, with some embarrassment about the topic, adamantly says that he doesn't go to sites like that. Taking this opportunity to express her thoughts directly, Roxanne turns to her son and says, "Hopefully you know, Jeremy, that if I ever see or have evidence that you're doing anything like that, then it all stops. You know, because it's a trust that you will, I hope, honor."

"I know, I know, I *know*, Mom!" Jeremy interrupts with increasing fervor and a red face.

Yet it does seem that Jeremy is not left entirely to self-monitoring. "I mean, sometimes he'll be watching something and I'll just say, 'Jeremy, that's disgusting, turn it off, change it,'" Roxanne notes.

Roxanne presents herself as a parent with a great interest in discussing issues and values with her son, much like the middle-class Richter and Dykstra families. Yet like the Olivers and unlike either the Richters or the

Dykstras, the Conners have a fairly small living space, making it relatively easy for Roxanne to know what Jeremy is watching, playing, or using the phone for when they are both in the house together, as they are on most evenings and weekends. It is therefore easier for Roxanne to demand an immediate change in behavior when they are together, but because they often aren't, she relies on the strategies of reinforcing her right to make it "all stop" if she learns of media consumption that does not meet her approval. Moreover, Jeremy's rights and even his ability to make good decisions are constrained within what his mother has established as acceptable boundaries. In this sense, Roxanne is like other would-be middle-class parents who rely on establishing a strong ethic of respect for parental wishes and prioritizing the good of the family over the desires of the individual. If Jeremy chooses, in his media consumption, to go against what his mother expresses as her preferences, they will not have a discussion about good decision making; he will be punished and his media privileges will be taken away. In this sense, parental authority over media use is clearer in a household like the Conners' than it is in either the Dykstra or the Richter household, despite the fact that middle-class families express more concern about media influences and institute more restrictions than do would-be middle-class families like the Conners. This is consistent with the style of parenting that sociologist Margaret Nelson equates with lower-income families and terms *parenting with limits*.[31]

For the most part, Roxanne sees herself as flexible and interested in Jeremy's media choices rather than judgmental, authoritarian, or strict. But then Roxanne reflects on a time when another mother called into question Roxanne's non-authoritarian approach. "I was telling a friend about taking Jeremy and his buddies to see [an R-rated] movie and my friend, who has a son that's two years older than Jeremy, turned to me with a straight face and said, 'Shame on you!' And she wasn't teasing me," Roxanne says. Roxanne was initially taken aback that another mother would challenge her right to make a decision regarding what films her son should be able to watch. "[But] I just have to laugh about that," Roxanne continues after describing this embarrassing moment. "I'm more lenient. And maybe I should be more—"

"No, you shouldn't," Jeremy interjects. Jeremy then makes a connection between what he perceives as his mother's relatively strict policies about media use with what he considers to be her strict approach to parenting in general. He complains about the fact that when he wants to invite a friend over, his mother insists on calling the friend's parents, or worse, she rejects his plan by noting that she doesn't know the friend's parents. "That's the way we are," says Jeremy's mother with a shrug, seeming quite comfortable asserting parental authority.

Interestingly, in the story about the mother who disapproved of letting a thirteen-year-old watch an R-rated film, Roxanne compares herself to a mother who emphasizes parental authority even more than she does. She is not comparing herself to mothers like Marcia Richter, who probably would express discomfort about the film but might be equally uncomfortable having to decide whether and how to forbid her sons from seeing it.

Like the children in the comfortably middle-class (or upper-middle-class) Dykstra and Richter families, Jeremy Conner has some restrictions on his media use. Also like the Dykstra and Richter families, in which texting during dinner is not allowed although it sometimes happens, Roxanne Conner sometimes allows Jeremy to indulge his media preferences despite her reservations. She even lets him watch television while completing his homework, just as some middle-class families allow their children to use instant messaging or texting while completing their homework. The rules about media use in the Conner family are similarly contingent on the rules about homework: as long as the homework is completed and there is no evidence of problems, there is little need felt for restriction, and self-monitoring is considered sufficient.

The Phone as a Tether

Marcia Richter and Janice Dykstra, much like Tammy Welton and Freda Nelson (chapter 6), seem to be mothers who want to devote themselves, and an inordinate amount of their time, to their children. They are part of a wider trend that sociologist Margaret Nelson terms *hyper-involved parenting*, reflected in the fact that the amount of time mothers spend on child care activities has risen steadily since 1965, even as more women have entered the workforce full-time.[32] Their use of technologies reflects this desire to remain in constant contact with their children, as each mother discusses the importance she places on receiving updates from children via text or phone call.[33] But the phone also becomes a way for children to assert their own rights, as witnessed in the story of Trent Richter's bending of school rules and Laurel Dykstra's bending of her parents' rules. Neither of these young people was punished for these acts, perhaps because they were able to play on their mothers' guilt as it related to an unspoken assumption that mothers should be always available to their children.

Like the young people in the Richter and Dykstra households, Jeremy Conner is also expected to utilize his mobile phone to keep his mother up to date on transportation, scheduling, and other details of daily life. But in the Conner household, there is no expectation that Roxanne should be always available to Jeremy; indeed, given her work demands, such availability is not possible. Having a mobile phone means that Roxanne can expect to be able to contact Jeremy when neither of them is at home; she feels that she does not have to be anxious about whether he is all right. In some ways, the use of the mobile phone as a "tether" to her provides a justification for not seeking after-school activities for Jeremy (which they would be hard pressed to afford), as making such arrangements as a single parent always involves extra labor on her part.[34] In this sense, the mobile phone, which provides a certain freedom for Jeremy to use his leisure time as he wishes, actually constrains him to spend time in settings and with people with whom he is already familiar. Unlike the Dykstra and Richter children, Jeremy has few activities other than the ones that he can arrange for himself, which inadvertently reinforces his small and somewhat closed social network of friends and acquaintances.

Alone Together and Together Alone: Coviewing and Participatory Learning

Neither the Dykstras nor the Conners could recall a single time when they engaged in participatory learning with media, defined as a time in which parents and children either played games together or somehow used digital technologies to learn something new together. However, other studies are demonstrating that parents are finding ways to develop meaningful interactions with their children through playing games and going online together, although joint sibling play is the more common joint mediated activity.[35] Right now, it seems that participatory learning may be occurring most frequently among families where one parent is involved in the information and technology industry, but research into this issue is ongoing.[36] Mobile apps and educational products such as Leapfrog offer opportunities for parents to spend time together, although little research yet demonstrates how often parents and children engage in these activities together, or how such time use compares to time spent in joint activities such as traditional book reading. The sales of family-friendly Wii games may be suggestive, but there is little evidence as of yet that these activities become focal points that bring together families that would not already be spending time together in other joint activities.[37] Still, research is finding that some families in the information technology sector are using specialized technologies that enable family members who are separated by distance to work together on joint projects, thus making it easier for children of divorced or two-parent households to connect with one another and do things together using tools of digital and mobile media.[38] Whether digital media platforms that encourage interaction will become a regular part of family life in the future is yet to be seen.

As noted earlier, Roxanne Conner expresses little interest in playing games with her son, although like the Grantmans, the Conners do spend time in their small living room watching television programs and films together. Due to the limits of time and finances, the Conners, like many would-be middle-class and less advantaged families, are usually in their own home when they are not at work or at school. In contrast, the Dykstras are rarely all at home together, and when they are, they only rarely watch television together in one room, apart from the occasional family movie night.[39]

In some ways, despite the large amounts of time that they spend together at sporting and church events, the Dykstra family's experiences with digital, mobile, and traditional media, like their practice of taking turns observing one another's participation in sports, is more individual. They do not participate together in activities so much as participate separately and sometimes stand on the sidelines for one another.

The Dykstra family's practice of engaging in separate media experiences, what Sherry Turkle labels the experience of being "alone together" in the home, is not unusual among middle-class families in the United States.[40] Whereas the amount of time U.S. families devote to television viewing has remained fairly stable across several decades, what has changed among middle-class families can be described in relation to what Jane Brown and her colleagues term the rise of "teenage bedroom culture."[41] Today, middle-class teens like the Dykstra girls and Richter boys live in what Sonia Livingstone describes as "media-rich environments," in which they may be participating in a text message thread, talking on a mobile phone, watching a television program, and downloading music, all while seated in front of a laptop computer doing schoolwork. Significantly, these activities increasingly take place in cars as teens travel between activities, or in teens' bedrooms rather than in the more public household spaces of living rooms or kitchens.[42] Middle- and upper-middle-class teens may be devoting more concentrated time to such activities, engaging in them in the rare hours when they are not involved in school or in extracurricular activities. And these media-rich environments that form a teen domain apart from parent life likely contribute to an environment in which middle-class young people feel that they have the right to engage in leisure and in self-expression as they please once they have met the expectations of empowerment set forth by their parents and the other adults in their lives. In contrast, with the rise in the number of single-parent families with meager options outside the home, less advantaged families may be spending more time together alone. In both cases, digital and mobile media seem to be supporting isolation: in the case of less advantaged families, isolation from larger communities, and in the case of more advantaged families, isolation in the form of enhanced individualism.

Conclusions

In the Dykstra and Richter families, media restrictions have to do with rules about time use and the challenge of fitting media use into a highly structured schedule. In contrast, Jeremy Conner's restrictions have more to do with his family's finances, their situation as a fairly isolated single-parent family, and his mother's desire to be an authoritative parent who is not as controlling as the helicopter parents from which she wishes to distinguish herself. Their talk about media is also somewhat different. While families like the Dykstras emphasize the importance of having their teens make good decisions about media so as to avoid unwanted consequences— recall Mark Dykstra's concern that a future employer might see inappropriate materials on a Facebook page—Roxanne Conner emphasizes that Jeremy needs to respect her views of what is appropriate, and pornography and demeaning depictions of women are not. Talk about media in the Conner home is less in relation to ideas and consequences of actions (such as the discussions about news in the Dykstra family) and more in relation to parental concerns about representations of violence, "blood and gore," sex, and similar topics.

Whereas talk seems to be related to the desire of the middle- and upper-middle-class mothers Marcia Richter and Janice Dykstra to be continuously available to their children for listening, encouragement, or guided supervision, talk with Roxanne Conner is about content and intended to reinforce what Roxanne hopes are her family's shared values. Jeremy is expected to know that if he views porn, which is programming beyond the bounds of acceptability according to Roxanne, then his media privileges will be curtailed. In contrast, the young women in the Dykstra family are encouraged to consider possible consequences outside of family life that come about as a result of bad decisions. In contrast to discussions about ideas and about possible negative consequences of one's actions that are part of an ethic of expressive empowerment, Roxanne, living out an ethic of respectful connectedness, wants Jeremy to feel enveloped in a loving and compassionate setting that will influence the decisions he makes. She also wants to be part of a community that shares her views of the world and of child rearing, and therefore expresses a sense of communal responsibility. Jeremy Conner's mother feels comfortable bending the rules regarding Jeremy's media use, but if he took it upon himself to decide not to follow school rules, as Trent Richter had, Roxanne might enforce a punishment in the form of restricted media use, rather than engage in a discussion of what happened, when, and why. In the Conner family, as is true in many less financially stable families who participated in this study, the rights of the individual are subsumed to the rights of the larger group, whether that's the family or the school.

Whereas the Dykstra and Richter families approach the task of mediating the media through an ethic that emphasizes empowerment and expressiveness, the Conner and Oliver families approach digital, mobile, and traditional media through an ethic of respectful connectedness, placing media use in the larger context of what is expected of a family member in terms of respect for parents' views and the importance of maintaining strong familial bonds by honoring family wishes over those of individual family members. Restrictive parental mediation, as well as active mediation or talk about media uses, takes place in relation to these overarching perspectives, which in turn are shaped by their lived realities and lived constraints. Parents with these differing approaches to communication and to family goals are not likely to adopt the same one-size-fits-all approach to mediating the media. Even if most parents are in agreement that restriction is good and talk about media use with children is better, these practices look quite different as parents consider what that talk is supposed to accomplish and how restriction is related to parental authority.

There are some new issues that emerge for parents in today's media environment, as suggested in the stories in this chapter. What digital and mobile media use seems to suggest is that technologies can be used to intensify what are already hyperintensive parenting practices. Middle- and upper-middle-class mothers who are concerned about providing their children with all the possible support they could need to become expressive and empowered adults may be utilizing digital and mobile media, and in particular mobile phones and social network sites, to monitor, care for, communicate with, and perhaps even spy on their children. This isn't going unnoticed by their children, as evidenced in Laurel Dykstra's reservations about her mother's interest in Facebook, and it's a topic that will surface again in this book.

Another new issue is that whereas digital and mobile media are making certain kinds of parent-child interaction possible through participatory learning, there is little evidence yet that this is a direction that will become important in the lives of families in the future. It's an approach that holds a great deal of promise, but because participatory learning presumes both time for joint activities and either the predisposition or skill required to engage in digital media together, it is difficult to see if it will be found appealing among parents other than those who are already hyperinvolved in their children's lives.

Restricting media, discussing it, and engaging in coviewing or media enhanced participatory learning with their children are not events that occur after parents have conducted an intentional evaluation of the possible negative or positive cognitive outcomes their children may experience because of media exposure. Parental decision making is much less conscious or rational than that and is rooted to a much greater extent in the goal of promoting well-being among family members. Sometimes parents did make intentional decisions about media use, of course. But parents seemed to be conscious of this decision making only when they felt the need to go against what they saw as the taken-for-granted approach of their friends and family members.

In many cases, parents like those in this chapter approached media use in a *reactive* mode: media only became an issue when a rule, whether an implicit or explicit one, was broken, bent, or challenged. For the most part, parental practices were connected to what seemed to be the most obvious route that presented itself in the moment rather than the most rational and well-thought-out route. Parental choices were shaped by the cultural milieu in which they lived, and thus whether they happened to live in a social environment that emphasized respectful connectedness or one that stressed expressive empowerment made a significant difference in what they chose to do in any given circumstance.

| Media Rich and Time Poor

*The Emotion Work of Parenting
in a Digital Age*

WHEN MELANIE BOUGHT HER preteen son, Sam, a PlayStation for Christmas, she suddenly found herself faced with several new problems in her middle-class home.[1] Although eleven-year-old Sam had been thrilled and surprised with the purchase, Melanie, a single mother of Latina and European American heritage who worked full-time, said that she soon grew weary of the fact that any request for him to stop playing seemed to escalate until she found herself screaming. "Every time I try to encourage him to do something else, he seems to act as if I'm punishing him," she said with frustration. Later, it was Sam's turn to experience frustration. When his younger sister expressed interest in the PlayStation, Melanie decided that nine-year-old Connie, too, should have some games that were her own and that she should have equal time on the gaming system. "Sam was spending too much time on it anyway," Melanie reasoned. The system was in the main room next to the kitchen, and as that room contained both the family's one computer and their one television hooked to the gaming system, it was the room to which both Sam and Connie naturally gravitated after school and after dinner.

Despite the heightened tensions the gaming system introduced for her family, Melanie recognized that playing had soon become a regular part of the family's routine. When she, Sam, and Connie were in their home, Melanie was usually making dinner, cleaning the house, doing work related to her job, or helping one of her children with homework. The PlayStation often provided Sam and Connie with something do to so that she could get things done.[2]

Still, Melanie almost constantly engaged in some kind of cost/benefit analysis involving the use of communication technologies in their home. She did not like them to use the PlayStation, television, and computer as much as they did. She also believed that it was worthwhile for Sam and Connie to help her clean the house and prepare food, although, as she said, this always involved more effort on her part than she wished. After all, Sam and Connie would much prefer to unwind in front of the television or gaming system rather than help her with the domestic work. So each afternoon and evening she weighed their media choices based on whether she felt she had enough energy to engage them in getting dinner ready or getting the house cleaned up. If she didn't have the patience for the possible struggle and supervision required, she switched on her favorite Internet radio station and got to the work of cleaning or preparing the meal, while the PlayStation, computer, and television kept Sam and Connie occupied. Such a decision might gain her the solitude she needed, but cost her in terms of guilty feelings about relying on entertainment media instead of engaging her growing children in household chores. Melanie therefore engaged in a kind of *emotion work* when it came to decisions about the communication technologies she and her children utilized. She thought she should feel bad about what she considered to be their excessive use of PlayStation and television, but she had other concerns as well; she needed to clean and make dinner, and she needed to decide whether she would feel better about herself as a parent if she got her preteen children to help around the house or if, due to her tiredness from her own work situation, her impatience coupled with their resistance would result in greater stress, frustration, and ultimately an unpleasant experience for them all.

Melanie and her family live in and express an ethic of expressive empowerment. Melanie wants to raise her children to be self-confident and self-reliant, and she tries to make decisions about how they will spend their time based on her belief that while it's important for children to have fun, it's also important that they learn to spend their time wisely.

This chapter considers the emotion work that parents perform as they make decisions regarding how they will regulate, restrict, or utilize digital, mobile, and traditional media in relation to their familial goals, and how they feel about managing these various tasks. I use the term "emotion work," following sociologist Arlie Hochschild, as a way to describe the emotion management that takes place in the household as parents (and in particular mothers) balance their own emotional needs with those of their children and spouses in the context of their busy lives together.[3] Parents like Melanie make decisions about regulating and overseeing media in relation to many factors such as the pressures of balancing work and family, the needs of their children, the taken-for-granted ways of being a "good parent" that are supported among their family and friends, and their own emotional state. We will explore what happens when parents adopt a particular approach to media as a way of enacting what they feel is a more balanced approach between work and parenting demands but which sets them at odds with many people in their social circles. Through the stories of the Blayne-Gallagher and Fallon families, this chapter explores how parents make these decisions and suggests a model for rethinking what in the previous chapter was termed "parental mediation." We begin with the reason many parents, like Melanie, feel caught in a bind with regard to the demands of work and parenting. They may be media rich, but they feel time poor.

U.S. Families and the Time Crunch

Numerous studies have documented the time crunch happening across the economic spectrum in today's families with children.[4] A key part of the busyness in family life in the years since World War II has been the rise in the number of women in the paid labor force and accompanying changes in gender roles and expectations. In 1960, 38 percent of women in the United States worked outside the home, but that number had risen to 59 percent by 2006. In 1970, almost 36 percent of couples in the United States were a part of dual-income families; by 2000, almost 60 percent were dual-income couples.[5] The combined total of the hours worked by parents has also been on the increase. In 1970, couples worked a combined total of 52.5 hours a week. By 2000, that figure had risen to 63.1 hours.[6]

Women enter the workforce in greater numbers, or work more hours during childbearing years, as a means of replacing the household income lost as a result of the stagnation in wages that economists date to 1973, arguably the beginning of globalization.[7] Those with less than a college degree have suffered even greater losses since then, as two-thirds of those without degrees experienced a 6 percent decline in real wages since 1973. And the Economic Policy Institute estimated in 2010 that wages in the industries where jobs were being created were on average 21 percent lower than the wages in industries where jobs were disappearing.[8] Not surprisingly, then, by 2006 there were more two-paycheck couples than there had been male breadwinners in 1970.[9] Because one's class status is often related to the earning power of a spouse or partner, women and their children stand to lose out economically when a divorce occurs. Their finances and their time away from work become more thinly stretched as they strive to remain in a neighborhood, school system, and social network of people whose incomes and assets may be significantly higher than their own.[10] Together, these economic shifts mean that more people in family groups experience longer work hours today than forty years ago.

Because of the demands on families, a variety of child care arrangements has arisen to meet the needs of families where two parents or a single parent works. Eighty percent of children under five whose mothers work full-time spend at least forty hours in some kind of child care arrangement, and 63 percent of children ages six to fourteen spend an average of twenty-one hours each week in child care with someone other than a parent. And because options for adolescents are more limited (particularly for those from lower-income families), it's estimated that 40 percent of fourteen-year-olds with working mothers spend time on their own when they're not in school.[11]

As a result of this increase in parental working hours and in children's supervised care between 1981 and 1997, children ages three to twelve experienced a decline in their free or unstructured time by 12 percent, or seven hours per week. They spend the bulk of their waking hours in school, day care, and after-school programs. They spend more time now in organized sports, hobbies, and outdoor activities, and they also spend more time doing homework, than did the young people and children of prior generations, meaning that most of their unstructured time occurs as they are being transported between structured activities.[12] They spend less time casually visiting with friends and they also spend less time talking to those in their homes.[13] With increasing suburban sprawl and time pressure on parents, there has also been a decline in the number of students who walk to school and an increase in the time spent in the car moving between these activities.[14]

Young people are not the only ones leading highly structured lives. With the rise in communication technologies that have enabled a 24/7 work environment, people are expected to adjust their home lives to accommodate the demands of their workplaces, changing their shifts or their hours worked to best benefit the companies that pay them, coordinating working hours between multiple jobs, or working from home in addition to work during usual business hours.[15] As a result, we have been left with shorter periods of free time. This is a finding that doesn't always show up on statistical measures of work and leisure time.[16] According to those studies, parents in the United States may actually have more cumulative minutes devoted to leisure than in the past. But the rapid interweaving of leisure with work activities has become a pattern that has replaced longer stretches of uninterrupted free time.[17] And today, communication technologies not only connect us with our employers but also are increasingly designed to provide ways for us to fill those spare minutes between demands.[18]

Even if our individual work hours have remained about the same as thirty years ago, family lives today have become characterized by a constant negotiation between the changing demands of work and family life. This situation has led to increased household dissonance and heralds an era of unprecedented household-level negotiations over work, gender, and family. Some, such as sociologist Arlie Hochschild, have argued that the rising rates of divorce and single parenting relate directly to these heightened tensions wrought by the demands of the workforce.[19]

Perhaps as a result of the increase in the amount of time young people spend alone at home or with caregivers who are not their parents, middle-class parents today report both a high level of concern about entertainment media options and a desire to be involved in their children's education and in their formalized extracurricular activities such as community sports leagues, choirs, orchestras, religious and community leadership events, or other activities, in what have been termed "intensified parenting activities."[20] These activities are expected of the parents who live in a cultural milieu that emphasizes an ethic of expressive empowerment, as we have already observed. It might be that mothers engage in these intensified parenting activities because they want to provide their children with the best possible chances for success, or as a way of demonstrating that they are needed, as sociologist Margaret Nelson has contends.[21] But intensified parenting affects both mothers and fathers. Whereas the amount of time mothers spend with their children has remained fairly consistent over the years, fathers in 2000 spent more than twice as much time with their children than did fathers in 1965 (60 minutes a day in 2000 compared to 24 minutes in 1965 for fathers, 102 minutes a day versus 90 minutes for mothers).[22] Middle-class families have experienced an increased sense of busyness as a result of at least three things: the proportion of time parents devote to work, the constant interweaving of work and family time, and the pressure felt to spend more time with their children to meet friends' and family members' expectations of what it means to be a "good" parent today.

Communication technologies have become an almost transparent part of how families manage their ongoing commitments as well as unexpected disruptions. Many middle- and upper-middle-class parents remain available to their workplaces through cell phones, smart phones, and Internet-connected laptops or tablets that can move with them from home to activities, as did Marcia Richter and Janice Dykstra (chapter 7). Less advantaged families, in contrast, are asked to respond more quickly to the changing needs of a dynamic workforce with fewer guarantees of work hours or stability. Parents across the socioeconomic spectrum thus manage their family and home life responsibilities from their work settings, as the boundaries between work and home lives increasingly overlap and blur.[23] Parents spend quite a bit of time developing coping strategies, relying on lists, calendars, smart phones, and other means to plan their time and manage the information and communication required in order to get through the countless activities and decisions that need to be made each day.[24] So even as these technologies help to address problems of management, they also become another source of demands on parents' time, as parents must work to keep the information in calendars and digital devices up to date and coordinate such information with other family members. Technologies have evolved to serve these needs, changing the landscape of family life and the coordination of its activities.

But these technologies have not alleviated the demands of emotion work. As we will see, both the Fallon and Blayne-Gallagher families were making valiant efforts to manage the time crunch, and to do so they were pursuing parenting styles that seemed to be at odds with those of their friends and family members. The Blayne-Gallagher family, whose members had access to a great deal of resources and were embedded in an upper-middle-class school and neighborhood culture of high achievement and expressive empowerment, were nevertheless the one family in my study whose teen daughter described her parents as "permissive." Daughters in the single-parent Fallon family, in contrast, learned to navigate choppy social waters as they moved back and forth between the expectations of their extended family members, who embraced a respectful connectedness approach, and their peers at school, who were much more supportive of their efforts at expressiveness and empowerment. Members in both families had to work at adjusting their presentation of their family's media policies so that they would not appear to be too out of sync with those of their friends and families, particularly in relation to how they spent their time together and separately. In this chapter, we consider how these families viewed their approaches to media in the context of their social milieus. Then, bringing together the insights of the previous three chapters, this chapter presents a revised model for how parents approach parenting issues that they feel are related to digital and mobile media.

The Blayne-Gallagher Family

For most parents interviewed in this study as well as in numerous other studies about parenting and the media, the dangers and risks of television and of the Internet loom large.[25] But, at least at first, the members of the Blayne-Gallagher family seemed to embrace a completely different approach. "The more you expose them to stuff, the better," said Gwen Blayne, mother of sixteen-year-old Maria and eleven-year-old Nigel Blayne-Gallagher. Gwen recognized that her views of media and leisure were out of step with many in her social circle. As she noted, "I'll be at school and I'll overhear other mothers going, 'She wanted to go see blah-blah-blah movie and I wouldn't allow it.' And I'm thinking, 'Oh, I took my daughter to see that.'"

The Blayne-Gallaghers are a biracial European American and African American upper-middle-class family living in a large city in the northeastern part of the United States, where Maria and Nigel's father, Stan, is in city government and their mother is a student in medical school.[26] As a biracial teen, Maria says that she views herself, like her mother, as somewhat out of step with her peers. Also like her mother, she relishes her ability to notice and embrace her differences.

A straight-A student, Maria is active in her mostly black urban high school's after-school activities, and regularly spend time reading weekly newsmagazines and watching news programs on television with her parents. The Blayne-Gallagher house is a favorite hangout place for her high school friends, as Maria explains, because in the living room there were many instruments that beckon interaction (didgeridoo, guitars, mariachis, tambourines, piano, drums). It is also a media-rich house, with a large-screen TV and a PlayStation in another main living area.

Maria had gotten an iPod earlier in the year as a gift, and her family had also given her several iTunes gift certificates so that she could download music without the threat of viruses. Maria did not mention that another benefit of having access to iTunes is legal downloading, which may have been more of a concern for her parents than for her. Like many other young people her age, Maria spends a fair amount of time texting, instant-messaging, and communicating with her friends through social network sites.

Maria's parents had purchased a mobile phone for her at the end of her ninth-grade year. Nigel got one at the same time (at the end of his fifth-grade year) so that Maria and Nigel could work out arrangements about getting home when both of their parents were busy. At first Gwen had expressed trepidation about getting them each a mobile phone, she says. But

Gwen is proud that they have used them to problem-solve without the help of their parents:

> The other day they actually used them! Nigel was supposed to go home on the train. He didn't have any money. So he called Maria on his cell. Hooked up with her, went over to her school, waited for her while she was doing her rehearsal and then they came home together. They worked that out all by themselves.

Gwen, in contrast with Marcia Richter and Janice Dykstra from the previous chapter, does not express a desire to have her children remain in constant contact with her through the mobile phone. Rather, she is pleased when Maria and Nigel use their cell phones to be in contact with each other and solve a problem without consulting her. This emphasis on expected self-reliance differs from what Maria and Nigel saw among their peers. As Maria notes, "My friends all think my family is pretty weird, in a really cool way . . . like all my friends who went to my junior high, all their parents are so friggin' uptight." Like others in their upper-middle-class neighborhood, Maria and her parents talk together about the media rules and guidelines that they think are appropriate and about how they feel about those rules. Both their mother and father share in the responsibility of working with Maria and Nigel to maintain those guidelines and to set up consequences for when those guidelines are not met. But Maria sees a difference between what her parents do and what happens in the homes of her friends, describing her parents' practices in terms of permissiveness. Not surprisingly, she is highly supportive of her parents' approach: "So we are not as strict. I think I am growing up so much happier. Thank you so much, Mom!"

In a separate interview, Maria's mother, Gwen, places their practices of parental authority in a framework that might better be described as flexible and responsive with limits rather than permissive, emphasizing the importance of warmth and caring: "I think being a parent is all about letting them know you are there, that you love them, you care, you will help them out," she says. "You want them to know that whatever they do is okay, that they can come to you. You give them the rules and guidelines and you expect them to follow that. But you know, you have to go day by day." Maria's mother and father are able to be flexible and responsive because, although Stan is in a high-powered position and Gwen is a medical student, they both have a great deal of autonomy in their workplaces. This means that they are able to work together to ensure that at least one of them is home much of the time when Maria and Nigel are home. To do this, sometimes they work late into the night; other times Stan and Gwen take turns with Maria and Nigel on the weekends or at their school events, or one or the other parent will take Maria and Nigel with them to city-related events in the evenings. In other words, this was a time-poor family, but also one that had access to freedoms and resources that many other families did not have. They could afford to resist their neighborhood's tendency to be hypervigilant about schools and leisure time, and they embrace an ethic of respectful connectedness as a choice.

The Blayne-Gallagher family places a great deal of emphasis on respecting others and thinking through how their actions affect not just themselves but also the lives and choices of those around them. It was not so much that "whatever" they did was "okay," as Maria describes her parents' approach, but rather that Gwen and Stan want their children to trust them enough to admit when they make mistakes, so that the parents can act as consultants as the children work out their own solutions or next steps—and those next steps would differ depending on the circumstances. Says Gwen, "You try to tell your kids, 'Use your brain. Question these things. What do you think is right? How would you judge these people and what do you base that on?'" Gwen says that she believes it is important to respect the dignity of all people. Then, with a note of irony, she adds laughingly, "I think my kids would agree with me, and they're right!"

Stan says that the family has "no rules" regarding digital and mobile media use: "I look at this differently. It's not about what they can't do, but about what they can get out of it, the media. Another way of looking at this policy question is that we want the kids getting more information, not to limit their information." With this statement, Stan acknowledges that his family's approach is distinct from that of other families in their social circles, who, he observes, spend a great deal of time supervising and controlling the environment for their children. Gwen and Stan want Nigel and Maria to have regular access to magazines and newspapers as well as to what is online, because they feel that the children will be more likely to open a magazine or paper out of a slight interest and become more intrigued by and informed about things they had not known that they were interested in. But of course, that access to magazines and newspapers was shaped by the parents' decisions regarding which publications were worthy of subscription. In the Blayne-Gallagher family, learning about different cultures was a highly valued part of their family life, and thus encouraging and sharing curiosity was a part of their individual and collective media experiences as well.

Gwen and Stan Blayne-Gallagher have a clear sense of right and wrong that they want to communicate to their children. In this regard they agree with the basic assumption that good parenting includes raising self-reliant and self-confident children and that restricting, discussing, consuming, and learning about media together is an important response. But Gwen and Stan are adamant about resisting the "culture of fear" that surrounds them. To them, focusing on risk and the darker side of humanity is counter to their spiritual and humanistic values. They specifically chose to live in an ungentrified urban neighborhood because they want their children to know that they should not live in fear of their neighbors just because those neighbors might be African American and poor.[27] In a separate interview, Gwen notes that when she sees Maria or Nigel watching something on television that she feels is insulting to women or to certain racial or ethnic groups, she insists that they turn it off, exercising restrictive mediation. Gwen also does not hesitate to criticize Maria's favorite late-night syndicated program, *Friends*, calling it "stupid . . . they are all white, rich, beautiful people," to which Stan adds, "That is the bad thing about *Friends*. The black person that shows up will be the one that buses the table." Maria contradicts this, noting that Ross, a central character on *Friends*, had dated a black woman, and that the program had portrayed biracial relationships. Gwen then recognizes Maria's observation and says, "Okay, well that's good," demonstrating to Maria that her views are heard and valued while also reaffirming Gwen's own perspective that inclusive representations of racial/ethnic diversity and biracial couples are desirable.

The Blayne-Gallaghers appreciate it when they find in popular media a range of voices and representations of people who are often underrepresented or disadvantaged. For example, Gwen explains that Maria's music choices are "fine," offering an implicit critique of some kinds of lyrics when she says of the music Maria prefers, "It's not violence against women. It is just rock. We may not like the music but it's not offensive." To this comment, Maria adds, "It's offensive if you're a corporate type of person," indicating her preference for music that challenges the authority of the large-scale music industry through its distribution as well as its lyrics. Maria is not interested in "testing" her parents' limits by trying to download or buy music that they might find offensive, but in turn, her parents are more willing than many to listen to Maria's choices of entertainment as their form of involvement in what researchers term active mediation. "Eminem, when he first came out, his lyrics were pretty out there and he said every word you can imagine and I used to think, 'He is so disgusting, don't you be listening to that crap,'" says Gwen. "And then

I started listening to his lyrics, and even though he said the *f*-word, he is brilliant. I just think he is totally brilliant." Maria appreciates this assessment, placing it in the framework of her parents' interest in giving things a chance before passing judgment. "That's the thing. Most adults don't ever give it a chance. If you listen to it, it's really pretty good," Maria notes.

Gwen says that while, like others in their neighborhood, they do not have specific rules about computer use, "we have an understanding that there is some stuff that is not appropriate for you." The family also employs a filtering system on the family computer, so Maria and Nigel are automatically blocked from certain sites. The parents see themselves as setting limits, and they utilize technology to help them in this task. This use of technology for setting limits did not seem unusual within upper-middle-class families in my study, as noted in chapter 1.

In contrast to the term "permissive," which Maria had used to express the distinction between her parents' approach to media and the approaches of parents who were, in Maria's words, more "uptight" about media, the Blayne-Gallagher parents utilize differing parental mediation strategies as the circumstances changed, sometimes engaging in restriction and sometimes in active discussion about their children's media choices, and sometimes sharing in media consumption so as to better understand their children's experiences and tastes. They view entertainment media as a language that opens opportunities for discussion rather than as either a distracting individual activity or an opportunity for parents to reinforce their own views. They take an interest in their children's media interests, keeping the computer in a public space in the home and subtly indicating through their occasional observations that they expect their children's online interactions to be in line with what the family espouses as its values.

But allowing their children to think of their parents as out of step with the mainstream also serves an important purpose in the Blayne-Gallagher family, whose members are by virtue of their biraciality often considered different by the white upper-middle-class majority that surrounds them. With their discussions about openness to media and their seemingly countercultural embrace of leisure, Maria and Nigel see themselves and their parents as rebelling against upper-middle-class norms—even as, to some extent, they actually embrace many of them. The Blayne-Gallaghers are engaging in emotion work as they consider the norms of the upper-middle-class regarding media and leisure and then take pride and pleasure in articulating a different approach. But like many upper-middle-class families, the Blayne-Gallaghers also struggle against the familiar time crunch and the need for individuals within the family to have separate as well as collective experiences within their home. This came up when Gwen voices what she says are her only regrets regarding digital media:

> Sometimes I feel that we really need to stop being so separate: Nigel is doing a game, Maria is doing her thing on the computer, and I'm watching something. We all need to come into the same room and play Scrabble. Do something together. And not every family occurrence can be about going to a movie. So that does come up for me a lot . . . It takes more energy to *not* do something related to media. It really does. You gotta create it. Think about what you are going to do and get everybody in the same room. It takes a lot more energy.

Whereas they do seem to resist the push to empowerment and expression, they still experience the phenomenon of being alone together with media in their house. In this statement, Maria's mother expresses a value in being "unplugged" from media culture. She also subtly acknowledges that being unplugged in their family context would mean engaging in emotion work: getting everyone on board with her idea of a joint leisure activity, and dealing with the possible disappointment of finding that others would prefer to do something else.[28] Unlike strict parents who are concerned about avoiding the negatives of popular culture, the Blayne-Gallaghers' desire to unplug grows out of the desire for a home environment in which mutual connection could be more wholeheartedly embraced. Wishing to replace movie night as the default family leisure activity was not particularly countercultural or out of step with the mainstream; sometimes Gwen, like many other mothers, found that she needed to engage in "emotional downsizing" regarding her expectations of connection with her children and spouse. This is a key strategy for dealing with the time crunch in her family, particularly because Gwen also prioritizes self-preservation in the face of her family's pressures. She regularly participates in yoga, meditation, and reading, and also travels with friends, prioritizing these activities as a way of both staying healthy and avoiding the burnout some mothers experience through constant participation in intensive parenting activities. Whereas the family's access to resources helps her to participate in these activities and to maintain a balance that seems much more difficult to achieve in less privileged families, she also prioritizes self-preservation to a much greater extent than others in her neighborhood and in her upper-middle-class milieu.

The Blayne-Gallaher family therefore engaged in at least two kinds of emotion work. When the family is in the home and engaged in separate activities, Gwen considers interrupting those activities to suggest some joint activity. Whether or not she actually makes the suggestion has to do with her sense of her own emotional needs and the needs of individual family members. The other kind of emotion work involves the family's awareness of how others in their circles perceive them. They mobilize a different approach to leisure and media than those around them, both as a way of reinforcing their own commitment to openness and as a means of allowing their children to rebel against norms. Other families with different values and priorities similarly found themselves performing emotion work as they negotiated between differing norms of what it means to be a good parent.

The Fallon Family

Wyonna Fallon is a single parent who lives with her two daughters, fourteen-year-old Jill and twelve-year-old Tami. All of them are of European American heritage.[29] While her daughters are in school, Wyonna is working toward a bachelor's degree in social work. She receives child support inconsistently, so to support her family she is also working two part-time jobs: as a baker in a local franchise of a national chain (work that she does for eight to ten hours on Saturday mornings beginning at 3:30 a.m.) and as a custodian at a nearby private Christian high school, which enables her daughters to attend tuition-free. The Fallons are navigating between the experiences of two differing sets of people: the middle- and upper-middle-class families of the Christian school the girls attend, and the less advantaged extended family and friends who had supported the family in their earlier years.

Sometimes the emotion work involved in moving between these two settings becomes evident. After school each day, Wyonna picks up her daughters and has them accompany her as she does her janitorial work. "Tami's so funny because she's only twelve and she doesn't know that it's not cool to be a janitor at school," Wyonna explains with a smile. "And so she walks around with the keys out of her back pocket on purpose so people can see them. She thinks it's really cool." Wyonna did not need to tell Jill that janitorial work isn't "cool"; Jill had learned that from her interactions with her middle- and upper-middle-class peers. But Wyonna has decided that having a job and enabling her daughters to attend the school mattered more than other people's views about her job. She encourages Jill to focus on having a positive attitude and ignoring what others might say. "She's not embarrassed, but she's not interested in helping out, either," Wyonna says.

Wyonna earned her GED after dropping out of high school at age sixteen to have her first child, a son who at twenty-two is a high school graduate working as a home health aide in a midwestern state near Wyonna's extended family. Wyonna left her second husband, Jill and Tami's father, seven years earlier to escape a situation of physical abuse. Wyonna's own father and mother had divorced when she was young. Her father had been a truck driver who delivered coal, and her mother had been a "housewife," as she describes her. Wyonna has four older sisters; each completed at least some college, and all still live in the town where they grew up.

The Fallons live in a small apartment in a midsized midwestern city. It is the fifth home they've lived in since Tami's birth twelve years earlier, and as they have been there for almost four years, all are anxious for Wyonna to complete her degree and find a more permanent job so that they can afford to stay in the area, which they like. When they are home and the weather is nice, Jill and Tami often go down to the nearby school's park. As Tami explains: "There's a hill and there's a little park down there. We usually have jumping contests. And there's a skate[board] park." Jill and Tami like to bike, Rollerblade, and run on the trails near their house. They are also avid readers, with interests in the Harry Potter series, the King Arthur legends, Anne McCaffrey's series *Dragonriders of Pern*, and other books about dragons and unicorns. At one point in the interview, Tami says jokingly, "Me and Jill are easily amused, I would say." "It's embarrassing how we're so easily amused," Jill chimes in, continuing: "One time after school we threw sticks in a tree and that was our amusement for an hour," she says, laughing along with Tami. "It was kind of fun," Tami adds, "and we also flip pop can tops." Their reading and outdoor activities, their mother feels, are far preferable to having them watch television anytime she is busy at work or doing school assignments. In fact, Wyonna had given away their television two years earlier, in part because she felt they all "watched way too much TV" but also in part because "cable is expensive." "We had a big-screen TV!" Tami exclaims. "Well, not big," Jill clarifies. "A twenty-seven-inch TV," Wyonna notes.

Although the family is religious, Wyonna emphasizes that she didn't give away the television for religious reasons. "I don't think that it's an evil that you have to have out of the house," she says. "Mostly it was those stupid commercials." She jokes that when she first gave away the television, she thought she was "quite self-righteous" about it. "But then I got over myself," she says, perhaps having decided that it wasn't socially appropriate in her circle of family and friends to express pride in her decision to no longer have access to cable television. Several in her family,

Wyonna says, had expressed shock at her decision, noting that they couldn't imagine going without television. Because Wyonna does not want to be interpreted as judgmental of others' decisions, she engages in emotion work to mask her feelings of pride and seeks a more acceptable explanation as to why they do not have television. She and the girls talk about the negative influence of television advertisements, which, they believe, make people more conscious of the need to buy things. At the prestigious middle- and upper-middle-class high school they attend, Jill discusses their lack of a television as a point of pride and distinction among her friends; Tami chooses to discuss it with her friends as a form of deprivation on the part of a strict mother. But Wyonna herself notes that it isn't as if they've eliminated all screen time; after all, they still have a fifteen-inch television with a built-in DVD player that they keep in the closet in Jill and Tami's room, and Wyonna does not restrict how often Jill and Tami view movies on it.[30] Sometimes all three of them squeeze into the small bedroom to watch one of the six dozen or so movies they own or another one they have rented. But more often, Jill and Tami watch while Wyonna is in the other room. They'd watched the same few movies over and over again so often that the girls had made up new lyrics to the songs in those movies.

Wyonna feels glad that their access to owned and rented movies is limited, noting that her usual bargain includes allowing the girls to pick out a film as long as both agree to it and as long as she is allowed to pick one out as well. This often means lengthy and heated discussions between the girls about which movies to watch. The fact that they had to agree and that they had to clear their selection with their mother meant that both of them self-censored based on what they believed their mother would find appropriate.

In the apartment's main room, the Fallons have an older desktop computer and a small portable stereo perched on a table behind the couch. Both Jill and Tami also have portable electronic games. Jill, Tami, and Wyonna all use the computer, with Wyonna emailing her sisters every day and Jill and Tami taking turns getting online to play games, go to the Neopets site, download music, or do schoolwork. They have a half-hour limit on the amount of time they spend on the computer, although Jill says that they often exceed the time limit. Then her mother "scowls at us once in a while when we're playing. Then she'll come in after a while and think of something else for use to do, and we'll have to go and do it." They are not allowed to chat, IM, or use social networking sites on the computer at all, although Jill is allowed to use email to keep in touch with a friend who has moved out of state. Neither Jill nor Tami is much bothered by this rule, as most of Jill's friends similarly are not allowed to have access to social networking sites due a school rule that forbids it.[31] Jill and Tami usually keep in touch with their friends through a low-cost cell phone that they share. Their school friends do not live in their neighborhood, and as Jill and Tami are either with their mother while she works or at home after school and in the evenings, they text or call their friends from those locations. Wyonna also has an inexpensive cell phone, used mainly to make arrangements with Jill and Tami and to allow them to keep in touch with her when she is at the bakery on Saturdays.

The family has online access through Wyonna's status as a student at a nearby university. Wyonna says apologetically, "I'm not real good at consistently monitoring it. A lot of times I'm not here." But the older daughter, Jill wants to present her mother in a positive light in the interview. She adds, "We do really good with the half an hour on the Internet, though. Homework isn't a problem anymore because when she cleans the high school, we stay there and do our homework then. So we get it done." Wyonna notes that she asks the girls to get their homework done, clean their room, and get their violin practice out of the way before they spend time watching movies. Jill, laughing, notes that frequently things don't happen in that order. "They *should* happen that way," Wyonna agrees, also laughing, again aiming to present herself as perhaps more relaxed about their interactions with entertainment media than her family practices would suggest. Wyonna believes that Jill and Tami's middle- and upper-middle-class school friends live with more media oversight, but because of the demands on her time from work and school, she is forced to trust their use of media to a great extent.

Still, the girls have more oversight than they used to. Jill and Tami used to spend a great deal of time playing video games, Wyonna says; in fact, that was why she quit her old Saturday job and took the one at the bakery that begins at three-thirty in the morning. She had decided that she wanted to spend more time home with the girls so that she could ensure that they didn't spend their days just watching television or playing video games. As Jill says of her mother's approach: "She wants us to be productive. Anything we do should be productive. Although a lot of times it isn't. It must help our future, I guess. The violin is productive."

Jill has internalized her mother's concerns about the productive use of time, a theme that was common among middle- and upper-middle-class families who had adopted an ethic of expressive empowerment. Even Jill's description of her leisure time on the computer evokes the idea that computer use can be positive and related to informal learning, a viewpoint more expressly articulated among middle- and upper-middle-class families than among less privileged families.[32] Jill says that she often likes to play around on the computer, particularly with graphics programs that enable her to draw and games that involve solving puzzles. Despite the fact that her uses of the computer could be viewed as "productive," Jill still feels that she spends "too much" time on the computer; "It's not a good thing," she says, shaking her head.

Yet even as talk of the "productive" use of free time echoes the middle- and upper-middle-class parental orientation toward the use of leisure time for empowerment, Wyonna also talks about the importance of family and respect, and the time they spend both on long road trips traveling to see her family and in their twice or three times weekly involvement in church activities: "I think it's important to have close friends that you can count on. Family, my mom, my sisters, their aunts . . . That's also why church is so important." Even the discussion of a future that includes college has less to do with securing a certain kind of job than with the ability to develop empathy for others, as Wyonna describes it: "It's not that you get left back [if you don't attend college], it's just that you learn about so many different places, different people, different views. . . . When you have that many different personalities in a room, you can learn a lot from that."

Rather than highlighting a connection between college and a better-paying job, as several of the families in chapter 6 did, Wyonna downplays the idea that she might get any economic benefit from attending college; perhaps she frames her decision to get her degree with reference to a reason that is more socially acceptable among her family and friends: to get along better with others. A quiet and unassuming woman, Wyonna seems to want to play down the efforts she is making to improve her life and the lives of her children, even as her commitment to her daughters is evident to them.

Wyonna's biggest priority is spending time with her daughters, encouraging them to follow through on responsibilities such as homework, cleaning their room, and violin practice. She cannot afford for her daughters to participate in the many after-school activities that parents such as the upper-middle-class Dykstras, Nelsons, and others pay for. There are no sports-related travel events and few vacations save for an occasional camping trip. College isn't a sure thing for them, given Wyonna's financial situation; although she says she hopes that they will attend university, she doesn't think it has to be "right after high school," in contrast to the middle- and upper-middle-class families who attend the private school with Jill and Tami. However, Wyonna is able to help her daughters structure their time in other ways.

Wyonna changed her own life and work situation to address a difficulty Jill had encountered several years earlier, when they'd first moved to their town. Even though she had initially said that she changed her work schedule so that she could oversee Jill and Tami's media use, she told a different story when alone with the interviewer later on. Jill had been the target of bullying at the public school she'd attended when they first arrived in the area. That had motivated Wyonna to begin looking into the Christian private school, and once she got the janitor's job there, both girls switched to that school.

The daughters clearly express great loyalty to their mother, even as they also recognize that their mother does not have the expertise to give them much guidance in the online realm. "Once, I changed the color of the tool bar and she got really mad," Jill says of her mother. When a family friend helped them set up a new computer, the friend showed Jill how it worked, with the understanding that Jill would then show her mother. And at one point when they are speaking with the interviewer together, Jill gently teases her mother about her lack of knowledge about computers, which leads to the relaying of what is clearly a story about computers that amused the whole family:

JILL: You see, my mom doesn't know computers. When we first got this [two years earlier], when she turned it on she held the button down. And when you hold the button down (laughing), it shuts the computer down. So she was holding it down and it turned on and turned off. And she had asked the computer support staff people about it.

WYONNA: I called them. And they said, "What are you doing?" And I said, "I'm pushing down on it." So you would think they would have understood what I meant. But evidently they didn't.

JILL: All she had to do was push and let go!

WYONNA: To make things worse, this computer support guy came to my house when all of my friends were over from church . . . and one friend, I said to him, "Look, this computer doesn't work."

JILL (LAUGHING HYSTERICALLY): And he turns it on!

WYONNA (LAUGHING): And he says, "Well, why are you holding the button down?" I felt so stupid. And then the computer support guy shows up. He goes, "Is there a problem with the computer?" And we're like, "No. Do you want a hamburger?"

Wyonna then transitions from this story into a brief reminiscence about that night at her apartment. "It was neat. They sat and played music and that was kind of cool. I've had a few things like that . . .," she says, her voice trailing off. Clearly, the family enjoys spending time together, although between work and school Wyonna's time is tight. Wyonna does not have the freedom to balance her work and family time, and she does not have the resources to support self-preservation to the extent that mothers like Gwen Blayne-Gallagher do.

Wyonna notes that her days are often very full and tiring: "It's hard with studying, and kids, and staying focused. It's just hard to get to them all. It's tiring to have all those jobs, even though they all seem to be part-time." Not surprisingly, perhaps, Wyonna has not found time to date. Her priority is raising her daughters.

Like many of the less advantaged families discussed in this book, the Fallons live in a small space with limited technology, making it necessary to share television time and alternate their use of the computer and the mobile phone. Like parents across the economic spectrum, Wyonna is concerned about the ways her daughters fill their free time with television and game playing; like several of the middle- and upper-middle-class parents, she speaks of these media as a waste of time. But because she does not have the resources to find alternative activities outside of their home, Wyonna often has to come up with alternatives to media use herself or allow her daughters to spend unsupervised time in their home or in nearby outdoor activities. Taking the girls with her to the school during her janitorial shift is one way she limits their access to media; not having cable television is another. And when they are all at home together, she occasionally interrupts their viewing or game playing, giving them a clear suggestion about something else that she wants them to do. All of this monitoring and restricting is somewhat easier to manage because she is working two part-time jobs that enable her to be home when the girls are home, and therefore in some ways her parenting style echoes that of the hypervigilant mothers who devote a great deal of time to oversight of children. But the family's income is quite low, and they live in a cramped apartment far from the girls' school because that's what they can afford, placing their experience at odds with that of many of the mothers whose children go to the private school Jill and Tami attend. Moreover, the Fallon family does not engage in much conversation about what the girls are finding online or watching on the screen, because, like Melanie (introduced at the beginning of this chapter), such activities usually take place while Wyonna is engaged in household work, studying for her classes, or, in a rare moment, doing something of her own preference.

Wyonna is striking in her willingness to make sacrifices for her daughters. But she has to limit their activities as well as her own so that she can keep their schedules coordinated. She works in the middle of the night so that she can be with them during their waking hours on the weekend. She has also made several moves so that her ex-husband would not be able to find her, and as a result, she is not interested in getting involved in online activities beyond emailing with her sisters. Wyonna Fallon is fortunate that she and her daughters have no health or other problems that might have upset this fragile balance.

Wyonna's family remains an important source of support, even if her primary communication with her sisters is via email. As in other families who rely on one another in part because of less access to resources, Jill and Tami Fallon spend a great deal of time together and act as enforcers of the family's media preferences. Wyonna is also fortunate that her daughters work well together, perhaps as an outgrowth of their felt need for mutual familial support. Her daughters appreciate the sacrifices Wyonna has made for them, and Jill fills the adult-like role of computer consultant for her mother with good humor and no loss of respect. Like other families from less advantaged backgrounds, the Fallons engage in communication practices that both are respectful and emphasize connection between family members. But they are also more expressive than many, and also place a great emphasis on encouraging empowerment through education.

The Fallons' story illustrates several ways in which less advantaged families perform the emotion work of parenting in relation to digital and mobile media. Wyonna believes that it is a good idea to limit her daughters' screen time. She also finds that doing certain things, such as eschewing cable, helps them stay within their meager family budget. Sometimes, such as when she or her daughter Jill are with Jill's friends and other people associated with Jill's school, this approach to screen time as a "waste of time" is welcomed. But when Wyonna speaks with her family and friends about the family's decision to get rid of their television, she finds that their response makes her feel as if she is behaving in a self-righteous way. Perhaps some in those circles equate television restriction and talk of more productive use of time with her decision to live far from her hometown, pursue college, get ahead in life, and eventually land a career that pays better than the jobs other members of her family have. Wyonna and her daughters have to perform emotion work to present their media use appropriately within differing social settings. And, as with the Blayne-Gallagher family, feeling not quite in step with their various social settings probably contributes to their strong bonds within the family. Both Wyonna Fallon and Gwen Blayne-Gallagher felt pressure to balance the various demands on their family's time and to justify their approaches in social circles that often did not share their views or experiences.

The Emotion Work of Parenting

In many ways, we tend to think of parenting as a rational process that involves adults who explore alternatives and then choose the most appropriate course of action. Many of our media theories about parental mediation tend to have this idea of the calm and rational parent at its core. But parenting, like all interpersonal relationships, involves emotions. And in the situation of familial relations, parents and children make decisions regarding how they will approach media and parental mediation not only based on an intentional awareness of cognitive outcomes but also based on the fact that they are interested in promoting and experiencing well-being. Being a self-conscious parent is touted throughout the self-help parenting literature: "think and then respond," or engage in "love and logic," as several popular parenting texts geared to middle-class Americans exhort.[33] This approach does not assume that people are rational; rather, it assumes that they are guided by emotions and must self-consciously adopt a rational position. Parenting advice books may be good indicators of the emotion work that parents engage in.

The emotion work the Blayne-Gallaghers and the Fallons performed differed in several ways. Gwen and Stan Blayne-Gallagher's children appreciated the fact that their parents took time to listen to their views about television programs and music. Sometimes these families had to make hard decisions that involved letting their children suffer consequences and figure things out on their own, as Nigel Gallagher learned when he forgot his subway fare and had no easy way to get home. Sometimes they felt less than happy with the decisions of other family members, as Gwen Blayne-Gallagher expressed in her wish for less separateness and more togetherness time with her family. But in both families, children felt honored, valued, trusted, and respected. These feelings encompassed much more than their digital and mobile media use. But the positive feelings about their relationships with their parents meant that the Blayne-Gallagher and Fallon children knew that they could show their parents what was happening in the media they consumed—and in Jill Fallon's case, she could even show her mother how the computer worked.

In each case, family members had to think about how they would engage in media use and how they would feel about that engagement in relation to the social settings in which they found themselves. Sometimes they felt that their own media practices were out of sync with the practices of others around them; in other ways, they felt affirmed in their approach. These feelings, as well as the positive feelings created within the family as a result of parental respect for the children's needs and views, were a key factor in how the parents approached issues of restriction, discussed media, and engaged in media together. But the families also differed somewhat in their means of relating to one another within the family, and that, too, can be seen as growing out of their different contexts. It's hard to imagine Wyonna Fallon allowing either of her daughters to find their own way home without subway fare, for instance, just as it was practically impossible for Gwen Blayne-Gallagher to take their children with her to medical school or for Stan to take them with him to city hall. Parental opportunities and choices for work both shaped and reinforced certain ways of parenting that, in turn, affected how they could incorporate digital, mobile, and traditional media into their individual and family lives.

Preteens and teenagers tend to see the world differently than adults, and parents adjust their expectations and emotions based on their experiences with this. Thus parents often talk about "choosing their battles" with their teenage children, as they know that they must work to feel patient and understanding in interactions with their children when their own time deficits and emotional needs might make them feel frustrated and angry, and they must consider the individual needs of family members as well as those of the larger family unit.[34] Parents like Melanie and Wyonna and even Gwen and Stan engage in what Hochschild calls "emotional downsizing," lowering expectations of interpersonal relationships as they seek a balance between work and family life.[35]

Consistent with my observation that upper-middle and middle-class families are oriented toward expressive family relationships, Hochschild has argued that middle-class families do more emotion management than less advantaged families.[36] But parents like Melanie and Wyonna, who interact with individuals and with families that are both more and less advantaged than they are, similarly reflect on their emotions about their family's media use and on whether and how to share them in differing circumstances.

When parents don't feel like (or don't have the energy for) being a "good parent," they sometimes engage in techniques of emotion work such as practicing slow breathing or counting to ten before speaking as a means of both relationship management and self-preservation. But "good parenting" in families like the Blayne-Gallaghers and Fallons also might mean consciously approaching media and leisure in ways that break from the harried pace and internalized demands of middle- and upper-middle-class motherhood.

Rethinking Parental Mediation in Relation to Emotion Work

Throughout the third section of this book, we have seen four concerns that guide parental actions regarding the mediation of the media: (1) concerns about the future of their children, (2) concerns about family connectedness or relationships between parents and children, (3) concerns about balancing work and family time, and (4) concerns regarding parental self-preservation and self-development. When media scholars think about parental mediation they focus mostly on the first concern, and occasionally on the second. Yet parents discussed each of these concerns in relation to certain parental mediation strategies, and they relied upon sometimes differing and sometimes overlapping rationales for why they engaged in the parental mediation strategies that they did (see Table 8.1). This grid presents a way of thinking about the various factors that come into play when parents and their children make decisions about how, when, and why they will engage in oversight of

TABLE 8.1 Dimensions of Parental Mediation

PARENTAL CONCERNS	STRATEGIES	DISCUSSED IN TERMS OF	RATIONALES
Future of kids	• Restrictive mediation	• Homework, health, peers, bad influences	"It's good parenting to restrict"
	• Active mediation	• Cognitive develop ment (stereotypes)	
Family connectedness	• Active mediation	• Trust	"Media are okay when meeting familial goals"
	• Coviewing	• Togetherness	
	• Calls, texts	• Fun	"It's good parenting to trust"
	• Participatory Learning	• Interaction, closeness	
Work/family time	• Keep busy	• Demands (school, sports, homework)	"Media are okay when meeting familial goals"
	• Keep in touch	• Checking in when not together	"It's good parenting to trust"
Self	• Keep busy	• Growing independence	"It's good parenting to trust"
		• Differing tastes	

children's media use—and how they might explain their decisions to others in their social circles.

First, parents were concerned about the future of their children, and this was often discussed in terms familiar to those concerned about the potentially negative effects of media on children's cognitive processes. When parents spoke about limiting gaming, phone, texting, and television time, they noted that they wished to do so for the sake of attention to homework, concerns about their children's physical health, and concerns about the bad influences that stereotypes and violence might have on their children's development of what they considered to be an appropriate and desirable worldview. When parents like Melanie and Wyonna and even Gwen and Stan spoke of media restrictions, they did so with a rationale that assumed that restricting media influences was good parenting. As noted earlier, this approach to parental mediation is well addressed in the existing literature.

Second, parents were concerned about family connectedness. Some mentioned the experience of sitting in the same room with everyone on different devices as an example of how technology seems to disrupt family connectedness. Parents more frequently spoke about how they used communication technologies to maintain family connectedness. Some families took these practices further than the passive coviewing and even active discussion suggested in parental mediation literature, embracing what the previous chapter discussed as *participatory learning*, in which both parents and children interact with one another and learn together through activities such as Wii Bowling, Guitar Hero, or Dance Dance Revolution.[37] However, neither Wyonna nor Melanie seems to have either an interest in engaging in these kinds of activities or the time to do so. Neither did most of the other parents interviewed in this book, except in rare and special circumstances such as holiday events or multigenerational birthday celebrations. Even the Blayne-Gallaghers devoted only minimal time to participatory learning activities. This may change as parents become more comfortable with technologies that lend themselves to these kinds of activities. It will be interesting to see how quickly the conversations about media might change because of the potential for digital media to encourage interaction among parents and their growing children. In some places, this conversation is already emphasizing positive possibilities for mutual learning and family connection, particularly in relation to the educational benefits of such interactions.[38]

Like the Blayne-Gallaghers, many families also spoke about the importance of developing trust between parents and teens that would enhance their relationships. Parents and young people offered two potentially competing rationales when they described why they embraced the parental mediation strategies related to these concerns, paraphrased here as the parental rationale of "Media are acceptable when they are directed toward meeting familial goals" and the young person's rationale of "It's good parenting to trust in a teen's good judgment."

The third concern that guided parental mediation strategies often was not articulated but provided an important lens through which these strategies were viewed: this was the concern of balancing work and family time. Parents and young people spoke indirectly of these concerns and their strategies regarding them, referring to the many after-school activities in which young people engaged, often while parents worked, and discussing the phone calls and text messages that allowed parents to stay in touch while meeting the demands of their job. The strategy of utilizing media to keep young people busy, and to keep them in contact with parents, were two important ways in which parents engaged in parental mediation strategies that had less to do with cognitive awareness of media and more to do with demands on parents' time.

Interestingly, parents often used the same kinds of rationales when they discussed how to utilize media both to keep kids busy and to keep in touch with their kids. Parents noted that they provided cell phones so that their children could stay in contact with them when they were apart, drawing upon the rationale that "Media are acceptable when they are directed toward meeting familial goals." They also accepted the fact that their children would sometimes utilize media in an unsupervised setting while the parents were otherwise engaged, drawing upon the rationale that "It's good parenting to trust in a teen's good judgment." Remaining unarticulated was the view that by allowing their young people to engage in unsupervised media time, media were being utilized to meet other familial goals, such as allowing a parent to go to work while the young person was at home, or providing a young person with an in-home activity while the parent engaged in preparing meals, paying bills, cleaning, or otherwise maintaining the household.

The final concern that guided parental mediation strategies was similarly not articulated explicitly, but also provided an important justification for parental mediation strategies. This was the concern for parental self-preservation and self-development. Often, discussions of strategies that addressed this concern surfaced in relation to the need to keep children busy while parents pursued their own interests or needs, and it was also discussed in relation to the different ways that parents and young people choose to spend their leisure time. The rationale that guided the strategy of keeping children busy (or allowing them to pursue their own separate interests) echoed earlier rationales: "It's good parenting to trust in a teen's good judgment."

Wyonna Fallon expressed concerns about her children's future and therefore restricted their media use in many ways, even though, due to the restrictions on her own time, her children engaged in heavy media use. Yet her daughter Jill defended her mother as a parent who practiced strict oversight of their media use, seeing in her mother's many efforts an ethic of respect and an emphasis on family connectedness that played into how each member of the family viewed their digital and mobile media use. The Blayne-Gallagher parents, Gwen and Stan, expressed concerns about their children's future, too. This led them to engage in both active and restrictive forms of parental mediation. The Blayne-Gallaghers put limitations on the websites that the children could visit, discussed the use of social networking sites and other websites, and talked about stereotypes they encountered in the children's favorite media content. Yet, interestingly, the family viewed themselves not as restrictive or strict but rather as permissive in relation to media. Assessing the Blayne-Gallagher family as permissive is possible only when their approach is contrasted with the level of anxiety and oversight that seems to have become common among middle- and upper-middle-class families when it comes to social networking sites, mobile phones, gaming systems, and other forms of entertainment and leisure. Rather than spending a great deal of time in structured activities away from home or at home engaged in "productive" uses of time, the Blayne-Gallagher children had a great deal of media available in the public spaces of their home, including magazines, computers, newspapers, music, television, additional electronic media, and musical instruments. The parents utilized media as a means of inviting young people—both their children and their children's friends—into relationships, thereby addressing their family's concern with connectedness. They also used communication technologies such as the mobile phone as a means of keeping connected with one another, and of balancing work and family life. Gwen and Stan's lives were quite busy with the demands of work, but because their children participated in individual media-related activities, the parents were able to pursue their own interests, which included reading and yoga.

Conclusion

We are indeed a nation that's media rich and time poor. We have come to need our media not only to keep our young people entertained while we're doing something else but also to keep our young people connected to us. Busy schedules necessitate short and frequent phone calls between children and Dad or (more frequently) Mom, discussing transportation, meal plans, and joint family activities. We use film and television as "family time," and we often share music or sometimes DVDs when we're in the car. We may have many different feelings about these media, and our social environments may help us to know what it means to be a "good parent" in relation to restricting, discussing, or sharing in media time with our children. But there is little doubt that the digital and mobile media give shape to our collective and individual lives and our feelings about how we enact our relationships with those closest to us.

Digital and mobile media both potentially solve and potentially exacerbate many dilemmas of contemporary family life. They can enable young people to check in more frequently with their parents and can make it easier to keep track of young people's activities and interactions. They can make new opportunities for intergenerational interactions possible and even desirable. But they are also sources of real distress, anxiety, and worry for a great many parents, because they provide more opportunities for autonomy and for risk taking, amplifying what has long been a source of concern about the preteen and teen years. Parenting practices have changed in relation to this increase in the autonomy of youth culture, but what has not changed is the desire on the part of both parents and young people to establish and maintain meaningful relationships, both within the family and outside it.

CHAPTER 9 | Parenting in a Digital Age

The Mediatization of Family Life
and the Need to Act

IN A POLEMICAL FIFTEENTH-CENTURY tract titled "In Praise of Scribes," the Benedictine monk Johannes Trithemius wrote with dismay about an invention by one of his contemporaries, Johann Gutenberg. The printing press was going to contribute to an inferior culture, Trithemius' manuscript argued.[1] Moreover, the young monks who had long pursued the arduous task of learning how to copy the *scriptoria* by hand would lose an important means of attaining moral character, as copying engaged them in activities of "diligence and industry."[2] Trithemius was early to notice and deplore the shift from a culture of the manuscript to what would become the culture of the printed word. It was a shift from a time in which only specialists within the institution of the Catholic Church could access and reproduce valuable manuscripts to a time when owners of the printing press could make market-based decisions about what might be considered valuable and worthy of reproduction. As historian Elizabeth Eisenstein has pointed out, there is an interesting irony in the story of Trithemius' diatribe against his culture's new form of communication. So as to ensure that his ideas were circulated widely, Trithemius sought out his local printer and had his own work printed for mass consumption.[3] He wanted to resist communication technology, but then again couldn't resist the advantages it had introduced for his own communication efforts. Now even his resistance is remembered in the process of cultural change in which he inevitably took part.

Parents in the United States today find themselves in the same bind. Many parents whose stories were described in this book lamented the extensive use of mobile phones, texting, and social networking sites in the lives of their children, and expressed concerns about the older media of television programs, music, and gaming as well. Most parents encouraged limited or supervised media use, either indirectly through the extensive scheduling of "better" uses of leisure time, as in the middle-class Nelson and Welton families, or directly in relation to sharing mobile phones or computers in small living spaces, as in the less advantaged Williams, Hagos, and Baylor families.

Yet parents have also found these media helpful in their own lives. Roxanne Conner was relieved when her son could contact her by mobile phone, as it meant that she had one fewer item on her long list of concerns as a single parent balancing the competing demands of work and home. The mothers of Renee Venuzzo and her friend were similarly relieved that their daughters had been able to call when the thirteen-year-olds encountered an unusual and scary situation in their local mall. And in some cases media were a preferred "safe" leisure alternative: Judy Cruz and Meghan Sealy believed that having their sons engage in endless gaming meant that they had fewer reasons to encounter the temptations in their own neighborhoods.

New media introduce new ways of doing things, and their incursion into the rhythms of family life is no exception. While some of the changes in family life are direct—for instance, we can now instantaneously communicate with one another from anywhere at any time—other changes to social behavior are less direct, as evidenced by the fact that we may not always *want* to communicate with one another from anywhere at any time. Danielle Oliver's mother wanted to be able to disconnect and shop on her own without having to answer phone calls or texts from her daughter or son, for instance. This book has suggested that different patterns and coping strategies have evolved out of social patterns and strategies that came before. We should not be too quick to jump to overarching statements regarding how digital and mobile media are making our family relationships more superficial, less intimate, or more separate. Rather than beginning with a specific hypothesis regarding how digital and mobile media might be making all of us more or less tightly knit as families or better or worse at communicating with one another, in this book I wanted to begin with the stories of families themselves, exploring how they are negotiating digital and mobile media in their everyday lives. The questions of the role of technology in the changing lives of families then became: Which aspects of social life are changing, and which are remaining the same? What particular shape do family lives take because of changes introduced with these new media? And what problems that may have existed prior to the introduction of these new media are now brought to the forefront and amplified? These are the questions answered in this concluding chapter as we review the stories of families in this study, what these stories say about how communication technologies are playing a role in social change, and what parents, legislators, teens, educators, and family members should be doing in response.

Family Communication Patterns in the Middle Class

People are experiencing digital and mobile media differently, and in relation to certain existing, long-standing patterns of inequity. Upper-middle-class families embrace an *empowering and expressive* ethic of family communication that has grown out of earlier patterns of family communication.[4] Their approach has shaped how technologies are relevant to and problematic within family situations. To ensure their children's happiness and safety in the present and to help them succeed in the future, parents such as the Weltons, Nelsons, Richters, and Dykstras schedule their growing children's leisure time with many empowering activities of personal enrichment. These parents effectively preclude extensive media use in their homes and also limit mediated communication between peers to a certain extent. Families like these rarely even watch a film or television program together, as today's upper-middle-class family usually owns several kinds of portable devices, ranging from e-readers and tablets to laptops and smart phones. Their individual schedules might be too rigid, but their options for media use when at home also mitigate against shared screen time except on rare occasions. The demands of family life, particularly the need to balance ever-increasing work demands with the demands of the individual children's enrichment activities, means that communication between family members is viewed in relation to efficiency: constantly changing situations demand that family members, in particular mothers, need to communicate details of transportation and home/life management and be available for such communication on an ongoing basis, as discussed by mothers in the upper-middle and middle-class Dykstra, Richter, and Kline families.

When upper-middle-class parents make decisions regarding how they will oversee their children's media use, they consider what they perceive to be their children's rights to independence, and they appreciate their children's willingness to make good decisions on their own. We saw this when Kirsty and Laurel's father, Mark Dykstra, talked about how he wanted his daughters to have the right to select their own music and was pleased when they shared their tastes with him, and when parents in the Blayne-Gallagher family were pleased that their children used their mobile phones to contact each other and solve their transportation problem without the help of their parents. Middle- and upper-middle-class families also encourage the expression of ideas and feelings within family relationships, enabling young people to feel supported and also special—and, to a greater or lesser extent, entitled.

Upper-middle-class young people are confident in their own ability to make decisions regarding digital and mobile media, and to utilize these media in their self-expression and identity construction. Jennifer Yu's use of Neopets for building her confidence as a writer exemplifies this, as does Taylor Billings' decision to change his online social networking profile to better reflect how he wanted his friends and acquaintances to understand him. Each of these young people and several others were able to draw upon the pragmatic, symbolic, and mythic dimensions of entertainment media and social, digital, and mobile media. The story of Korinna and her oversharing not-friend Marta was similarly an example of how these media become woven into peer practices of defining and identifying oneself in opposition to others, and of how important peer acceptance becomes in the preteen and teen years.

Problems can emerge from this sense of independence and rights cultivated in the upper-middle-class family communication ethic of empowerment and expressiveness, however. When Trent Richter's mother refrained from disciplining her son for breaking school rules because she felt complicit in his decision to answer the phone during class, and when Kayla Torelli effectively shielded her mother from her risky online and offline activities, we see examples of parents who have difficulty finding their footing in the midst of changing child-parent relationships. Their desire to parent in a non-authoritarian way combines with the tendency to privilege their children's individual rights over the rights of family members, and this leaves them with questions about when and whether to assert parental authority and how to intervene in troubling behaviors. Upper-middle-class parents are more familiar with digital and mobile media than are less advantaged parents, but they are still likely to encounter unfamiliar situations. This unfamiliarity becomes one more source of tension that is then accentuated in relation to rights (including the right of parents to expect their children to respect them as people, even if not as authoritarian family leaders). When parents feel unsure about intervention because something about digital or mobile media and their children's behavior puzzles them, their children may feel less need to consult with or reference their parents regarding their own behaviors. This apprehension can inadvertently reinforce a sense of self-focus, narcissism, or entitlement to independence.

If we were to look only at troubling stories like those of Trent Richter and Kayla Torelli, then we would not get a full picture of the teen middle- and upper-middle-class experience. Whereas some might wish to suggest that digital and mobile media help middle- and upper-middle-class youth attain independence and autonomy from their parents, the opposite seems to be true. Middle- and upper-middle-class young people use their mobile devices to rely on their parents for support and guidance far longer into their post-high-school years than was possible in previous generations, and parents use technology to stay connected and even to spy on their older children.[5] And as this book has attested, mobiles and even social networking sites are enabling "helicopter parenting" among middle- and upper-middle-class parents, allowing parents to snoop on their children's online profiles and, in extreme cases such as that of cyberbullying mom-and-daughter duo Lori and Sarah Drew, to intervene in strikingly inappropriate ways. Tolerating questionable behaviors or helicoptering in the effort to help children avoid problems can contribute to the middle- and upper-middle-class young person's sense of entitlement and the sense that he or she is special and beyond the rules. Media do not cause these young people to be more narcissistic, but many factors in their lived experience, including media, combine to foster this environment of self-focus. Of course, media can be drawn upon to help young people develop a sense of awareness and appreciation for others, as seen in the middle-class Blayne-Gallagher family, whose media use encouraged discussion about caring for those who were different from them. But this approach requires middle-class families to perform a certain kind of emotion work, developing a narrative about why they might want to resist individualism and consumerism in favor of valuing their contributions to the whole family, and opting for anti-corporate or anti-globalization ideals. We will have more to say about this below. First, however, we need to consider how digital and mobile media uses unfold differently among the would-be middle-class and less advantaged families in this study.

Family Communication Ethics in Would-Be Middle-Class and Less Advantaged Families

I have termed the "would-be middle class" those families that would have had higher income levels, more purchasing power, better housing, and possibly more education if they had not experienced intervening circumstances such as divorce, ill health, or unemployment. The less advantaged families include those whose household incomes have been below $50,000 a year for at least three years in a row, and they are more likely to have experienced chronic unemployment, poverty, discrimination, or a history of alcohol, drug, or sexual abuse in their families. These families embrace an *ethic of respectful connectedness* in their style of family communication that guides how they think about the potential risks of digital and mobile media. As is true of middle-class families, these patterns grow out of both the specific contexts of their home environments and what are taken to be commonsense beliefs about how parents should relate to their children. And as with middle-class families, this ethic of respectful connectedness shapes how technologies become relevant to or problematic within family situations.

Like upper-middle and middle-class families, would-be middle-class and less advantaged families worry about their children's welfare in the present and the future. Many parents in this study undertook extraordinary measures to help their children pursue interests and develop abilities, like Avis Grantman's advocacy for her daughter Nina's participation in her school's special computer program, Louisa and John Cortez's enrollment of their daughter Tanya in a school program for high achievers, and Wyonna Fallon's job change that enabled her daughters to attend a private school after a bullying incident in the public school. Even with these and other special activities, for the most part less advantaged and would-be middle-class families did not have the resources to pursue the intensive extracurricular scheduling that structured the lives of preteens and teens in the middle-class and upper-middle-class families of this study. Sometimes, parental intervention alone wasn't enough, as highlighted in the high social costs Tanya Cortez encountered when her cousins mocked her desire to improve herself, thinking that she was trying to be better than they were. Sometimes, as in the case of single mother Meghan Sealy (chapter 3), the demands of work lives precluded parents from intervening more directly when problems occurred. Even though Meghan had followed her son, Dell, through his school for a day to ensure his attendance, she had to return to work or risk not getting paid, and unfortunately she found few resources that could support her effort to get her son to stay in school—especially when watching MTV and playing games at home were much more attractive than the alternatives.

Young people in these families had more unstructured leisure time, often in smaller family quarters. This meant that they often spent more time with siblings and extended family members, reinforcing a sense of connection within families. They did not always enjoy this particular connection, but it was related to the family's scarce resources. Like Caleb Baylor, Deshonelle Williams, and Iskinder Hagos, young people in these families shared mobile phones, often with their siblings and sometimes with their parents as well. Like upper-middle-class families, these parents and children, too, used mobile phones to make various arrangements regarding transportation, work, and school, but shared phones tended to remain with the mothers in these families (or in Iskinder's case, his father), as the parent was the connective node for family arrangements and thus was perceived to need them the most. Siblings were expected to look out for one another, as Montana Odell did for her younger brother, Thad, and as Rosalia and other young women did as they oversaw their younger siblings' media use. They served as experts about the online realm for parents, and shared in punishments when they allowed their siblings to deviate from household expectations regarding digital and mobile media. Family members sometimes viewed television time as "family time," as was the case in the Grantman, Conner, and Fallon homes, and, when available, sometimes used televisions and computers in separate rooms as a means of finding a bit of private space in an otherwise crowded home life, as Wyonna Fallon, Caleb Baylor, Avis Grantman, and Nancy Oliver each mentioned.

As previous research has demonstrated, less advantaged families tend to embrace stronger parental forms of authority, perhaps in response to the heightened risks that their children encounter. By and large, preteens and teens in the would-be middle-class and less advantaged families in this study were expected to respect the authority of their parents. Many, like Blake and Katie Polanski and Carmen Rodriguez, as well as Montana Odell and Gabriela Richards, did so without difficulty, viewing their parents' oversight of digital and mobile media as an expression of their parents' desire to counteract the many disadvantages and shortcomings they found in their schools, neighborhoods, and communities. Together, family members shared critiques of these environments and, as in the discussion among the Polanski family members who were unhappy with Blake's school experience, and Avis and Nina Grantman's experiences with crumbling infrastructures of neighborhood and community organizations. These critiques seemed to bring family members closer together and to encourage them to trust in one another rather than in the school or neighborhood programs that had too frequently failed them. This, too, reinforced the importance of connectedness within these families, and encouraged family members to look to siblings and extended family members for support in how they would incorporate digital and mobile media into their lives.

When would-be middle-class and less advantaged parents make decisions regarding how they will oversee their children's media use, they prioritize the needs of the entire family over those of the individual. Children in these families seemed less likely to claim the right to make their own decisions and more likely to see their own practices in relation to family priorities, such as when Deshonelle Williams discussed the need to "stick up for her friends and family" when online. Some related family digital and mobile media practices to specific communities of identification, such as when Bina and Sunita discussed the restrictions on their mobile phone use in relation to their parents' cultural and religious values that advocated restricting young women from contacting those beyond their families. Some of these young people therefore also saw their practices in relation to the norms of the larger community of identification of which they were a part, such as when Santosh Sadasankar discussed his experiences of racism that had encouraged him to elect high privacy levels and make his online materials and his mobile phone number available only to those he knew well. Whereas several young people from would-be middle-class and less advantaged families created online social profiles and texted frequently with friends, sometimes these young people found that others in their social circles were less forthcoming, as Iskinder Hagos discovered when he found that few of his acquaintances from either his new home or his old one were on Facebook. In these instances, class difference intersected with racial and ethnic difference, as might be expected in the U.S. context, where class and race tend to overlap. But as other recent studies of U.S. families have found, when members of the same racial and ethnic backgrounds had differing economic experiences, distinct differences emerged between them.[6]

Like the family communication ethic of the upper-middle-class families, some similar challenges arose with respect to the would-be middle-class and less advantaged families' ethic of respectful connectedness. Sometimes, when parents were overly intrusive and authoritarian, older teens rebelled quietly, as Caleb Baylor did within his restrictive, conservative family. Other young people in chapter 3 like Winona and Eduardo did so more directly, claiming the right to oversee their own mobiles because they paid for them. But such actions could come at great cost, as illustrated in Veronica Domentary's move out of her mother's house. Her move resulted in financial independence that made it impossible for her to pursue her goal of community college. The stakes in rebellion could be high among would-be middle-class and less advantaged youth.

Another great challenge to these families was that because they had learned to rely on one another in the face of crises, they had fewer resources at hand to support them when they encountered unfamiliar circumstances, such as those introduced with digital and mobile media. Of course, one could also turn this claim around and state, as many of these families did, that there were fewer resources available, which is why they relied upon those they knew. As noted earlier, would-be middle-class and less advantaged parents were less likely to be familiar with digital and mobile media than were middle- and upper-middle-class parents. This lack of familiarity did not necessarily undermine their sense of parental authority, however. In these families, children had rights, but in relation to the family overall. Parents felt disempowered by the circumstances in which they found both themselves and their children. If anything, their authority was reinforced because of this joint disempowerment, as many parents seemed more than willing to do what they could on behalf of their children, and at least some of their children respected that desire. These young people may have been immersed in a digital culture that encouraged narcissism, but in many ways they were also not a part of this culture. Young people like Iskinder and Santosh had experienced digital culture as a conduit for the same racism and classism they experienced in offline settings, and thus found immersion in it less desirable. As argued earlier, digital and mobile media do not so much cause narcissism in upper-middle-class culture so much as serve as one among many factors that foster an environment for self-focus, and it is also the case that cultures in which would-be middle-class and less advantaged young people find themselves are defined as much by their skepticism toward these media as their embrace of them. Rather than serving as a platform for digital democracy and enhanced diversity, then, digital and mobile media can be experienced as one more avenue that can drive a wedge between young people and the opportunities they seek.

Social Class and the Mediatization of Family Life

Social class makes a difference in how families and individuals approach and incorporate digital, mobile, and entertainment media into their lives. It's not that people somehow adhere to a way of doing things because they consciously make choices based on their class location, or that they are predetermined to act in certain ways because of their location in the stratified economic system of U.S. society. Rather, what this book has argued is that families find themselves with different, and sometimes limited, options regarding how they will address themselves to the challenges they face in their everyday lives. When Avis Grantman, John Cortez, and other parents recognized that their children had more computer savvy than they did, they sought insight and help from friends and family on how to guide their children. This was one way in which a coping strategy evolved that met the perceived needs of families in similar economic circumstances yet from different racial and ethnic backgrounds and with different lived experiences. Those families were not interacting with other families, nor was each creating an idiosyncratic response. They were drawing upon a common pool of cultural experiences and taken-for-granted commonsense ideas about how families rely upon familial connections when facing difficulties— approaches from a common cultural toolkit that is reproduced in would-be middle-class and less advantaged families and which takes a particular form in relation to the needs introduced with the new situation of digital and mobile media.

In seeking to understand the role of media in social change, how are we to understand the interlocking mechanisms—human, technological, and institutional—through which particular changes have come about? A series of case studies like those we have explored in this book has the benefit of providing a specific story line, a narrative through which we might interrogate particularities within a more general theory. Case studies also have the benefit of bringing to the fore the need for definitions and further questions of the general theory, such as, in this case: Whose families are we talking about? Which media do we have in mind? And what do we mean by change?

In this book, I have advocated looking at specific families of differing socioeconomic backgrounds, and I have argued that we can't make blanket statements about how today's digital and mobile media are changing all families in the same way. We can hardly ignore the observable differences between upper-middle-class families and those families whose incomes, assets, education, and life situations currently place them outside the bounds of the middle class. This should tell us something about the role of media in social change. In the case of families, digital and mobile media are reinforcing trends toward a deeply divided society in which certain ideals and images of an ever-consuming and time-poor middle-class life are normalized, even as more and more families find themselves hard pressed to meet those normalized expectations—or any expectations of a life that might be lived with some minimal measure of security. Families are utilizing digital and mobile media to address themselves to the problems of a risk-filled and time-poor society, even as our uses of these communication technologies further contribute to supporting a commercialized environment that we find inhumane in its ravenous needs for consumption and exploitation. We want technologies that solve our problems and address our felt needs for connection, but these same technologies also tempt parents to engage in surveillance in ways that were not possible before and may not be desirable or effective. We want technologies that make life easier, but the ones we use also create more work, particularly for already overburdened mothers. We want technologies that assist us in guiding our children as unique individuals, yet we risk inculcating in them a sense that others are sources of competition rather than members of a community in which, in an important sense, we will fail or thrive together. We are responsible for the technologies our culture is creating, yet the technological environment we have created is beyond our control—or seemingly so. Is this the kind of change we want to see in our culture and in our lives?

Scholars are currently employing the somewhat awkward term "mediatization" to denote studies that consider how various media forms are playing a role in social change.[7] The definition of mediatization I have developed in this book is this: mediatization may be understood as the process by which collective uses of communication media extend developments of media products, contribute to new forms of action and interaction in the social world, and give shape to how we think of humanity and our place in the world.[8] I have argued that in order to understand the role of media in social change, we have to look at communication practice and the ethic that informs and guides that practice. Mediatization can help us to raise questions that are subtler than whether the media are or are not contributing to social change, focusing our attention on how media are contributing to social change that is already under way, and how media might be facilitating cultural production (including, in this case, the production of family communication norms) that, in turn, contributes to, extends, and intensifies such existing social trends. We need to understand how communication media mediate, just as we need linguistics to understand how language mediates or material cultural studies to understand how cultural products mediate. This allows us to better understand the nature of changes within society, culture, and power so that, in turn, we can take responsibility for addressing what is disempowering and empowering in our collective lives.[9]

In his book *No Sense of Place*, media scholar Joshua Meyrowitz proposed that electronic media have tended to "reshape the everyday behaviors associated with group identity, socialization, and hierarchy by undermining print-era patterns of what different types of people know about, and relative to, each other."[10] Digital and mobile media continue and extend the changes brought about with earlier media, challenging parents and young people to develop new norms, especially in relation to autonomy and trust. In middle- and upper-middle-class families, changes in digital and mobile media are extending the trend toward less authoritarian parent-child relationships and may eventually facilitate a shift from top-down styles of parenting to more flexible, collaborative, and relational ones. But the role of these media in relation to parental authority is different in would-be middle-class and less advantaged families, where the stakes are higher and the challenges weightier. In these families, digital and mobile media are extending the trend toward greater familial focus and more social isolation. Although there has been a tendency for theorists to assume that middle-class parents are bellwethers for change and that technology is an equalizer, it may be that differences in parenting styles are becoming more rather than less distinct over time. As a society, we will have to work hard to address ourselves to these differences.

What Technology Is Not Changing: Risks and Needs

So what is changing, and what is not changing, as a result of the introduction of digital and mobile media in family life? First let's consider what is not changing. As discussed in chapter 1, digital and mobile media are not amplifiers of the weightiest risks our children face. We have not seen an increase in teen suicide, teen pregnancy, illegal drug use, or sexual activity since the introduction of the Internet and the mobile phone. This book has pointed out that even though digital and mobile media can play a role in each of these behaviors, these media can also serve as avenues through which young people can have access to more help, support, and advocacy than ever before. These media can be a positive conduit for young people, helping those who feel marginalized or different in their homes and schools to connect with others like them.

Young people have needs that relate to their particular stage in life, and this, too, is not changing as a result of new technologies. Young people need to feel accepted by peers, attractive to prospective intimates, and distinct from others. Digital and mobile media can provide new locations where young people feel the pain of rejection and discrimination, but this is because these locations have also become important platforms for young people as they try out different ways of performing their identities and connecting with others.

What Is Changing and What Needs Our Attention

The Digital Trail

Because young people's identity work is occurring online and with mobile devices, young people must be made aware of what danah boyd has identified as four key characteristics of digital media, as discussed in chapter 1: persistence, constant mutability, scalability, and searchability.[11] Young people must learn to be aware of the persistence of their digital trail, and parents can take a role in helping them to learn to manage this. Throughout their lives, young people will manage not only the materials they make available to others online but also the materials that others make available about them. Because this digital trail persists and remains visible to others, they also are continually viewing their digital trail through differing lenses as they go through different life experiences. *What will my future employer think if she looks at my fraternity photos? What will that cute guy in my science class think of the childhood photos my mom posted?* Any possible new visitor to one's profile or new life situation will trigger a felt need to re-create one's self-representation, as Taylor's story illustrated in chapter 4. Young people also need to be encouraged to act responsibly when posting information and photos about others. Parents need to discuss how such posting can quickly scale beyond their control, as illustrated in the story of the Star Wars kid discussed in chapter 1 and in the stories of online harassment discussed in chapter 5. "Pause before you post" is the mantra suggested by the Cyberbullying Research Center, and it's a good one for parents to discuss with their children as they interact online and through texting.

The Digital Tether

The needs of young people haven't changed, but their social activities are more publicly accessible and observable through social networking sites and text messages. Moreover, it's much easier for young people to text or call their parents for advice and feedback, a fact that may be contributing to an extended adolescence, as Barbara Hofer and Abigail Sullivan Moore have argued.[12] In 2009, about 13 percent of young adults ages twenty-five to thirty-four lived with their parents, up nearly 20 percent from the number at that age who lived with their parents in 1982.[13] A number of scholars and commentators have bemoaned the tendency for young adults to remain dependent on their parents well into their twenties. Some have connected this development with helicopter parenting, as illustrated with recent book titles such as *A Nation of Wimps: The High Cost of Invasive Parenting* and *The Price of Privilege: How Parental Pressure and Material Advantage Are Creating a Generation of Disconnected and Unhappy Kids*[14]. Others acknowledge that a weak economy is also surely a factor in the young adult's return to the nest, and argue that a longer launch time is beneficial for young people overall.[15] While there is no set time when young adults need to live apart from their parents' support, there does come a time when parents need their children to help them in their aging years. Technologies can facilitate connections between generations and can make it easier to help our loved ones weather change, with support flowing from parent to child or in the reverse direction. Whether the development of delayed independence is a positive or negative one in relation to other adult developmental needs is unclear at this point, although it's clear that technologies are playing a significant role in fostering connections and longer periods of dependence between family members.

It's quite possible that today's generation of adults know much more about the activities of their children than previous generations did. This knowledge, as I argued in chapter 1, is a source of anxiety for parents, even as parents see this surveillance as something that is both necessary and protective of their children.[16] Some parents find that they can use data from sources such as Microsoft's Family Safety program to identify the sites their children have visited in order to initiate conversations with their children and to provide them more emotional support. Technologies like these both seem to heighten anxiety and provide tools for nipping potential problems in the bud. As a middle-class parent, I deeply understand the appeal of utilizing surveillance, and I have many friends who use these tools not for discipline but rather to remain in-touch, aware, and responsive parents. Personally, I'm more concerned about how intrusiveness can backfire and can contribute to raising overly dependent and self-focused young people. I am resisting the urge to participate in surveillance, although I often feel like a neglectful parent among my more attentive middle- and upper-middle-class friends. That feeling creates emotion work for parents like me who want to understand themselves as "good parents," an idea with specific meanings in relation to specific cultural groups, and yet who find themselves at odds with their main reference group.

Intensified Emotion Work

Whether parents see these tools as helpful or intrusive, the media-saturated environment of today's parenting has introduced an intensified level of emotion work that is required of both parents and young people in their relationships with each other. As noted in chapter 1, we are all surrounded by information and must access, process, and interpret that information and develop new ways of knowing that may include monitoring ourselves and others in new ways.[17]

Parents have to decide how much surveillance is appropriate and how much is a violation of children's privacy. Parents also have to consider their own self-representation both online and off, and they have to negotiate when and how to turn over to their children the rights to their own digital trail.[18] Because their children can maintain easy and frequent contact with them well into their young adult years, parents must think about how to negotiate changes in autonomy and independence that are key to the parent-child relationship. Importantly, parents also have to consider how they will interact with their children about their digital and mobile media use at various points in their lives together, recognizing that what seems unfamiliar to parents is not necessarily so for young people. And because family members and friends may not approach media in the same ways, parents need to adjust their self-presentations about parenting for differing audiences, as illustrated in the stories of Gwen and Stan Blayne-Gallagher and Wyonna Fallon.

The fact that emotion work seems to fall disproportionately on mothers is nothing surprising. Women have long managed both the "second shift," or the work of managing the household, as well as the "third shift," which is the term Arlie Hochschild uses to refer to the emotion work of helping children to feel secure and cared for in the midst of juggling parental responsibilities of work and home.[19] But as this workload increases with the new and potentially constant demands of digital and mobile media, the time constraints that result from work and intensive parenting may place great demands on a relationship with a partner.[20] This is an important area of concern for women who may feel compelled to choose between the needs of children and the needs of a partner.[21] Mobile phones and digital calendars can help manage time, but rather than securing more time for the maintenance of relationships, they make it easier than ever for work demands to intrude upon family time. Moreover, the rise of the flexible and always-connected workplace has escalated the role of work as a central organizing force in a family's life.

The digital trail, the digital tether, and the resultant increased emotion work of parents and young people are the key dimensions of the mediatization of U.S. families. Two other dimensions of mediatization are less felt but, I believe, are equally if not more significant for us as a society: increasing isolation between social classes and exacerbated inequality. U.S. society's emphasis on individualism and achievement existed before our current technological environment, and our collective uses of digital and mobile media follow patterns that have deepened the divides that have long separated us.

Increasing Isolation

Although the Internet has ushered in a whole new era of connectedness and connectibility, it's easy to lose sight of who is not participating in these connections and what the consequences of nonparticipation might be.

There is an irony in the fact that we feel more interconnected than ever, even as our experiences of class-related separation are more pronounced now than they have been in many decades. Sherry Turkle uses the phrase "alone together" to point to the phenomenon of people in the same space using technologies to connect with people who are elsewhere.[22] As this book pointed out in chapter 2, among would-be middle-class and less advantaged families, being "together alone" also seems to be true. Because these media eat up more and more of our time as we connect with one another through Twitter, Facebook, texting, and a host of other sites, we need to be more intentional than ever before about connecting with those whose life experiences differ from our own, particularly because such connections often need to be made offline. It's been interesting to see a rise in organizations such as WorldPulse, which brings people from developing countries directly into contact with those in the developed world, and Global Voices Online, which provides language translations so that people can hear directly from those most affected by world events.[23] Such organizations help to bridge the gap between the available sea of information about differing cultures and the felt need to connect with human beings on a personal level. Such efforts to connect require intentionality and opportunity, and for lasting change they require continuity as well.

Exacerbated Inequality

As this book has demonstrated, experiences with digital and mobile media differ dramatically according to social and economic resources. Chapter 6 described how these differences have become embedded in an ethic of respectful connectedness, and chapter 5 detailed why efforts at inclusion of marginalized communities are about more than access and opportunity. It's important that we give up the myth that technological proficiency will level the playing field. It's equally important that we consider how to address the gaps that remain between the digital haves and have-nots.

What aspects of digital and mobile media are required for life in today's networked society? Access will continue to be an issue, and corporations will continue to press for more ways to develop products for an elite audience. In 2011, advocacy groups scored a major victory when Verizon lost in its latest effort to legalize a two-tiered Internet in which some content providers could pay for higher-speed delivery of their online materials. While Verizon's plan would be profitable for the company, it would also make much of the Internet inaccessible or interminably slow, effectively giving large corporations greater access to customers than smaller or start-up businesses and individuals who couldn't pay the proposed fee. Advocacy groups scored another victory for access with the protests against the Stop Online Privacy Act, which would have put decisions about free speech and censorship in the hands of corporations. Efforts are under way to expand the Universal Service Fund's Lifeline program, which has long ensured that families unable to afford it have received basic telephone service. Under the proposed expansion, families would also be eligible to receive broadband service regardless of whether they could afford to pay for it.[24] Each of these recent efforts showcases the growing movement in media reform and the connection between media freedoms and the ability of all people to have access to these media.

Implications for the Future

I have discussed what I believe are some of the benefits as well as some of the costs of the different ways in which parents from less advantaged and middle-class, and upper-middle-class families go about their parenting tasks in relation to digital, mobile, and entertainment media. In some ways, this book serves as a critique of the fact that too often, unexamined middle-class assumptions have framed our understandings of how parents "should" approach media in the lives of their children.

I have also attempted to point out that in our discussions about parenting in a digital age, the fears regarding digital and mobile media that middle- and upper-middle-class people express are not only focused on the media themselves but also an expression of their fears of loss: lost wages, lost security, lost hope for a more comfortable and secure future for their children. This fear of loss is what is making it difficult for middle-class parents to participate in any discussion regarding how to build bridges between young people of differing economic circumstances. Middle- and upper-middle-class parents may be concerned about those less fortunate than they are, but ultimately they feel compelled to ensure that their children will be among the few who attain top spots in the Ivy League and the new economy. Arising from the research featured in this book are a number of suggestions that are relevant for the discussion of how parenting in a digital age is different from parenting in the past, and how we might play a more collaborative role in designing the media ecology of the future. We need to change our parenting, change the conversation about media, change the situation for young people, and change the media themselves.

Change Our Parenting

This book has demonstrated that despite the debates about overparenting and helicopter parenting as facilitated by and through communication technologies, too often parents are letting their anxieties about the unknown fuel decision making. How are parents across the economic spectrum to respond to these new challenges? Researchers have identified several best practices for parents who want to foster respectful and connected relationships with their young people without veering into the realm of surveillance that can seem so attractive.

Make Monitoring Less Work-Intensive and More Rule-Specific

As noted in previous chapters, some middle- and upper-middle-class parents seem to be at a loss as to how to create boundaries regarding digital and mobile media, in part because they are focused on their children's paths to empowerment and expressiveness and they therefore want to respect the rights their children have as they learn to make their own decisions. But there are some best practices that are recommended by experts. First, experts generally suggest putting off a child's use of mobile phones and social networking sites for as long as possible. Once it's become necessary or unavoidable to incorporate these media into family life, phones, laptops, and gaming sites all come with parental controls that enable parents to limit the numbers that can be called and received, the sites that can be visited, and the hours spent on systems. Read *A Parent's Guide to Facebook 2.0* and *A Parent's Guide to Google Plus* as well as other helpful guides made available for free through the website ConnectSafely.org.

When your child first gets a mobile phone, ask if you can view the child's texting and online activities. Come to an agreement together about how you will be able to look at their texts and under what circumstances. Mention that your desire to look at their texts is not meant to be an invasion of privacy, but a way for you both to familiarize yourselves with what can be sent and received among peers. Such interactions can also help you discuss advertising and applications that cost money, and can give your child an opportunity to teach you the latest time-saving and fun uses.

Rather than expecting a parent (usually the mother) to go through the record of every keystroke a child enters on a keyboard, consider relying on a less direct system of observation. Expect that laptops, tablets, and other devices will be used in public areas of the home, and keep chargers in your bedroom so that devices are parked there overnight. In addition to saving parents the time required for surveillance, these practice also discourage distraught young people from seeking late-night solace in places where they're not always likely to find it.

Discuss Media Content Both with and Away from the Media

If it's important for you to feel "in the know" about the media environment your children are experiencing, find sites that you can regularly visit for helpful information. CommonSenseMedia.org and NetFamilyNews.org are two sites that offer reviews, recommendations, and news items that will help you feel informed and also give you conversation topics to share with your children.

When your children are giving you a tour of mobile apps or online sites, don't be overly critical, but don't be afraid to be critical, either. To model and encourage critical viewing of online materials, ask them to show you online materials that they think are "fake." Ask them to teach you about privacy settings for Facebook and other social networking sites, and ask them why you have heard that "friends only" is a good option for most people. Ask if they've seen cyberbullying or drama online or in texts between friends, and what they've done about it. If they show you something you find offensive, ask them to talk about what they think about it, and don't be afraid to respectfully tell them why you don't find it appropriate.

Model the Behavior You Want

In one interview with a junior-high-age boy, I asked for insights into how he would know when people might be spending too much time with media, expecting that he would discuss a younger brother or a games-obsessed friend. Instead, he said, "You know, I think about my dad. I wish my dad would put his mobile phone away and just enjoy watching me play soccer once in a while." If we want our own children to value our time with them, we need to model that we are not spending time with them only because we don't currently have a more interesting or demanding call to take or email to answer.

Come to an agreement together about appropriate times and places to use digital and mobile media. Use the Family Internet and Mobile Media Agreement in Appendix C as a place to start the conversation.

Parents often think that we are modeling how to spend time productively, while young people simply see us as "doing our jobs," whether that work is paid or unpaid. What they also need to see is how we value our relationships with them. In what is perhaps my own most difficult personal challenge in this area, I've decided that I'm not going to suggest limiting my children's screen time unless I'm prepared to offer an alternative that demands that I, too, stop what I'm doing in favor of a different activity. This has required me to keep on hand a list of activities that we can do together, including hiking, bicycling, board games, listening to music together, baking, participating in an art or craft project together, or gaming. I believe that my frustration with what I'm tempted to see as their misuse of free time is related to my *own* frustration at the lack of free time I feel I have. I've decided that recognizing that frustration can be a trigger for me to reset my own priorities and get back to the important task of spending unstructured time having fun and interacting with my children.

Prioritize Time Together

This is advice specifically for middle- and upper-middle-class families. Parents like Gwen Blayne-Gallagher remind us of how easy it is to fall into the pattern of rushing between scheduled activities and settling into separate mediated activities when we're home together. Many middle- and upper-middle-class mothers in this study voiced concern about wasting time watching movies, even as young people consistently mentioned movie night as a time for family bonding. It can be challenging to find activities that everyone wants to do together, but as we saw in stories of several families that shared media time because they could not afford other activities, media can form a common bond that crosses generations and is often not too taxing for tired and overburdened parents.

In addition to movie night, invite your children and possibly even their friends to participate in activities such as Dance Dance Revolution, Guitar Hero, or Wii Sports. Select a television program that everyone can watch, and make a commitment to viewing it together on a regular basis. Sharing stories and having fun together are important when you're in your home, because young people need opportunities to experience their homes not only as places where homework and sleep happen or where everyone does separate activities.

Let Your Children Take the Lead

If you have a gaming system, let your teen walk you through Halo, Super Mario Brothers, or Fruit Ninja, or have your younger child introduce you to the world of Club Penguin or Webkinz. Challenge your children to take the lead on family-related digital projects, whether it's documenting the family vacation or making a video holiday card and distributing it through YouTube. Ask for a tour of music sites. Don't expect that you have to be the expert on everything. If you let them lead you through Facebook, Twitter, or other sites, you will also have opportunities to hear what they think about these online locations and applications, and you can then participate in more productive conversations about your own concerns with their digital practices and digital identity.

Use Media for Empowerment

This is advice for upper- and middle-class parents, but also for parents who have more limited access to digital and mobile media. As discussed in chapter 3, many parents are already using media in positive ways, using entertainment media as a platform for discussions of morality and employing mobile phones and social networking sites as pragmatic means to increase the frequency of communication. But parents can go further. As Cathy Davidson suggests in her book *Now You See It: How the Brain Science of Attention Will Transform the Way We Live, Work, and Learn*, parents need to experiment with user-friendly software programs such as Scratch, a program that lets parents and children build their own computer games.[25] She believes that collaborative and participatory learning between parents and children enables parents to learn along with their children. Building relationships of trust between parents and children gives adults opportunities to provide guidance to young people, but also allows them to listen and learn from young people, whose life experiences have their own trajectories.

Change the Conversation About the Media

Concerns about media and children are always to some extent concerns about both individual children and our fears for the future of society. Yet with the introduction of digital and mobile media, we have an opportunity to change the conversation from one that is guided by fear to one of realism and possibility.

Changing the discussion about the media would also enable us to recognize that the media are not the sole cause of change or even a primary one. The media contribute to ongoing trends; they mediate; and because they have certain affordances, they help to reinforce some practices and make others less attractive. Perhaps more than anything else, the introduction of new communication technologies can provide a moment of reflection and a wake-up call for our society, giving us a way to take the cultural temperature. This process of reflection might lead us to different questions. Rather than asking how Internet is or is not making us more narcissistic or isolated, we might ask instead why society is accepting a move toward greater self-focus and less compassion on the part of the upper-middle-class, and why we are allowing those who are already marginalized to become more so. What would it look like to have media policies that mitigated against further movements in these directions?

An excellent example of an approach that begins by addressing public concerns and then goes on to reframe the debate occurs in the report on U.K. media and families by Sonia Livingstone and Ranjana Das.[26] After an introduction that acknowledges that media have become thoroughly embedded in the everyday lives of European families, the report opens with a section titled "What Are Media Effects?" A brief yet conclusive review of the literature ends by noting that media effects are rarely supported by evidence in a straightforward way, and that media effects depend on other factors. In other words, communication technologies do not raise the level of risk for young people, and our research should not begin with the assumption that they do.

Change the Situation for Young People

If our digital and mobile media uses are helping to produce a society that is more divided than ever before, then we have a responsibility to our children to help them (and us) recognize and address this fact. For middle-class young people, we need to figure out ways to utilize media to develop a sense of connection with those whose life experiences differ from theirs. Involvement in media production can be a powerful way to do this. Schools, religious organizations, and other community programs can provide ways for young people to explore issues of inequity, moving beyond a charity impulse to a mentality of alliance. Less advantaged young people need more opportunities to develop their own voices and to see connections with the voices and concerns of others. They can learn to see that what they are experiencing is not fair and that something needs to be done about this. Involvement in media production can also help youth to explore these things. We need efforts that enable young people to learn how to express their concerns and interests in ways that address the real inequities they experience.

As noted earlier, it may be that digital and mobile media are providing us with new ways of thinking about who we are in relation to one another. In a variety of work environments, within education, and across scholarly disciplines today, we see a turn from the hierarchical relationship to a networked and relational model of interaction.[27] For instance, to challenge the assumption that things always progress from the bottom up in hierarchical fashion, the philosophers Gilles Deleuze and Felix Guattari have suggested the metaphor of the rhizome, an underground plant stem that spreads horizontally rather than vertically and puts out roots and shoots in multiple directions. These philosophers suggest that, rather than seeing interactions as competitions for control and resources in a one-way route to progress, we can consider how we continually learn from and interact with one another, like the orchid and the wasp; we are mutually dependent upon one another, even though the characteristics of that dependence will vary with each relationship. Wikipedia is a great example of how we're beginning to conceive of the benefits of sharing ideas and relying upon a community of people who are sticklers for detail to help us manage the overflow of possible things we should know about.[28] But for all the hype surrounding applications such as Wikipedia, there are also stories of how our increasingly interconnected ways of being can be misused and can result in unforeseen consequences.[29] This, too, is something we need to consider when we think about how being a part of a network is reshaping parenting and parent-teen relationships.

Change the Media, Change the Culture

This chapter opened with the story of Trithemius, the forlorn scribe who sought to spread his message about printing's dire effects by printing and distributing his disapproval. It is time, now, for parents to consider how we might employ the metrics of digital and mobile media to address the concerns we have about the role of media in our children's lives. In the television age, a great deal of energy was focused on regulating the content of television, although few substantive policies were enacted.[30] Advocates claim greater success in encouraging the development of programming for children than in implementing regulations that would limit advertising to children.[31] And yet, with the rise of digital media, new concerns have arisen regarding the regulation of children's spaces online, from sites such as Club Penguin, Webkinz, and Disney Online, which bridge online play and commercial products, to sites such as Facebook, which identify certain of your purchases and promote goods to you and those in your social network based on those purchases.[32]

In the field of media studies, television policy quickly became a specialized field. To be engaged in discussions of policy, one needed to be conversant with the structure of the Federal Communications Commission, the Federal Trade Commission, network and cable television, and often federal and state legislation. And even though the 1970s had seen the development of restrictions on the amount and type of advertising allowed during children's television and the kinds of programming permissible during certain hours, the Telecommunications Act of 1996 largely reversed decades of television policy, promoting the interests of the market at the expense of the public.[33] We have seen the results of this deregulation in the flood of children's media and consumer goods tie-ins and cross-promotions, a decrease in diversity in media content, a decrease in women-and ethnic-minority-owned media, continued irregular service coverage in impoverished rural areas, and a decline in media content that serves local needs and interests.[34]

Policies guiding mobile communication and the Internet are evolving much more quickly, and more publicly, than did policies governing television. There are also several organizations that have come into being to assist people in sorting out the various laws, corporations, and citizens' advocacy groups involved in changing, or establishing, policies. Free Press and the Benton Foundation are two that are worth following.

Of course, not many parents will feel that they have the time or the interest to delve into the particulars of policy making. What is important to recognize, and what this book has sought to highlight, is that the problem with media today, as media critics such as Robert McChesney have argued, is not only related to what is available to children on television screens, gaming devices, and mobile downloads. The problems rest in a system that creates, supports, and reinforces our reliance on capitalism with ever-increasing consumption at its core. The overwhelming and unchecked power of corporate interests to dictate the terms of American society is, of course, the same root problem identified by sociologists of family and labor such as Arlie Hochschild, Stephanie Coontz, and Barbara Ehrenreich. And yet sociologists in the United States have tended to view media through the established lens of "effects on individuals," concentrating on what individual parents should do rather than drawing connections between this corporate incursion and the need for media reform. A case in point is the popular sociological work by Juliet Schor titled *Born to Buy: The Commercialized Child and the New Consumer Culture*. Schor argues that the encroachment of commercialism is changing childhood, and that marketing to children needs more governmental regulation rather than industry self-regulation. Yet rather than discuss media ownership regulation and how parents can work together as an alliance to negotiate the current commercialized media environment, she, like those in older models of mass communication research, has taken this concern into an individualistic framework, advocating for more study of the effects of advertising on children and for more policies that govern what gets put on the air. These are important issues, but I argue that they do not get at the root of the problem. We need to consider why media corporations want to make products that appeal to children and adolescents. The answer is that young people are a profitable audience. If media industries were regulated and held accountable for their role in fostering the public good rather than regulated and held accountable for their ability to maximize profits for shareholders, we might have a different media landscape. We might come to expect more profit sharing from corporations that benefit from selling things to us and to our children; we might expect a greater movement of resistance when corporations such as Verizon propose a two-tiered Internet that will further disadvantage those who cannot afford to pay for access. We might come to question why we ever believed that a policy environment emphasizing the importance of competition between corporations would result in a media environment that serves the best interests of public life. In short, we would realize that whether for pragmatic purposes of connecting us to one another, symbolic purposes of helping us to draw upon cultural resources to identify ourselves in our relations with others, or mythic purposes of creating meaningful stories for an equitable life together, the media hold more value to us as a society than simply their potential to earn money for stockholders.

Conclusion

Just like Trithemius, parents are tempted to lash out against new technologies that were not a part of their own growing-up experiences. Yet these technologies actually provide parents with new means for connecting with and creating stronger bonds with our children. These new opportunities do not come without their own dilemmas, as I've discussed in relation to the digital trail, the digital tether, the emotion work of parenting, and the social experiences of increased isolation and exacerbated inequality. What lies ahead for us as parents and as a society has a great deal to do with how we think of our role in relation to the technologies we create and the uses to which we allow those technologies to be put. Communication technologies are not luxuries for the few. We have to find ways to ensure that broadband access is available and viewed as necessary for everyone. At the same time, we also have to find ways for middle- and upper-middle-class parents to view technologies and, more important, leisure and family time as necessary.

The last decade has seen tremendous changes in the economic fortunes of U.S. families. Those on Wall Street, who were never fully trusted by those on Main Street, gambled and lost on a massive commodity boom that decimated people's retirement savings and reversed decades of housing property values. If ever there were a time when the public might reconsider the value of regulation, this is it. We were told that reduced regulation was good for the economy, and this proved to be a lie. And yet the United States has barely changed its regulation of the financial industry in this country, let alone launched a consideration of how international trade and inequitable working and labor conditions outside the United States are contributing to the lower wages and disappearing jobs of American families.

In order to address the concerns that our increasingly mediated and risk-dominated society demands, then, we must rethink the ways that societal institutions support our parents and children. As a society, we have been willing to think about the implications of media content, but we have done little to regulate the environment of digital and mobile media to ensure that many different life experiences are accounted for, in terms of both access and representations. If we truly want to counter the commercialization of childhood, we need to recognize that there are links between an unregulated marketplace that places profit above public welfare and sells to children and an unregulated marketplace that outsources jobs, keeps wages artificially low, and makes it difficult for families to meet their basic needs. Solutions to the problems that the digital and mobile media have brought to our attention will not lie in creating policies about media alone, nor will they rest in family policy alone. We must start to consider how policies advocating media reform and policies addressed to family life intersect and overlap with one another. The digital and mobile media that are so much a part of our lives may seem inevitable, but the particular forms they take and the organizational patterns governing the industries that make and distribute them are not. It is up to us to choose how these media will fit into our collective lives and how they will shape the lives of our children and families in the future.

APPENDIX A | Methodology

T O EXPLORE HOW FAMILIES from various backgrounds negotiated the introduction of new media into their home lives, I worked with a variety of research assistants to conduct in-depth and focus group interviews and observations with a total of 343 people over the course of eleven years (2001–12).[1] These interviews took place in urban, suburban, and rural areas near New York City, Washington, D.C., Cleveland, Denver, Seattle, San Francisco, and Los Angeles. We interviewed a total of 194 teens and preteens between the ages of eleven and eighteen, as well as eighty-six of their parents and sixty-three of their younger siblings. We conducted repeated interviews with fifty family groups and also asked several of the teens we met in these family groups as well as some teens from other locales to put together discussion groups with their friends, resulting in twenty discussion groups.

The earliest interviews (2001–6) were conducted by Monica Emerich, Curtis Coats, Michele Miles, Denice Walker, Christof Demont-Heinrich, Scott Webber, and AnnaMaria Russo as part of a project overseen by Stewart Hoover and myself at the University of Colorado. All of the interviewers were doctoral students at the time of the interviewing, and they interviewed forty-six family groups, interviewing the families together and then individual family members separately in Seattle, Washington, D.C., Denver, and Los Angeles. Michele, Monica, and Scott then also conducted nine focus groups with thirty-five members of the friendship circles of some of the young people from those original family groups.

Working with Rachel Monserrate, Caroline Davidson, Colette Holst, Alexis Lynn, and Deidre Helton of the University of Denver, nine focus groups and eight additional in-depth interviews (2007–12) were conducted with a total of sixty young people.[2] Students in the University of Denver's Qualitative Research Methods classes of 2009, 2010, and 2011 conducted additional interviews and observations with four family groups (eight parents, eight teens), and I conducted two informal discussion group interviews with twenty-four parents, adding another forty people to the sample. These interviews were conducted in three different urban and suburban areas in Colorado. About a third of this group were young people and parents from lower-income and would-be middle-class families and two-thirds were in middle- and upper-middle-class families.

Twenty-four of the fifty family groups participating in this study had annual house-hold incomes that fell below the U.S. Census-determined median household income of $48,201, and eighteen were above that median. One-third of the teen discussion groups were held in neighborhoods where the average household income was at or below the national median. Twenty of the households interviewed were headed by a single parent. Thirty-three of the families described themselves as European American or Caucasian, fourteen as bi- or multiracial; there was one each of families describing themselves as African American, Latino, and Asian.[3] The racial/ethnic background of the teens in the discussion groups was thirty-nine European American, seventeen Latino, six African American, two Asian, and seventeen bi- or multiracial.[4]

In the family groups, we interviewed parents and teens together and then separately, seeking to gain insights into how new media fit into their everyday lives and how they negotiated conflicts that emerged in relation to these technologies in their family lives. Teens in discussion groups spoke of how they utilized digital media in their everyday lives, discussing family policies as well as conflicts about the technology that had occurred.

Interviewees were located through referrals from various "gatekeepers," including educators, workplace associates, and officials who worked in several non-profit agencies focused on helping disadvantaged families. Interviewees were also located through the researchers' acquaintance and friendship networks. Family groups that had been interviewed were asked to assist the researchers in finding additional interviewees. Families were recruited using what Lindlof and Taylor have termed "maximum variation sampling," in which each family or discussion group was expected to add a contrasting element to the overall sample.[5] All names of interviewees were changed. Six of the youth focus groups were organized with the help of a young person who took on the task of organizing meetings with friends in their social networks. All participants were compensated for their involvement in this research, receiving a gift card in the amount of between $15 and $100 depending on the time commitment and level of involvement of the participants. The various interrelated projects received approval from the University of Colorado and University of Denver Institutional Review Boards.

Data Analysis

Analysis of the data began immediately after the first family group was interviewed and continued concurrently with data collection. Topics pertaining to use, rules, and tensions related to new media in the lives of teens and their parents were coded and discussed using a constant comparative method as described by Glaser and Strauss.[6] Consistent with Michael Agar's argument that we not break apart data but rather consider narratives in context, I kept all of the interviews and other research materials in large three-ring binders organized chronologically so that I could periodically read through the entire data record.[7] I then began coding the data by writing comments in the transcript margins as a means of initially identifying and highlighting categories for analysis, and I frequently returned to these notes.[8] The interview data in the transcripts were also analyzed using a social constructionist approach that Baumberg has termed "narratives-in-interaction."[9] This method of analysis suggests that the researcher should pay attention not only to what is said, but also to what is not said, and why certain statements might have been made in a particular context to elicit a desired response among a specific audience. This approach differs from traditional narrative analysis, as Baumberg writes: "Rather than seeing narratives as intrinsically oriented toward coherence and authenticity, and inconsistencies and equivocations as an analytic nuisance, the latter are exactly what is most interesting. They offer a way into examining how storytellers are bringing off and managing their social identities in context."[10] There are two levels of analysis in this approach, therefore: first, a consideration of and written comment on the transcript regarding what is said, and second, a consideration of why a particular story or statement might be deployed and how it might then be understood between speaker and audience. Such an approach helpfully leads to a focus on the socially constructed nature of the discourses through which parents and their children speak, both to each other and to those who are interviewing them about their practices in relation to one another.[11]

My research team and I produced a one- or two-page index for each interview, highlighting topics discussed and identifying where they could be located in the transcript materials. To further ease the process of locating key passages, I developed what my research team and I termed an *analytical index guide* for each family, individual, or group of individuals interviewed. The analytical index guide was an expanded version of the one- or two-page index that included short passages from the interview identified by topic in the order in which they occurred within the interview. The analytical index guide thus enabled us to consider several pertinent topics in the order in which they occurred in the interviews while also reducing the data, as the guide eased the process of recalling the context and overall flow of each individual interview while enabling the quick review of conversations pertaining to pertinent categories.[12] The analytical index guides thus produced a new set of shortened data materials that remained separate from the overall corpus of data, yet maintained the order and context of the original interviews. Both the one-page indexes and the analytical index guides were placed before each interview transcript in a binder organized by interview groups so that I could move easily between one-page summaries, excerpted passages organized by category, and entire transcripts.

Identifying Patterns in the Data

The first pattern to emerge in the data related to socioeconomic status. It became clear early on that differences of income, neighborhood, and resources for families made a large difference in the resources of time and money that families were able to bring to the process of negotiating about digital and mobile media in their homes. This of course is consistent with research on the digital divide and access to technologies.[13] This level of analysis led to several articles that I co-authored with colleagues on how people from differing socioeconomic backgrounds experience such things as the digital divide and their sense of how access to computers and the Internet might or might not assist in helping their young people to achieve their eventual economic goals.[14] Another interesting finding was that in more disadvantaged families, parents relied on both older siblings and on extended family members to help monitor digital and mobile media use (see chapter 5).

Next, I looked for patterns among the statements made by teens and tweens between the ages of eleven and eighteen about how digital and mobile media fit into their everyday practices. Practices surrounding friendships quickly emerged as the most salient of uses.[15] I introduced the idea of constant contact as the organizing principle that seemed to guide how young people related to one another, as many of the young people noted that they felt as if they were either in constant contact or constantly contactable by their primary peer group.[16] I was also seeing things that had already been established in research, such as the fact that whereas teen and tween girls enjoyed interacting through writing, teen and tween boys seemed to prefer interacting through gaming. Additionally, teens and tweens were finding ways to utilize the digital realm to experiment with reaching out and attempting to establish relationships with people of both genders.[17] And teens and tweens compared the number of contacts they had on buddy and chat lists as well as on mobile phone lists as a means of quantifying their popularity.[18] The character of the communication between boys and girls differed as well, as boys tended to enjoy conflicts and girls were more inclined to ask for feedback on materials they posted online.

Another theme that emerged in conversations with teens about their digital and mobile media use involved the importance of how they negotiated use in relation to parental constraints.[19] Several teens reported that their parents were concerned about supervision and had therefore encouraged or mandated use of the computer in their home's main room. Teens developed work-arounds such as switching or closing screens or even developing false screens so that they could quickly hide their online conversations or other activities from parents who came too close to the screen. Once social networking became part of the landscape, some teens developed secondary Facebook pages so that they could share one with their parents and adults and reserve a second one for more private communication among their peers.[20] One of the most extreme and intriguing cases of work-arounds was described by Rivka Ribak. In a paper she developed with an M.A. student in Haifa, they analyzed a young Palestinian woman whose boyfriend purchased her a cell phone that she kept hidden from her family but with which she could remain in contact with him against her family's wishes.[21]

After considering teen practices, I then looked at parental practices that seemed to group together, and found that there were similarities according to the age of the children in the families. Several of the parents of younger children used the term "strict" to describe their household rules regarding when and how their children could access and utilize digital and mobile media. Some parents used this term to refer to the establishment of transparent and consistent rules regarding expectations of media use, whereas others used it to assert their parental decision-making authority over household media practices. Problems with this strict approach sometimes emerged when young people reached the age of about eleven or twelve. At that point, many young people entered into more serious negotiations with their parents as they voiced their own views and attempted to make their own decisions regarding media consumption and practices. I noticed that "trust" was a word that parents and teens used to discuss how they handled these negotiations of privilege and autonomy, as parents felt that teens and preteens needed to earn their trust and teens and preteens both desired to be trusted and to find that the adults in their lives could be trusted to follow through on their promises regarding digital and mobile media (see chapter 2). Trust remained a pertinent term for older teens and their parents as well, although ownership and independence emerged as sites of struggle and negotiation, as older teens sometimes purchased their own cell phones or, in the case outlined in chapter 5, claimed the computer technology as their own as they moved out of the residence of their parent(s).

Time was a category that received a great deal of attention among both parents and young people. Parents worried about whether they had enough time with their children and discussed issues such as helping their children to occasionally "unplug." Both children and parents felt constantly pressed for time (as discussed in the introduction and in chapter 3). Sometimes, digital and especially mobile media seemed to be very much a part of their efforts to solve the time problem, as parents texted or called children from work to remind them of commitments or simply to check in, and children texted, chatted, and called friends and family members when they were traveling between activities. At other times, the digital and mobile media seemed to exacerbate the problem of time shortage, especially as parents lamented the constant contact with peers via texting or social network sites that they believed ate into family-time activities such as dinners out or movie nights. Such constant contact between peers sometimes caused last-minute changes to plans that affected other family members as well.

A theme that I returned to at several points in the process of identifying patterns was that of differing notions of authority. Despite the fact that some parents of younger children seemed interested in maintaining strict lines of authority, not all parents were interested in developing and maintaining a hierarchical relationship with their children, and not all teens were engaged in a constant battle of resistance to parental authority. I found that in some of the most hierarchically (and patriarchally) organized families, some children were compliant and other children were resistant to the ways in which parents exerted authority and established and maintained digital and mobile media practices.Differences in responses to parental styles could be found even in the same families (see chapter 5).[22] One of the interesting patterns to emerge was that the children who seemed least interested in resisting parental authority when it came to views and practices regarding digital and mobile media were those whose parent or parents embraced a democratic and child-centered view (see chapters 7 and 8). An especially striking finding was that this lack of conflict over digital and mobile media seemed to emerge even in families where there was a serious technological and generational gap in competence within the digital realm (chapter 8).[23]

I end this appendix with where the book begins, in an effort to make more transparent the process of how one gets from what John Seidel terms the tasks of observing, collecting, and thinking about things to this particular book.[24]

| Parents, Children, and the Media Landscape: Resources

Websites and Organizations

CommonSenseMedia.org: Offers age-specific reviews for television programs, websites, video games, books, and music. They also offer information on public policy affecting the media environment. The site is funded by foundations, educational organizations, parents, and individuals.

NetFamilyNews: Provides a review of the latest news on technologies that affect the lives of families and children, including reviews of parent guides to Facebook and Google Plus, information on privacy and safety laws and issues, and school and library policy concerns. The site is funded by private companies serving the family market as well as individuals and educators. The editor of NetFamilyNews is Anne Collier, a writer and journalist with expertise in Internet safety who is also executive director of the Tech Parenting Group.

ConnectSafely.org: Much of the content on this site is drawn from NetFamilyNews but is organized topically in a user-friendly way. There's also an active and unmonitored parent forum, which means the discussion and advice range from helpful to questionable.

GetNetWise: Contains a large repository of video tutorials that help parents to set privacy and search settings on the computers their children use. Provides online safety guides and an excellent explanation of the kinds of risks children are likely to encounter online at different ages.

Media Awareness Network: Based in Canada, this site offers resources on digital literacy for parents and educators. Their e-parenting tutorial includes the topics "online research and homework," "online relationships," "inappropriate content," "online marketing," and "too much time online." They are supported by telecommunications companies in Canada and in the United States and are endorsed by numerous educational organizations.

NetSmartz: A commercially supported site that is part of the National Center for Missing and Exploited Children, this site offers up-to-date Internet safety presentations given by law enforcement officials. The site includes real-life stories and resources that let young people learn to identify dangers online.

Motherlode: Adventures in Parenting: This is a *New York Times* parenting blog, found at parenting.blogs.nytimes.com. If you long to participate in intelligent conversations about how parenting relates to the latest news (remember the guy who shot nine bullets into his daughter's laptop after a disrespectful Facebook post?), this is the place to go. You'll need a *New York Times* subscription (either print or online) to access this blog, but it's worth it, as you'll find it a refreshing and unique place to discuss online parenting as well as a host of other issues contemporary parents face.

Ongoing Sources for Research into Parents, Children, and Media

PewInternet.Org: The Pew Internet and American Life Project issues monthly reports on trends in Internet and mobile phone use as well as research on special topics of interest.

Joan Ganz Cooney Center: The people who brought us *Sesame Street* are now conducting research on how to maximize technology's potential for learning and development among young people.

Digital Media and Learning: This site features entries from scholars who are studying digital media use in the everyday lives of young people and their families, and educators who are putting into practice new and innovative ideas about technology's role in learning.

The GoodPlay Project: A research effort based at Harvard that's exploring the ethical implications of decision making among young people online.

danah boyd: A researcher at Microsoft, danah has been dubbed "high priestess of the Internet" by *Financial Times*. Her blog includes reviews of her research, which focuses on young people (specifically teens) and privacy.

Sonia Livingstone: Based in the U.K., Sonia is the preeminent researcher of children, families, and the Internet in the world and makes available on her website numerous reports that set the standards for research in this area.

Media Policy Organizations

FreePress.Net: If you're puzzled about SOPA or why Verizon wants to change legislation to make the Internet faster for some providers than others, this is the site that will break it down for you. Information ranges from policy-specific discussions on how advocacy groups are lobbying the Federal Communications Commission to tips on what you can do to help you and your child understand which corporations are profiting most from the current privacy rules that are making parents especially nervous.

National Conference for Media Reform: This annual event brings together educators, activists, media creators, and policy makers who are interested in making media safer and more accessible for everyone.

APPENDIX C | Family Digital and Mobile Media Agreement

IN ORDER FOR THIS agreement to be effective, parents as well as children should be encouraged to sign it. The goal of working through this agreement is to demonstrate and practice mutual respect as well as to initiate discussions about why certain rules are considered respectful to others, both within the family and outside it.

Time Together

1. I agree to spend _____ hours per week doing activities with only my family members.
   Signed: _____

2. I agree that when I am at the dinner table with my family (whether at home or else-where), I will put my phone and other devices away and I will not return to them until we have finished cleaning up after the meal.
   Signed: _____

3. I agree that the following locations will be no-technology zones:
   Signed: _____

Mutual Support

4. I agree that I will tell someone in the family if I experience something online that makes me feel bad or if I find something that I feel is inappropriate.
   Signed: _____

5. I agree that no matter what I am doing, I will answer the phone when I see that a family member has sent our unique passcode via text.
   Signed: _____

Respecting the Rights of Others

1. I will download or use copyrighted materials only when they are legal to download or I have sought and received permission to use them.

Signed: _____

2. I will not fill out surveys or questionnaires online and will not give out specific information about where I live or where I go during the day.

Signed: _____

3. I will give credit to others when I cite, quote, or copy their ideas or images from an online source.

Signed: _____

4. I won't copy, paste, and send a message to someone else if that message was meant only for me.

Signed: _____

Limits

1. I agree that I will ask permission when I'd like to view what someone else has been doing online or elsewhere. I agree that I will not hide what I am doing online and on my phone from other members of my family.

Signed: _____

2. I agree that I will not share personal information that I wouldn't be willing to see broadcast on our local television news.

Signed: _____

3. I agree to limit time on the computer to _____ hours per week.

Signed: _____

4. I agree to limit time on game devices to _____ hours per week.

Signed: _____

5. I agree that I am responsible for remembering my own password, and I will not share it with anyone beyond my family.

Signed: _____

6. I agree that I will practice respectful and responsible behavior, and I will not insult other people or send mean messages online, in a text, or in a comment.

Signed: _____

7. I agree that I will not purchase anything online or enter a credit card for any reason without asking a parent first.

Signed: _____

Opportunities

1. I agree that I will ask someone else in my family to teach me how to do _____ thing(s) per week.

Signed: _____

NOTES

Preface: The Parent App and the Parent Trap

1. Amanda Lenhart, *Teens, Cell Phones and Texting*, Pew Internet and American Life project, April 20, 2011; Amanda Lenhart, Mary Madden, Aaron Smith, Kirsten Purcell, Kathryn Zickuhr, and Lee Rainie, *Teens, Kindness, and Cruelty on Social Network Sites*, Pew Internet and American Life Project, November 9, 2011; Amanda Lenhart, "It's Personal: Similarities and Differences in Online Social Network Use Between Teens and Adults," presentation at the annual meeting of the International Communication Association, May 23, 2009; Amanda Lenhart, Mary Madden, and Aaron Smith, *Teens and Social Media*, Pew Internet and American Life Project, http://pewinternet.org (retrieved January 20, 2008); Amanda Lenhart, *Teens, Video Games, and Civics*, Pew Internet and American Life Project, http://pewinternet.org (retrieved October 1, 2008).

2. Sara Kessler, "Six Valuable SNs (Social Networks) for Parents," *Mashable*, January 21, 2011, http://mashable.com/2011/01/21/parenting-social-networks (retrieved January 31, 2012).

3. MediaSmarts (2012, May 29). *Young Canadians in a Wired World, Phase III: Talking to Youth and Parents about Life Online.* Available: http://mediasmarts.ca/research-policy. Retrieval: July 19, 2012. See also discussion of this study at Anne Collier, "WHAT has 'online safety' wrought (with parents)? *NetFamilyNews.org.* Available: http://www.netfamilynews.org/?p=31663. Retrieval: July 19, 2012; See also Randstad Workmonitor Report (2012, March 3). *Technology may be eroding work-life balance: survey.* VietnamNet. vn/Xinhuanet. Available: http://english.vietnamnet.vn/en/world-news/19651/technology-may-be-eroding-work-life-balance--survey.html. Retrieval: July 19, 2012.

4. On "good-enough parenting," see, for example, Becky Beaupre Gillespie and Hollee Schwartz Temple, *Good Enough Is the New Perfect: Finding Happiness and Success in Modern Motherhood* (New York: Harlequin, 2011).

5. Margaret Nelson, *Parenting Out of Control* (New York: New York University Press, 2010).

6. Barbara K. Hofer and Abigail Sullivan Moore, *The iConnected Parent: Staying Close to Your Kids in College (and Beyond) While Letting Them Grow Up* (New York: Free Press/Simon and Schuster, 2010).

7. See Sonia Livingstone, *Young People and New Media* (London: Routledge, 2002).

8. On the concept of affordances, or the practices that technologies either curb or make possible, see I. Hutchby, "Technologies, Texts, and Affordances," *Sociology* 35, 2 (2001): 441–56.

9. This is a position articulated in feminist theories of the social construction of technology, notably Judy Wajcman, *Technofeminism* (Cambridge: Polity Press, 2004). Wajcman is interested in how women's uses of technology relate both to women's continued experiences of discrimination and oppression and to their prospects for emancipation.

10. Carolyn Marvin, *When Old Technologies Were New: Thinking About Electric Communication in the Late Nineteenth Century* (New York: Oxford University Press, 1990), 5.

11. The term "gradations of digital inclusion" is introduced in Sonia Livingstone and Elizabeth Helsper, "Gradations of Digital Inclusion: Children, Young People, and the Digital Divide," *New Media and Society* 9, 4 (2008): 671–96.

12. Marina Primorac, "F&D Spotlights Widening Gap Between Rich and Poor," *IMF Survey Magazine: In the News*, September 12, 2011, www.imf.org/external/pubs/ft/survey/so/2011/NEW091211A.htm.

13. Roger Silverstone, Eric Hirsch, and David Morley, "Information and Communication Technologies and the Moral Economy of the Household," in Roger Silverstone and Eric Hirsch, eds., *Consuming Technologies*, 15–31 (London: Routledge, 1992).

14. Mary Field Belenky, Blythe McVicker Clinchy, Nancy Rule Goldberger, and Jill Mattuck Tarule, *Women's Ways of Knowing: The Development of Self, Voice, and Mind* (New York: Basic Books, 1997).

15. My favorite book in this regard is religious studies scholar Robert Orsi's *Between Heaven and Earth: The Religious Worlds People Make and the Scholars Who Study Them* (Princeton, NJ: Princeton University Press, 2006).

Chapter 1: Risk, Media, and Parenting in a Digital Age

1. See, e.g., Don Tapscott, *Growing Up Digital: The Rise of the Net Generation* (New York: McGraw-Hill, 1999); John Palfrey, *Born Digital: Understanding the First Generation of Digital Natives* (New York: Basic Books, 2008); Amanda Lenhart, *Generation IM: Teens and Technology*, Pew Internet and American Life Project, 2003, http://pewinternet.org (retrieved August 28, 2011).

2. Rivka Ribak argues that mobile phones serve as a kind of security blanket both for parents and for young people, as they enable parents to give more independence to children while keeping them tethered to them electronically. See Rivka Ribak, "Remote Control, Umbilical Cord and Beyond: The Mobile Phone as a Transitional Object," *British Journal of Developmental Psychology* 27, 1 (March 2009): 183–96.

3. See Deborah Feyerick and Sheila Steffen, "'Sexting' Lands Teen on Sex Offender List," April 7, 2009, http://articles.cnn.com/2009-04-07/justice/sexting.busts_1_phillip-alpert-offender-list-offender-registry?_s=PM:CRIME (retrieved August 28, 2011).

4. Michele L. Ybarra, Cheryl Alexander, and Kimberly J. Mitchell, "Depressive Symptomatology, Youth Internet Use, and Online Interactions: A National Survey," *Journal of Adolescent Health* 36 (2005): 9–18.

5. Nicholas Carr, *The Shallows: What the Internet Is Doing to Our Brains* (New York: W. W. Norton, 2010); Maggie Jackson and Bill McKibben, *Distracted: The Erosion of Attention and the Coming Dark Age* (New York: Prometheus, 2009).

6. List from a talk given by David Finkelhor, "The Internet, Youth Deviance, and the Problem of Juvenoia," www.vimeo.com/16900027 (retrieved August 28, 2011). This talk was reviewed in Anne Collier, "Juvenoia, Part I: Why Internet Fear Is Overrated," www.netfamilynews.org/?p=30220 (retrieved August 28, 2011).

7. Ibid.

8. Ibid.

9. Ibid.

10. danah boyd, "Social Network Sites as Networked Publics: Affordances, Dynamics, and Implications," in Zizi Papacharissi, ed., *A Networked Self: Identity, Community, and Culture on Social Network Sites*, 39–58 (New York: Routledge, 2010). Note that boyd was writing specifically about social network sites; I believe that her observations are relevant for characteristics of the digital environment in general.

11. Ibid.

12. Ibid.

13. Ibid.

14. Lynn Harris, "ChatRoulette: Should Parents Worry About the New Internet Sensation?" report on Babble.com, www.babble.com/kid/chatroulette-parental-controls (retrieved July 16, 2010).

15. Associated Press, "Iowa Teen's Suicide Prompts Strong Anti-Bullying Statement," *Christian Science Monitor*, April 23, 2012, www.csmonitor.com/The-Culture/Family/2012/0423/Iowa-teen-s-suicide-prompts-strong-anti-bullying-statement (retrieved April 24, 2012).

16. B. Glassner, *The Culture of Fear: Why Americans are Afraid of the Wrong Things* (New York: Basic Books, 2010).

17. Ashley Korslein and KREM.com, "'Sexting' Takes on New, More Dangerous Form," KVUE.com, March 29, 2012, www.kvue.com/news/Sexting-takes-on-new-more-dangerous-form--144908715.html (retrieved April 22, 2012).

18. S. E. Voumvakis and R. V. Ericson, *News Accounts of Attacks on Women: A Comparison of Three Toronto Newspapers* (Toronto: University of Toronto Centre of Criminology, 1984).

19. Brian Spitzberg and Michelle Cadiz, "The Media Construction of Stalking Stereotypes," *Journal of Criminal Justice and Popular Culture* 9, 3 (2002): 28–149.

20. George Gerbner, Larry Gross, M. Jackson-Beeck, S. Jeffries-Fox, and Nancy Signorielli, "Cultural Indicators Violence Profile No. 9," *Journal of Communication* 28, 3 (1978): 176–207.

21. The NBC program *To Catch a Predator* is perhaps the apex of examples, but almost every television network or local station has aired some version of the "parents, be worried" story.

22. Matt Richtel, "Hooked on Gadgets, and Paying a Mental Price," *New York Times*, June 6, 2010; Jane M. Healy, *Endangered Minds: Why Children Don't Think and What We Can Do About It* (New York: Simon and Schuster, 1999).

23. Several youth organizations have been trying to put Internet-related "stranger danger" in perspective; see, e.g., the Girl Scouts' site, http://lmk.girlscouts.org/Online-Safety-Topics/Online-Sexual—Predators/The-Facts.aspx; and the *School Library Journal*'s website, www.schoollibraryjournal.com/article/CA6420413.html (retrieved August 28, 2011).

24. Lenore Skenazy, *Free Range Kids: How to Raise Safe, Self-Reliant Children* (San Francisco: Jossey-Bass, 2010).

25. Melanie Hick, "Study: Parents Don't Care if Kids Play Violent Video Games," *Huffington Post UK*, April 11, 2012, www.huffingtonpost.co.uk/2012/04/11/study-parents-dont-care-if-kids-play-violent-video-games_n_1416853.html?ref=uk (retrieved April 22, 2012).

26. D. Finkelhor, H. A. Turner, R. K. Ormrod, and S. L. Hamby, "Trends in Childhood Violence and Abuse Exposure: Evidence from Two National Surveys," *Archives of Pediatrics and Adolescent Medicine* 164, 3 (2010): 238–42.

27. Lori Takeuchi, *Families Matter: Designing Media for a Digital Age*, Joan Ganz Cooney Center at Sesame Workshop, May 2011, www.joanganzcooneycenter.org (retrieved August 28, 2011).

28. On helicopter parenting, see Foster Kline and Jim Fay, *Parenting with Love and Logic: Teaching Children Responsibility* (Colorado Springs, CO: Piñon Press, 1990).

29. The study of the shift from *Gemeinschaft* to *Gesellschaft* has been a central concern of sociologists from the field's earliest traditions, rooted in studies by Durkheim, Marx, Weber, and Tonnies, among others. In recent years, contributions to the understanding of the network society have come notably from Jan Van Dijk, *The Network Society: Social Aspects of New Media* (London: Sage, 1999) and Manuel Castells, *The Rise of the Network Society, vol. 1: The Information Age* (New York: John Wiley and Sons, 1996). See also Barry Wellman's work on the rise of networked individualism, e.g., Barry Wellman, Anabel Quan-Haase, Jeffrey Boase, Wenhong Chen, Keith Hampton, Isabel Isla de Diaz, and Kakuko Miyata, "The Social Affordances of the Internet for Networked Individualism," *Journal of Computer Mediated Communication* 8, 3 (2003), http://jcmc.indiana.edu/vol8/issue3/wellman.html (retrieved August 28, 2011).

30. Living with risk is not new, as Beck points out that we have always lived with a certain amount of risk in our lives due to circumstances beyond our control. As life became increasingly complex over the course of the past several hundred years, however, Western society developed ever more complex systems meant to guard against risks, both those that were natural and those that resulted from human behavior. Ulrich Beck, *Risk Society: Towards a New Modernity* (London: Sage, 1992). See also Roger Silverstone, *Media and Morality: On the Rise of the Mediapolis* (Cambridge: Polity Press, 2006).

31. Paul Virilio, *Speed and Politics: An Essay on Dromology*, trans. Mark Polizzotti (Los Angeles: Semiotext(e), 1977). Virilio argues that the risk society has been related to the development of sophisticated military systems that have supported both governments and countergovernment activities.

32. Terhi Rantanen, "Giddens and the 'G' Word: An Interview with Anthony Giddens." *Global Media and Communication* 1, 1 (2005): 63–77.

33. Anthony Giddens, *The Consequences of Modernity* (Cambridge: Polity Press, 1990). In this and subsequent writings, Giddens develops his theory of structuration, which attempts to explain the relationship between individual agency and social structure. He argues that society provides the structures that give shape to how people live and the choices we can make. We learn society's "rules" as we grow into the culture, but these rules do not determine everything about how we will live. Thus, the structure is like a language in which there are ways of using words that create familiar sentences, and some freedom to create new sentences using existing words. This theory attempts to explore why and how social change can occur, and gives a way to think about the relationship between micro choices and macro change.

34. See, e.g., Phillip Brown, Hugh Lauder, and David Ashton, *The Global Auction: The Promises of Education, Jobs, and Incomes* (New York: Oxford University Press, 2010).

35. Gillian Tett, "The Rise of the Middle Class—Just Not Ours," *Atlantic*, July/August 2011, 63.

36. Henry Giroux, *Youth in a Disposable Society: Democracy or Disposability?* (New York: Palgrave Macmillan, 2010). See also David Nasaw, ed., *Schooled to Order: A Social History of Public Schooling in the United States* (New York: Oxford University Press, 1981). The latter argues that the United States inherited a system that was built to create a citizenry that respected order, not one that participated in democratic decision making.

37. My favorite critiques of how the media support a certain view of the middle class include the 2007 film *Class Dismissed: How TV Frames the Working Class*, available from the Media Education Foundation (and featuring the work of Pepi Leistyna), and the film *People Like Us: Social Class in America*, a documentary aired on and distributed by PBS. See also Lynn Spiegel, *Make Room for TV: Television and the Family Ideal in Postwar America* (Chicago: University of Chicago Press, 1992).

38. Lisa McGirr, "The New Suburban Poverty," *New York Times*, March 19, 2012, http://campaignstops.blogs.nytimes.com/2012/03/19/the-new-suburban-poverty (retrieved April 25, 2012).

39. Gerardo was part of a group discussion about social media that took place in his school during the fall of 2011.

40. Laurence Steinberg, *The Ten Basic Principles of Good Parenting* (New York: Simon and Schuster, 2004).

41. As I will note in the chapter that follows, the ethic of expressive empowerment shares common ground with what Annette Lareau terms "concerted cultivation" and Margaret Nelson has referred to as "out-of-control parenting." Nelson is critical of parents who expect their children to rely upon them for advice and sees this as a tactic that can undermine children's independence.

42. Carly Shuler, *iLearn II: An Analysis of the Education Category on Apple's App Store*, Joan Ganz Cooney Center at Sesame Workshop, www.joanganzcooneycenter.org/Reports-33.html (retrieved January 29, 2012).

43. This is the basis of the media ecology school of thought, articulated most famously in Marshall McLuhan, *Understanding Media: The Extensions of Man* (Cambridge, MA: MIT Press, 1994 [1964]). See also Joshua Meyrowitz, *No Sense of Place: The Impact of Electronic Media on Social Behavior* (New York: Oxford University Press, 1985); Neil Postman, *Amusing Ourselves to Death: Public Discourse in the Age of Show Business* (New York: Penguin, 1985); Sherry Turkle, *Alone Together: Why We Expect More from Technology and Less from Each Other* (New York: Basic Books, 2011). A significant number of scholars in the fields of media history, cultural studies, and the social construction of technology also contribute to understandings of media's role in social change. See, e.g., Carolyn Marvin, *When Old Technologies Were New: Thinking About Electric Communication in the Late Nineteenth Century* (New York: Oxford University Press, 1988); James Carey, *Communication as Culture: Essays on Media and Society* (New York: Routledge, 1988); Raymond Williams, *Television: Technology and Cultural Form* (London: Fontana, 1974). Following Roger Silverstone, I am defining communication media as part

of the "general texture of experience" in everyday life, as he uses that phrase. The media are conduits, languages, and environments, according to Silverstone, who argues that the study of media foregrounds how meanings move through and across time and space and how certain institutions participate in what he calls the "production of enchantment." The definition of media can extend from the present-day smart mobile phone back to language itself. Thus while the phrase "communication media" does not refer only to what we think of as today's contemporary mobile, digital, and entertainment media, it also includes these things. Roger Silverstone, *Why Study the Media?* (London: Sage, 1999).

44. Meyrowitz, *No Sense of Place.*

45. Ibid., 8. Basing his work on Meyrowitz's theory and approach, Neil Postman developed a similar argument in his book *The Disappearance of Childhood* (New York: Random House, 1994).

46. My approach thus seeks to follow that of Raymond Williams, *Technology and Cultural Form* (London: Fontana, 1974). As will be discussed in chapter 9, there are several interrelated theories that have built upon this approach since Williams' work. Mediation, mediatization theory, and domestication theory all address this concern for the relationship between technologies, human practices, and social change, and there are also important insights in the fields of actor-network theory and cultural sociology that similarly explore these issues.

47. Martin Hilbert and Priscila López, "The World's Technological Capacity to Store, Communicate, and Compute Information," *Science* 332, 6025 (2011): 60–65.

48. Martin Hilbert, "World_info_capacity_animation," YouTube, June 11, 2011, www.youtube.com/watch?v=iIKPjOuwqHo.

49. Ibid.

50. Ibid.

51. Robert Kegan, *In over Our Heads: The Mental Demands of Modern Life* (Cambridge, MA: Harvard University Press, 1998).

52. Ruth Schwartz Cowan, *More Work for Mother: The Ironies of Household Technology from the Open Hearth to the Microwave* (New York: Basic Books, 1985).

53. Stewart Hoover, Lynn Schofield Clark, and Diane Alters, *Media, Home, and Family* (New York: Routledge, 2004).

54. "Emotion work" is a term coined by sociologist Arlie Russell Hochschild. See her "Emotion Work, Feeling Rules, and Social Structure," *American Journal of Sociology* 85, 3 (November 1979): 551–75.

55. Anthony Giddens, *Modernity and Self-Identity: Self and Society in the Late Modern Age* (Stanford, CA: Stanford University Press, 1991), xxxix.

56. John Palfrey and Urs Gasser, *Born Digital: Understanding the First Generation of Digital Natives* (New York: Basic Books, 2010).

57. This book therefore follows in the tradition of research known as domestication of technology, which asserts that technologies are first integrated into everyday life, and then the users and the wider environment adapt accordingly. See, e.g., Roger Silverstone and Eric Hirsch, *Consuming Technologies: Media and Information in Domestic Spaces* (London: Routledge, 1992). I remain reluctant to utilize the phrase "domestication of technologies" to describe my work for two reasons. First, I am troubled by the term itself, which tends to be gendered and classed (e.g., in the United States, a "domestic" is a person, usually female, who provides care for children and has responsibility for household tasks, and

who has little legal protections when it comes to working conditions). I wonder if there is an implicit metaphorical suggestion that technology is tamed or put in its place, much as women of lower economic means once were and continue to be. Second and perhaps more important, I believe that the dynamics of the growing-up years suggest that technology is never "tamed," but is instead always new, untamed, and surprising for families as different children age into the preteen and teen years. This is partly because children find new uses of these technologies as they age, and also because the media industries are constantly striving to find new markets and hence developing new products that appeal to the key demographic of preteens and teens. I prefer the broader if more clumsy term "mediatization" to describe this interaction between uses of communication technologies and the shaping of the larger social environment, as I detail more fully in chapter 9.

58. John Horrigan, *The Mobile Difference: Wireless Connectivity Has Drawn Many Users More Deeply into Digital Life*, Pew Internet and American Life Project, March 2009, http://pewinternet.org; Joseph Straubhaar, "Constructing a New Information Society in the Tropics: Examining Brazilian Approaches to Information and Communication Technology (ICTs) Through the Lens of the User and Non-user," paper presented to the annual meeting of the International Communication Association, Boston, May 2011; Kenneth R. Wilson, Jennifer S. Wallin, and Christa Reiser, "Social Stratification and the Digital Divide," *Social Science Computer Review* 21 (2003): 133; Caroline Anstey, "New Technology Can Democratize Development," *Guardian*, November 29, 2011; Florence Jaumotte, Subir Lall, Chris Papageorgiou, and Petia Topalova, "Technology Widening Rich-Poor Gap," *IMF Survey Magazine: IMF Research*, October 10, 2007, www.imf.org/external/pubs/ft/survey/so/2007/res1010a.htm.

59. Sonia Livingstone and Elizabeth Helsper, "Gradations in Digital Inclusion: Children, Young People, and the Digital Divide," *New Media and Society* 9, 4 (2008): 671–96. Livingstone also addresses class differences in *Children and the Internet* (Cambridge: Polity Press, 2009).

60. This is a common critique in media studies. See Livingstone, *Children and the Internet*; Ellen Seiter, *The Internet Playground* (New York: Peter Lang, 2007); Silverstone, *Media and Morality*; Joseph Straubhaar, Jeremiah Spence, Zeynep Tufekci, and Roberta G. Lenz, eds., *Inequality in the Technopolis: Race, Class, Gender, and the Digital Divide in Austin* (Austin: University of Texas Press, 2012); K. Facer, J. Furlong, R. Furlong, and R. Sutherland, *Screenplay: Children and Computing in the Home* (New York: Routledge, 2003).

61. Nicholas Carr, *The Big Switch: Rewiring the World, from Edison to Google* (New York: W. W. Norton, 2008); Evgeny Morozov, *The Net Delusion: The Dark Side of Internet Freedom* (New York: Public Affairs, 2011).

62. For a long time, the United States was thought of as a middle-class nation because of the belief that in the United States economic opportunity was open to all.

63. New York Times, *Class Matters* (New York: Times Books, 2005).

64. Paul Fussell, "Class: A Touchy Subject," in *Class: A Guide Through the American Status System* (New York: Simon and Schuster, 1983), www.pbs.org/peoplelikeus/resources/essays6.html (retrieved June 3, 2010). Fussell also argued that how one thinks about class is often related to one's class position. Those in the middle class are most anxious about the topic because they worry about slipping down a rung or two. This is, he suggests, because middle-class people tend to believe that one's class status is determined by one's

occupation, and in turn, one's occupation is determined by one's education and one's will or self-determination. In contrast, he argues, upper-class people think of class in relation to taste, style, intelligence, and behavior, and lower-class people tend to think of class in relation to the amount of money people have.

65. Daniel Larison, "Santorum's Classless Society," *American Conservative*, July 28, 2010, www.amconmag.com/larison/2010/07/28/santorums-classless-society (retrieved June 17, 2011).

66. Six distinct social classes are identified in relation to stratification: the wealthy capitalist class (constituting approximately 1.5 percent of the U.S. population, many of whom inherited wealth), the upper-middle-class (15 percent, consisting of highly educated professionals and managers), the lower middle class (32 percent, consisting of sales professionals and craftsmen, most with college degrees, who have some autonomy in their work), the working class (32 percent, consisting of clerical, transportation, industrial, and health care workers with low job security and often no higher education), and a lower class constituted of the working poor and the chronically unemployed (12–20 percent). Things become somewhat complicated because each class definition has its own stigma. Upper- and upper-middle-class people prefer to think of themselves as middle-class to avoid being considered pretentious; lower-middle-class and working-class people with stable salaries consider themselves middle-class rather than working-class because the term "working class" has long been associated with the increasingly outsourced jobs of blue-collar factory workers. These self-definitions are also complicated in relation to marital patterns and gendered patterns of employment. Men tend to pursue and hold occupations that are higher-paying than the occupations more frequently held by women. See, e.g., the discussion of the "ruling class" and the "country class" in Angelo M. Codevilla, "America's Ruling Class—and the Perils of Revolution," *American Spectator*, July/August 2010, http://spectator.org/archives/2010/07/16/americas-ruling-class-and-the# (retrieved August 25, 2011). See also William Thompson and Joseph Hickey, *Society in Focus* (Upper Saddle River, NJ: Pearson, 2005); Dennis Gilbert, *The American Class Structure* (Belmont, CA: Wadsworth, 1998); Leonard Beeghley, *The Structure of Social Stratification in the United States* (Upper Saddle River, NJ: Pearson, 2004); David Autor, Lawrence F. Katz, and Melissa S. Kearney, "Trends in U.S. Wage Inequality: Revising the Revisionists," *Review of Economics and Statistics* 90, 2 (May 2008): 300–23. The employment situation in June 2011 is based on data from the Bureau of Labor Statistics, U.S. Department of Labor, and cited in Motoko Rich, "Job Growth Falters Badly, Clouding Hope for Recovery," *New York Times*, July 8, 2011. See also Michael C. Dawson, "Severe Hardship, Dashed Hopes: Room for Debate," *New York Times*, July 25, 2011.

67. Amy Chua, *Battle Hymn of the Tiger Mother* (New York: Penguin, 2011); Pamela Druckerman, *Bringing Up Bebe* (New York: Penguin, 2012).

68. Annette Lareau, *Unequal Childhoods: Class, Race, and Family Life* (Berkeley: University of California Press, 2003).

69. See Lynn Schofield Clark, "Question to Tiger (and All) Mothers: Why Is Leisure Bad?" *Parenting in a Digital Age*, January 24, 2011, http://digitalparenting.wordpress.com.

70. Hannah Rosin, "Mother Inferior?" *Wall Street Journal*, January 15, 2011.

71. Pierre Bourdieu, *Outline of a Theory of Practice* (Cambridge: Cambridge University Press, 1977); Pierre Bourdieu, *Distinction: A Social Critique of the Judgement of Taste* (London: Routledge, 1984).

72. As is probably clear by this point, I am avoiding the term "working class" because I believe that it tends to be eschewed as pejorative and historically has referenced a community of blue-collar workers whose population size and influence have been in decline for several decades. Neither "blue collar" nor "pink collar" seems to speak to jobs in retail and food sales, health care, and the military that, according to the U.S. Bureau of Labor Statistics, are the most common jobs in the United States today. I am also using the phrase "middle class" in a way that echoes its use by people in my study and in my university classrooms, who tend to think of the middle class in relation to lifestyle choices rather than in relation to household incomes, parents' educational levels, or parents' professions. It is therefore not a precise term so much as a cultural marker.

73. Clifford Geertz built upon Max Weber's idea of culture in his phrase "Man is an animal suspended in webs of significance he himself has spun." Clifford Geertz, "Thick Description: Toward an Interpretive Theory of Culture," in *The Interpretation of Cultures* (New York: Basic Books, 1977), 5. Ann Swidler, "Culture in Action: Symbols and Strategies," *American Sociological Review* 51, 2 (April 1986): 273–86.

74. Allison Pugh, *Longing and Belonging: Parents, Children, and Consumer Culture* (Berkeley: University of California Press, 2009).

75. Margaret Nelson, *Parenting Out of Control* (New York: New York University Press, 2010).

76. Wendy Griswold, "The Fabrication of Meaning: Literary Interpretation in the United States, Great Britain, and the West Indies," *American Journal of Sociology* 92 (1987): 1077–117.

77. On differing cultural interpretive communities, see Stanley Fish, *Is There a Text in This Class?* (Cambridge, MA: Harvard University Press, 1980), 147–74. On how subcultures subvert styles of the elite for their own identity ends, see Dick Hebdige, *Subculture: The Meaning of Style* (London: Methuen, 1979). On how working-class young people experience schooling differently than middle-class young people in Britain, see Paul Willis, *Learning to Labor: How Working Class Kids Get Working Class Jobs* (Farnborough, UK: Saxon House, 1977).

78. Brene Brown, "The Power of Vulnerability," *TEDx Houston*, June 2010, www.youtube.com/watch?v=X4Qm9cGRub (retrieved April 22, 2012).

Chapter 2: Cyberbullying Girls, Helicopter Moms, and Internet Predators

1. Kim Zetter, "Experts Say MySpace Suicide Indictment Sets 'Scary' Precedent," *Wired*, May 15, 2008, http://blog.wired.com/27bstroke6/2008/05/myspace-indictm.html (retrieved December 17, 2008); Derek Kravitz, "MySpace Suicide Expands Web Law," *Washington Post*, November 28, 2008.

2. The story is compelling across socioeconomic contexts, of course, but I'd argue it gained significant attention due to the fact that its protagonists (or antagonists) were middle-class, and news organizations tend to favor stories about middle-class individuals, not least because these are their primary audiences.

3. Mike Celizic, "Parents of MySpace Hoax Victim Seek Justice," *Today*, November 19, 2007, http://today.msnbc.msn.com/id/21882976/?GT1=10547 (retrieved December 17, 2008).

4. See, e.g., "MySpace Suicide Reaction: Outrage! Outrage! Outrage!" *Death by 1000 Papercuts*, November 14, 2007, http://deathby1000papercuts.blogspot.com/2007/11/myspace-suicide-reaction-outrage.html; Nordette Adams, "Megan Meier, MySpace, Bad

Parents and Sick Adults: When Should Cyberbullying Be Considered a Crime?" *BlogHer*, November 18, 2007, www.blogher.com/megan-meier-myspace-bad-parents-and-sick-adults-when-should-cyberbullying-be-considered-crime; Moe, "If You Can Handle a Really Depressing Teen Suicide Story Right Now," Jezebel, November 14, 2007, http://jezebel.com/gossip/hell-is-other-people/if-you-can-handle-a-really-depressing-teen-suicide-story-right-now-322888.php. Note that the names of the alleged perpetrators of the hoax were deleted from the comments below most of these and other stories.

5. Celizic, "Parents of MySpace Hoax Victim Seek Justice."

6. "Judge Postpones Lori Drew Sentencing, Weighs Acquittal," *Wired*, May 18, 2009, www.wired.com/threatlevel/2009/05/drew_sentenced.

7. Rep. Linda Sanchez introduced the Megan Meier Cyberbullying Prevention Act in May 2008 as HR 6123. The bill was referred to the Subcommittee on Crime, Terrorism, and Homeland Security in July of that year. See www.opencongress.org/bill/110-h6123/show (retrieved October 6, 2010).

8. Steve Pokin, "Dardenne Prairie Officials Plan to Make Cyberspace Harassment a Crime," *St. Louis Suburban Journals*, November 15, 2007, http://suburbanjournals.stltoday.com/articles/2007/11/15/news/doc473c629800bb7940817680.txt (retrieved October 6, 2010).

9. See Missouri Revised Statutes, Chapter 565, Offenses Against the Person, Section 565.225, www.moga.mo.gov/statutes/C500-599/5650000225.HTM (retrieved October 6, 2010).

10. "Helicopter parenting" is a term coined by Jim Fay in *Helicopters, Drill Sergeants, and Consultants: Parenting Styles and the Messages They Send* (Golden, CO: Love and Logic Press, 1994).

11. "MySpace Suicide Reaction: Outrage! Outrage! Outrage!"

12. Ibid.

13. Statistics on the topic of cyberbullying range widely, given that studies rely upon self-reports and define cyberbullying in differing ways. See, e.g., the Cyberbullying Research Center, http://cyberbullying.us (retrieved August 27, 2011).

14. "Parents Say Fake Online 'Friend' Led to Girl's Suicide," *CNN*, November 17, 2007.

15. danah boyd, "Reflections on Lori Drew, Bullying, and Solutions to Helping Kids," *Apophenia*, November 30, 2008, www.zephoria.org/thoughts/archives/2008/11/30/reflections_on.html (retrieved August 27, 2011).

16. Caroline and Kayla (not their real names) are both European American young people, separated by a few years but also by the fact that Kayla was a high school student and Caroline a college senior at the time of this interview. Several years have passed since the encounter narrated here, and Kayla is now a young adult who survived her teen years and is rebuilding her relationship with her mother, according to Caroline.

17. See Glynis M. Breakwell, *Coping with Threatened Identities* (London: Routledge, 1986).

18. Margaret Nelson critiques this approach among upper-middle-class parents in *Parenting Out of Control* (New York: New York University Press, 2010).

19. These categories come from Richard O'Connor, author of *Undoing Perpetual Stress: The Connection Between Depression, Anxiety, and 21st Century Illness* (New York: Berkley, 2005). O'Connor, in "Permissive Parenting," Focus Adolescent Services,

also notes that permissiveness is sometimes associated with poverty, illness, or substance abuse, which makes parents feel overwhelmed with the tasks of parenting. See http://www.focusas.com/Permissive.html (retrieved June 20, 2009).

20. This is a finding of the Pew study as well. Amanda Lenhart, *Teens and Sexting, A report of the Pew Internet and American Life Project*, December 15, 2009. Available: http://pewinternet.org/Reports/2009/Teens-and-Sexting.aspx. Retrieval: July 19, 2012. See also Amanda Lenhart, Mary Madden, Aaron Smith, Kristen Purcell, Kathryn Zickuh, Lee Rainie, *Teens, Kindness, and Cruelty on Social Network Sites: A report of the Pew Internet and American Life Project*, November 9, 2011. Available: http://pewinternet.org/Reports/2011/Teens-and-social-media.aspx, Retrieval: July 19, 2012. See also Sonia Livingstone, Leslie Haddon and Anke Gorzig. *Children, risk, and safety on the Internet*. London: Polity, 2012.

21. Ibid. This study that found that teens by and large know what to do when someone approaches them inappropriately online.

22. Sonia Livingstone and Magdalena Bober, *UK Children Go Online: Listening to Young People's Experiences* (London: LSE Report, 2003).

23. danah boyd & Eszter Hargittai, "Facebook Privacy Settings: Who Cares?" *First Monday* 15, 8 (August 2010), www.uic.edu/htbin/cgiwrap/bin/ojs/index.php/fm/article/view/3086/2589 (retrieved August 27, 2011).

24. Andrea, who was one of my students and then a sophomore at the University of Denver, conducted three group interviews with friends of her younger sisters in February 2007, under my supervision.

25. Pew study. Lenhart, *Teens and Sexting*.

26. Personal conversation, July 2009.

27. Personal conversation with teachers, August 2009.

28. Margaret Nelson argues that middle- and upper-middle-class families are less interested in tracking devices than are lower-income families, but this may have been an artifact of the time in which she completed her studies. In recent years, use of technologies such as GPS tracking and online monitoring have become much more acceptable among middle- and upper-middle-class parents.

29. Nelson, *Parenting Out of Control*.

30. danah boyd, "Taken Out of Context: American Teen Sociality in Networked Publics," Ph.D. dissertation, University of California, Berkeley, 2008.

31. Harvard study on parents and kids. Rafi Santo, Carrie James, Katie Davis, Shira Lee Katz, Linda Burch and Barry Joseph, *Meeting of Minds: Cross-Generational Dialogue of the Ethics of Digital Life*. A report of Global Kids, Common Sense Media, and Harvard University's GoodPlay Project, December, 2009. Available: http://dmlcentral.net/resources/3981.

32. Perri Klass, "Seeing Social Media as More Portal than Pitfall," *New York Times*, January 9, 2012.

33. Richard Weissbord, *The Parents We Mean to Be: How Well-Intentioned Adults Undermine Children's Moral and Emotional Development* (New York: Houghton Mifflin Harcourt, 2009).

34. See, e.g., Richard Perez-Pena, "More Complex Picture Emerges in Rutgers Student's Suicide," *New York Times*, August 12, 2011.

35. Ashley Surdin, "States Passing Laws to Combat Cyberbullying," *Washington Post*, January 1, 2009.

36. Andy Carvin, "CA Legislation Criminalizes Campus Cyberbullying," *Learning Now*, August 29, 2008, www.pbs.org/teachers/learning.now/2008/08/ca_legislation_criminalizes_ca.html (retrieved August 27, 2011).

37. Three of the six students involved in the case of Phoebe Prince, who committed suicide after bullying online and off, faced trial in December 2010. The other three are to be tried at a later time. Edecio Martinez, "Phoebe Prince Update: Bullying-Suicide Case in Court," *CBS News*, September 24, 2010, www.cbsnews.com/8301-504083_162-20017512-504083.html (retrieved October 7, 2010).

38. Beth Lloyd and Colleen Curry, "Dharun Ravi's Own Words Led to Conviction, Juror Tells ABC News," *ABC 20/20*, March 16, 2012.

39. See, e.g., Parry Aftab, *The Parent's Guide to Protecting Your Children in Cyberspace* (New York: McGraw-Hill, 1999).

40. Michele Ybarra and Kimberly Mitchell, "Youth Engaging in Online Harassment: Associations with Caregiver-Child Relationships, Internet Use, and Personal Characteristics," *Journal of Adolescence* 27 (2004): 319–36.

41. On how discussions about youth pathologies can underscore discourses of control and containment, see Janet L. Finn, "Text and Turbulence: Representing Adolescence as Pathology in the Human Services," *Childhood* 8, 2 (May 2001): 167–91.

Chapter 3: Strict Parents, Gamer High School Dropouts, and Shunned Overachievers

1. Thomas Hine, *The Rise and Fall of the American Teenager* (New York: Bard/Avon, 1999); David Buckingham, *After the Death of Childhood: Growing Up in an Age of Electronic Media* (London: Polity, 2000).

2. Diana Baumrind, "Current Patterns of Parental Authority," *Developmental Psychology* 4, 1 (part 2) (1971): 1–103; Diana Baumrind, "The Influence of Parenting Style on Adolescent Competence and Substance Use," *Journal of Early Adolescence* 11 (1991): 56–95; E. Maccoby, "The Role of Parents in the Socialization of Children: An Historical Overview," *Developmental Psychology* 28 (1992): 1006–17; Laurence Steinberg, "We Know Some Things: Parent-Adolescent Relationships in Retrospect and Prospect," *Journal of Research on Adolescence*, 11, 1 (2001): 1–19.

3. Matthew Eastin, Bradley Greenberg, and Linda Hofshire, "Parenting the Internet," *Journal of Communication* 56 (2006): 486–504.

4. Sonia Livingstone and Ellen J. Helsper, "Parental Mediation and Children's Internet Use," *Journal of Broadcasting and Electronic Media* 52, 4 (2008): 581–99.

5. Stewart Hoover, Lynn Schofield Clark, and Diane Alters, *Media, Home, and Family* (New York: Routledge, 2004); Sonia Livingstone, *Children and the Internet: Great Expectations, Challenging Realities* (Cambridge: Polity, 2009).

6. Margaret Nelson, *Parenting Out of Control: Anxious Parents in Uncertain Times* (New York: New York University Press, 2010).

7. On differences in approaches to parental authority that vary by socioeconomic status and ethnic background, see J. G. Smetana, "Adolescents' and Parents' Conceptions of Parental Authority," *Child Development* 59 (1988): 321–35; B. Bradford Brown, Jeremy P. Bakken, Jacqueline Nguyen, and Heather G. Von Bank, "Sharing Information About Peer Relations: Parent and Adolescent Opinions and Behaviors in Hmong and African American Families," *New Directions for Child and Adolescent Development* 116 (Summer 2007): 67–82.

8. Brown, Bakken, Nguyen, and Von Bank note in "Sharing Information" that disadvantaged African American families tend to have more egalitarian relationships than other ethnic groups due to the matriarchal nature of these families and the response to the perception of danger in disadvantaged neighborhoods. See also N. Sudarkasa, "African American Families and Family Values," in Harriet P. McAdoo, ed., *Black Families*, 3rd ed. (Thousand Oaks, CA: Sage, 1997). These differences are discussed further in chapter 5.

9. Carmen took part in a group interview in March 2008. I served as facilitator of that interview group.

10. City-data.com profile (retrieved August 3, 2011).

11. Annette Lareau, *Unequal Childhoods: Class, Race, and Family Life* (Berkeley: University of California Press, 2003).

12. City-data.com profile (retrieved August 3, 2011). Caleb and his family were interviewed by Scott Webber when Scott was a doctoral student at the University of Colorado.

13. Veronica and Norma Domentary were interviewed by Monica Emerich in 2006, when Monica was a doctoral student at the University of Colorado.

14. Meghan and Dell Sealy were interviewed by Christof Demont-Heinrich in late 2002, when Christof was a doctoral student at the University of Colorado.

15. Mizuko Ito, Heather Horst, et al., *Hanging Out, Messing Around, Geeking Out: Living and Learning with New Media* (Cambridge, MA: MIT Press, 2009).

16. Stanley Cohen, *Folk Devils and Moral Panics* (London: MacGibbon and Kee, 1972); Dick Hebdige, *Subculture: The Meaning of Style* (London: Methuen, 1979).

17. Researcher danah boyd argues that young people from more "controlling or tumultuous households" tend to approach social networking sites as a means of escape more than do young people whose family relationships seem healthy. See her "Taken Out of Context: American Teen Sociality in Networked Publics," Ph.D. dissertation, University of California, Berkeley, 2008.

Chapter 4: Identity 2.0

1. Steph Kline and her family were first interviewed by Monica Emerich in 2004. I have changed the word "computer" to "laptop" so that the text appears less dated, as I believe that this story is about how Steph responds to her parents in relation to their decision to move the computer, and the specific technology of the computer does not change the meaning of the story.

2. Steph's story appeared in Lynn Schofield Clark, "The Constant Contact Generation: Exploring Teen Friendship Networks Online," in Sharon Mazzarella, ed., *Girl Wide Web* (New York: Peter Lang, 2008).

3. Global Kids, Inc., The GoodPlay Project of Harvard University's Project Zero, and Common Sense Media, *Meeting of Minds: Cross-Generational Dialogue on the Ethics of Digital Life*, John D. and Catherine T. MacArthur Foundation, October 2009.

4. Victoria Rideout, Ulla G. Foehr, and Donald Roberts, "Generation M2: Media in the Lives of 8-to 18-Year-Olds," Kaiser Family Foundation, January 20, 2010, www.kff.org/entmedia/mh012010pkg.cfm (retrieved July 16, 2010).

5. Ibid.

6. Amanda Lenhart, Kristen Purcell, Aaron Smith, and Kathryn Zickuhr, *Social Media and Mobile Use Among Teens and Young Adults*, Pew Internet and American Life Project, February 3, 2010, http://pewinternet.org (retrieved June 27, 2011).

7. Ibid.

8. Rideout, Foehr, and Roberts, "Generation M2."

9. Ibid.

10. Amanda Lenhart, Rich Ling, Scott Campbell, and Kristen Purcell, "Teens and Mobile Phones," Pew Internet and American Life Project, April 20, 2010, www.pewinternet.org/Reports/2010/Teens-and-Mobile-Phones/Summary-of-findings.aspx (retrieved July 18, 2010).

11. World mobile use has doubled since 2000. "Infosync: Reporting from the Digital Frontier," www.infosyncworld.com/news/n/5636.html (retrieved July 16, 2010; no longer available).

12. "Five Billion People to Use Cell Phones in 2010: UN," *Independent* (UK), February 16, 2010, www.independent.co.uk/life-style/gadgets-and-tech/news/five-billion-people-to-use-mobile-phones-in-2010-un-1900768.html (retrieved July 16, 2010).

13. The Globalist syndication services, www.theglobalist.com/globalicons/syndication/sample.htm (retrieved July 16, 2010).

14. Lee Rainie, "How Media Consumption Has Changed Since 2000," presentation given at the Newhouse School's Monetizing Online Business conference, 2010, www.pewinternet.org/~/media/Files/Presentations/2010/Jun/2010%20-%20062410%20-%20syracuse%20newhouse%20MOB%20conf%20NYC%20pdf.pdf (retrieved July 16, 2010).

15. Colin Campbell, *The Romantic Ethic and the Spirit of Modern Consumerism* (Oxford: Blackwell, 1987).

16. There is so much literature on this that it's difficult to single anything out. See, e.g., Roger Silverstone, *Media and Morality: The Rise of the Mediapolis* (Cambridge: Polity, 2006).

17. Sonia Livingstone and Magdalena Bober similarly identify three characteristics of the Internet, noting that it serves as "a conduit, a language, and an environment." I use the term "pragmatic" to describe the conduit function and the term "symbolic" to describe the language function or the way in which things such as cell phone cases become more than a conduit as they enable owners to communicate something of identity symbolically. I add the term "mythic" to recognize that Internet content is often similar or identical to the content of television, films, and music, media long recognized by Silverstone and others for their mythic dimensions. I have folded Livingstone and Bober's use of the term "environment" into the conduit or pragmatic function, as communicating through these technologies is no longer experienced as distinct from other ways in which communication occurs interpersonally. In effect, there is no longer a distinction between offline and online environments, which may be a measure of how these technologies become somewhat invisible to us over time as "conduits," or as pragmatically useful objects. See Sonia Livingstone and Magdalena Bober, *UK Children Go Online: Listening to Young People's Experiences* (London: LSE Report, 2003).

18. Rich Ling, *The Mobile Connection: The Cell Phone's Impact on Society* (San Francisco: Morgan Kaufmann, 2004).

19. Allison Pugh, *Longing and Belonging: Parents, Children, and Consumer Culture* (Berkeley: University of California Press, 2009).

20. See, e.g., Ellen Seiter, *Sold Separately: Children and Parents in Consumer Culture* (New Brunswick, NJ: Rutgers University Press, 1995); Marsha Kinder, ed., *Kids' Media Culture* (Durham, NC: Duke University Press, 1999).

21. The girl for whom I use the name "Jennifer" here wrote about this experience as a contributor to a special issue of the *Journal of Virtual Worlds* that I co-edited with Sun Sun Lim. This is an excerpt from an unpublished version of her paper, used with permission. For her own interpretation, see Stephanie Louise Lu, "Growing Up with Neopets: A Personal Case-Study," *Journal of Virtual Worlds* 3, 2 (December 2010), http://jvwresearch.org/index.php/past-issues/32-virtual-worlds-for-kids.

22. Mimi Ito and Heather Horst, "Neopoints, and Neo Economies: Emergent Regimes of Value in Kids' Peer-to-Peer Networks," paper presented at the annual meeting of the American Anthropological Association, November 16, 2006, www.itofisher.com/mito/itohorst.neopets.pdf (retrieved January 30, 2012).

23. COPPA laws restrict online interaction to those who are over the age of thirteen.

24. Personal correspondence, May 2010.

25. Mizuko Ito et al., *Hanging Out, Messing Around, Geeking Out* (Cambridge, MA: MIT Press, 2009).

26. Mary Celeste Kearney documents the various ways in which young women create media as a form of personal expression and, to a greater or lesser degree, a political statement, in Mary Celeste Kearney, *Girls Make Media* (New York: Routledge, 2006). See also Sharon Mazzarella, ed., *Girl Wide Web 2.0* (New York: Peter Lang, 2010).

27. Alexis Lynn interviewed Taylor three times in 2009. See Alexis Lynn, "The Digitally Born Identity," M.A. thesis, University of Denver, 2009.

28. For an overview of arguments regarding the role of media in identity-construction, see Douglas Kellner, *Media Culture: Cultural Studies, Identity and Politics Between the Modern and Postmodern* (New York: Routledge, 1995); Meenakshi Gigi Durham and Douglas Kellner, *Media and Cultural Studies: Keyworks* (London: Wiley-Blackwell, 2005).

29. "Mook" and "midriff" were the terms marketers used to describe the teen archetypes of the early 1990s, as documented in the excellent PBS *Frontline* episode "The Merchants of Cool," February 27, 2001. The episode focused on how marketers conduct research on teen life in an effort to tie products to admired teen archetypes and sell teen culture back to itself for a profit.

30. See, e.g., Stuart Hall and Tony Jefferson, eds., *Resistance Through Rituals: Youth Subcultures in Postwar Britain* (London: Routledge, 1990).

31. On cultivating and negotiating micro-celebrity, see Theresa Senft, "Fame to Fifteen: Re-framing Celebrity," TED Salon talk, London, November 2, 2010, www.terrisenft.net (retrieved August 29, 2011); Theresa M. Senft, "Sex, Spectatorship, and the 'Neda' Video: A Biopsy," in Hille Koskela and J. Macgregor Wise, eds., *New Visualities, New Technologies: The New Ecstasy of Communication* (Oxford: Blackwell, 2011).

32. Global Kids, GoodPlay Project, and Common Sense Media, *Meeting of Minds*.

33. Naomi Klein's manifesto *No Logo* is an excellent description of how difficult, and yet how necessary, it is for young people to gain a critical distance from the commercial realities that surround them the way water surrounds fish. See Naomi Klein, *No Logo* (London: Picador, 2009).

34. Korinna and her friends were interviewed as part of an undergraduate research project led by Caroline Davidson at the University of Denver in spring 2009.

35. Joe and Rashad participated in a focus group interview in Denver in February 2012.

36. David Brake, "Shaping the 'ME' in MySpace: The Framing of Profiles on a Social Network Site," in Knut Lundby, ed., *Digital Storytelling, Mediatized Stories*, 285–300 (New York: Peter Lang, 2008).

37. Erik Erickson, *Identity: Youth and Crisis* (New York: Norton, 1968); G. Stanley Hall, *Adolescence* (New York: Appleton, 1904).

38. These questions of "Who am I?" and "What should I therefore do?" are directly related to Western culture's construction of the subject and the concept of the self, which in turn are rooted in the idea of the "sovereign individual." The sovereign individual first emerged in political thought during the time of the Enlightenment and served as a justification for the dismantling of the former feudal order in favor of capitalism. Enlightenment thinkers challenged previous understandings of the subject, which had been based in relation to a deity and king, arguing instead for a subject capable, as Kant argued, of making cognitive, moral, and aesthetic judgments autonomously. Kant and Hume both argued for the importance of the subject's perceptions of the world, an idea that became important to Milton, Locke, Bentham, Jefferson, and later John Stuart Mill, all of whom advocated a government that would not restrain individual reason. The point is that the idea of the "self" is not easily separated from the social system in which we're located in the West, and recent ideas of the self have been critical of the historical relationship between individualism and capitalism. See, e.g., Thomas Streeter, *The Net Effect: Romanticism, Capitalism, and the Internet* (New York: New York University Press, 2010).

39. Victor Strasburger and his colleagues have argued that television presents a limited number of occupational options, for instance, and argues that teens may "sell themselves short based on what they see on TV." See Victor Strasburger, Barbara J. Wilson, and Amy Jordan, *Children, Adolescents, and the Media* (Thousand Oaks, CA: Sage, 2008), 11. However, this view places a great deal of emphasis on the role of media content in influencing young people's perceptions without acknowledging the relationships between the symbolic forms circulated in the media and the limitations that really do exist in our society based on factors such as racial and gendered assumptions and histories.

40. Susannah Stern, "Producing Sites, Exploring Identities: Youth Online Authorship," in David Buckingham, ed., *Youth, Identity, and Digital Media*, 95–118 (Cambridge, MA: MIT Press, 2008).

41. Carol Gilligan, *In a Different Voice* (Cambridge, MA: Harvard University Press, 1982).

42. William A. Corsaro, *The Sociology of Childhood*, 2nd ed. (Thousand Oaks, CA: Pine Forge, 2004); Paula Fass and Mary Ann Mason, *Childhood in America* (New York: New York University Press, 2000); Stephen Mintz, *Huck's Raft: A History of American Childhood* (Cambridge, MA: Harvard University Press, 2004); Viviana A. Rotman Zelizer, *Pricing the Priceless Child: The Changing Social Value of Children* (New York: Basic Books, 1985). This is a central point for David Buckingham; see *After the Death of Childhood* (London: Polity, 2000) and *Youth, Identity, and Digital Media*. Stern, "Producing Sites," makes this point as well.

43. Sociologist Ann Swidler refers to these unconscious, taken-for-granted approaches as "strategies of action." See Ann Swidler, "Culture in Action: Symbols and Strategies," *American Sociological Review* 51, 2 (1986): 273–86.

44. See Richard Jenkins, *Social Identity* (London: Routledge, 2004); Judith Butler, *Gender Trouble* (London: Routledge, 1990).

45. Corsaro, *Sociology of Childhood.*

46. British cultural studies looked at how young people drew upon the commercial environment to formulate and maintain subcultural identities. This was one example of a body of research that looked at young people not as recipients of adult socialization but as people who were agents on their own terms. See Hall and Jefferson, eds., *Resistance Through Rituals*; Angela McRobbie, *Feminism and Youth Culture: From "Jackie" to "Just Seventeen"* (London: Macmillan, 1990); Dick Hebdige, *Hiding in the Light: On Images and Things* (London: Routledge, 1989).

47. Sociologists have been particularly interested in how differing people construct self-identities in relation to various racial/ethnic, class, gender, and other groups. Standpoint theories, such as those of feminist scholars, highlight how experiences as members of certain groups shape further experiences and thus world views. See Donna Haraway, "Situated Knowledges: The Science Question in Feminism and the Privilege of Partial Perspective," *Feminist Studies* 14 (1988): 575–99; Nancy Hartsock, *Money, Sex, and Power: Toward a Feminist Historical Materialism* (New York: Longman, 1983). Others have noted that we must consider not only memberships in groups, which can essentialize experiences, but rather intersectionalities of differing identities, exploring how identity work can be less permanent and more strategic and contextual. See Mary C. Waters, *Ethnic Options: Choosing Identities in America* (Berkeley: University of California Press, 1990). Moreover, a great deal of research has been devoted to identity multidimensionality, or how identity is complex and multifaceted. Modernity "embeds us in multiple thought communities simultaneously, giving us a complex web of sociomental affiliations that shapes our own sense of self," as sociologist Wayne Brekhus has noted. See Wayne Brekhus, "Trends in the Qualitative Study of Social Identities." *Sociology Compass* 2/3 (2008): 1059–78.

48. danah boyd, "Why Youth (Heart) Social Network Sites: The Role of Networked Publics in Teenage Social Life," in David Buckingham, ed., *Youth, Identity, and Digital Media*, John D. and Katherine T. MacArthur Foundation Series on Digital Media and Learning (Cambridge, MA: MIT Press, 2008). See also danah boyd, "Taken Out of Context: American Teen Sociality in Networked Publics," Ph.D. dissertation, University of California, Berkeley, 2008.

49. Erving Goffman was the first to discuss identity in relation to display. See his *The Presentation of Self in Everyday Life* (New York: Anchor, 1959).

50. Shayla Thiel Stern notes the way in which theories of representation complicate notions of identity in her study of adolescent girls and instant messaging. See her *Instant Identity: Adolescent Girls and the World of Instant Messaging* (New York: Peter Lang, 2007).

51. Theresa Senft, *Camgirls: Celebrity and Community in the Age of Social Networks* (New York: Peter Lang, 2008). See also Sherry Turkle, *Life on the Screen* (New York: Simon and Schuster, 1995).

52. Google, "Zeitgeist 2010: How the World Searched," www.google.com/intl/en/press/zeitgeist2010 (retrieved July 20, 2011).

53. Rebekah Willett has made this argument; see her "Consumer Citizens Online: Structure, Agency and Gender in Online Participation," in David Buckingham, ed., *Youth, Identity and Digital Media*, 49–70 (Cambridge, MA: MIT Press, 2008), www.mitpressjournals.org/toc/dmal/-/6.

54. NPD Group, "Children Are Exposed to and Adopting Electronic Devices at Earlier Ages," press release, www.npd.com/press/releases/press_070605.html, June 5, 2007 (retrieved July 22, 2011).

55. Sun Sun Lim and Lynn Schofield Clark, "Virtual Worlds as a Site of Convergence for Children's Play," *Journal of Virtual Worlds* 3, 2 (2010), http://journals.tdl.org/jvwr/article/view/1897.

56. NPD Group, "While the Majority of Mobile Devices Used by Parents and Kids Have Fewer than 20 Apps for Children, Close to 10 Percent Have More than 60," press release, September 20, 2010, www.npd.com/press/releases/press_100920a.html (retrieved July 22, 2011).

57. This was the focus of the Networked Participation workshop, hosted by the Joan Ganz Cooney Center and CISCO in November 2011.

58. "Emotion work" is a term used by sociologist Arlie Hochschild and will be discussed more thoroughly in chapter 8.

59. Sherry Turkle, *Alone Together: Why We Expect More from Technology and Less from Each Other* (New York: Basic Books, 2011), 172.

60. Ibid., 280.

61. See Christopher Lasch, *The Culture of Narcissism* (New York, Norton, 1979); David Riesman, Nathan Glazer, and Reuel Denney, *The Lonely Crowd: A Study of the Changing American Character* (New Haven, CT: Yale University Press, 1950); see also Turkle, *Alone Together*, 177.

Chapter 5: Less Advantaged Teens, Ethnicity, and Digital and Mobile Media

1. Mike was a senior at the University of Denver when he served as a volunteer at Denver High School in fall 2011.

2. Lisa Tripp also observed that educational opportunities frequently emerged in discussions of digital and mobile media use among Latino immigrant families. See Lisa Tripp, "The Computer Is Not for You Looking Around, It Is for Schoolwork: Challenges for Digital Inclusion as Latino Immigrant Families Negotiate Children's Access to the Internet," *New Media and Society* 13 (2011): 552–67.

3. Patricia Ann Banks, *Represent: Art and Identity Among the Black Upper Middle Class* (New York: Routledge, 2009); Maria Chavez, *Everyday Injustice: Latino Professionals and Racism* (Lanham, MD: Rowman and Littlefield, 2001); William A. V. Clark, *Immigrants and the American Dream: Remaking the Middle Class* (New York: Guilford Press, 2003); Karyn Lacy, *Blue-Chip Black: Race, Class, and Status in the New Black Middle Class* (Berkeley: University of California Press, 2007); Gregory Rodriguez, "The Emerging Latino Middle Class," Institute for Public Policy, Pepperdine University, 1996.

4. Ben Rooney, "Recession Worsens Racial Wealth Gap," *CNN Money*, July 26, 2011, http://money.cnn.com/2011/07/26/news/economy/wealth_gap_white_black_hispanic/index.htm?cnn=yes&;hpt=hp_t2 (retrieved August 25, 2011).

5. Ibid.

6. Ibid.

7. "U.S. Population Projections: 2005–2050—Pew Hispanic Center," Pewhispanic. org (retrieved February 4, 2012); Tena Starr, "Mexican Farmworker's Life Like Living in a 'Golden Cage,'" *Chronicle* (Barton, VT), April 28, 2010, 12.

8. N. Sudarkasa, "African American Families and Family Values," in H. P. McAdoo, ed., *Black Families*, 3rd ed. (Thousand Oaks, CA: Sage, 1997).

9. N. Way, "Between Experiences of Betrayal and Desire: Close Friendships Among Urban Adolescents," in B. J. R. Leadbetter and N. Way, eds., *Urban Girls* (New York: New York University Press, 1996).

10. L. M. Burton, K. W. Allison, and D. Obeidallah, "Social Context and Adolescence: Perspectives in Development Among Inner-City African American Teens," in L. J. Crockett and A. C. Crouter, eds., *Pathways Through Adolescence* (Mahwah, NJ: Erlbaum, 1995).

11. Alan Riding, *Distant Neighbors* (New York: Vintage Books, 1989); A. R. Del Castillo, "Covert Cultural Norms and Sex/Gender Meaning: A Mexico City Case," *Urban Anthropology* 22, 3–4 (1993): 237–58.

12. Y. Flores Niemann, A. J. Romero, J. Arredondo, and V. Rodriguez, "What Does It Mean to Be 'Mexican'? Social Construction of an Ethnic Identity," *Hispanic Journal of Behavioral Sciences* 22, 1 (1999): 47–60; P. J. Guamaccia and O. Rodriguez, "Concepts of Culture and Their Role in the Development of Culturally Competent Mental Health Services," *Hispanic Journal of Behavioral Sciences* 18, 4 (1996): 419–33; M. A. Lara-Cantu, "A Sex Role Inventory with Scales for 'Machismo' and 'Self-Sacrificing Women,'" *Journal of Cross-Cultural Psychology* 20 (1989): 396–98; S. L. Lindsley, "Communication and 'the Mexican Way': Stability and Trust as Core Symbols in Maquiladoras," *Western Journal of Communication* 63, 1 (1999): 1–31; W. F. Strong, J. S. McQuillen, and J. D. Hughey, "En el Laberinto de Machismo: A Comparative Analysis of Macho Attitudes Among Hispanic and Anglo College Students," *Howard Journal of Communications* 5, 1–2 (1994): 18–35; J. B. Torres, "Masculinity and Gender Roles Among Puerto Rican Men: Machismo on the U.S. Mainland," *American Journal of Orthopsychiatry* 68, 1 (1998): 16–26.

13. A. J. Fuligni, "Authority, Autonomy, and Parent-Adolescent Conflict and Cohesion: A Study of Adolescents from Mexican, Chinese, Filipino, and European Backgrounds," *Developmental Psychology* 34 (1998): 782–97; A. J. Fuligni, T. Yip, and V. Tseng, "The Impact of Family Obligation on the Daily Activities and Psychological Well-Being of Chinese American Adolescents," *Child Development* 73, 1 (2002): 302; Z. B. Xiong and D. F. Detzner, "Southeast Asian Fathers' Experiences with Adolescents: Challenges and Change," *Hmong Studies Journal* 6 (2005): 1–23; M. Zhou and I. C. Bankston, *Growing Up American: How Vietnamese Children Adapt to Life in the United States* (New York: Russell Sage Foundation, 1998).

14. "Frequently Requested Statistics on Immigrants and Immigration in the United States," *Migrant Immigration Source*, Migration Policy Institute, www. migrationinformation.org/USfocus/display.cfm?ID=818 (retrieved February 4, 2012).

15. B. Bradford Brown, Jeremy P. Bakken, Jacqueline Nguyen, and Heather G. Von Bank, "Sharing Information About Peer Relations: Parent and Adolescent Opinions and Behaviors in African American and Hmong Families," *New Directions for Child and Adolescent Development* 116 (Summer 2007): 67–82.

16. K. Rick and J. Forward, "Acculturation and Perceived Intergenerational Difference Among Hmong Youth," *Journal of Cross-Cultural Psychology* 23, 1 (1992): 85–94.

17. J. W. Berry and D. Sam, "Acculturation and Adaptation," in J. W. Berry, M. H. Segal, and C. Kagitcibaci, eds., *Handbook of Cross-Cultural Psychology*, vol. 3: *Social Behavior and Applications*, 2nd ed. (Boston: Allyn and Bacon, 1997).

18. U.S. Department of Commerce, *A Nation Online: How Americans Are Expanding Their Use of the Internet* (Washington, DC: U.S. GPO, 2002).

19. A review of these reports, and a contesting of their findings, was issued for the Leadership Conference on Civil Rights Education Fund in 2005. See Robert W. Fairlie, "Are We Really a Nation Online? Ethnic and Racial Disparities in Access to Technology and Their Consequences," www.civilrights.org/publications/nation-online (retrieved July 21, 2011).

20. The Technology Opportunities Program and Community Technology Centers Program were discontinued in 2002.

21. Paul DiMaggio, Eszter Hargittai, Coral Celeste, and Steven Shafer, "Digital Inequality: From Unequal Access to Differentiated Use," in Kathryn Neckerman, ed., *Social Inequality*, 355–400 (New York: Russell Sage Foundation, 2004).

22. Fairlie, "Are We Really a Nation Online?" 3, 7, 8.

23. Mark Warschauer, *Technology and Social Inclusion: Rethinking the Digital Divide* (Cambridge, MA: MIT Press, 2003). See also A. Clement and L. Shade, "The Access Rainbow: Conceptualizing Universal Access to the Information/Communication Infrastructure," in M. Gurstein, ed., *Community Informatics*, 32–51 (Hershey, PA: Idea Publishing, 2000). See also Lisa Nakamura, "Interrogating the Digital Divide: The Political Economy of Race and Commerce in New Media," in P. Howard and S. Jones, eds., *Society Online: The Internet in Context*, 71–83 (Thousand Oaks, CA: Sage, 2004); Maria Bakardjieva and R. Smith, "The Internet in Everyday Life," *New Media and Society* 3 (2001): 67–83; L. Kvasny, "Cultural (Re)production of Digital Inequality in a US Community Technology Initiative," *Information, Communication and Society* 9, 2 (2006): 160–181; Ronald Rice and Carolyn Haythornthwaite, "Perspectives on Internet Use: Access, Involvement, and Interaction," in L. Lievrouw and S. Livingstone, eds., *Handbook of New Media: Social Shaping and Consequences of ICTs*, 2nd ed., 92–113 (London: Sage, 2006); Jan Dijk, *The Deepening Divide: Inequality in the Information Society* (Thousand Oaks, CA: Sage, 2005). The term "gradations in digital inclusion" is introduced in Sonia Livingstone and Elizabeth Helsper, "Gradations in Digital Inclusion: Children, Young People and the Digital Divide," *New Media and Society* 9, 4 (2007): 671–96.

24. Eszter Hargittai, "Digital Na(t)ives? Variation in Internet Skills and Uses Among Members of the 'Net Generation,'" *Sociological Inquiry* 80, 1 (2010): 92–113; Paul DiMaggio and Bart Bonikowski, "Make Money Surfing the Web? The Impact of Internet Use on the Earnings of U.S. Workers," *American Sociological Review* 73 (2008): 227–50; DiMaggio et al., "Digital Inequality."

25. Hargittai, "Digital Na(t)ives?"

26. Fred Rothbaum, Nancy Martland, and Joanne Beswick Jannsen, "Parents' Reliance on the Web to Find Information About Children and Families: Socio-economic Differences in Use, Skills, and Satisfaction," *Journal of Applied Developmental Psychology* 29 (2008): 118–28. See also Sun Sun Lim and Y. L. Tan, "Parental Control of New Media

Usage—the Challenges of Infocomm Literacy," *Australian Journal of Communication* 31, 1 (2004): 95–102.

27. Sonia Livingstone and Elspeth Helsper, "Gradations in Digital Inclusion: Children, Young People and the Digital Divide," *New Media and Society* 9, 4 (2007): 671–96; Henry Jenkins, R. Purushotma, K. Clinton, M. Weigel, and A. Robinson, *Confronting the Challenges of Participatory Culture: Media Education for the 21st Century* (Chicago: MacArthur Foundation, 2006), www.projectnml.org/files/working/NMLWhitePaper.pdf.

28. "Demographics of Internet Users May 2011," Pew Internet and American Life Project, http://pewinternet.org/Static-Pages/Trend-Data/Whos-Online.aspx (retrieved February 4, 2012). The number of nonusers has declined only slightly in recent years, from approximately 25 percent to 22 percent of the U.S. population. See C. Zhang, M. Callegaro, and M. Thomas, "More than the Digital Divide? Investigating the Differences Between Internet and Non-Internet Users," Midwest Association of Public Opinion Research, Chicago, 2008, cited in Hargittai, "Digital Na(t)ives?"

29. Amanda Lenhart, S. Arafeh, A. Smith, and A Macgill, *Writing, Technology and Teens* (Washington, DC: Pew Internet and American Life Project, 2008), www.pewinternet.org/PPF/r/247/report_display.asp (retrieved July 21, 2011).

30. Amanda Lenhart, Rich Ling, Scott Campbell, and Kirsten Purcell, *Teens and Mobile Phones*, Pew Internet and American Life Project, 2011, pewinternet.org.

31. Craig S. Watkins, *The Young and the Digital: What the Migration to Social Network Sites, Games, and Anytime, Anywhere Media Means for Our Future* (Boston: Beacon, 2009).

32. Craig Watkins (ibid.) has pointed out that whereas ethnic young people who lack access to laptops are able to use their mobile phones for consumption, they are less likely to use them for creative activities.

33. Tripp, "The Computer Is Not for You Looking Around"; Gretchen Livingston, *Latinos and Digital Technology*, 2010, Pew Hispanic Center, http://pewhispanic.org/reports/report.php?ReportID=134; Susannah Fox and Gretchen Livingston, *Latinos Online*, Pew Hispanic Center and Pew Internet and American Life Project, March 2007, www.pewinternet.org/PPF/r/204/report_display.asp (retrieved July 21, 2011); J. Benítez, "Transnational Dimensions of the Digital Divide Among Salvadoran Immigrants in the Washington DC Metropolitan Area," *Global Networks* 6, 2 (2006): 181–99. See also V. Rojas, J. Straubhaar, J. Spence, D. Roychowdhury, O. Okur, J. Pinon, and M. Fuentes-Bautista, "Communities, Cultural Capital and Digital Inclusion: Ten Years of Tracking Techno-Dispositions," in J. Straubhaar, ed. *Inequity in the Technopolis: Race, Class, Gender, and the Digital Divide in Austin* (Austin: University of Texas Press, 2012).

34. Watkins, *The Young and the Digital*.

35. Ibid.

36. Iskinder was interviewed by first by Katie Kremer as part of a qualitative research methods class at the University of Denver, and later by Lynn Sywyj, research assistant at the University of Denver, in spring and summer of 2011. Data on Iskinder's home area obtained from city-data.com.

37. Ethiopian communities west of Addis Ababa have been the site of several ethnic-related incidences of violence. See, e.g., www.genocidewatch.org/Ethiopia%20US%20Government%20Wants%20Gambella%20Violence%20Investigated.htm.

38. N. Landale, K. Thomas, and J. Van Hook, "The Living Arrangements of Children of Immigrants," *Future of Children* 21, 1 (2011): 43–70.

39. I interviewed Kamlai informally in winter 2012.

40. Bina was interviewed by Lynn Swywj in fall 2011.

41. Katie Kremer interviewed Bina Dhakal as part of a qualitative research methods class at the University of Denver in spring 2011.

42. Ibid.

43. Heather Smith interviewed Santosh as part of a qualitative research methods class at the University of Denver in spring 2011.

44. Tracy Scherr and Jim Larson, "Bullying Dynamics Associated with Race, Ethnicity, and Immigration Status," in Shane R. Jimerson, Susan M. Swearer, and Dorothy L. Espelage, eds., *Handbook of Bullying in Schools: An International Perspective*, 223–34 (New York: Routledge, 2010). Little research has explored racial/ethnic dynamics in relation to cyberbullying, although existing research suggests that online patterns of bullying correlate with offline patterns. See, e.g., M. L. Ybarra, M. Diener-West, and P. J. Leaf, "Examining the Overlap in Internet Harassment and School Bullying: Implications for School Intervention," *Journal of Adolescent Health* 41, 6 (2007): 42–50; J. Wolak, M. L. Ybarra, K. Mitchell, and D. Finkelhor, "Current Research Knowledge About Adolescent Victimization via the Internet," *Adolescent Medicine* 18 (2007): 325–41.

45. This is discussed in Lynn Schofield Clark and Lynn Swywj, "Mobile Intimacies in the U.S. Among Refugee and Recent Immigrant Teens and Their Parents," *Journal of Feminist Media Studies*, 2012.

46. Mateo Lopez was interviewed by Lynn Sywyj and Carrie Miller as part of a qualitative research methods class at the University of Denver in spring 2011. The summary of his story was first drafted by Alexandra Gardner from the same class.

47. This is consistent with findings regarding higher levels of restriction among parents of lower-income families. See, e.g., Burton, Allison, and Obeidallah, "Social Context and Adolescence"; M. Cruz-Santiago and J. I. Ramírez García, "'Hay Que Ponerse en los Zapatos del Joven': Adaptive Parenting of Adolescent Children Among Mexican-American Parents Residing in a Dangerous Neighborhood," *Family Process* 50, 1 (2011): 92–114.

48. Heather Horst and Daniel Miller, *The Cell Phone: An Anthropology of Communication* (London: Berg, 2006).

49. Deshonelle Williams was interviewed by Carrie Miller in April 2011.

50. Skyview Academy High School Accountability Report, 2006–7, 2007–8, Colorado Department of Education, http://acsd1.k12.co.us; "College Board Announces Expansion of EXCELerator Schools project to Denver, CO, and Hillsborough County, FL (Tampa)," January 23, 2007, http://press.collegeboard.org/releases/2007/college-board-announces-expansion-excelerator8482160schools-project-denver-co-and-hills-borou.

51. South High School demographic data available: www.piton.org/index.cfm?fuseaction=SchoolFacts.Summary&;School_ID=288.

52. The researcher danah boyd has also observed the importance of critical mass in her explanation of why some young people switched from MySpace to Facebook. See danah boyd, "Taken Out of Context: Teen Sociality in Networked Publics," Ph.D. dissertation, University of California at Berkeley, 2008.

53. TaRhonda Thomas interviewed Monique as part of a qualitative research methods class at the University of Denver in spring 2011.

54. See, e.g., Qing Li, "New Bottle but Old Wine: A Research of Cyberbullying in Schools," *Computers in Human Behavior* 23, 4 (July 2007): 1777–91; Justin W. Patchin and Samecr Hinduja, "Bullies Move Beyond the Schoolyard," *Youth Violence and Juvenile Justice* 4, 2 (April 2006): 148–69.

55. Written comments submitted by a student anonymously as part of a school-based program on cyberbullying, spring 2011. Cited in Heather Smith and Katie Roberts-Kremer, "Cyberbullying," University of Denver, 2011.

56. Ibid.

57. Some young people used "dirty kids" or "DK" when referring to young people who bathed or changed clothes infrequently as a result of impoverished home situations. See boyd, "Taken Out of Context."

58. Researcher danah boyd has argued that this is true of most young people, who go on social networking sites to interact with people they already know. By including these stories here, I wish to highlight the barriers that similarly shape the ways that young people from less privileged backgrounds encounter the social groups to which they do and do not feel that they have (or would want) access.

59. Mary Madden and Aaron Smith, "Reputation Management and Social Media," Pew Internet and American Life Project, 2010, www.pewinternet.org/Reports/2010/Reputation-Management.aspx (retrieved July 26, 2010).

60. Kevin Lewis, Jason Kaufman, and Nicholas Christakis, "The Taste for Privacy: An Analysis of College Student Privacy Settings in an Online Social Network," *Journal of Computer-Mediated Communication* 14, 1 (2008): 79–100. See also Fred Stutzman and Jacob Kramer-Duffield, "Friends Only: Examining a Privacy-Enhancing Behavior in Facebook," *Proceedings of the 28th International Conference on Human Factors in Computing Systems*, 2010, 1553–62. Both are cited in danah boyd and Eszter Hargittai, "Facebook Settings: Who Cares?" *First Monday* 15, 8 (August 2010).

61. boyd and Hargittai, "Facebook Settings."

62. Lim and Tan, "Parental Control of New Media Usage."

63. Researcher Monica Emerich interviewed the Odell family. The two children had different fathers, and hence differing racial/ethnic identifications: Montana was part Native American, and Thad was part African American. Monica Emerich also interviewed the Richards family. Focus group interviews were conducted by Lynn Schofield Clark, Caroline Davidson, Alexis Lynn, and Colette Holst in 2007–8.

64. Monica Emerich also interviewed the Richards family. Marvin Richards' case has been highlighted in studies of masculinity, parenting, and religious values conducted by Stewart Hoover and Curtis Coats, who shared this data. See Stewart Hoover, *Religion in a Media Age* (London: Routledge, 2006).

65. See, e.g., Brown et al., "Sharing Information"; Sudarkasa, "African American Families."

66. Rosalia Jiminez and Sofia Hernandez were interviewed by me, Alexis Lynn, and Colette Holst in a high school focus group during the spring of 2008.

67. John Timmer, "Let Them Use AOL: Upper Class Searchers Prefer Google," *Ars Technica*, March 27, 2008, http://arstechnica.com/old/content/2008/03/let-them-use-aol-upper-class-searchers-prefer-google.ars (retrieved September 29, 2010).

68. This finding echoes the gap of "infocomm illiterate" parents and their more technologically comfortable children in Singapore, according to Lim and Tan, "Parental Control of New Media Usage."

69. K. Facer, J. Furlong, R. Furlong, and R. Sutherland, *Screenplay: Children and Computing in the Home* (New York: Routledge, 2003).

Chapter 6: Communication in Families

1. Members of the Welton family were interviewed in 2008–9 by Robert Peaslee, then a research assistant in the Teens and the New Media @ Home project and the Media, Meaning, and Work project at the University of Colorado–Boulder.

2. This is the basis of the media ecology school of thought, articulated most famously in Marshall McLuhan, *Understanding Media: The Extensions of Man* (Cambridge, MA: MIT Press, 1994 [1964]). See also Joshua Meyrowitz, *No Sense of Place: The Impact of Electronic Media on Social Behavior* (New York: Oxford University Press, 1985); Neil Postman, *Amusing Ourselves to Death: Public Discourse in the Age of Show Business* (New York: Penguin, 1985); Sherry Turkle, *Alone Together: Why We Expect More from Technology and Less from Each Other* (New York: Basic Books, 2011). A significant number of scholars in the fields of media history, cultural studies, and the social construction of technology also contribute to understandings of media's role in social change. See, e.g., Carolyn Marvin, *When Old Technologies Were New: Thinking About Electric Communication in the Late Nineteenth Century* (New York: Oxford University Press, 1988); James Carey, *Communication as Culture: Essays on Media and Society* (New York: Routledge, 1988); Raymond Williams, *Television: Technology and Cultural Form* (London: Fontana, 1974). Following Roger Silverstone, I am defining communication media as part of the "general texture of experience" in everyday life, as he uses that phrase. The media are conduits, languages, and environments, according to Silverstone, who argues that the study of media foregrounds how meanings move through and across time and space and how certain institutions participate in what he calls the "production of enchantment." The definition of media can extend from the present-day smart mobile phone back to language itself. Thus while the phrase "communication media" does not refer only to what we think of as today's contemporary mobile, digital, and entertainment media, it also includes these things. Roger Silverstone, *Why Study the Media?* (London: Sage, 1999).

3. Annette Lareau, *Unequal Childhoods: Class, Race, and Family Life* (Berkeley: University of California Press, 2003).

4. Stephen Chaffee, Jack McLeod, and Dennis Wackman first outlined differences in family communication patterns in "Family Communication Patterns and Adolescent Political Participation," in J. Dennis, ed., *Socialization to Politics* (New York: John Wiley, 1973). They argued that some families (particularly middle-class ones) tend to be concept-oriented, emphasizing the development of expressiveness, whereas other families are socio-oriented, emphasizing the importance of getting along with others. Lareau in *Unequal Childhoods* has also observed the importance within middle-class families of learning to express one's views.

5. On the risks and opportunities of digital media for children, see Sonia Livingstone, *Children and the Internet: Great Expectations, Challenging Realities* (London: Polity Press, 2009).

6. Lori Takeuchi and Reed Stevens, *The New Coviewing: Designing for Learning Through Joint Media Engagement*, Joan Ganz Cooney Center, December 2011, http://joanganzcooneycenter.org/Reports-32.html.

7. Heather Horst, "Families," in Mizuko Ito et al., *Hanging Out, Messing Around, Geeking Out: Living and Learning with New Media* (Cambridge, MA: MIT Press, 2010).

8. Laurence Steinberg, *The Ten Basic Principles of Good Parenting* (New York: Simon and Schuster, 2004).

9. Carly Shuler, *iLearn II: An Analysis of the Education Category on Apple's App Store*, Joan Ganz Cooney Center at Sesame Workshop, January 2012, http://joanganzcooneycenter.org/Reports-33.html (retrieved January 29, 2012).

10. Chaffee, McLeod, and Wackman, "Family Communication Patterns and Adolescent Political Participation."

11. Roger Silverstone, David Morley, Andrea Dahlberg, and Sonia Livingstone, "Families, Technologies, and Consumption: The Household and Information and Communication Technologies," CRICT discussion paper, Brunel University, 1989.

12. See, e.g., the discussion in chapter 1 of the research of Annette Lareau, Allison Pugh, Margaret Nelson, and Wendy Griswold.

13. James Lull, "Family Communication Patterns and the Social Uses of Television," in *Inside Family Viewing: Ethnographic Research on Television's Audiences*, 49–61 (London: Routledge, 1990). His first articulation of these differences is James Lull, "The Social Uses of Television," *Human Communication Research* 6, 3 (1980): 197–209.

14. Members of the Grantman-Lane family were first interviewed in 2004 by Monica Emerich, then a research assistant in the Teens and the New Media @ Home project and the Media, Meaning, and Work project at the University of Colorado–Boulder. Emerich is author of *The Gospel of Sustainability: Media, Market and LOHAS* (Urbana: University of Illinois Press, 2011).

15. I use the phrase "would-be middle class" in reference to the financial instability many experience as a measure of distance from middle-class culture. Sociologist Barbara Ehrenreich also discusses the underemployed and the "anxiously employed" as part of this would-be middle class. See Barbara Ehrenreich, "If There's a War on the Middle Class, I'm Enlisting to Fight for It!" *United Professionals*, n.d., www.unitedprofessionals.org/tag/bait-and-switch (no longer available online).

16. The views of would-be middle-class and less advantaged parents concerning communication media represent a source of ambivalence about the processes and accomplishment of "natural growth" in which parents of less means tend to trust. In this sense, the approach I am outlining here aims to build on Lareau's theory of how working-class and poor parents trust in the "natural" processes of their child's development.

17. Lisa Tripp has also found that less advantaged Latino families view media as "safe" for unsupervised consumption. See Lisa Tripp, "The Computer Is Not for You to Be Looking Around, It Is for Schoolwork: Challenges for Digital Inclusion as Latino Immigrant Families Negotiate Children's Access to the Internet," *New Media and Society* 13, 4 (2011): 552–67.

18. See Chaffee, McLeod, and Wackman, "Family Communication Patterns and Adolescent Political Participation."

19. Lareau, *Unequal Childhoods*, has also noted the sense of "distance, distrust, and constraint" in the institutional experiences of less advantaged younger children and their families.

20. Committee on Public Education, American Academy of Pediatrics, "Media Education." *Pediatrics* 104, 2 (August 1999).

21. See, e.g., Joanne Cantor and M. L. Mares, "The Effects of Television on Children and Family Emotional Well-Being," in Jennings Bryant, ed., *Television and the American Family*, 2nd ed. (Mahwah, NJ: Erlbaum, 2001); see also National Institute of Mental Health, *Television and Behavior: Ten Years of Scientific Progress and Implications for the Eighties*, vol. 1 (Rockville, MD: U.S. Department of Health and Human Services, 1982).

22. Lareau, *Unequal Childhoods*.

23. See, e.g., Lynn Schofield Clark, "Digital Media and the Generation Gap: Qualitative Research on U.S. Teens and Their Parents," *Information, Communication, and Society* 12 (2009): 388–407.

24. Leonard Beeghley, *The Structure of Social Stratification in the United States* (Boston: Pearson, 2004).

25. The Nelson family members were interviewed in 2005 and 2006 by Monica Emerich, who served as a research associate at the University of Colorado.

26. Barbara Ehrenreich, *Fear of Falling: The Inner Life of the Middle Class* (New York: Pantheon, 1989).

27. The Polanski family members were interviewed in 2005 by Curtis Coats, who served as a research associate at the University of Colorado.

28. Amanda Lenhart, Rich Ling, Scott Campbell, and Kirsten Purcell, *Teens and Mobile Phones*, Pew Internet and American Life Project, April 20, 2010, http://pewinternet.org/Reports/2010/Teens-and-Mobile-Phones.aspx (retrieved August 28, 2011).

29. On one Missionary College blog about setting up businesses as a form of mission, a student writes of the "Ten Deadly Sins" of approaching a business as a mission. The seventh "deadly sin" is "the temptation of pride." "Having people work for you can make you prideful," the author wrote. "The antidote? A wife." The author credits another writer for coining this joke, and then adds, "It's funny because it's true." This is an obvious example of a conservative view of gender roles, as it assumes that the reader and businessperson is a male, and that the role of the female is to be supportive (or at least a check on the male's pride). See http://blogs.globeservebusiness.com/business-as-mission (retrieved August 28, 2011).

30. Many conservative Christians view the online environment as one that is culturally polluted; hence the need for "discernment" guided by a commitment to one's own conservative Christianity. Blake himself acknowledged that he had often given in to the "temptation" of viewing pornography online—which in many ways reinforced his view that the online environment was one of danger and needed to be navigated with the help of the compass of conservative Christianity.

31. This is consistent with the observations of W. Bradford Wilcox regarding what he terms "soft patriarchs" within conservative Christianity. See W. Bradford Wilcox, *Soft Patriarchs, New Men: How Christianity Shapes Fathers and Husbands* (Chicago: University of Chicago Press, 2004).

32. Dave and Judy Cruz were interviewed by Scott Webber, who was a doctoral student at the University of Colorado in 2002.

33. On the importance of weak social ties to one's prospects for greater employment opportunities, see Mark S. Granovetter, "The Strength of Weak Ties," *American Journal of Sociology* 78, 6 (May 1973): 1360–80.

34. This is the point that British sociologist Paul Willis made in the book *Learning to Labor: How Working Class Kids Get Working Class Jobs* (New York: Columbia University Press, 2001).

35. This is a central argument in Cathy N. Davidson, *Now You See It: How the Brain Science of Attention Will Transform the Way We Live, Work, and Learn* (New York: Penguin, 2011). See also Brigid Barron, "Interest and Self-Sustained Learning as Catalysts of Development: A Learning Ecology Perspective," *Human Development* 49 (2006): 193–224.

36. In the Quest2Learn middle school, game design leads the curriculum. Reviewed in Stephanie Olsen, "Education: Video Games Mix Cool with Purpose," *New York Times*, November 1, 2009. See also the Digital Youth Network, affiliated with the Chicago Public Libraries: http://digitalyouthnetwork.org (retrieved August 28, 2011).

37. In an important study, Jean Anyon documented differences in educational approaches in working-class, middle-class, and affluent areas that demonstrated an emphasis on conformity and rote learning in less advantaged schools and creativity and individualized encouragement in the schools with more advantages. See Jean Anyon, "Social Class and the Hidden Curriculum of Work," *Journal of Education* 162, 1 (Fall 1980).

38. See Barry Wellman, Aaron Smith, Amy Wells, and Trace Kennedy, *Networked Families*, Pew Internet and American Research Project, 2008, http://www.pewinternet.org/Reports/2008/Networked-Families.aspx.

39. This is the primary point of David Finkelhor's research, as discussed in the previous chapter.

Chapter 7: How Parents Are Mediating the Media in Middle-Class and Less Advantaged Homes

1. Nancy, Danielle, and Adam Oliver were first interviewed by Scott Webber and Denise Walker in 2002. Scott and Denise were research assistants for the Teens and the New Media @ Home research project at the University of Colorado. They also worked with Stewart Hoover's Symbolism, Meaning, and the New Media @ Home project.

2. Amanda Lenhart, Kristen Purcell, Aaron Smith, and Kathryn Zickuhr, "Social Media and Mobile Internet Use Among Teens and Young Adults," Pew Internet and American Life Project, 2010, http://67.192.40.213/~/media/Files/Reports/2010/PIP_Social_Media_and_Young_Adults_Report_Final_with_toplines.pdf; R. Ling, *The Mobile Connection: The Cell Phone's Impact on Society* (San Francisco: Morgan Kauffman, 2004).

3. Arlie Russell Hochschild, *The Time Bind: When Work Becomes Home and Home Becomes Work* (New York: Holt, 2001).

4. Jill Dierberg interviewed the Richter family in 2009 as part of a graduate-level qualitative research methods class at the University of Denver.

5. Margaret Nelson, *Parenting Out of Control: Anxious Parents in Uncertain Times* (New York: New York University Press, 2010).

6. See, e.g., Annette Lareau, *Unequal Childhoods: Class, Race, and Family Life* (Berkeley: University of California Press, 2003).

7. F. E. Barcus, "Parental Influence on Children's Television Viewing," *Television Quarterly* 4 (1969): 63–73; J. R. Brown and O. Linne, "The Family as Mediator of Television's Effects," in R. Brown, ed., *Children and Television*, 184–98 (Beverly Hills, CA: Sage, 1976); M. Hochmuth, "Children's Radio Diet," *Quarterly Journal of Speech* 33, 2 (1947): 249–57; Wilber Schramm, Jack Lyle, and Edwin B. Parker, *Television in the Lives of Our Children* (Toronto: University of Toronto Press, 1961); J. M. McLeod, M. A. Fitzpatrick, C. J. Glynn, and S. F. Fallis, "Television and Social Relations: Family Influences and Consequences for Interpersonal Behavior," in D. Pearl, L. Bouthillet, and J. Lazar, eds., *Television and Behavior: Ten Years of Scientific Progress and Implications for the Eighties*, HHS Publication No. ADM 82-1196 (Washington, DC: U.S. Government Printing Office, 1982), 2:272–86.

8. E. Maccoby, "Why Do Children Watch Television," *Public Opinion Quarterly* 18, 3 (1954): 239–44; P. Burr and R. Burr, "Television Advertising to Children: What Parents Are Saying About Government Control," *Journal of Advertising* 5, 4 (1976): 37–41; A. Caron and S. Ward, "Gift Decisions by Kids and Parents," *Journal of Advertising Research* 15, 4 (1974): 15–20; S. Banks and R. Gupta, "Television as a Dependent Variable, for a Change," *Journal of Consumer Research* 7, 3 (1980): 327–30; J. Webster, J. Pearson, and D. Webster, "Children's Television Viewing as Affected by Contextual Variables in the Home," *Communication Research Reports* 3, 1 (1986): 1–8.

9. A. Dorr, P. Kovaric, and C. Doubleday, "Parent-Child Coviewing of Television," *Journal of Broadcasting and Electronic Media* 33, 1 (1989): 35–51; E. Kay, *The ACT Guide to Television or . . . How to Treat TV with TLC* (Boston: Beacon, 1979); C. A. Lin and D. J. Atkin, "Parental Mediation and Rulemaking for Adolescent Use of Television and VCRs," *Journal of Broadcasting and Electronic Media* 33 (1989): 53–67; B. Logan and K. Moody, eds., *Television Awareness Training: The Viewer's Guide for Family and Community* (New York: Media Action Research Center, 1977); A. Nathanson, "Identifying and Explaining the Relationship Between Parental Mediation and Children's Aggression," *Communication Research* 26, 6 (1999): 124–43; P. M. Valkenburg, M. Krcmar, A. L. Peeters, and N. M. Marseille, "Developing a Scale to Assess Three Styles of Television Mediation: Instructive Mediation, Restrictive Mediation, and Social Coviewing," *Journal of Broadcasting and Electronic Media* 43, 1 (1999): 52–67.

10. A. Nathanson, "The Immediate and Cumulative Effects of Television Mediation on Children's Aggression," Ph.D. dissertation, University of Wisconsin–Madison, 1998; Nathanson, "Identifying and Explaining the Relationship"; Valkenburg et al., "Developing a Scale." Note that Eastin and colleagues prefer the term *evaluative mediation* rather than *active mediation*; see M. S. Eastin, B. Greenberg, and L. Hofshire, "Parenting the Internet," *Journal of Communication* 56 (2006): 486–504. Valkenburg and colleagues (1999) prefer *instructive mediation* and *social coviewing*. I have suggested that participatory learning is an emergent strategy in Lynn Schofield Clark, "Parental Mediation Theory for the Digital Age," *Communication Theory*, in press.

11. A. Nathanson, W. P. Eveland, H. S. Park, and B. Paul, "Perceived Media Influence and Efficacy as Predictors of Caregivers' Protective Behaviors," *Journal of Broadcasting and Electronic Media* 46, 3 (2002): 385–411; E. W. Austin, D. F. Roberts, and C. Nass, "Influences of Family Communication on Children's Television-Interpretation

Processes," *Communication Research* 17 (1990): 545–64; R. J. Desmond, J. L. Singer, and D. G. Singer, "Family Mediation: Parental Communication and the Influences of Television on Children," in J. Bryant, ed., *Television and the American Family* (Hillsdale, NJ: Erlbaum, 1990). On the benefits of discussing aggression for child socialization, see R. J. Beck and D. Wood, "The Dialogic Socialization of Aggression in a Family's Court of Reason and Inquiry," *Discourse Processes* 16, 3 (1993): 341–63.

12. E. W. Austin, "Exploring the Effects of Active Parental Mediation of Television Content," *Journal of Broadcasting and Electronic Media* 37 (1993): 147–58.

13. A. Isaacs and A. Koerner, "Linking Familial Typologies: An Investigation of the Relationship Between Parenting Styles and Family Communication Patterns," paper presented to the International Communication Association, Chicago, 2008; A. Koerner and M. A. Fitzpatrick, "Understanding Family Communication Patterns and Family Functionings: The Roles of Conversation Orientation and Conformity Orientation," *Communication Yearbook* 26 (2002): 37–69; A. F. Koerner and M. A. Fitzpatrick, "Family Communication Patterns Theory: A Social Cognitive Approach," in D. O. Braithwaite and L. A. Baxter, eds., *Engaging Theories in Family Communication: Multiple Perspectives*, 50–65 (Mahwah, NJ: Lawrence Erlbaum Associates, 2006).

14. Nathanson, "Identifying and Explaining."

15. Ibid.; see also M. L. Hoffman, "Moral Development," in P. H. Mussen, ed., *Carmichael's Manual of Child Psychology*, 3rd ed., 2:261–360 (New York: Wiley, 1970).

16. A. Nathanson, "The Unintended Effects of Parental Mediation of Television on Adolescents," *Mediapsychology* 4 (2002): 207–30.

17. L. Baxter, C. Bylund, R. Imes, and T. Routsong, "Parent-Child Perceptions of Parental Behavioral Control Through Rule-Setting for Risky Health Choices During Adolescence," *Journal of Family Communication* 9 (2009): 251–71.

18. Curtis Coats interviewed the Chang family in 2006. Curtis was a research assistant for the Teens and the New Media @ Home research project at the University of Colorado. He also worked with Stewart Hoover's Symbolism, Meaning, & the New Media @ Home project.

19. Eastin, Greenberg, and Hofshire, "Parenting the Internet"; Valkenburg et al., "Developing a Scale"; R. Warren, "Parental Mediation of Children's Television Viewing in Low Income Families," *Journal of Communication* 55 (2005): 847–63.

20. Austin, Roberts, and Nass, "Influences of Family Communication"; Valkenburg et al., "Developing a Scale."

21. Bocking and Bocking. Saskia and Tabea Bocking, Parental mediation of television. *Journal of Children and Media* 3(3), 286–302. See also Stewart M. Hoover, *Religion in a Media Age* (London: Routledge, 2006). Hoover argues that parents in the United States have a difficult time drawing connections between family media practices and the values they wish to impart to their children.

22. W. P. Davison, "The Third-Person Effect in Communication," *Public Opinion Quarterly* 47, 1 (1983): 1–15; C. Hoffner and M. Buchanan, "Parents' Responses to Television Violence: The Third-Person Perception, Parental Mediation, and Support for Censorship," *Media Psychology* 4 (2002): 231–52; M. Krcmar and J. Cantor, "The Role of Television Advisories and Ratings in Parent-Child Discussion of Television Viewing Choices," *Journal of Broadcasting and Electronic Media* 41, 3 (1997): 393–411; P. C. Meirick, J. Sims, E. Gilchrist, and S. Croucher, "All the Children Are Above

Average: Parents' Perceptions of Education and Materialism as Media Effects on Their Own and Other Children," *Mass Communication and Society* 12, 2 (2009): 217–37; Nathanson et al., "Perceived Media Influence"; Y. Tsfati, R. Ribak, and J. Cohen, *"Rebelde Way* in Israel: Parental Perceptions of Television Influence and Monitoring of Children's Social and Media Activities," *Mass Communication and Society* 8 (2005): 3–22.

23. Sonia Livingstone and Ellen J. Helsper, "Parental Mediation of Children's Internet Use," *Journal of Broadcasting and Electronic Media* 52, 4 (2008): 581–99; J. A. Robinson and J. Kim, "Modeling the Relationship Between Family Media Use, Perceived Media Influence, and Rulemaking," paper presented to the International Communication Association, New Orleans, 2004.

24. E. W. Austin, C. Knaus, and A. Meneguelli, "Who Talks How to Their Kids About TV: A Clarification of Demographic Correlates of Parental Mediation Patterns," *Communication Research Reports* 14, 4 (1997): 418–30; J. R. Brown, K. W. Childers, K. E. Bauman, and G. Koch, "The Influence of New Media and Family Structure on Young Adolescents' Television and Radio Use," *Communication Research* 17, 1 (1990): 65–82; R. Warren, P. Gerke, and M. A. Kelly, "Is There Enough Time on the Clock? Parental Involvement and Mediation of Children's Television Viewing," *Journal of Broadcasting and Electronic Media* 46, 1 (2002): 87–112.

25. Joseph Brown interviewed the Dykstra family in 2009 as part of a graduate-level qualitative research methods class at the University of Denver.

26. See Nelson, *Parenting Out of Control.*

27. On how young people conceive of Facebook and MySpace as realms to which young people have "rights," see danah boyd, "Taken Out of Context: American Teen Sociality in Networked Publics," Ph.D. dissertation, University of California at Berkeley, 2008; David Brake, "Shaping the 'Me' in MySpace: The Framing of Profiles on a Social Network Site," in Knut Lundby, ed., *Digital Storytelling, Mediatized Stories: Self-Representations in New Media,* 285–300 (New York: Peter Lang, 2008).

28. Barry Wellman, Aaron Smith, Amy Wells, and Trace Kennedy, *Networked Families,* Pew Internet and American Life Project, 2008, http://pewinternet.org.

29. Jill Allen was interviewed in 2004 by Scott Webber, a doctoral student at the University of Colorado.

30. The Conner family was interviewed in the fall of 2002 by Denice Walker, a doctoral student at the University of Colorado.

31. Nelson, *Parenting Out of Control.*

32. Margaret K. Nelson, "Helicopter Moms, Heading for a Crash," *Washington Post,* July 4, 2010.

33. "There's an App for That: Mediating the Mobile Moms and Connected Careerists Through Smartphones and Networked Individualism," *Journal of Feminist Media Studies,* special issue on mobile intimacies, forthcoming.

34. Psychologist Barbara Hofer uses the term *electronic tether* to describe the way in which mobile phones enable college students to remain in contact with their parents when they have moved out of their parents' homes. Their initial study found that college freshmen contacted their parents ten times a week; a later study found that this use of the electronic tether was common among college students throughout their four years of university life. See *The iConnected Parent: Staying Close to Your Kids in College (and Beyond) While Letting Them Grow Up* (New York: Simon and Schuster/Free Press, 2010).

A summary of the iConnected Parent study is located at www.middlebury.edu/newsroom/experts/hofer/node/24561 (retrieved April 29, 2012).

35. Lori Takeuchi and Reed Stevens, *The New Coviewing: Designing for Learning Through Joint Media Engagement*, Joan Ganz Cooney Center, Fall 2011; P. Nikken, J. Jansz, and S. Schouwstra, "Parents' Interest in Videogame Ratings and Content Descriptors in Relation to Game Mediation," *European Journal of Communication* 22, 3 (2007): 24–143; Erika W. Austin, "Effects of Family Communication on Children's Interpretation of Television," in J. Bryant and J. A. Bryant, eds., *Television and the American Family*, 377–96 (Mahwah, NJ: Lawrence Erlbaum Associates, 2001); R. Stevens, T. Satwicz, and L. McCarthy, "In Game, in Room, in World: Reconnecting Video Game Play to the Rest of Kids' Lives," in K. Salen, ed., *Ecology of Games* (Cambridge, MA: MIT Press, 2008).

36. Brigit Barron, C. K. Martin, Lori Takeuchi, and R. Fithian, "Parents as Learning Partners in the Development of Technological Fluency," *International Journal of Learning and Media* 1, 2 (2009): 55–77.

37. Edward Downs, "How Can Wii Learn from Video Games? Examining Relationships Between Technological Affordances and Socio-cognitive Determinates on Affective and Behavioral Outcomes," Ph.D. dissertation, Pennsylvania State University, 2008.

38. S. Yarosh, S. Cuzzort, H. Muller, and G. D. Abowd, "Developing a Media Space for Remote Synchronous Parent-Child Interaction," paper presented at the IDC Conference, Como, Italy, 2009.

39. Janna Jones, "When the Movie Started, We All Got Along: Generation Y Remembers Movie Night," *Media International Australia* 139 (May 2011): 96–102.

40. Sherry Turkle, *Alone Together: Why We Expect More from Technology and Less from Each Other* (New York: Basic Books, 2011).

41. Angela McRobbie and Jenny Garber, "Girls and Subcultures," in Stuart Hall and Tony Jefferson, eds., *Resistance Through Rituals: Youth Subcultures in Post-War Britain*, 209–22 (New York: Routledge, 1976).

42. Sonia Livingstone first discussed the "media-rich environment" of middle-class households in *Young People and New Media* (London: Routledge, 2002).

Chapter 8: Media Rich and Time Poor

1. I first discussed this with Melanie in December 2008, and our conversation continued into 2009. Melanie's was a biracial Latino and European American middle-class family living in the Southwest.

2. Ellen Seiter has written about the ways in which single parents utilize digital media as a means of organizing their children's time while they attend to the work of maintaining a household. See Ellen Seiter, *Television and New Media Audiences* (Oxford: Clarendon, 2000).

3. Arlie Russell Hochschild, "Emotion Work, Feeling Rules and Social Structure," *American Journal of Sociology* 85, 3 (1979): 551–75.

4. M. Turcotte, "Time Spent with Family During a Typical Work Day 1986 to 2006," Canadian Social Trends, Statistics Canada—Catalogue No. 11-08 (2007), www.statcan.ca/english/freepub/11-008-XIE/2006007/pdf/11-008-XIE20060079574.pdf (retrieved June 23, 2010); M. A. Milkie, M. J. Mattingly, K. M. Nomaguchi, S. M. Bianchi, and J. P. Robinson, "The Time Squeeze: Parental Statuses and Feelings About Time with Children,"

Journal of Marriage and Family 66, 3 (2004): 739–61; M. J. Mattingly and L. C. Sayer, "Under Pressure: Gender Differences in the Relationship Between Free Time and Feeling Rushed," *Journal of Marriage and Family* 68, 1 (2006): 205–21. Juliet Schor has claimed that those in the United States work roughly two months more each year than do workers in Germany or France. She also argues the Americans take fewer vacation days than the inhabitants of any other country in the developed world. Juliet Schor, *The Overworked American: The Unexpected Decline of Leisure* (New York: Basic Books, 1992).

5. Jerry A. Jacobs and Kathleen Gerson, *The Time Divide: Work, Family, and Gender Inequality* (Cambridge, MA: Harvard University Press, 2004).

6. Kathleen Gerson, *The Unfinished Revolution* (New York: Oxford University Press, 2010).

7. Richard Posner, "American Wage Stagnation," *The Becker-Posner Blog*, April 18, 2010, http://uchicagolaw.typepad.com/beckerposner/2010/04/american-wage-stagnationposner. html (retrieved July 28, 2010). The trend toward wage decline has only continued in recent years, as the median U.S. household income fell by 4 percentage points between 1997 and 2008 after adjusting for inflation.

8. AFL-CIO, "Exporting America," www.aflcio.org/issues/jobseconomy/exportingamerica/ outsourcing_problems.cfm (retrieved July 28, 2010).

9. Gerson, *The Unfinished Revolution*.

10. Steven P. Martin, "Growing Evidence for a 'Divorce Divide'? Educational and Marital Dissolution Rates in the U.S. Since the 1970s," Russell Sage Foundation, n.d., http://www.russellsage.org/sites/all/files/u4/Martin_0.pdf.

11. Eugene Smolensky and Jennifer Appleton Grootman, eds., *Working Families and Growing Kids: Caring for Children and Adolescents* (Washington, DC: National Academies Press, 2003), www.nap.edu/openbook.php?record_id=10669&;page=R1.

12. Roland Sturm, "Childhood Obesity—What We Can Learn from Existing Data on Societal Trends, Part I," *Preventing Chronic Disease* 2, 1 (2005): A12.

13. M. McPherson, L. Smith-Lovin, and M. E. Brashears, "Social Isolation in America: Changes in Core Discussion Networks over Two Decades," *American Sociological Review* 71(June 2006): 353–75.

14. Ibid. Sturm, "Childhood Obesity," also cites data from the 1999 Kaiser Family Foundation study that found, among other things, that computer gaming goes up and TV watching goes down among boys ages nine to twelve.

15. Arlie Russell Hochschild, *The Time Bind: When Work Becomes Home and Home Becomes Work* (New York: Henry Holt, 1997).

16. Ken Anderson and Tye Rattenbury, "Laptop, Netbook and MID Study Data: The Realities of Usage," paper presented to the Intel Developers Forum, San Francisco, CA, 2009. See also Ken Anderson, Dawn Nafus, Tye Rattenbury, and Ryan Aipperspach, "Numbers Have Qualities Too: Experiences with Ethno-Mining," in *Proceedings of EPIC*, 2009.

17. Anderson and Rattenbury, *Laptop, Netbook and MID Study Data*; Anderson et al., "Numbers Have Qualities Too."

18. See, e.g., Matt Richtel, "Digital Devices Deprive Brain of Downtime," *New York Times*, August 24, 2010.

19. Between 1985 and 2000, the percentage of the population living in households with married partners and children declined from 31 to 23 percent of all families, according to U.S. Census, *Statistical Abstract* (Washington, DC: Census Bureau, 2008), table 1304.

20. Charles N. Darrah, James M. Freeman, and J. A. English-Lueck. *Busier than Ever! Why American Families Can't Slow Down* (Stanford, CA: Stanford University Press, 2007).

21. Margaret Nelson, *Parenting Out of Control: Anxious Parents in Uncertain Times* (New York: New York University Press, 2010).

22. National Research Council and Institute of Medicine, *Working Families and Work Policies*, 32–36, cited in Darrah, Freeman, and English-Lueck, *Busier than Ever!*

23. Barry Wellman, Aaron Smith, Amy Wells, and Tracy Kennedy, *Networked Families*, report of the Pew Internet and American Life Project, October 19, 2008, http://pewinternet.org/Reports/2008/Networked-Families.aspx (retrieved May 15, 2012).

24. Darrah, Freeman, and English-Lueck, *Busier than Ever!*

25. See, e.g., Kathryn Rose and Pam Frame Pearlman, *The Parent's Guide to Facebook* (n.p.: CreateSpace, 2011); Don Pearson, *iParent: Gender Trends, Online Friends and the Soul of Your Child* (Grand Rapids, MI: Pot-boilers, 2011); Nancy Willard, *Cyber-Safe Kids, Cyber-Savvy Teens* (San Francisco: Jossey-Bass, 2007).

26. On biracial identity in the United States, see Nancy Foner, *Islands in the City: West Indian Immigration to New York* (Berkeley: University of California Press, 2001); Nancy Foner and G. Fredrickson, eds., Not Just Black and White: Historical and Contemporary Perspectives on Immigration, Race, and Ethnicity in the United States (New York: Russell Sage Foundation, 2004); M. Vickerman, Cross Currents: West Indian Immigrants and Race (New York: Oxford University Press, 1999).

27. This is an insight interviewer Monica Emerich shared about the family in 2012, as she remains in contact with them.

28. M. Borba, "Plugged-in Reduces Family Time: Parenting in a Digital World," February 4, 2011, www.micheleborba.com/blog/2011/02/04/is-a-plugged-in-world-reducing-childrens-empathy; Sasha, "It's National TV Turn-Off Week," Parenting.com, April 20, 2010, www.parenting.com/blogs/show-and-tell/it-s-national-tv-turn-week.

29. Christof Demont-Heinrich first interviewed the Fallon family in 2002 when working as a graduate student research associate at the University of Colorado.

30. Actually, it was a television with a built-in VCR, but for the flow of the chapter I have changed this to DVD so that the story would appear less dated.

31. Some private schools in the United States have rules forbidding the use of social networking sites. See "Brooklyn Girls School Bans Facebook," *Algemeiner*, March 23, 2012, www.algemeiner.com/2012/03/23/brooklyn-girls-school-bans-facebook (retrieved May 15, 2012).

32. See, e.g., Mizuko Ito et al., *Hanging Out, Messing Around, Geeking Out: Living and Learning with Digital Media* (Cambridge, MA: MIT Press, 2010).

33. Foster Cline and Jim Fay, *Parenting with Love and Logic: Teaching Children Responsibility* (Colorado Springs, CO: NavPress, 2006).

34. See, e.g., Scott Sells, *Parenting Your Out-of-Control Teenager: 7 Steps to Reestablish Authority and Reclaim Love* (New York: St. Martin's Press, 2001); Tom McMahon, *Teen Tips: A Survival Guide for Parents with Kids 11–19* (New York: Simon and Schuster, 2003).

35. Hochschild, *The Time Bind.*

36. Hochschild, "Emotion Work," 552.

37. Lynn Schofield Clark, "Parental Mediation Theory for a Digital Age," *Communication Theory*, 2011.

38. See, e.g., Cathy Davidson, *Now You See It.: How the Brain Science of Attention will Transform the Way we Live, Work, and Learn* (New York: Viking, 2011).

Chapter 9: Parenting in a Digital Age

1. Johannes Trithemius, *In Praise of Scribes*, ed. Klaus Arnold (1974), 65, cited in Bernard J. Hibbits, "Yesterday Once More: Skeptics, Scribes, and the Demise of Law Reviews," *Akron Law Review* 30, 267 (1996), http://www.law.pitt.edu/hibbitts/akron.htm (retrieved December 11, 2006). Trithemius referred specifically to the inferiority of printed versus handmade books.

2. Ibid.

3. Elizabeth Eisenstein, *The Printing Press as an Agent of Change*, vol. 1 (Cambridge: Cambridge University Press, 1979).

4. As noted in chapter 6, this style of parenting was first observed by communication researchers Jack McLeod and Stephen Chaffee.

5. See, e.g., Barbara K. Hofer and Abigail Sullivan Moore, *The iConnected Parent: Staying Close to Your Kids in College (and Beyond) While Letting Them Grow Up* (New York: Free Press, 2010).

6. Sociologist Annette Lareau also acknowledges that race matters, but still notices that it seems less powerful than how parents use language, how parents oversee their children's time, how families are connected to other social organizations and societal institutions, and the strategies they use for intervening in their children's education. Those, she says, are all more strongly patterned in relation to class. She found that middle-class kids, both black and white, fought with siblings and talked back to their parents, whereas these behaviors were not permitted among working-class and less advantaged families. See Annette Lareau, *Unequal Childhoods: Class, Race, and Family Life in the U.S.*, 2nd ed. (Berkeley: University of California Press, 2011).

7. See, e.g., Friedrich Krotz and Andreas Hepp, "A Concretization of Mediatization: How Mediatization Works and Why 'Mediatized Worlds' Are a Helpful Concept for Empirical Mediatization Research," presented at the Symposium on Mediatization, Bremen, Germany, September 3, 2011.

8. This definition is first introduced in Lynn Schofield Clark, "Considering Mediatization Through a Case Study of J + K's Big Day (The JK Wedding Entrance Dance): A Response to Stig Hjarvard," *Culture and Religion*, 2011. This definition borrows from but also elaborates upon John Thompson's idea of "mediazation" introduced in *Media and Modernity: A Social Theory of the Media* (Stanford, CA: Stanford University Press, 1995). I place this citation in the footnotes to avoid even more possible confusion of "mediatization," "mediation," and "mediazation" as terms that describe somewhat overlapping yet somewhat distinct processes. The difference between my work and Thompson's is twofold. First, I am interested in exploring the affordances of technology, or what particular communication technologies make possible at specific times. Therefore, my work aims to incorporate an historical understanding of social change into Thompson's social theory. Second, I am interested in how collective human actions double back to intensify the development of independent media industries and their circulation.

9. Sonia Livingstone suggests the syllogism between media studies' interests in studying how communication media mediate, linguists' interests in studying how language mediates, and consumption studies' interests in studying how material goods mediate. I thank her for this insight. See Sonia Livingstone, *Children and the Internet* (London: Polity, 2009).

10. Joshua Meyrowitz, *No Sense of Place* (New York: Oxford University Press, 1985). This summary of his work is taken from Joshua Meyrowitz, "Media Evolution and Cultural Change," in John R. Hall, Laura Grindstaff, and Ming-Cheng Lo (eds.), *Handbook of Cultural Sociology*, 52–63 (London: Routledge, 2010).

11. See danah boyd, "Taken Out of Context: American Teen Sociality in Networked Publics," Ph.D. dissertation, University of California, Berkeley, 2008.

12. Hofer and Moore, *The iConnected Parent.*

13. Barbara Ray, "Adulthood: What's the Rush? The Truth About 21st Century 20 Somethings," *Psychology Today*, November 4, 2010.

14. Madeline Levine, *The Price of Privilege: How Parental Pressure and Material Advantage Are Creating a Generation of Disconnected and Unhappy Kids* (New York: Harper, 2008); Hara Estroff Marano, *A Nation of Wimps: The High Cost of Invasive Parenting* (New York: Broadway Books, 2008).

15. Richard Settersten and Barbara Ray, *Not Quite Adults: Why 20-Somethings are Choosing a Slow Path to Adulthood, and Why It's Good for Everyone* (New York: Bantam, 2010).

16. Margaret Nelson, *Parenting Out of Control: Anxious Parents in Uncertain Times* (New York: New York University Press, 2010).

17. Stig Hjarvard relates this monitoring to David Riesman's notion of the other-directed character presented in Riesman's *The Lonely Crowd*. See Stig Hjarvard, *En verden af medier. Medialiseringen af politik, sprog, religion og leg* [A world of media. The mediatization of politics, language, religion and play] (Frederiksberg: Samfundslitteratur, 2008).

18. Tama Leaver, "The Ends of Online Identity," presentation to the Association of Internet Researchers, Seattle, WA, October 2011.

19. Arlie Russell Hochschild, *The Time Bind: When Work Becomes Home and Home Becomes Work* (New York: Metropolitan Books, 1997).

20. Demie Kurz, *For Richer, For Poorer: Mothers Confront Divorce* (New York: Routledge, 1995).

21. See Nelson, *Parenting Out of Control.*

22. Sherry Turkle, *Alone Together: Why We Expect More from Technology and Less from Each Other* (New York: Basic Books, 2011).

23. See http://worldpulse.com and http://globalvoicesonline.org.

24. "Free Press: More Work to Be Done to Solve Broadband Problem," January 9, 2012, www.freepress.net/press-release/2012/1/9/free-press-more-work-be-done-solve-broadband-adoption-problem (retrieved February 9, 2012).

25. Cathy Davidson, *Now You See It: How the Brain Science of Attention Will Transform the Way We Live, Work, and Learn* (New York: Viking, 2011).

26. Sonia Livingstone and Ranjana Das, POLIS Media and Family Report, LSE Research Online, 2010. Available: http://eprints.lse.ac.uk/30156/1/family_and_media_report_(LSERO_version).pdf. Retrieval: July 19, 2012.

27. See, e.g., Chris Boem, *Hierarchy in the Forest: The Evolution of Egalitarian Behavior* (Cambridge, MA: Harvard University Press, 1999); Jeanne M. Brett, *Negotiating Globally: How to Negotiate Deals, Resolve Disputes, and Make Decisions Across Cultural Boundaries* (Hoboken, NJ: John Wiley and Sons, 2007); Richard Wilkinson, *The Impact of Inequality: How to Make Sick Societies Healthier* (New York: Routledge, 2005).

28. See Axel Bruns, *Blogs, Wikipedia, Second Life, and Beyond: From Production to Produsage* (New York: Peter Lang, 2008); Yochai Benkler, *The Wealth of Networks: How Social Production Transforms Markets and Freedom* (New Haven: Yale University Press, 2007); Clay Shirky, *Here Comes Everybody: The Power of Organizing Without Organizations* (New York: Penguin, 2009); Don Tapscott and Anthony Williams, *Wikinomics: How Mass Collaboration Changes Everything* (New York: Portfolio, 2008).

29. John Seigenthaler, once assistant to Attorney General Robert Kennedy, writes of his harrowing experience in what has since become a classic story of how Wikipedia can be used in unfounded character assassination that is untraceable and hence leaves its creator unaccountable. John Seigenthaler, "A False Wikipedia 'Biography,'" *USA Today*, November 11, 2005.

30. Dale Kunkel and Bruce Watkins, "Evolution of Children's Television Regulatory Policy," *Journal of Broadcasting and Electronic Media* 31, 4 (1987): 369–89.

31. See, e.g., Barrie Gunter and Jill L. McAleer, *Children and Television: The One-Eyed Monster?* (New York: Routledge, 1990).

32. On regulating virtual worlds, see Sarah Grimes, "Kids' Ad Play: Regulating Children's Advergames in the Converging Media Context," *Journal of Communication Law and Policy* 8, 12 (2008): 162–78. On Facebook and privacy laws, see danah boyd and Eszter Hargittai, "Facebook Privacy Settings: Who Cares?" *First Monday* 15, 8 (August 2010), www.uic.edu/htbin/cgiwrap/bin/ojs/index.php/fm/article/view/3086/2589 (retrieved August 27, 2011).

33. See, e.g., Consumers Union, "Lessons from the 1996 Telecommunications Act: Deregulation Before Meaningful Competition Spells Consumer Disaster," www.consumersunion.org/telecom/lessondc201.htm (retrieved August 30, 2011). See also Free Press, *Changing Media: Public Interest and Policies for the Digital Age* (n.d.), http://www.freepress.net/files/changing_media.pdf.

34. Robert McChesney and Mark Crispin Miller, *Rich Media, Poor Democracy* (film/DVD), Media Education Foundation, 2003.

Appendix A: Methodology

1. Much of the research for this project was conducted at the University of Colorado as part of the Teens and the New Media @ Home project, under the direction of the author, and the parallel Religion, Meaning and the New Media @ Home project, under the direction of Stewart Hoover. Focus groups and interviews conducted between 2007 and 2012 were under the direction of the author at the University of Denver.

2. In 2009, Alexis Lynn, an M.A. student at the University of Denver, conducted in-depth and repeated interviews with six young people for her thesis, and shared her transcripts for inclusion in this manuscript.

3. Here is the breakdown of the bi- and multiracial families interviewed: five European American and Hispanic, four European American and African American, one European

American and Native American, one European American and Asian, one African American and Native American, and one Hispanic, Native American, and European American.

4. Although we do not know the exact household income of all of the young people who participated in the discussion group interviews, we strove for a breakdown that would be similar to that of the family household income, with five groups from lower-income neighborhoods, six from lower-middle-income neighborhoods, and nine from middle- to upper-middle-income neighborhoods.

5. Thomas R. Lindlof and Bryan C. Taylor, *Qualitative Communication Research Methods*, 2nd ed. (Thousand Oaks, CA: Sage, 2002).

6. Barney G. Glaser and Anselm L. Strauss, *The Discovery of Grounded Theory: Strategies for Qualitative Research* (Chicago: Aldine, 1967). Although the terms are less scientific, I like John Seidel's description of qualitative research as an iterative process of "noticing, collecting, and thinking," which begins by making observations, writing field notes, tape-recording interviews, and gathering documents so as to produce a record of things noticed. Then I code passages within the record by highlighting, underlining, and making margin notes on transcripts and other materials. See John V. Seidel, "Qualitative Data Analysis," Appendix E of the manual for The Ethnograph, vol. 4 (data analysis software), copyright 1998, and available at www.qualisresearch.com.

7. Michael Agar, "The Right Brain Strikes Back," in N. Fielding and R. Lee, eds., *Using Computers in Qualitative Research*, 181–94 (Newbury Park, CA: Sage Publications, 1991).

8. Kathy Charmaz uses the grounded theory tradition and advocates marking the data several times and then studying the markings across cases for patterns. Kathy Charmaz, "The Grounded Theory Method: An Explication and Interpretation," in Robert M. Emerson, ed., *Contemporary Field Research: A Collection of Readings*, 109–28 (Boston: Little, Brown, 1983).

9. M. Baumberg, "Narrative Discourse and Identities," in J. C. Meister, T. Kindt, W. Schernus, and M. Stein, eds., *Narratology Beyond Literary Criticism* (Berlin: Walter de Gruyter, 2004), 213–37.

10. Ibid., 122.

11. See also Stewart Hoover, Lynn Schofield Clark, and Diane Alters, *Media, Home, and Family* (New York: Routledge, 2004).

12. The importance of reducing the data is discussed in Lindlof and Taylor, *Qualitative Communication Research Methods*.

13. Eszter Hargittai, "Digital Na(t)ives? Variation in Internet Skills and Uses Among Members of the 'Net Generation,'" *Sociological Inquiry* 80, 1 (2010): 92–113; Amanda Lenhart, *Generation IM: Teens and Technology*, Pew Internet and American Life Project, 2003, http://pewinternet.org (retrieved August 28, 2011); Mark Warschauer, *Technology and Social Inclusion: Rethinking the Digital Divide* (Cambridge, MA: MIT Press, 2003); Susan C. Herring, "Questioning the Generational Divide: Technological Exoticism and Adult Constructions of Online Youth Identity," in David Buckingham, ed., *Youth, Identity, and Digital Media*, 71–92 (Cambridge, MA: MIT Press, 2008).

14. L. S. Clark, C. Demont-Heinrich, and S. Webber, "Parents, ICTs, and Children's Prospects for Success: Interviews along the Digital 'Access Rainbow,'" *Critical Studies in Media Communication* 22, 5 (2005): 409–26; L. S. Clark, C. Demont-Heinrich, and S. Webber, "Ethnographic Interviews on the Digital Divide," *New Media and Society* 6, 4

(2004): 529–47. See also Scott Webber and Lynn Schofield Clark, "Dreams and Means: Ethnographic Analysis of Disadvantaged Young People and the Digital Divide," presented to the Shaping the Network Society conference, Seattle, WA, May 2002; L. S. Clark, C. Demont-Heinrich, and S. Webber, "Ethnographic Interviews on the Digital Divide," presented to the International Communication Association, San Diego, May 2003; S. Webber and L. S. Clark, "Buying In and Left Behind," presented to the Association of Internet Researchers, Toronto, October 2003; C. Demont-Heinrich, L. S. Clark, and S. Webber, "Computers and Success," presented to the Association of Internet Researcher, Toronto, October 2003.

15. We also began looking at how teens and preteens discussed the use of the Internet for educational purposes. L. S. Clark, M. Miles, and K. Lustyik, "Seek the Truth (but Let the Search Engine Find It)," paper presented at the annual meeting of the International Communication Association, New Orleans, May 2004.

16. L. S. Clark, "The Constant Contact Generation: Exploring Teen Friendship Networks Online," in S. Mazzarella, ed., *Girl Wide Web* (New York: Peter Lang, 2005). See also L. S. Clark, "Teen Friendship Networks Online," presented to the International Communication Association, San Diego, May 2003; L. S. Clark, "The Constant Contact Generation: Interview-Based Material from Teens," presented at the Digital Kids Symposium, sponsored by the MacArthur Foundation, June 2005.

17. See danah boyd, "Why Youth (Heart) Social Network Sites: The Role of Networked Publics in Teenage Social Life," in David Buckingham, ed., *Youth, Identity, and Digital Media* (Cambridge, MA: MIT Press, 2008).

18. Richard Ling and Birgitte Yttri, "Hyper-Coordination via Mobile Phones in Norway," in James Katz and Mark Aarhus, eds., *Perpetual Contact: Mobile Communication, Private Talk, Public Performance*, 139–69 (Cambridge: Cambridge University Press, 2002).

19. L. S. Clark, "How Baby Boomers View the Media as a Cultural Resource for Parenting," presented to the Association for Education of Journalism and Mass Communication, Kansas City, July 2003.

20. Clark, "The Constant Contact Generation"; Sonia Livingstone, *Young People and New Media* (London: Routledge, 2002); Rivka Ribak, "Remote Control, Umbilical Cord and Beyond: The Mobile Phone as a Transitional Object," *British Journal of Developmental Psychology* 27, 1 (2009): 183–96.

21. Ribak, "Remote Control."

22. L. S. Clark, "Spiritual Support from Afar: The Case of Caleb Baylor and E-Mail," paper presented at the Fourth Public International Conference on Media, Religion, and Culture, Louisville, KY, September 2004.

23. Lynn Schofield Clark, "Digital Media and the Generation Gap: Qualitative Research on U.S. Teens and Their Parents," *Information, Communication, and Society* 12 (2009): 388–407; L. S. Clark, "Digital Media and the Generation Gap," presented at the annual meeting of the Association of Internet Researchers, October 2008.

24. See John V. Seidel, "Qualitative Data Analysis," Appendix E of the manual for *The Ethnograph* v. 4 (data analysis software), copyright 1998, and available for download at: http://www.qualisresearch.com.

BIBLIOGRAPHY

AFL-CIO. Still Nickel and Dimed and (Not) Getting by in America. August 17, 2011. http://www.aflcio.org/Blog/Corporate-Greed/Still-Nickel-and-Dimed-and-Not-Getting-by-in-America. (retrieved May 15, 2012).

Aftab, Parry. 1999. *The Parent's Guide to Protecting Your Children in Cyberspace.* New York: McGraw-Hill.

Agar, Michael. 1991. The Right Brain Strikes Back. In N. Fielding and R. Lee, eds., *Using Computers in Qualitative Research*, 181–94. Newbury Park, CA: Sage Publications.

Anderson, Ken, Dawn Nafus, Tye Rattenbury, and Ryan Aipperspach. 2009. Numbers Have Qualities Too: Experiences with Ethno-mining. In *Ethnographic Praxis in Industry Conference Proceedings*, American Anthropological Association.

Anderson, Ken, and Tye Rattenbury. 2009. Laptop, Netbook and MID Study Data: The Realities of Usage. Presented to the Intel Developers Forum, San Francisco, CA.

Anstey, Caroline. 2011. New Technology Can Democratize Development. *Poverty Matters* (blog), *Guardian*, November 29. www.guardian.co.uk/global-development/poverty-matters/2011/nov/29/technology-can-democractise-development?INTCMP=SRCH (retrieved January 25, 2012).

Anyon, Jean. 1980. Social Class and the Hidden Curriculum of Work. *Journal of Education* 162, 1: 67–93.

Austin, Erica W. 1993. Exploring the Effects of Active Parental Mediation of Television Content. *Journal of Broadcasting and Electronic Media* 37: 147–58.

Austin, Erica W., C. Knaus, and A. Meneguelli. 1997. Who Talks How to Their Kids About TV: A Clarification of Demographic Correlates of Parental Mediation Patterns. *Communication Research Reports* 14, 4: 418–30.

Austin, Erica W., Roberts, D. F. and Nass, C. 1990. Influences of Family Communication on Children's Television-Interpretation Processes. *Communication Research* 17: 545–64.

Autor, David, Lawrence F. Katz, and Melissa S. Kearney. 2008. Trends in U.S. Wage Inequality: Revising the Revisionists. *Review of Economics and Statistics* 90, 2: 300–23.

Bakardjieva, Maria, and R. Smith. 2001. The Internet in Everyday Life. *New Media and Society* 3: 67–83.

Banks, Patricia Ann. 2009. *Represent: Art and Identity Among the Black Upper Middle Class*. New York: Routledge.

Banks, S., and R. Gupta. 1980. Television as a Dependent Variable, for a Change. *Journal of Consumer Research* 7, 3: 327–30.

Barcus, F. E. 1969. Parental Influence on Children's Television Viewing. *Television Quarterly* 4: 63–73.

Barron, Brigid. 2006. Interest and Self-Sustained Learning as Catalysts of Development: A Learning Ecology Perspective. *Human Development* 49: 193–224.

Barron, Brigid, C. K. Martin, Lori Takeuchi, and R. Fithian. 2009. Parents as Learning Partners in the Development of Technological Fluency. *International Journal of Learning and Media* 1, 2: 55–77.

Baxter, L., C. Bylund, R. Imes, and T. Routsong. 2009. Parent-Child Perceptions of Parental Behavioral Control Through Rule-Setting for Risky Health Choices During Adolescence. *Journal of Family Communication* 9: 251–71.

Beaupre Gillespie, Becky, and Hollee Schwartz Temple. 2011. *Good Enough Is the New Perfect: Finding Happiness and Success in Modern Motherhood*. New York: Harlequin.

Beck, R. J., and D. Wood. 1993. The Dialogic Socialization of Aggression in a Family's Court of Reason and Inquiry. *Discourse Processes* 16, 3: 341–63.

Beeghley, Leonard. 2004. *The Structure of Social Stratification in the United States*. Boston: Pearson.

Belenky, Mary Field, Blythe McVicker Clinchy, Nancy Rule Goldberger, and Jill Mattuck Tarule. *Women's Ways of Knowing: The Development of Self, Voice, and Mind*. 10th anniversary ed. New York: Basic Books, 1997.

Benítez, J. 2006. Transnational Dimensions of the Digital Divide Among Salvadoran Immigrants in the Washington DC Metropolitan Area. *Global Networks* 6, 2: 181–99.

Benkler, Yochai. 2007. *The Wealth of Networks: How Social Production Transforms Markets and Freedom*. New Haven, CT: Yale University Press.

Berry, J. W., and D. Sam. 1997. Acculturation and Adaptation. In J. W. Berry, M. H. Segal, and C. Kagitcibaci, eds., *Handbook of Cross-Cultural Psychology*, vol. 3: *Social Behavior and Applications*. 2nd ed. Boston: Allyn and Bacon.

Boem, Chris. 1999. *Hierarchy in the Forest: The Evolution of Egalitarian Behavior*. Cambridge, MA: Harvard University Press.

Bourdieu, Pierre. 1984. *Distinction: A Social Critique of the Judgement of Taste*. London: Routledge.

———. 1977. *Outline of a Theory of Practice*. Cambridge: Cambridge University Press.

boyd, danah. 2008. Reflections on Lori Drew, Bullying, and Solutions to Helping Kids. *Apophenia*, November 30. www.zephoria.org/thoughts/archives/2008/11/30/reflections_on.html (retrieved August 27, 2011).

———. 2010. Social Network Sites as Networked Publics: Affordances, Dynamics, and Implications. In Zizi Papacharissi, ed., *A Networked Self: Identity, Community, and Culture on Social Network Sites*, 39–58. New York: Routledge.

———. 2008. Taken Out of Context: American Teen Sociality in Networked Publics. Ph.D. dissertation, University of California at Berkeley.

———. 2008. Why Youth (Heart) Social Network Sites: The Role of Networked Publics in Teenage Social Life. In David Buckingham, ed., *Youth, Identity, and Digital Media*. MacArthur Foundation Series on Digital Learning. Cambridge, MA: MIT Press. http://www.mitpressjournals.org/toc/dmal/-/6.

boyd, danah, and Eszter Hargittai. 2010. Facebook settings: Who Cares? *First Monday* 15, 8.

Brake, David. 2008. Shaping the "Me" in MySpace: The Framing of Profiles on a Social Network Site. In Knut Lundby, ed., *Digital Storytelling, Mediatized Stories: Self-Representations in New Media*, 285–300. New York: Peter Lang.

Breakwell, Glynis M. 1986. *Coping with Threatened Identities*. London: Routledge.

Brekhus, Wayne. 2008. Trends in the Qualitative Study of Social Identities. *Sociology Compass* 2/3: 1059–78.

Brett, Jeanne M. 2007. *Negotiating Globally: How to Negotiate Deals, Resolve Disputes, and Make Decisions Across Cultural Boundaries*. Hoboken, NJ: John Wiley and Sons.

Brown, B. Bradford, Jeremy P. Bakken, Jacqueline Nguyen, and Heather G. VonBank. 2007. Sharing Information About Peer Relations: Parent and Adolescent Opinions and Behaviors in African American and Hmong Families. *New Directions for Child and Adolescent Development* 116: 67–82.

Brown, Jane R., K. W. Childers, K. E. Bauman, and G. Koch. 1990. The Influence of New Media and Family Structure on Young Adolescents' Television and Radio Use. *Communication Research* 17, 1: 65–82.

Brown, Jane R., and O. Linne. 1976. The Family as Mediator of Television's Effects. In R. Brown, ed., *Children and Television*, 184–98. Beverly Hills, CA: Sage.

Brown, Phillip, Hugh Lauder, and David Ashton. 2010. *The Global Auction: The Promises of Education, Jobs, and Incomes*. New York: Oxford University Press.

Bruns, Axel. 2008. *Blogs, Wikipedia, Second Life, and Beyond: From Production to Produsage*. New York: Peter Lang.

Buckingham, David. 2000. *After the Death of Childhood: Growing Up in the Age of Electronic Media*. London: Polity.

———, ed. 2008. *Youth, Identity, and Digital Media*. Cambridge, MA: MIT Press.

Burr, P., and R. Burr. 1976. Television Advertising to Children: What Parents Are Saying About Government Control. *Journal of Advertising* 5, 4: 37–41.

L. M. Burton, K. W. Allison, and D. Obeidallah. 1995. Social Context and Adolescence: Perspectives in Development Among Inner-City African American Teens. In L. J. Crockett and A. C. Crouter, eds., *Pathways Through Adolescence*. Mahwah, NJ: Erlbaum.

Butler, Judith. 1990. *Gender Trouble*. London: Routledge.

Campbell, Colin. 1987. *The Romantic Ethic and the Spirit of Modern Consumerism*. Oxford: Blackwell.

Cantor, Joanne, and M. L. Mares. 2001. The Effects of Television on Children and Family Emotional Well-Being. In Jennings Bryant, ed., *Television and the American Family*. 2nd ed. Mahwah, NJ: Erlbaum.

Carey, James. 1988. *Communication as Culture: Essays on Media and Society*. New York: Routledge.

Caron, A., and S. Ward. 1974. Gift Decisions by Kids and Parents. *Journal of Advertising Research* 15, 4: 15–20.

Carr, Nicholas. 2010. *The Shallows: What the Internet Is Doing to Our Brains*. New York: W. W. Norton.

———. 2008. *The Big Switch: Rewiring the World, from Edison to Google*. New York: W. W. Norton.

Carvin, Andy. 2008. CA Legislation Criminalizes Campus Cyberbullying. *Learning Now*. August 29. www.pbs.org/teachers/learning.now/2008/08/ca_legislation_criminalizes_ca. html (retrieved August 27, 2011).

Castells, Manuel. 1996. *The Rise of the Network Society*. London: Wiley-Blackwell.

Celizic, Mike. 2007. Parents of MySpace Hoax Victim Seek Justice. *Today*. November 19. http://today.msnbc.msn.com/id/21882976/?GT1=10547 (retrieved December 17, 2008).

Chaffee, Stephen, Jack McLeod, and Dennis Wackman. 1973. Family Communication Patterns and Adolescent Political Participation. In J. Dennis, ed., *Socialization to Politics*. New York: John Wiley.

Charmaz, Kathy. 1983. The Grounded Theory Method: An Explication and Interpretation. In Robert M. Emerson, ed., *Contemporary Field Research: A Collection of Readings*, 109–28. Boston: Little, Brown.

Chavez, Maria. 2001. *Everyday Injustice: Latino Professionals and Racism*. Lanham, MD: Rowman and Littlefield.

Chua, Amy. 2011. *Battle Hymn of the Tiger Mother*. New York: Penguin Press.

Clark, Lynn Schofield. 2008. The Constant Contact Generation: Exploring Teen Friendship Networks Online. In Sharon Mazzarella, ed., *Girl Wide Web*. New York: Peter Lang.

———. 2009. Digital Media and the Generation Gap: Qualitative Research on U.S. Teens and Their Parents. *Information, Communication, and Society* 12: 388–407.

———. 2011. Considering Mediatization Through a Case Study of J + K's Big Day (The JK Wedding Entrance Dance): A Response to Stig Hjarvard. *Culture and Religion* 12(2): 167–84.

———. 2011. Question to Tiger (and All) Mothers: Why Is Leisure Bad? *Parenting in a Digital Age* (blog), January 24. http://digitalparenting.wordpress.com.

Clark, Lynn Schofield, and Lynn Swywj. 2012. Mobile Intimacies in the U.S. Among Refugee and Recent Immigrant Teens. *Journal of Feminist Media Studies*.

Clark, William A. V. 2003. *Immigrants and the American Dream: Remaking the Middle Class*. New York: Guilford Press.

Clement, Andrew, and Leslie Regan Shade. 2000. The Access Rainbow: Conceptualizing Universal Access to the Information/Communication Infrastructure. In M. Gurstein, ed., *Community Informatics*, 32–51. Hershey, PA: Idea Publishing.

Codevilla, Angelo M. 2010. America's Ruling Class—and the Perils of Revolution. *American Spectator*, July/August. http://spectator.org/archives/2010/07/16/americas-ruling-class-and-the# (retrieved August 25, 2011).

Cohen, Stanley. 1987. *Folk Devils and Moral Panics: The Creation of the Mods and the Rockers*. London: Blackwell.

Collier, Anne. 2011. *Juvenoia, Part I: Why Internet Fear Is Overrated*. NetFamilyNews. Org. www.netfamilynews.org/?p=30220 (retrieved August 28, 2011).

Committee on Public Education, American Academy of Pediatrics. 1999. Media Education. *Pediatrics* 104, 2.

Corsaro, William A. 2010. *The Sociology of Childhood*. 3rd ed. Thousand Oaks, CA: Sage.

Cowan, Ruth Schwartz. 1985. *More Work for Mother: The Ironies of Household Technology from the Open Hearth to the Microwave*. New York: Basic Books.

Cruz-Santiago, M., and J. Ramirez Garcia. 2011. "Hay Que Ponerse en los Zapatos del Joven": Adaptive Parenting of Adolescent Children Among Mexican-American Parents Residing in a Dangerous Neighborhood. *Family Process* 50, 1: 92–114.

Darrah, Charles N., James M. Freeman, and J. A. English-Lueck. 2007. *Busier than Ever! Why American Families Can't Slow Down.* Stanford, CA: Stanford University Press.

Davidson, Cathy N. *Now You See It: How the Brain Science of Attention Will Transform the Way we Live, Work, and Learn.* New York: Penguin, 2011.

Davison, W. P. 1983. The Third-Person Effect in Communication. *Public Opinion Quarterly* 47, 1: 1–15.

Dawson, Michael C. 2011. Severe Hardship, Dashed Hopes: Room for Debate. *New York Times*, July 25.

Del Castillo, A. R. 1993. Covert Cultural Norms and Sex/Gender Meaning: A Mexico City Case. *Urban Anthropology* 22, 3/4: 237–58.

DiMaggio, Paul, and Bart Bonikowski. 2008. Make Money Surfing the Web? The Impact of Internet Use on the Earnings of U.S. Workers. *American Sociological Review* 73: 227–50.

DiMaggio, Paul, Eszter Hargittai, Coral Celeste, and Steven Shafer. 2004. Digital Inequality: From Unequal Access to Differentiated Use. In Kathryn Neckerman, ed., *Social Inequality*, 355–400. New York: Russell Sage Foundation.

Dorr, A., P. Kovaric, and C. Doubleday. 1989. Parent-Child Coviewing of Television. *Journal of Broadcasting and Electronic Media* 33, 1: 35–51.

Downs, Edward. 2008. How Can Wii Learn from Video Games? Examining Relationships Between Technological Affordances and Socio-Cognitive Determinates on Affective and Behavioral Outcomes. Ph.D. dissertation, Pennsylvania State University.

Eastin, Michael S., B. Greenberg, and L. Hofshire. 2006. Parenting the Internet. *Journal of Communication* 56: 486–504.

Ehrenreich, Barbara. 1989. *Fear of Falling: The Inner Life of the Middle Class.* New York: Pantheon Books.

———. If There's a War on the Middle Class, I'm Enlisting to Fight for It! United Professionals. www.unitedprofessionals.org/tag/bait-and-switch (retrieved August 25, 2011).

Eisenstein, Elizabeth. 1979. *The Printing Press as an Agent of Change,* vol. 1. Cambridge: Cambridge University Press.

Erickson, Erik. 1968. *Identity: Youth and Crisis.* New York: Norton.

Facer, Keri, J. Furlong, R. Furlong, and R. Sutherland. 2003. *Screenplay: Children and Computing in the Home.* New York: Routledge.

Fairlie, Robert W. 2005. Are We Really a Nation Online? Ethnic and Racial Disparities in Access to Technology and Their Consequences. Report for the Leadership Conference on Civil Rights Education Fund. www.civilrights.org/publications/nation-online (retrieved July 21, 2011).

Fass, Paula, and Mary Ann Mason. 2000. *Childhood in America.* New York: New York University Press.

Fay, Jim. 1994. *Helicopters, Drill Sergeants, and Consultants: Parenting Styles and the Messages They Send.* Golden, CO: Love and Logic Press, 1994.

Feyerick, Deborah, and Sheila Steffen. 2009. "Sexting" Lands Teen on Sex Offender List. CNN, April 7. http://articles.cnn.com/2009-04-07/justice/sexting.busts_1_phillip-alpert-offender-list-offender-registry?_s=PM:CRIME (retrieved August 28, 2011).

Finkelhor, David. 2010. The Internet, Youth Deviance, and the Problem of Juvenoia. October 22. www.vimeo.com/16900027 (retrieved August 28, 2011).

Finkelhor, David, H. A. Turner, R. K. Ormrod, and S. L. Hamby. 2010. Trends in Childhood Violence and Abuse Exposure: Evidence from Two National Surveys. *Archives of Pediatrics and Adolescent Medicine* 164, 3: 238–42.

Finn, Janet L. 2001. Text and Turbulence: Representing Adolescence as Pathology in the Human Services. *Childhood* 8, 2: 167–91.

Fish, Stanley. 1980. *Is There a Text in This Class?* Cambridge, MA: Harvard University Press.

Fox, Susannah, and Gretchen Livingston. 2007. *Latinos Online*. Washington, DC: Pew Hispanic Center and Pew Internet and American Life Project. www.pewinternet.org/PPF/r/204/report_display.asp (retrieved February 4, 2012).

Fuligni, A. J. 1998. Authority, Autonomy, and Parent-Adolescent Conflict and Cohesion: A Study of Adolescents from Mexican, Chinese, Filipino, and European Backgrounds. *Developmental Psychology* 34: 782–97.

Fuligni, A. J., T. Yip, and V. Tseng. 2002. The Impact of Family Obligation on the Daily Activities and Psychological Well-Being of Chinese American Adolescents. *Child Development* 73, 1: 302.

Fussell, Paul. 1983. Class: A Touchy Subject. In *Class: A Guide Through the American status system*. New York: Simon and Schuster.

Geertz, Clifford. 1977. Thick Description: Toward an Interpretive Theory of Culture. *The Interpretation of Cultures*. New York: Basic Books.

Gerson, Kathleen. 2010. *The Unfinished Revolution*. New York: Oxford University Press.

Giddens, Anthony. 1990. *The Consequences of Modernity*. Cambridge: Polity Press.

———. 1991. *Modernity and Self-Identity: Self and Society in the Late Modern Age*. Stanford, CA: Stanford University Press.

Gilbert, Dennis. 1998. *The American Class Structure*. New York: Wadsworth.

Gilligan, Carol. 1982. *In A Different Voice*. Cambridge, MA: Harvard University Press.

Girl Scouts. Online Safety Topics. http://lmk.girlscouts.org/Online-Safety-Topics/Online-Sexual—Predators/The-Facts/Stranger-Danger—The-Real-Risks.aspx (retrieved August 28, 2011).

Giroux, Henry. 2010. Youth in a Disposable Society: Democracy or Disposability? London: Palgrave Macmillan, 2010.

Glaser, Barney G., and Anselm L. Strauss. 1967. *The Discovery of Grounded Theory: Strategies for Qualitative Research*. Chicago: Aldine.

The Globalist. n.d. Cell Phones and Globalization. www.theglobalist.com/globalicons/syndication/sample.htm (retrieved July 16, 2010).

Global Kids, Inc., GoodPlay Project of Harvard University's Project Zero, and Common Sense Media. 2009. *Meeting of Minds: Cross-Generational Dialogue on the Ethics of Digital Life*. John D. and Catherine T. MacArthur Foundation.

Goffman, Irving. 1959. *The Presentation of Self in Everyday Life*. New York: Anchor Books.

Google. 2011. Zeitgeist 2010: How the World Searched. www.google.com/intl/en/press/zeitgeist2010 (retrieved July 20, 2011).

Granovetter, Mark S. 1973. The Strength of Weak Ties. *American Journal of Sociology* 78, 6: 1360–80.

Griswold, Wendy. 1987. The Fabrication of Meaning: Literary Interpretation in the United States, Great Britain, and the West Indies. *American Journal of Sociology* 92: 1077–117.

Guamaccia, P. J., and O. Rodriguez. 1996. Concepts of Culture and Their Role in the Development of Culturally Competent Mental Health Services. *Hispanic Journal of Behavioral Sciences* 18, 4: 419–33.

Gunter, Barrie, and Jill L. McAleer. 1990. *Children and Television: The One-Eyed Monster?* New York: Routledge.

Hall, G. Stanley. 1904. *Adolescence.* New York: Appleton.

Hall, Stuart, and Tony Jefferson, eds. 1990. *Resistance Through Rituals: Youth Subcultures in Postwar Britain.* London: Routledge.

Haraway, Donna. 1988. Situated Knowledges: The Science Question in Feminism and the Privilege of Partial Perspective. *Feminist Studies* 14: 575–99.

Hargittai, Eszter. 2010. Digital Na(t)ives? Variation in Internet Skills and Uses Among Members of the "Net Generation." *Sociological Inquiry* 80, 1: 92–113.

Harris, Lynn. 2010. ChatRoulette: Should Parents Worry About the New Internet Sensation? Babble.com. February 26. www.babble.com/kid/chatroulette-parental-controls (retrieved July 16, 2010).

Hartsock, Nancy. 1983. *Money, Sex, and Power: Toward a Feminist Historical Materialism.* New York: Longman.

Healy, Jane M. 1999. *Endangered Minds: Why Children Don't Think and What We Can Do About It.* New York: Simon and Schuster.

Hebdige, Dick. 1979. *Subculture: The Meaning of Style.* London: Methuen.

Hibbits, Bernard. 1996. Yesterday Once More: Skeptics, Scribes, and the Demise of Law Reviews. *Akron Law Review* 30, 267. www.law.pitt.edu/hibbitts/akron.htm (retrieved December 11, 2006).

Hilbert, Martin. 2011. World_Info_Capacity_Animation. YouTube. www.youtube.com/watch?v=iIKPjOuwqHo (retrieved January 3, 2012).

Hilbert, Martin, and Priscila Lopez. 2011. The World's Technological Capacity to Store, Communicate, and Compute Information. *Science* 332, 6025: 60–65.

Hjarvard, Stig. 2008. *En verden af medier. Medialiseringen af politik, sprog, religion og leg* [A world of media. The mediatization of politics, language, religion and play]. Frederiksberg: Samfundslitteratur.

Hochmuth, M. 1947. Children's Radio Diet. *Quarterly Journal of Speech* 33, 2: 249–57.

Hochschild, Arlie Russell. 1979. Emotion Work, Feeling Rules and Social Structure. *American Journal of Sociology* 85, 3: 551–75.

———. 2001. *The Time Bind: When Work Becomes Home and Home Becomes Work.* New York: Holt.

Hofer, Barbara K., and Abigail Sullivan Moore. 2010. *The iConnected Parent: Staying Close to Your Kids in College (and Beyond) While Letting Them Grow Up.* New York: Free Press.

Hoffman, M. L. 1970. Moral Development. In P. H. Mussen, ed., *Carmichael's Manual of Child Psychology*, vol. 2, 261–360. 3rd ed. New York: Wiley.

Hoover, Stewart M. 2006. *Religion in a Media Age.* London: Routledge.

Hoover, Stewart, Lynn Schofield Clark, and Diane Alters. 2004. *Media, Home, and Family.* New York: Routledge.

Horrigan, John. 2009. *The Mobile Difference: Wireless Connectivity Has Drawn Many Users More Deeply into Digital Life.* Pew Internet and American Life Project. http://pewinternet.org (retrieved December 12, 2011).

Horst, Heather. 2010. Families. In Mizuko Ito et al., *Hanging Out, Messing Around, Geeking Out: Living and Learning with New Media.* Cambridge, MA: MIT Press.

Horst, Heather, and Daniel Miller. 2006. *The Cell Phone: An Anthropology of Communication*. London: Berg.

Hutchby, Ian. 2001. Technologies, Texts, and Affordances. *Sociology* 35, 2: 441–56.

Infosync. 2010. Reporting from the Digital Frontier. www.infosyncworld.com/news/n/5636 .html (retrieved July 16, 2010).

Isaacs, A., and A. Koerner. 2008. Linking Familial Typologies: An Investigation of the Relationship Between Parenting Styles and Family Communication Patterns. Paper presented to the International Communication Association, Chicago.

Ito, Mizuko, and Heather Horst. 2009. Neopoints, and Neo Economies: Emergent Regimes of Value in Kids' Peer-To-Peer Networks. Presentation to the American Anthropological Association Meetings. www.itofisher.com/mito/itohorst.neopets .pdf (retrieved January 30, 2012).

Ito, Mizuko, et al. 2010. *Hanging Out, Messing Around, Geeking Out: Living and Learning with Digital Media*. Cambridge, MA: MIT Press.

Jackson, Maggie, and Bill McKibben. 2009. *Distracted: The Erosion of Attention and the Coming Dark Age*. New York: Prometheus.

Jacobs, Jerry A,. and Kathleen Gerson. 2004. *The Time Divide: Work, Family, and Gender Inequality*. Cambridge, MA: Harvard University Press.

Jaumotte, Florence, Subir Lall, Chris Papageorgiou, and Petia Topalova. 2007. Technology Widening Rich-Poor Gap. *IMF Survey Magazine: IMF Research*, October 10. www.imf.org/external/pubs/ft/survey/so/2007/res1010a.htm (retrieved January 25, 2012).

Jenkins, Henry, R. Purushotma, K. Clinton, M. Weigel, and A. Robinson. 2006. *Confronting the Challenges of Participatory Culture: Media Education for the 21st Century*. Chicago: MacArthur Foundation. www.projectnml.org/files/working/NMLWhitePaper.pdf.

Jenkins, Richard. 2004. *Social Identity*. London: Routledge.

Jones, Janna. 2011. When the Movie Started, We All Got Along: Generation Y Remembers Movie Night. *Media International Australia* 139: 96–102.

Kay, E. 1979. *The ACT Guide to Television or . . . How to Treat TV with TLC*. Boston: Beacon Press.

Kearney, Mary Celeste. *Girls Make Media*. New York: Routledge, 2006.

Kegan, Robert. 1998. *In over Our Heads: The Mental Demands of Modern Life*. Cambridge, MA: Harvard University Press.

Kellner, Douglas. 1995. *Media Culture: Cultural Studies, Identity and Politics Between the Modern and Postmodern*. New York: Routledge.

Kessler, Sara. 2011. Six Valuable SNs (Social Networks) for Parents. *Mashable*, January 21. http://mashable.com/2011/01/21/parenting-social-networks (retrieved January 31, 2012).

Kinder, Marsha, ed. 1999. *Kids' Media Culture*. Durham, NC: Duke University Press.

Klass, Perri. 2012. Seeing Social Media as More Portal than Pitfall. *New York Times*, January 9.

Kline, Foster, and Jim Fay. 1990. *Parenting with Love and Logic: Teaching Children Responsibility*. Colorado Springs, CO: Pinon Press.

Koerner, Ascan F., and M. A. Fitzpatrick. 2006. Family Communication Patterns Theory: A Social Cognitive Approach. In D. O. Braithwaite and L. A. Baxter, eds., *Engaging Theories in Family Communication: Multiple Perspectives*, 50–65. Mahwah, NJ: Lawrence Erlbaum Associates.

Kravitz, Derek. 2008. MySpace Suicide Expands Web Law. *Washington Post*, November 28.

Krcmar, M., and J. Cantor. 1997. The Role of Television Advisories and Ratings in Parent-Child Discussion of Television Viewing Choices. *Journal of Broadcasting and Electronic Media* 41, 3: 393–411.

Krotz, Friedrich, and Andreas Hepp. 2011. *A Concretization of Mediatization:* How Mediatization Works and Why "Mediatized Worlds" Are a Helpful Concept for Empirical Mediatization Research. Paper presented at the Symposium on Mediatization, Bremen, Germany, September 3.

Kunkel, Dale, and Bruce Watkins. 1987. Evolution of children's television regulatory policy. *Journal of Broadcasting and Electronic Media* 31, 4: 369–89.

Kurz, Demie. 1995. *For Richer, for Poorer: Mothers Confront Divorce*. New York: Routledge.

Kvasny, Lynette. 2006. Cultural (Re)production of Digital Inequality in a US Community Technology Initiative. *Information, Communication and Society* 9, 2: 160–81.

Lacy, Karyn. 2007. *Blue-Chip Black: Race, Class, and Status in the New Black Middle Class*. Berkeley: University of California Press.

Landale, N., K. Thomas, and J. Van Hook. 2011. The Living Arrangements of Children of Immigrants. *Future of Children* 21, 1: 43–70.

Lara-Cantu, M. A. 1989. A Sex Role Inventory with Scales for "Machismo" and "Self-Sacrificing" Women. *Journal of Cross-Cultural Psychology* 20: 396–98.

Lareau, Annette. 2003. *Unequal Childhoods: Class, Race, and Family Life*. Berkeley: University of California Press.

Larison, Daniel. 2010. Santorum's Classless Society. *American Conservative*, July 28. www.amconmag.com/larison/2010/07/28/santorums-classless-society (retrieved June 17, 2011).

Lasch, Christopher. 1979. *The Culture of Narcissism*. New York: W. W. Norton.

Leaver, Tama. 2011. The Ends of Online Identity. Paper presented to the Association of Internet Researchers, Seattle, WA, October.

Lenhart, Amanda. 2003. *Generation IM: Teens and Technology*. Pew Internet and American Life Project. http://pewinternet.org (retrieved August 28, 2011).

———. 2009. It's Personal: Similarities and Differences in Online Social Network Use Between Teens and Adults. Paper presented at the annual meeting of the International Communication Association, May 23.

———. 2011. *Teens, Cell Phones and Texting*. Pew Internet and American Life Project. http://pewinternet.org (retrieved April 23, 2011).

———. *Teens, Video Games, and Civics*. 2008. Pew Internet and American Life Project. http://pewinternet.org (retrieved October 1, 2008).

Lenhart, Amanda, S. Arafeh, A. Smith, and A. Macgill. 2008. *Writing, Technology and Teens*. Pew Internet and American Life Project. www.pewinternet.org/PPF/r/247/report_display.asp (retrieved July 21, 2011).

Lenhart, Amanda, Rich Ling, Scott Campbell, and Kirsten Purcell. 2010. Teens and Mobile Phones. Pew Internet and American Life Project. http://pewinternet.org/Reports/2010/Teens-and-Mobile-Phones.aspx (retrieved July 18, 2011).

Lenhart, Amanda, Mary Madden, and Aaron Smith. 2008. *Teens and Social Media*. Pew Internet and American Life Project. http://pewinternet.org (retrieved January 20, 2008).

Lenhart, Amanda, Mary Madden, Aaron Smith, Kirsten Purcell, Kathryn Zickuhr, and Lee Rainie. 2011. *Teens, Kindness, and Cruelty on Social Network Sites*. Pew Internet and American Life Project. http://Pewinternet.org (retrieved January 4, 2012).

Lenhart, Amanda, Kirsten Purcell, Aaron Smith, and Kathryn Zickuhr. 2010. Social Media and Mobile Internet Use Among Teens and Young Adults. Pew Internet and American Life Project. http://pewinternet.org (retrieved April 23, 2010).

Lewis, Kevin, Jason Kaufman, and Nicholas Christakis. 2008. The Taste for Privacy: An Analysis of College Student Privacy Settings in an Online Social Network. *Journal of Computer-Mediated Communication* 14, 1: 79–100.

Li, Qing. 2007. New Bottle but Old Wine: A Research of Cyberbullying in Schools. *Computers in Human Behavior* 23, 4: 1777–91.

Lim, Sun Sun, and Y. L. Tan. 2004. Parental Control of New Media Usage—the Challenges of Infocomm Literacy. *Australian Journal of Communication* 31, 1: 95–102.

Lin, C. A., and Atkin, D. J. 1989. Parental Mediation and rulemaking for Adolescent Use of Television and VCRs. *Journal of Broadcasting and Electronic Media* 33: 53–67.

Lindlof, Thomas R., and Bryan C. Taylor. 2002. *Qualitative Communication Research Methods.* 2nd ed. Thousand Oaks, CA: Sage.

Lindsley, S. L. 1999. Communication and "the Mexican Way": Stability and Trust as Core Symbols in Maquiladoras. *Western Journal of Communication* 63, 1: 1–31.

Ling, Rich. 2004. *The Mobile Connection: The Cell Phone's Impact on Society.* San Francisco, CA: Morgan Kauffman.

Livingston, Gretchen. 2010. *Latinos and Digital Technology.* Pew Hispanic Center. http://pewhispanic.org/reports/report.php?ReportID=134 (retrieved February 4, 2012).

Livingstone, Sonia. 2002. *Young People and New Media.* London: Routledge.

———. 2009. *Children and the Internet: Great Expectations, Challenging Realities.* London: Polity.

Livingstone, Sonia, and Ellen J. Helsper. 2008. Gradations of Digital Inclusion: Children, Young People, and the Digital Divide. *New Media and Society* 9, 4: 671–96.

———. 2008. Parental Mediation of Children's Internet Use. *Journal of Broadcasting and Electronic Media* 52, 4: 581–99.

Logan, B., and K. Moody, eds. 1977. *Television Awareness Training: The Viewer's Guide for Family and Community.* New York: Media Action Research Center.

Lu, Stephanie Louise. 2010. Growing Up with Neopets: A Personal Case-Study. *Journal of Virtual Worlds* 3, 2. http://jvwresearch.org/index.php/past-issues/32-virtual-worlds-for-kids.

Lull, James. 1990. Family Communication Patterns and the Social Uses of Television. *Inside Family Viewing: Ethnographic Research on Television's Audiences*, 49–61. London: Routledge.

———. 1980. The Social Uses of Television. *Human Communication Research* 6, 3: 197–209.

Lynn, Alexis. 2009. The Digitally Born Identity. M.A. thesis, University of Denver.

Maccoby, E. 1954. Why Do Children Watch Television. *Public Opinion Quarterly* 18, 3: 239–44.

Madden, Mary, and Aaron Smith. 2010. *Reputation Management and Social Media.* Pew Internet and American Life Project. www.pewinternet.org/Reports/2010/Reputation-Management.aspx (retrieved July 26, 2010).

Martin, Steven P. 2010. Growing Evidence for a "Divorce Divide"? Educational and Marital Dissolution Rates in the U.S. Since the 1970s. *Report of the Russell Sage Foundation* 67: 211–26.

Marvin, Carolyn. 1990. *When Old Technologies Were New: Thinking About Electric Communication in the Late 19th Century.* New York: Oxford University Press.

Mattingly, M. J., and L. C. Sayer. 2006. Under Pressure: Gender Differences in the Relationship Between Free Time and Feeling Rushed. *Journal of Marriage and Family* 68, 1: 205–21.

Mazzarella, Sharon, ed. 2010. *Girl Wide Web 2.0.* New York: Peter Lang.

McChesney, Robert, and Mark Crispin Miller. 2003. *Rich Media, Poor Democracy* (film/DVD). Media Education Foundation.

McLeod, J. M., M. A. Fitzpatrick, C. J. Glynn, and S. F. Fallis. 1982. Television and Social Relations: Family Influences and Consequences for Interpersonal Behavior. In D. Pearl, L. Bouthillet, and J. Lazar, eds., *Television and Behavior: Ten Years of Scientific Progress and Implications for the Eighties,* vol. 2: 272–86. HHS Publication No. ADM 82–1196. Washington, D.C.: U.S. Government Printing Office.

McLuhan, Marshall. 1994. *Understanding Media: The Extensions of Man.* Cambridge, MA: MIT Press.

McMahon, Tom. 2003. *Teen Tips: A Survival Guide for Parents with Kids 11–19.* New York: Simon and Schuster.

McPherson, M., Smith-Lovin, L., and M. E. Brashears. 2006. Social Isolation in America: Changes in Core Discussion Networks over Two Decades. *American Sociological Review* 71: 353–75.

McRobbie, Angela. 1990. *Feminism and Youth Culture: From "Jackie" to "Just Seventeen."* London: Macmillan.

McRobbie, Angela, and Jenny Garber. 1976. Girls and Subcultures. In Stuart Hall and Tony Jefferson, eds., *Resistance Through Rituals: Youth Subcultures in Post-War Britain,* 209–22. New York: Routledge.

Meirick, P. C., J. Sims, E. Gilchrist, and S. Croucher. 2009. All the Children Are Above Average: Parents' Perceptions of Education and Materialism as Media Effects on Their Own and Other Children. *Mass Communication and Society* 12, 2: 217–37.

Meyrowitz, Joshua. 1985. *No Sense of Place: The Impact of Electronic Media on Social Behavior.* New York: Oxford University Press.

———. 2010. Media Evolution and Cultural Change. In John R. Hall, Laura Grindstaff, and Ming-Cheng Lo, eds., *Handbook of Cultural Sociology,* 52–63. London: Routledge.

Migration Policy Institute. 2012. Frequently Requested Statistics on Immigrants and Immigration in the United States. *Migrant Information Source.* www.migrationinformation.org/USfocus/display.cfm?ID=818 (retrieved February 4, 2012).

Milkie, M. A., J. M. Mattingly, K. M. Nomaguchi, S. M. Bianchi, and J. P. Robinson. 2004. The Time Squeeze: Parental Statuses and Feelings About Time with Children. *Journal of Marriage and Family* 66, 3: 739–61.

Mintz, Stephen. 2004. *Huck's Raft: A History of American Childhood.* Cambridge, MA: Harvard University Press.

Morozov, Evgeny. 2011. *The Net Delusion: The Dark Side of Internet Freedom.* New York: Public Affairs.

Nakamura, Lisa. 2004. Interrogating the Digital Divide: The Political Economy of Race and Commerce in New Media. In Phillip Howard and Stephen Jones, eds., *Society Online: The Internet in Context,* 71–83. Thousand Oaks, CA: Sage.

Nasaw, David, ed. 1981. *Schooled to Order: A Social History of Public Schooling in the United States*. New York: Oxford University Press.

Nathanson, Amy. 1998. The Immediate and Cumulative Effects of Television Mediation on Children's Aggression. Ph.D. dissertation, University of Wisconsin–Madison.

———. 1999. Identifying and Explaining the Relationship Between Parental Mediation and Children's Aggression. *Communication Research* 26, 6: 124–43.

———. 2002. The Unintended Effects of Parental Mediation of Television on Adolescents. *Mediapsychology* 4: 207–30.

Nathanson, Amy, W. P. Eveland, H. S. Park, and B. Paul. 2002. Perceived Media Influence and Efficacy as Predictors of Caregivers' Protective Behaviors. *Journal of Broadcasting and Electronic Media* 46, 3: 385–411.

National Institute of Mental Health. *Television and Behavior: Ten Years of Scientific Progress and Implications for the Eighties*, vol. 1. Rockville, MD: U.S. Department of Health and Human Services.

Nelson, Margaret. 2010. Helicopter Moms, Heading for a Crash. *Washington Post*, July 4.

———. 2010. *Parenting Out of Control: Anxious Parents in Uncertain Times*. New York: New York University Press.

New York Times. 2005. *Class Matters*. New York: Times Books.

Niemann, Yolanda Flores, Andrea J. Romero, Jorge Arredondo, and Victor Rodriguez. 1999. What Does It Mean to Be "Mexican"? Social Construction of an Ethnic Identity. *Hispanic Journal of Behavioral Sciences* 22, 1: 47–60.

Nikken, P., J. Jansz, and S. Schouwstra. 2007. Parents' Interest in Videogame Ratings and Content Descriptors in Relation to Game Mediation. *European Journal of Communication* 22, 3: 24–143.

O'Connor, Richard. 2006. *Undoing Perpetual Stress: The Missing Connection Between Depression, Anxiety, and 21st Century Illness*. New York: Berkeley.

Olsen, Stephanie. 2009. Education Video Games Mix Cool with Purpose. *New York Times*, November 1.

Orsi, Robert. 2006. *Between Heaven and Earth: The Religious Worlds People Make and the Scholars Who Study Them*. Princeton, NJ: Princeton University Press.

Palfrey, John, and Urs Gasser. 2008. *Born Digital: Understanding the First Generation of Digital Natives*. New York: Basic Books.

Patchin, Justin W., and Samecr Hinduja. 2006. Bullies Move Beyond the Schoolyard. *Youth Violence and Juvenile Justice* 4, 2: 148–69.

Perez-Pena, Richard. 2011. More Complex Picture Emerges in Rutgers Student's Suicide. *New York Times*, August 12.

Pew Internet and American Life Project. 2012. Demographics of Internet Users May 2011. http://pewinternet.org/Static-Pages/Trend-Data/Whos-Online.aspx (retrieved February 4, 2012).

Pokin, Steve. 2007. Dardenne Prairie Officials Plan to Make Cyberspace Harassment a Crime. *St. Louis Suburban Journals*, November 15. http://suburbanjournals.stltoday.com/articles/2007/11/15/news/doc473c629800bb7940817680.txt (retrieved October 6, 2010).

Posner, Richard. 2010. American Wage Stagnation. *The Becker-Posner Blog*, April 18. http://uchicagolaw.typepad.com/beckerposner/2010/04/american-wage-stagnation-posner.html (retrieved July 28, 2010).

Postman, Neil. 1985. *Amusing Ourselves to Death: Public Discourse in the Age of Show Business*. New York: Penguin.

————. 1994. *The Disappearance of Childhood*. New York: Random House.

Primorac, Marina. 2011. F&D Spotlights Widening Gap Between Rich and Poor. *IMF Survey Magazine: In the News*, September 12. www.imf.org/external/pubs/ft/survey/so/2011/NEW091211A.htm (retrieved January 23, 2012).

Pugh, Allison. 2009. *Longing and Belonging: Parents, Children, and Consumer Culture*. Berkeley: University of California Press.

Rainie, Lee. 2010. How Media Consumption Has Changed Since 2000. Paper presented at the Newhouse School's Monetizing Online Business conference. www.pewinternet.org/~/media/Files/Presentations/2010/Jun/2010%20-%20062410%20-%20syracuse%20newhouse%20MOB%20conf%20NYC%20pdf.pdf (retrieved July 16, 2010).

Rantanen, Terhi. 2005. Giddens and the "G" Word: An Interview with Anthony Giddens. *Global Media and Communication* 1, 1: 63–77.

Ray, Barbara. 2010. Adulthood: What's the Rush?: The Truth About 21st Century 20 Somethings. *Psychology Today*, November 4. www.psychologytoday.com/blog/adulthood-whats-the-rush/201011/is-blaming-parents-failure-launch-red-herring (retrieved February 8, 2012).

Relax News. 2010. Five Billion People to Use Cell Phones in 2010: UN. *Independent* (UK), February 16. www.independent.co.uk/life-style/gadgets-and-tech/news/five-billion-people-to-use-mobile-phones-in-2010-un-1900768.html (retrieved July 16, 2010).

Ribak, Rivka. 2009. Remote Control, Umbilical Cord and Beyond: The Mobile Phone as a Transitional Object. *British Journal of Developmental Psychology* 27, 1: 183–96.

Rice, Ronald, and Carolyn Haythornthwaite. 2006. Perspectives on Internet Use: Access, Involvement, and Interaction. In Leah Lievrouw and Sonia Livingstone, eds., *Handbook of New Media: Social Shaping and Consequences of ICTs*, 92–113. 2nd ed. London: Sage.

Rich, Motoko. 2011. Job Growth Falters Badly, Clouding Hope for Recovery. *New York Times*, July 8.

Richtel, Matt. 2010. Digital Devices Deprive Brain of Downtime. *New York Times*, August 24.

————. 2010. Hooked on Gadgets, and Paying a Mental Price. *New York Times*, June 6.

Rick, K., and J. Forward. 1992. Acculturation and Perceived Intergenerational Difference Among Hmong Youth. *Journal of Cross-Cultural Psychology* 23, 1: 85–94.

Rideout, Victoria, Ulla G. Foehr, and Donald Roberts. 2010. Generation M2: Media in the Lives of 8- to 18-Year-Olds. Kaiser Family Foundation. www.kff.org/entmedia/mh012010pkg.cfm (retrieved July 16, 2010).

Riding, Alan. 1989. *Distant Neighbors*. New York: Vintage Books.

Riesman, David, Nathan Glazer, and Reuel Denney. 1950. *The Lonely Crowd: A Study of the Changing American Character*. New Haven, CT: Yale University Press.

Robinson, J. A., and J. Kim. 2004. Modeling the Relationship Between Family Media Use, Perceived Media Influence, and Rulemaking. Paper presented to the International Communication Association, New Orleans, LA.

Rodriguez, Gregory. 1996. *The Emerging Latino Middle Class*. Pepperdine University, Institute for Public Policy.

Rojas, V., J. Straubhaar, J. Spence, D. Roychowdhury, O. Okur, J. Pinon, and M. Fuentes-Bautista. Forthcoming. Communities, Cultural Capital and Digital Inclusion: Ten Years of Tracking Techno-Dispositions. In Joseph Straubhaar, ed., *Austin Technopolis*. Austin, TX: University of Texas Press.

Rooney, Ben. 2011. Recession Worsens Racial Wealth Gap. CNN Money, July 26. http://money.cnn.com/2011/07/26/news/economy/wealth_gap_white_black_hispanic/index.htm?cnn=yes&hpt=hp_t2 (retrieved August 25, 2011).

Rosin, Hannah. 2011. Mother Inferior? *Wall Street Journal*, January 15.

Rothbaum, Fred, Nancy Martland, and Joanne Beswick Jannsen. 2008. Parents' Reliance on the Web to Find Information About Children and Families: Socio-economic Differences in Use, Skills, and Satisfaction. *Journal of Applied Developmental Psychology* 29: 118–28.

Scherr, Tracy, and Jim Larson. 2010. Bullying Dynamics Associated with Race, Ethnicity, and Immigration Status. In Shane R. Jimerson, Susan M. Swearer, and Dorothy L. Espelage, eds., *Handbook of Bullying in Schools: An International Perspective*, 223–34. New York: Routledge.

Schor, Juliet. 1992. *The Overworked American: The Unexpected Decline of Leisure*. New York: Basic Books.

Schramm, Wilbur, Jack Lyle, and Edwin B. Parker. 1961. *Television in the Lives of Our Children*. Toronto: University of Toronto Press.

Seidel, John V. 1998. Qualitative Data Analysis. Appendix E of the manual for *The Ethnograph*, vol. 4 (data analysis software), www.qualisresearch.com.

Seiter, Ellen. 1995. *Sold Separately: Children and Parents in Consumer Culture*. New Brunswick, NJ: Rutgers University Press.

———. 2000. *Television and New Media Audiences*. Oxford: Clarendon.

———. 2007. *The Internet Playground*. New York: Peter Lang.

Sells, Scott. 2001. *Parenting Your Out-of-Control Teenager: 7 Steps to Reestablish Authority and Reclaim Love*. New York: St. Martin's Press.

Senft, Theresa. 2008. *Camgirls: Celebrity and Community in the Age of Social Networks*. New York: Peter Lang.

———. 2010. Fame to Fifteen: Re-framing Celebrity. TED Salon talk, London, November 2.

———. 2012. Love in the Time of Snuff: Critical Internet Studies Meets the "Neda Video." In Hille Koskela and J. Macgregor Wise, eds., *New Visualities, New Technologies: The New Ecstasy of Communication*. Oxford: Blackwell.

Settersten, Richard, and Barbara Ray. 2010. *Not Quite Adults: Why 20-Somethings Are Choosing a Slow Path to Adulthood, and Why It's Good for Everyone*. New York: Bantam.

Shirky, Clay. 2009. *Here Comes Everybody: The Power of Organizing Without Organizations*. New York: Penguin.

Shuler, Carly. 2012. *iLearn II: An Analysis of the Education Category on Apple's App Store*. Joan Ganz Cooney Center at Sesame Workshop. www.joanganzcooneycenter.org/Reports-33.html (retrieved January 29, 2012).

Silverstone, Roger. 1999. *Why Study the Media?* London: Sage.

———. 2006. *Media and Morality: On the Rise of the Mediapolis*. London: Polity.

Silverstone, Roger, and Eric Hirsch. 1992. *Consuming Technologies: Media and Information in Domestic Spaces*. London: Routledge.

Silverstone, Roger, David Morley, Andrea Dahlberg, and Sonia Livingstone. Families, Technologies, and Consumption: The Household and Information and Communication Technologies. CRICT discussion paper, Brunel University, 1989.

Skenazy, Lenore. *Free Range Kids: How to Raise Safe, Self-Reliant Children*. San Francisco: Jossey-Bass, 2010.

Smith, Heather, and Katie Roberts-Kremer. 2011. Cyberbullying. Unpublished paper.

Smolensky, Eugene, and Jennifer Appleton Grootman, eds. 2003. *Working Families and Growing Kids: Caring for Children and Adolescents*. Washington, DC: National Academies Press.

Spiegel, Lynn. 1992. *Make Room for TV: Television and the Family Ideal in Postwar America*. Chicago: University of Chicago Press.

Starr, Tena. 2010. Mexican Farmworker's Life Like Living in a "Golden Cage." *Chronicle* (Barton, VT), April 28.

Steinberg, Laurence. 2004. *The Ten Basic Principles of Good Parenting*. New York: Simon and Schuster.

Stern, Susannah. 2008. Producing Sites, Exploring Identities: Youth Online Authorship. In David Buckingham, ed., *Youth, Identity, and Social Media*, 95–118. John D. and Katherine T. MacArthur Foundation Series on Digital Media and Learning. Cambridge, MA: MIT Press. http://www.mitpressjournals.org/toc/dmal/-/6.

Straubhaar, Joseph. 2011. Constructing a New Information Society in the Tropics: Examining Brazilian Approaches to Information and Communication Technology (ICTs) Through the Lens of the User and Non-User. Paper presented to the annual meeting of the International Communication Association, Boston, MA.

Straubhaar, Joseph, Jeremiah Spence, Zeynep Tufekci, and Roberta G. Lenz, eds. 2012. *Inequality in the Technopolis: Race, Class, Gender, and the Digital Divide in Austin*. Austin: University of Texas Press.

Strasburger, Victor, Barbara J. Wilson, and Amy Jordan. 2008. *Children, Adolescents, and the Media*. Thousand Oaks, CA: Sage.

Streeter, Thomas. 2010. *The Net Effect: Romanticism, Capitalism, and the Internet*. New York: New York University Press.

Strong, W. F., J. S. McQuillen, and J. D. Hughey. 1994. En el Laberinto de Machismo: A Comparative Analysis of Macho Attitudes Among Hispanic and Anglo College Students. *Howard Journal of Communications* 5, 1–2: 18–35.

Sturm, Roland. 2005. Childhood Obesity—What We Can Learn from Existing Data on Societal Trends, Part I. *Preventing Chronic Disease* 2, 1: A12.

Stutzman, Fred and Jacob Kramer-Duffield. 2010. Friends Only: Examining a Privacy-Enhancing Behavior in Facebook. *Proceedings of the 28th International Conference on Human Factors in Computing Systems*, 1553–62. New York: Association for Computing Machinery.

Sudarkasa, N. 1997. African American Families and Family Values. In H. P. McAdoo ed., *Black Families*. 3rd ed. Thousand Oaks, CA: Sage.

Surdin, Ashley. 2009. States Passing Laws to Combat Cyberbullying. *Washington Post*, January 1.

Swidler, Ann. 1986. Culture in Action: Symbols and Strategies. *American Sociological Review* 51, 2: 273–86.

Takeuchi, Lori. 2011. *Families Matter: Designing Media for a Digital Age*. Joan Ganz Cooney Center at Sesame Workshop, www.joanganzcooneycenter.org (retrieved August 28, 2011).

Takeuchi, Lori, and Reed Stevens. *The New Coviewing: Designing for Learning through Joint Media Engagement*. Joan Ganz Cooney Center, fall 2011.

Tapscott, Don. 1999. *Growing Up Digital: The Rise of the Net Generation*. New York: McGraw-Hill.

Tapscott, Don, and Anthony Williams. 2008. *Wikinomics: How Mass Collaboration Changes Everything*. New York: Portfolio.

Tett, Gillian. 2011. The Rise of the Middle Class—Just Not Ours. *Atlantic*, July/August, 63.

Thiel, Shayla. 2007. *Instant Identity: Adolescent Girls and the World of Instant Messaging.* New York: Peter Lang.

Thompson, John. 1995. *Media and Modernity: A Social Theory of the Media.* Stanford, CA: Stanford University Press.

Thompson, William, and Joseph Hickey. 2005. *Society in Focus.* Boston, MA: Pearson.

Timmer, John. 2008. Let Them Use AOL: Upper Class Searchers Prefer Google. *Ars Technica.* http://arstechnica.com/old/content/2008/03/let-them-use-aol-upper-class-searchers-prefer-google.ars (retrieved September 29, 2010).

Torres, J. B. 1998. Masculinity and Gender Roles Among Puerto Rican Men: Machismo on the U.S. Mainland. *American Journal of Orthopsychiatry* 68, 1: 16–26.

Tripp, Lisa. 2011. The Computer Is Not for You to Be Looking Around, It Is for Schoolwork: Challenges for Digital Inclusion as Latino Immigrant Families Negotiate Children's Access to the Internet. *New Media and Society* 13, 4: 552–67.

Turcotte, M. 2007. Time Spent with Family During a Typical Work Day 1986 to 2006. Canadian Social Trends, Statistics Canada—Catalogue No. 11–08. www.statcan.ca/english/freepub/11-008-XIE/2006007/pdf/11-008-XIE20060079574.pdf (retrieved June 23, 2010).

Turkle, Sherry. 1995. *Life on the Screen.* New York: Simon and Schuster.

———. 2011. *Alone Together: Why We Expect More from Technology and Less from Each Other.* New York: Basic Books.

U.S. Department of Commerce. 2002. *A Nation Online: How Americans Are Expanding Their Use of the Internet.* Washington, DC: U.S. Government Printing Office.

Valkenburg, Patti M., M. Krcmar, A. L. Peeters, and N. M. Marseille. 1999. Developing a Scale to Assess Three Styles of Television Mediation: Instructive Mediation, Restrictive Mediation, and Social Coviewing. *Journal of Broadcasting and Electronic Media* 43, 1: 52–67.

Van Dijk, January. 2006. *The Network Society.* London: Sage.

———. 2005. *The Deepening Divide: Inequality in the Information Society.* Thousand Oaks, CA: Sage Publications.

Virilio, Paul. 1977. *Speed and Politics: An Essay on Dromology.* Trans. Mark Polizzotti. New York: Semiotext(e).

Wajcman, Judy. 2004. *Technofeminism.* Cambridge: Polity Press.

Warren, Ron. 2005. Parental Mediation of Children's Television Viewing in Low Income Families. *Journal of Communication* 55: 847–63.

Warren, Ron, P. Gerke, and M. A. Kelly. 2002. Is There Enough Time on the Clock? Parental Involvement and Mediation of Children's Television Viewing. *Journal of Broadcasting and Electronic Media* 46, 1: 87–112.

Warschauer, Mark. 2003. *Technology and Social Inclusion: Rethinking the Digital Divide.* Cambridge, MA: MIT Press.

Waters, Mary C. 1990. *Ethnic Options: Choosing Identities in America.* Berkeley: University of California Press.

Watkins, Craig S. 2009. *The Young and the Digital: What the Migration to Social Network Sites, Games, and Anytime, Anywhere Media Means for Our Future.* Boston: Beacon.

Way, N. 1996. Between Experiences of Betrayal and Desire: Close Friendships Among Urban Adolescents. In B. J. R. Leadbetter and N. Way, eds., *Urban Girls.* New York: New York University Press.

Webster, J., J. Pearson, and D. Webster. 1986. Children's Television Viewing as Affected by Contextual Variables in the Home. *Communication Research Reports* 3, 1: 1–8.

Wellman, Barry, Anabel Quan-Haase, Jeffrey Boase, Wenhong Chen, Keith Hampton, Isabel Isla de Diaz, and Kakuko Miyata. 2003. The Social Affordances of the Internet for Networked Individualism. *Journal of Computer Mediated Communication* 8, 3. http://jcmc.indiana.edu/vol8/issue3/wellman.html (retrieved August 28, 2011).

Wellman, Barry, Aaron Smith, Amy Wells, and Trace Kennedy. 2008. *Networked Families*. Pew Internet and American Research Project. www.pewinternet.org/Reports/2008/Networked-Families.aspx.

Wilcox, W. Bradford. 2004. *Soft Patriarchs, New Men: How Christianity Shapes Fathers and Husbands*. Chicago: University of Chicago Press.

Wilkinson, Richard. 2005. *The Impact of Inequality: How to Make Sick Societies Healthier*. New York: Routledge.

Willett, Rebekah. 2008. Consumer Citizens Online: Structure, Agency and Gender in Online Participation. In D. Buckingham, ed., *Youth, Identity and Digital Media*, 49–70. Cambridge, MA: MIT Press. http://www.mitpressjournals.org/toc/dmal/-/6.

Williams, Raymond. 1974. *Technology and Cultural Form*. London: Fontana.

Willis, Paul. 1977. *Learning to Labor: How Working Class Kids Get Working Class Jobs*. London: Saxon House.

Wilson, Kenneth R., Jennifer S. Wallin, and Christa Reiser. 2003. Social Stratification and the Digital Divide. *Social Science Computer Review* 21, 2: 133–43.

Wolak, J., M. L. Ybarra, K. Mitchell, and D. Finkelhor. 2007. Current Research Knowledge About Adolescent Victimization via the Internet. *Adolescent Medicine* 18: 325–41.

Xiong, Z. B., and D. F. Detzner. 2005. Southeast Asian Fathers' Experiences with Adolescents: Challenges and Change. *Hmong Studies Journal* 6, 1–23.

Ybarra, Michele L., Cheryl Alexander, and Kimberly J. Mitchell. 2005. Depressive Symptomatology, Youth Internet Use, and Online Interactions: A National Survey. *Journal of Adolescent Health* 36: 9–18.

Ybarra, Michele L., M. Diener-West, and P. J. Leaf. 2007. Examining the Overlap in Internet Harassment and School Bullying: Implications for School Intervention. *Journal of Adolescent Health* 41, 6: 42–50.

Ybarra, Michele and Kimberly Mitchell, 2004. Youth Engaging in Online Harassment: Associations with Caregiver-Child Relationships, Internet use, and Personal Characteristics. *Journal of Adolescence* 27: 319–36.

Zelizer, Vivianna. 1985. *Pricing the Priceless Child: The Changing Social Value of Children*. New York: Basic Books.

Zetter, Kim. 2008. Experts Say MySpace Suicide Indictment Sets "Scary" Precedent. *Wired*, May 15. http://blog.wired.com/27bstroke6/2008/05/myspace-indictm.html (retrieved December 17, 2008).

Zhang, C., M. Callegaro, and M. Thomas. 2008. More than the Digital Divide? Investigating the Differences between Internet and Non-Internet Users. Paper presented at the Midwest Association of Public Opinion Research, Chicago.

Zhou, M., and I. C. Bankston. 1998. *Growing Up American: How Vietnamese Children Adapt to Life in the United States*. New York: Russell Sage Foundation.

INDEX

Adolescence. *See* teenagers
Alone Together. See Turkle, Sherry
Anderson, Ken, 268nn16, 17
Apps, 128, 169
Austin, Erika, 264n11, 265nn20, 24,
    266n35
Authority, 19, 36, 45, 47
    Challenging, 52–54, 69, 70, 101, 162,
        249n17
    And class, 207, 248n7
    And ethnicity, 101, 248n8, 255nn13,
        15
    Parental, 36, 50, 53, 68–71, 99, 101,
        104, 107, 129, 141–44, 156–57,
        167–68, 172, 181, 183, 204, 207,
        209, 212
    Parental uncertainty about, 35,
        167, 204
    Respecting, 50, 51, 70, 99, 101, 141,
        143, 156, 207
    Teen over adult, 101
    And teen autonomy (freedom), 50, 55,
        104, 126

Bakardjieva, Maria, 256n23
Barron, Brigid, 262n35, 266n36
Beck, Ulrich. *See* risk society
Biracial, 56, 114, 116, 125, 180, 183, 184,
    267n1, 269n26

boyd, danah, 6, 7, 22, 91, 92, 114, 213,
    234, 239nn10, 15, 247nn23, 30,
    249n17, 253n48, 258nn52, 57,
    259nn58, 60, 61, 266n27, 270n11,
    272n32, 274n17
Brake, David, 251n36, 266n27
Buckingham, David, 248n1, 252nn40,
    42, 253nn48, 53, 273n13,
    274n17

Chaffee, Stephen, 129, 260nn4, 10,
    261n18, 270n4
Child care, 36, 111, 165, 168, 177
Chua, Amy, 22–23, 244n67
Class, 20–27, 176, 243n64, 244n66
    Absence in digital and mobile media
        research accounts, 5, 21, 22
    Building bridges between differing,
        217
    And culture, 24
    Definitions, x, xv
    Distinctions and media use, 21, 50,
        131, 136–38, 148, 151–53,
        168–73, 179, 190, 195, 203, 206,
        217
    And education, 263n37
    And ethics of communication, xvi
    And ethnicity and race, 71, 99, 100,
        270n6

Class (*continued*)
  And identity and media, 245n77,
    259n58
  Increasing isolation between, 20, 216
  Less advantaged, 21, 23, 50, 70, 71, 99,
    103, 111–18, 131, 151–53,
    163–68, 205–9, 212, 222,
    261nn16, 17
  Media constructions of, 14, 241n37,
    245n2
  And media audiences, 8, 14, 245n2
  Middle, 14, 19, 24, 26, 28, 34, 38, 41,
    42, 47, 71, 76, 91, 99, 103, 118,
    133–38, 151–53, 158, 174, 178,
    243nn62, 64
  Mobility, lack of, 21
  Upper-middle class, 16, 22, 24, 31, 34,
    41, 48, 50, 71, 76, 81, 99, 110,
    120, 125–29, 134–38, 148,
    154–55, 160–63, 168–70, 178–86,
    205
  Working class, 130, 244n66, 245nn70,
    72, 77, 261n16, 263n37, 270n6
  Would-be middle class, xv, 16, 21–25,
    50, 70, 71, 99, 118, 130, 131–34,
    138–44, 151–53, 184, 186–92,
    205, 207, 244n66, 261n16
Clementi, Tyler, 47
Concept-oriented family communication,
    129, 134, 260n4
Concerted cultivation, 22–23, 127, 128,
    130, 134, 135, 159, 241n41
  Vs. natural growth parenting, 131,
    261n16
Corsaro, William, 91, 252n42
Cultural milieu, xi, xii, xiv, 16, 24, 69, 91,
    92, 128, 129, 173, 178, 179, 185
Cultural toolkit, 133, 210, 252n43
Cyberbullying, 28–31, 32, 47, 113, 246n4,
    247n37
  Research Center, 246n13
  Definition of, 246n13
  And racism, 108, 113
  Meghan Meier case, 28–31
  Legislation penalizing, 46, 246nn7–9
  See also Clementi, Tyler

Darrah, Charles, 268nn20, 22, 24
Davidson, Cathy, 221, 262n35, 271n25
Deviance and youth, 69, 248n41
Digital
  Divide, 102, 238n11, 243n58, 255n19,
    see also Straubhaar, Joseph
  And ethnicity, 102–3
  Expertise of teens vs. parents, 114–21,
    134, 162, 191
  Media, and after-school programs,
    146
  Media, characteristics of, 7, 15,
    239n10, 250n17
    In perpetual beta, 7, 15
    Persistence, 7, 15
    Scalability, 7, 15
    Searchability, 7, 15
  Media, functions of, 250n7
  Media, and immigrant uses, 104
  Media, and interest-driven participa-
    tion, 62, 71, 77, 83
  Media, and privacy levels. *See*
    Facebook privacy levels
  Ownership, 224
    And access, 99
    Policy, 224
  Trail, 19, 213, 215
  Tether, 213, 213, 215, 238n2
  See also Media; Technology
DiMaggio, Paul, 256n21

Eastin, Michael, 265n13
Ehrenreich, Barbara, 138, 224
Eisenstein, Elizabeth, 201
Emerich, Monica, 249n1, 259nn63, 64,
    261n14, 262n25, 269n27
Emotional downsizing, 185, 195
Emotion work, 93, 254n58
  Of parenting, 93, 174–200, 214
Entitlement
  And narcissism, 96, 204, 205, 209
  Teen sense of, 58–61, 139, 205, 209
  Parents' sense that teens are entitled to
    individual rights, 156, 157, 163,
    204
Erickson, Erik, 90–91

Ethic
  Definition, 76, 118
  of expressive empowerment, xii, 16, 21, 31, 47, 91, 125–29, 153–55, 160, 172, 173, 175, 178, 179, 189, 203–5, 218, 241n41
  And risk, 134–38, 148, 241n41
  And religion, 143
  of respectful connectedness, xii, 16, 21, 23, 50, 69, 99, 118–19, 126, 129–34, 148, 149, 153, 172, 179, 182, 193, 205–9, 216
  And respecting parental authority, 141
  And risk, 148–49

Facebook, 8, 11, 15, 31–38, 43, 45, 55, 78, 80, 86–88, 94, 103, 105–12, 114, 116, 118, 126, 142, 161–63, 171, 173, 208, 216, 218, 219, 221, 224, 230, 266n27
  And Facebook Parenting viral video, 118–19
  And identity, 87–88. See also Identity and media
  And self-censorship, 110
  And risk, 15
  Privacy levels, 37, 114
Families
  African American, 100
  Definitions, 176–79
  Ethnic groups and U.S. demographics, 100
  Extended, 111
  Latino, 101
  Recent immigrant, 101
  Statistics in U.S., 176
  And time pressures, 176
Family communication, 126, 129, 133, 203, 206–8, 211, 260n4
Feminism
  And standpoint theory, 253n47
  And technology, 237n9
Finkelhor, David, 6, 238n6, 240n26, 263n39
Fitzpatrick, Mary Ann, 263n7, 264n13

Gerson, Kathleen, 267n5, 268n9
Giddens, Anthony, 18–19, 240nn32, 33
Gunter, Barrie, 272n3
Gutenberg, Johann, 201

Habitus, 23, 210
Hargittai, Eszter, 114, 247n23, 256n21, 256nn24, 25, 27, 259nn60, 61
Haythornthwaite, Carolyn, 256n23
Helicopter parenting. See Parenting, Helicopter
Helsper, Elizabeth, 238n11, 243n59, 256n27, 265n23
Hochschild, Arlie, 152, 175, 178, 195, 215, 224, 242n54, 254n58, 263n3, 268n15, 269nn35, 36
Hofer, Barbara, 213, 237n6, 266n34, 270n5, 270n12
Hoover, Stewart, 259n64, 263n1, 265nn18, 21, 272n1, 273n11
Horst, Heather, 81, 249n15, 258n48, 260n7

Identity, 19, 80, 83–86, 90–95, 204, 211–13, 221, 239n10, 242n55, 245n77, 250n17, 251n27, 28, 252n42, 252n44, 253nn47–53, 254n3, 255n12, 269n26, 271n18, 273n13
  And media, 78–97, 212, 213, 245n77, 251nn28, 29, 31, 252n39, 252n46
  And self, 251n38
  And standpoint theory, 253n47
Inequality, economic and social, 20, 21, 71, 215–17
Information, access to, 17–18
Interest-driven participation, 62, 71, 77, 83
Ito, Mimi, 81, 83, 249n15, 251nn22, 25, 260n7, 269n32

Jordan, Amy, 252n39

Kaiser Family Foundation study, 78, 249n4, 268n14

Kearney, Mary Celeste, 251n26
Koerner, Ascan, 264n13

Lareau, Annette, 22, 24, 127, 133,
 241n41, 244n68, 249n11, 260nn3,
 4, 261nn12, 16, 19, 22, 263n6,
 270n6
Lenhart, Amanda, 237n1, 238n1, 249n6,
 249n10, 257nn29, 30, 262n28,
 263n2, 273n13
Leisure, 138, 145, 202 203
 Countercultural embrace of, 184
Lievrouw, Leah, 256n23
Lim, Sun Sun, 253n55, 256n26, 259nn62,
 68
Limits on screen time, recommended,
 132, 220
Ling, Richard, 249n10, 250n18, 257n30,
 262n28, 263n2,
Livingstone, Sonia, xii, 170, 222, 237n7,
 238n11, 243n59, 60, 247n22,
 248nn4, 5, 250n17, 256nn23, 27,
 260n5, 261n11, 265n23, 267n42,
 270n9, 271n26, 274nn18, 20
Lull, James, 129, 135, 261n13

Marvin, Carolyn, xii, 238n10, 241n43,
 260n2
Mazzarella, Sharon, 249n2, 251n26,
 273n16
McLeod, Jack, 129, 260nn4, 10, 261n18,
 263n7, 270n4
Media. *See also* Digital Media, Technology
 Conglomerates, 78–79, 224–26
 And critique of commercialism,
 251n33
 As "cultural pollution," 142
 Definition, 241n43, 260n2
 Functions
 Mythic, 79, 83, 93, 99, 225
 Pragmatic, 79, 83, 84, 90, 93, 99,
 225
 Symbolic, 79, 83, 84, 90, 93,
 99, 225
 And identity. *See* Identity
 And negative effects on children, 157

Ownership, 224
 And access, 99
 Policy, 224
 And passive consumption, 135
 As a more positive use of time than
 alternatives, 145–47
 Use, statistics
 youth, viii, 78, 102–3
 parents, viii, 78
 Use by children, enabling self-time for
 parents, 165
 Use for children's empowerment,
 221–23
Media ecology. *See* Medium theory
Mediatization, 211, 242n46, 242n57, 270n8
Medium theory, 241n43. *See also* Media
 and social change
Methods, 259n2
 Qualitative research, 25, 253n47,
 257nn36, 41, 43, 258nn46, 53,
 262n23, 263n4, 266n25, 272nn5,
 6, 273nn6, 7, 8, 12, 274nn23, 24.
 See also Appendix A.
 Researcher reflexivity, 26
 Sample, 24, 272nn1–4
 Women's ways of knowing, xiv
Meyrowitz, Joshua, 16–17, 211, 241n43,
 242n44, 45, 259n2, 270n10
Mobile phone, vii, 4, 10, 12, 16, 18, 51,
 52, 53, 58, 71, 78, 79, 96, 98,
 103–10, 113, 130, 136, 141, 116,
 120, 121, 144, 149, 151–59, 161,
 163, 164, 169, 170, 172, 180, 181,
 192, 199–203, 207, 208, 212, 215,
 218–21, 238n2, 242n43, 249n10,
 250n12, 257n32, 262n28, 266n34,
 274nn18, 20
 Acquisition by children, 152
 Shared among family members, 103,
 132, 149, 161, 171, 207,
 Monitoring by parents, 41, 76, 166, 168,
 189, 192, 215, 218, 247n28,
 265n22, 271n17
 See also Surveillance
Moral economy of the household, xiv
Morley, David, xiv, 261n11

Mothers
　And blame, 47, see also Parenting,
　　morally correct
　As desirable target market, 8
　And emotion work, 18, 101, 126, 159,
　　162, 168, 171, 175, 178, 185, 192,
　　203, 207, 211, 215, 220, 244n69
　Single, 36, 271n20
　And work, 177
Movie night, 170, 185, 220

Nathanson, Amy, 264nn9, 10, 11,
　265nn14, 16, 22
Nakamura, Lisa, 256n23
Negative outcomes and media use, 6, 60,
　65, 90, 97, 132, 157, 172, 188, 197
Nelson, Margaret, 24, 41, 50, 156, 167,
　168, 178, 237n5, 241n41, 245n75,
　246n18, 247nn28, 29, 248n6,
　261n12, 263n5, 266nn26, 31, 32,
　268n21, 271n16
Neopets, 81–91, 93–94, 188, 204, 250n21,
　251n22
No Sense of Place, see Meyrowitz,
　Joshua

Overparenting, see Parenting

Parent App, vii, 5, 20, 45, 71, 99, 121,
　128, 148, 149, 266n33
Parental mediation, 60, 152–53, 157–68,
　176, 184, 194, 196, 248n4,
　264nn9, 10, 12, 265nn15, 19, 22,
　23, 24, 269n37
　Restriction, 158–68, 197, 199
　Discussion (or active mediation), 158,
　　171, 199
　Coviewing, 158, 169–71
　Participatory learning, 158, 169, 197
Parenting
　And authority. *See* authority
　And difficulties setting boundaries, 35
　And growing up, 12
　And rules. *See* Rules
　And trust. *See* Trust
　And warmth, 49–51, 53, 61, 69, 139

Authoritarian, 49, 68, 167, 208
Authoritative, 49, 65, 69
"Good" or "good enough," 18, 66, 126,
　129, 175, 178, 186, 195, 200, 214
Helicopter, 30, 47, 49, 156, 166, 171,
　205, 213, 218, 240n28, 246n10,
　266n32
Hyper-involved, 168
Morally correct, 11
Neglectful, 49
Out-of-control parenting. *See* Nelson,
　Margaret
Overparenting, 41–45, 218
Permissive, 49, 160, 167, 179, 184,
　247n19
Reflexive, 18
Strict, 51, 56, 61, 68, 199
　And warmth, 61
Parents
　And Facebook, 43–44
　Helicopter. *See* Parents, Helicopter
　See also Teens, hiding online
　　information from parents
　Pew Internet & American Life. *See*
　　Lenhart, Amanda
Predators, online, 8, 12, 33, 45, 47
　Teen experiences with, 37–40
Privacy
　Desire for, 113
　Invasion of, 42–44, 95, see also
　　Clementi, Tyler
　See also Facebook privacy levels
Problem-solving among teens, 181
Pugh, Allison, 24, 80

Rhizome, 223
Religion
　And family media choices, 105, 140,
　　142, 265n21
　And media rules, 144, 259n64
　And web searching, 143
Research
　Sample, 24
Respect, 100, 140, 182, 194
　Of parents by teens, 65, 107,
　　118–19

Respect (*continued*)
Of teens by parents, 47, 118–19
See also Ethic, respectful
connectedness
Restrictions
And cultural norms of parenting, 107,
110–11
on media use, 49–61, 69
See also Parental mediation, restriction
Ribak, Rivka, 238n2, 274nn20, 21
Rice, Ronald, 256n23
Risk, 3, 12, 147, 183
Amplifier, 6
And communication technology as risk
amplifier, 6, 212
And digital media, 3–4, 15, 260n5
And economics, 14–15, 99, 137, 149
And opportunities of digital media,
260n5
And risk society, 5, 12–14, 240nn30,
31
And schooling, 138
Media construction of, 7–10, 239nn21,
23, 24
Media as mitigator of risk, 147, 202
See also Ethic, expressive
empowerment
Risky online behavior, 32–37, 47, 70
Rules, 34, 42, 50, 51, 54, 60, 69, 99, 101,
106, 108, 111, 117, 139, 155, 158,
159, 161, 162, 164, 168, 172, 181,
182, 184, 204, 205, 240n33,
242n54, 267n3, 269n31
And conservative values, 262nn29, 30
And religion, 108, 143–44
Mobile phone, 51, 108, 161

Schor, Juliet, 255
"second shift" the, 215. *See also*
Hochschild, Arlie
Seiter, Ellen, 250n20
Senft, Theresa, 251n31
Shade, Leslie, 256n23
Siblings and technological oversight,
116–18
Silverstone, Roger, 129, 240n30, 241n43

Socio-oriented family communication,
129, 260n4
Stern, Suzannah, 252n40
Straubhaar, Joseph, 243n60
Sullivan Moore, Abigail, 213, 237n6,
266n34, 270n5, 270n12
Surveillance
Using technology for monitoring
children, 41, 211, 214, 215, 219,
247n28
And society, 48

Takeuchi, Lori, 240n27, 260n6, 266n35,
36
Technology. *See also* Digital Media,
Media
Domestication of, 242n57
And educational benefits, 131
And memory, 17
Shared among family members, 192,
207
And social change, 209–26, 237n8,
240n33, 241n43
Social construction of, 237n9
Used to manage time, 215
Workaround, 237n9
Teens
And discussing moral values, 11, 63,
158, 221
And identity. *See* identity
And sense of entitlement, 58–62
And moral development, 46, 158, 221,
252
And narcissism, 97
And workarounds with parents, 54,
70
Hiding information from parents, 47,
54
Texting
And parental lenience, 155
Parental views of, 125
With parents, 161
Time
And changing demands of work and
family, 177–78
Crunch, 176–77, 184

Decline in uninterrupted leisure time, 177

    Productive use of, 189

Tripp, Lisa, 254n2, 257n33

Trust, 51–52, 64, 68, 133

Turkle, Sherry, 21, 96, 170, 216, 254n61

Valkenburg, Patti, 264nn9, 10, 265n20

Warmth and parenting, see Parenting

Warren, Ron, 265n19, 266n24

Weissbord, Richard, 46

Wellman, Barry, 240n29

Willett, Rebekah, 253n53

Willis, Paul, 262n34

Women in the workforce, 176

Workaround. *See* Teens